VOLUME **2**

CONTENTS

RATING **6**
MY GIRLFRIEND AND BROKEN HEARTS.............1

RATING **7**
MY GIRLFRIEND AND THE SEA (1)...................27

RATING **8**
MY GIRLFRIEND AND THE SEA (2)...................47

RATING **9**
MY GIRLFRIEND AND THE SEA (3).................68

RATING **10**
MY GIRLFRIEND AND THE SEA (4).................87

RATING **11**
MY GIRLFRIEND AND THE POCKY GAME............107

RATING **12**
MY GIRLFRIEND AND A STREET-PUNK FIGHT......135

RATING **13**
MY FRIEND AND MY GIRLFRIEND...................155

RATING **14**
MY GIRLFRIEND AND THE SEA (5)...................175

RENT-A-GIRLFRIEND

REIJI MIYAJIMA

RATING **6**
MY GIRLFRIEND AND BROKEN HEARTS

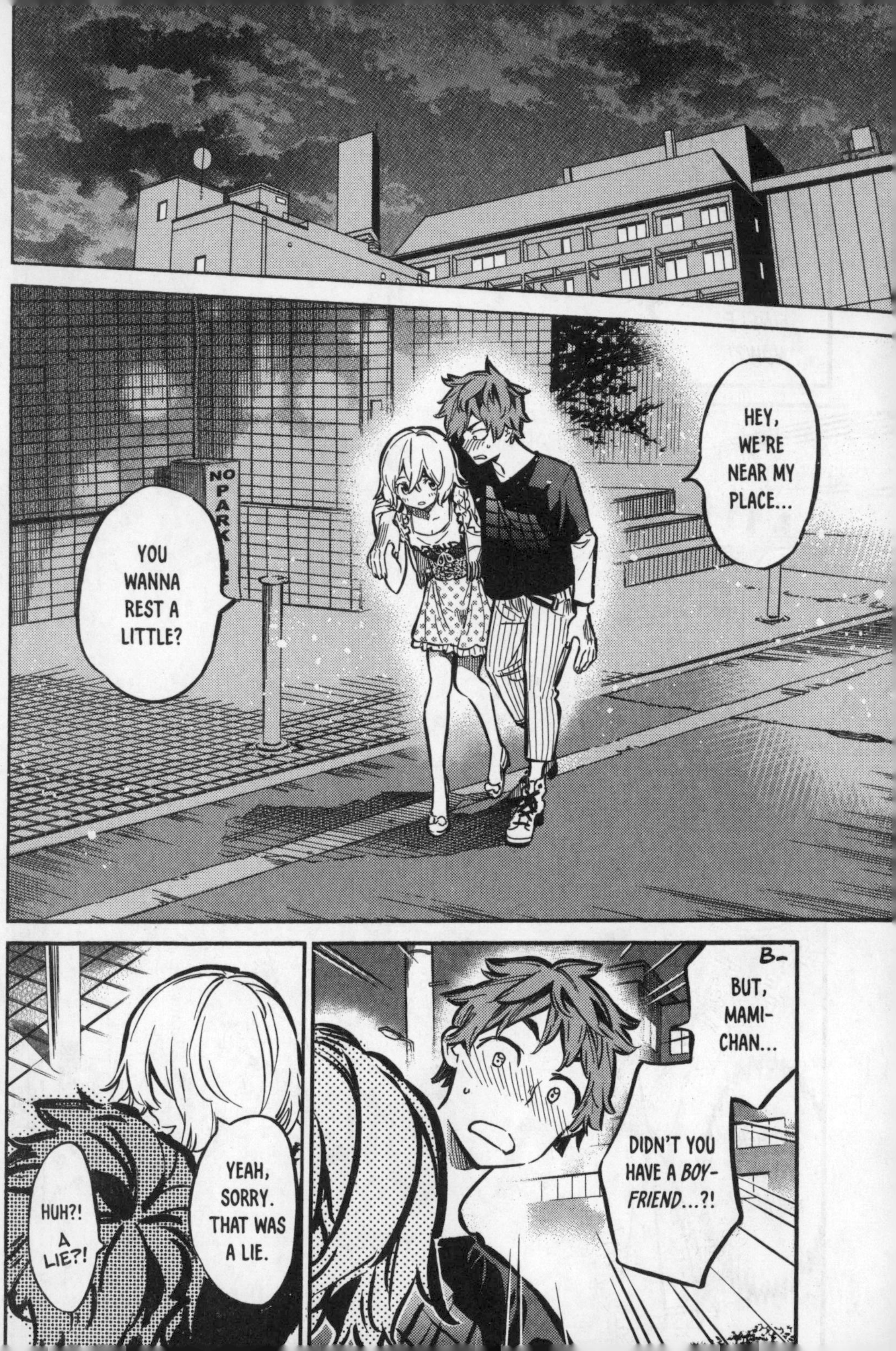
HEY, WE'RE NEAR MY PLACE...
YOU WANNA REST A LITTLE?
NO PARK
B-
BUT, MAMI-CHAN...
DIDN'T YOU HAVE A *BOY-FRIEND*...?!
YEAH, SORRY. THAT WAS A LIE.
HUH?! A LIE?!

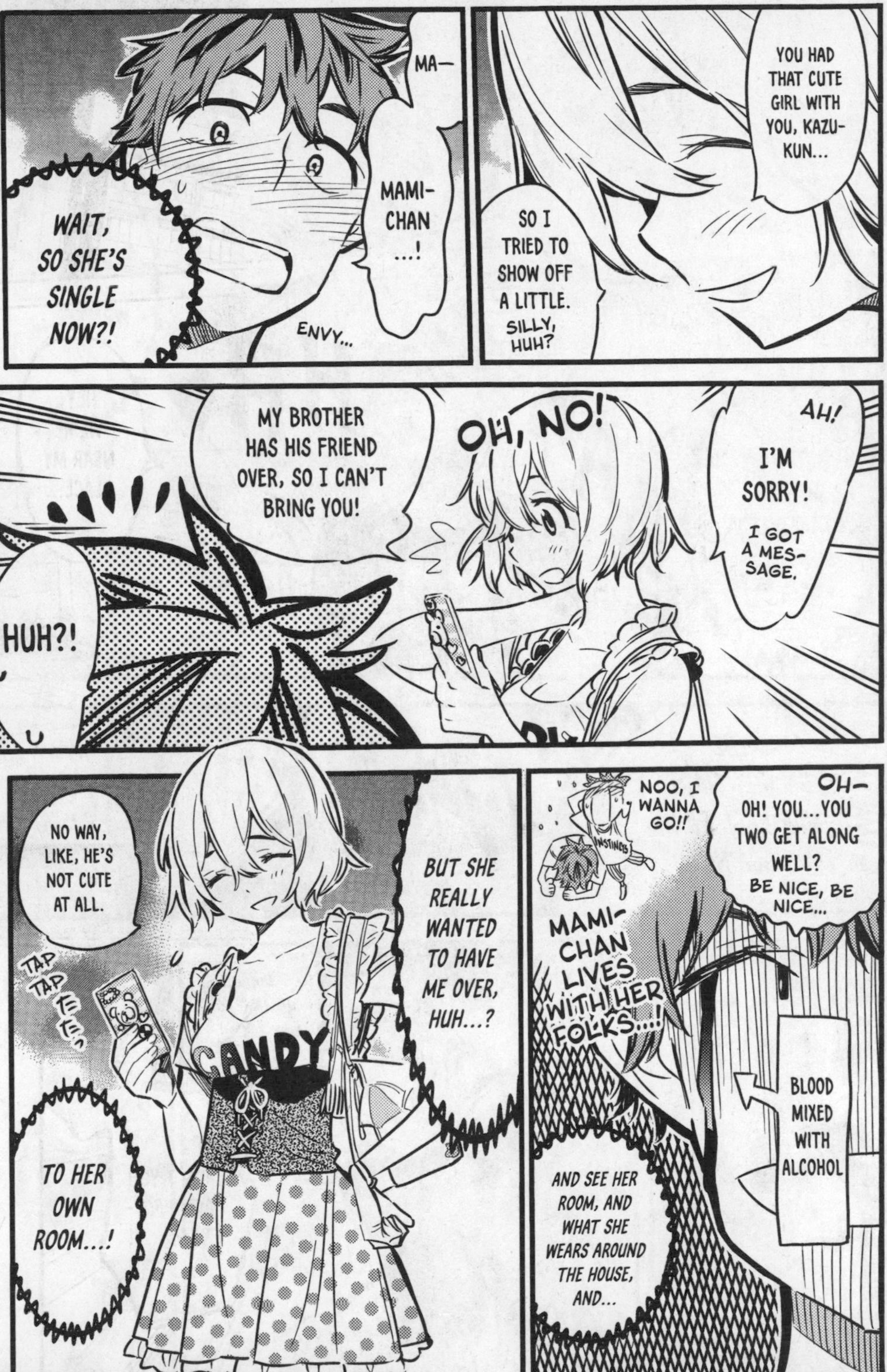
YOU HAD THAT CUTE GIRL WITH YOU, KAZU-KUN...
SO I TRIED TO SHOW OFF A LITTLE.
SILLY, HUH?
MA—
MAMI-CHAN...!
ENVY...
WAIT, SO SHE'S SINGLE NOW?!
AH!
I'M SORRY!
I GOT A MESSAGE.
OH, NO!
MY BROTHER HAS HIS FRIEND OVER, SO I CAN'T BRING YOU!
...!!
HUH?!
OH—OH! YOU...YOU TWO GET ALONG WELL?
BE NICE, BE NICE...
NOO, I WANNA GO!!
MAMI-CHAN LIVES WITH HER FOLKS...!
BLOOD MIXED WITH ALCOHOL
AND SEE HER ROOM, AND WHAT SHE WEARS AROUND THE HOUSE, AND...
BUT SHE REALLY WANTED TO HAVE ME OVER, HUH...?
NO WAY, LIKE, HE'S NOT CUTE AT ALL.
TAP TAP
CANDY
TO HER OWN ROOM...!

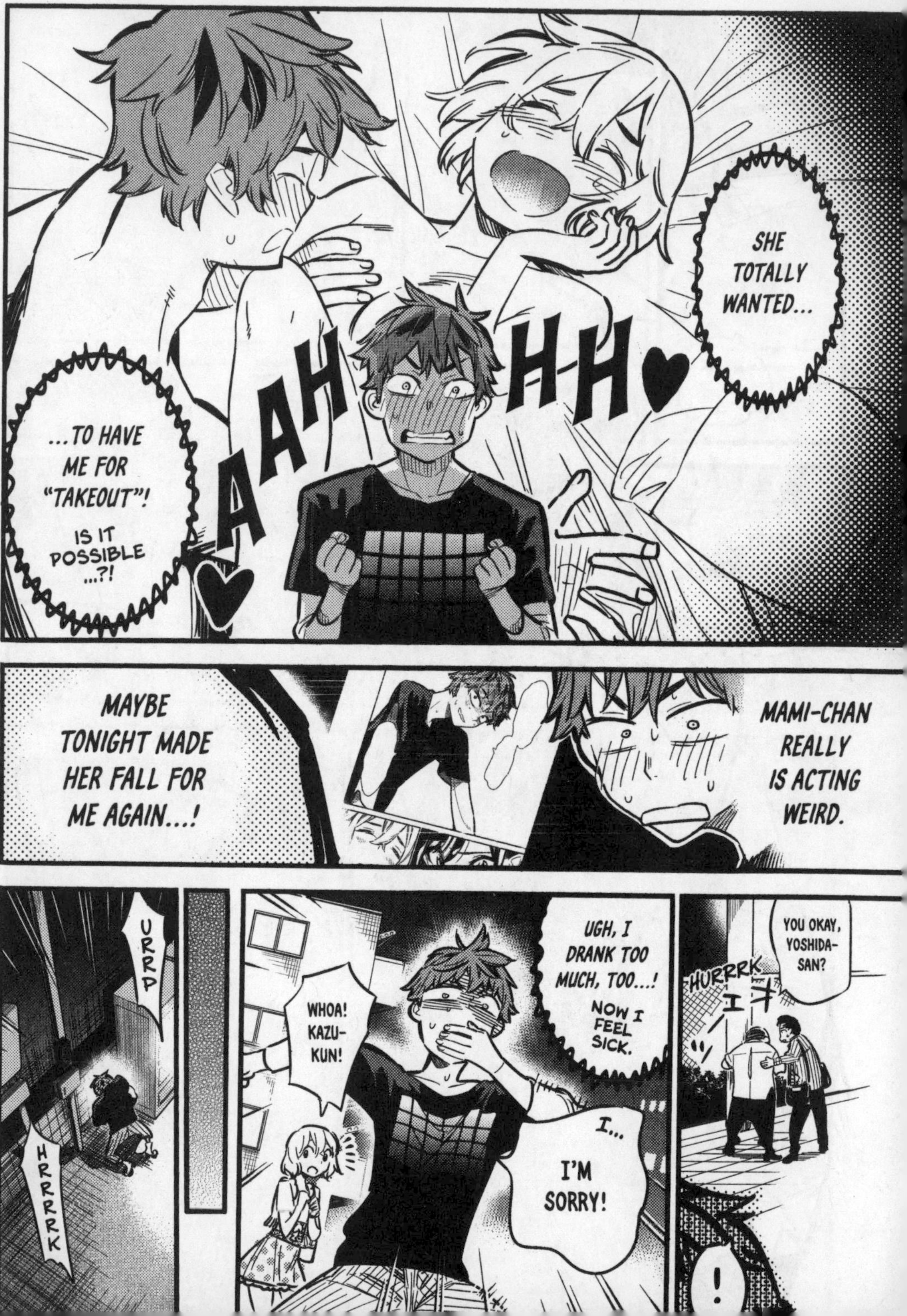
SHE TOTALLY WANTED...
AAHHH♥
...TO HAVE ME FOR "TAKEOUT"!
IS IT POSSIBLE ...?!
MAMI-CHAN REALLY IS ACTING WEIRD.
MAYBE TONIGHT MADE HER FALL FOR ME AGAIN...!
YOU OKAY, YOSHIDA-SAN?
HURRRK
UGH, I DRANK TOO MUCH, TOO...!
NOW I FEEL SICK.
WHOA! KAZU-KUN!
I...
I'M SORRY!
URRP
HRRRRK

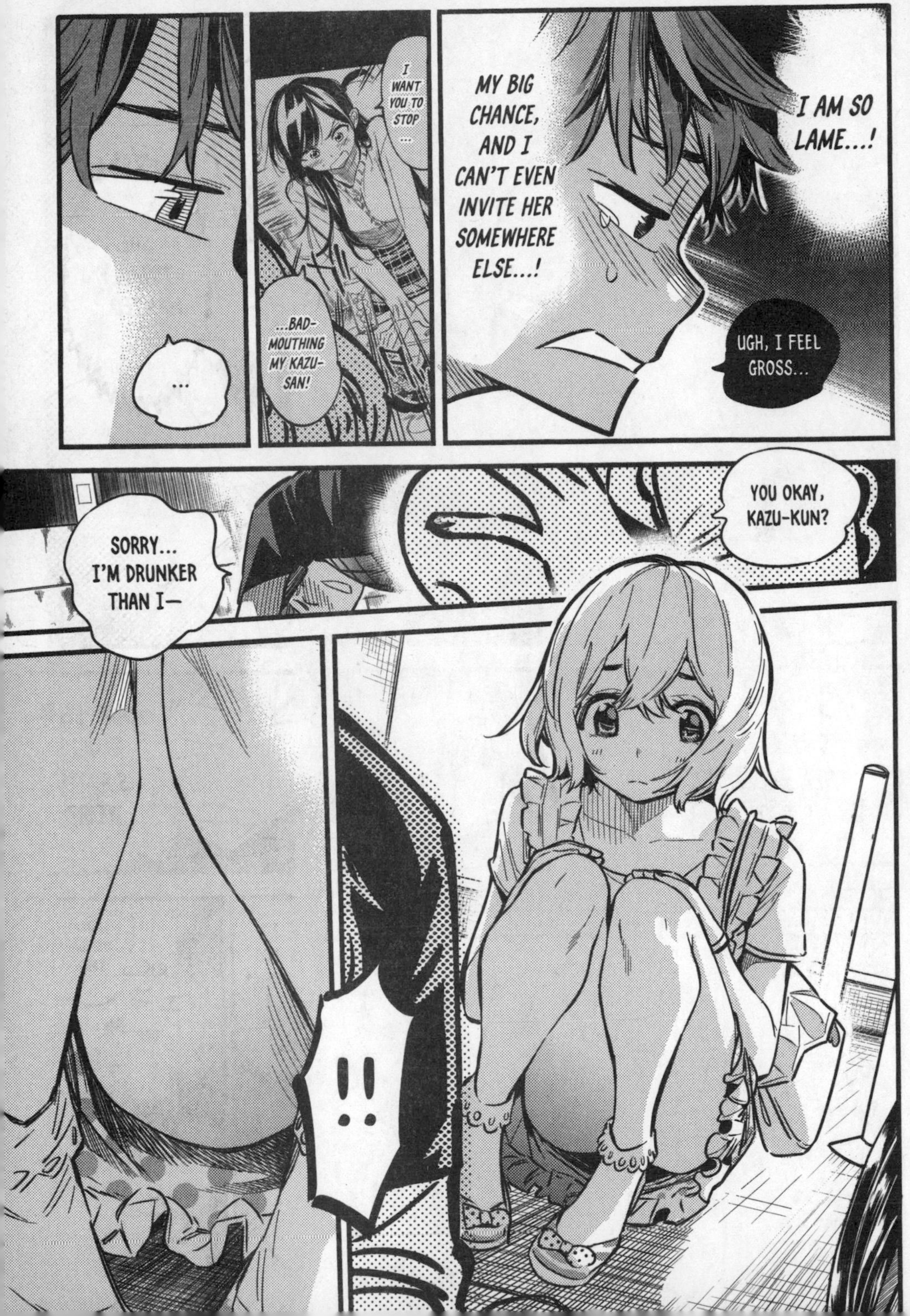
I AM SO LAME...!
MY BIG CHANCE, AND I CAN'T EVEN INVITE HER SOMEWHERE ELSE...!
UGH, I FEEL GROSS...
I WANT YOU TO STOP ...
...BAD-MOUTHING MY KAZU-SAN!
...
YOU OKAY, KAZU-KUN?
SORRY... I'M DRUNKER THAN I—
!!

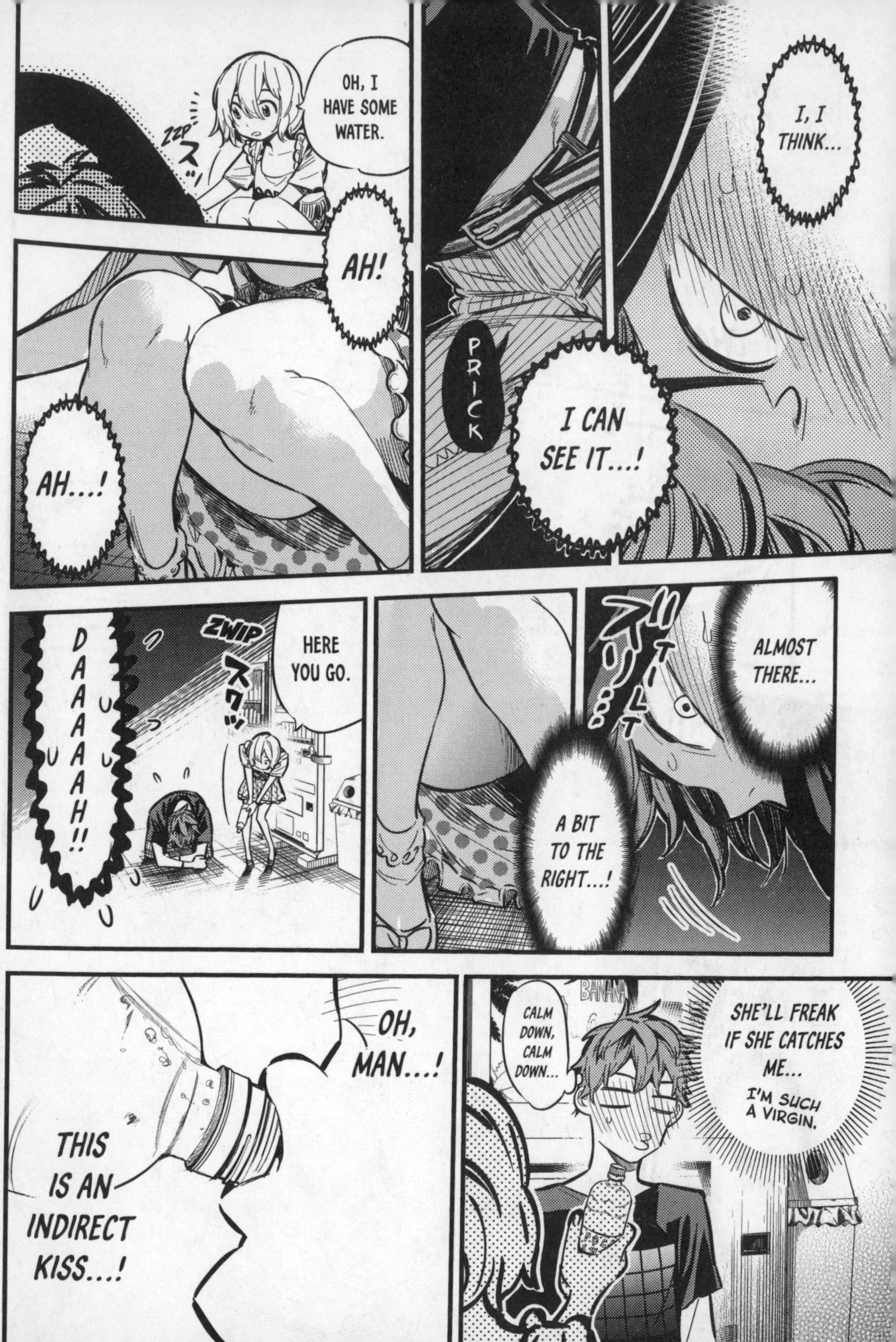
I, I THINK...
PRICK
I CAN SEE IT...!
OH, I HAVE SOME WATER.
ZZP
スッ
AH!
AH...!
ALMOST THERE...
TILT
A BIT TO THE RIGHT...!
ZWIP
HERE YOU GO.
DAAAAAAAH!!
BANANA
SHE'LL FREAK IF SHE CATCHES ME...
I'M SUCH A VIRGIN.
CALM DOWN, CALM DOWN...
OH, MAN...!
THIS IS AN INDIRECT KISS...!

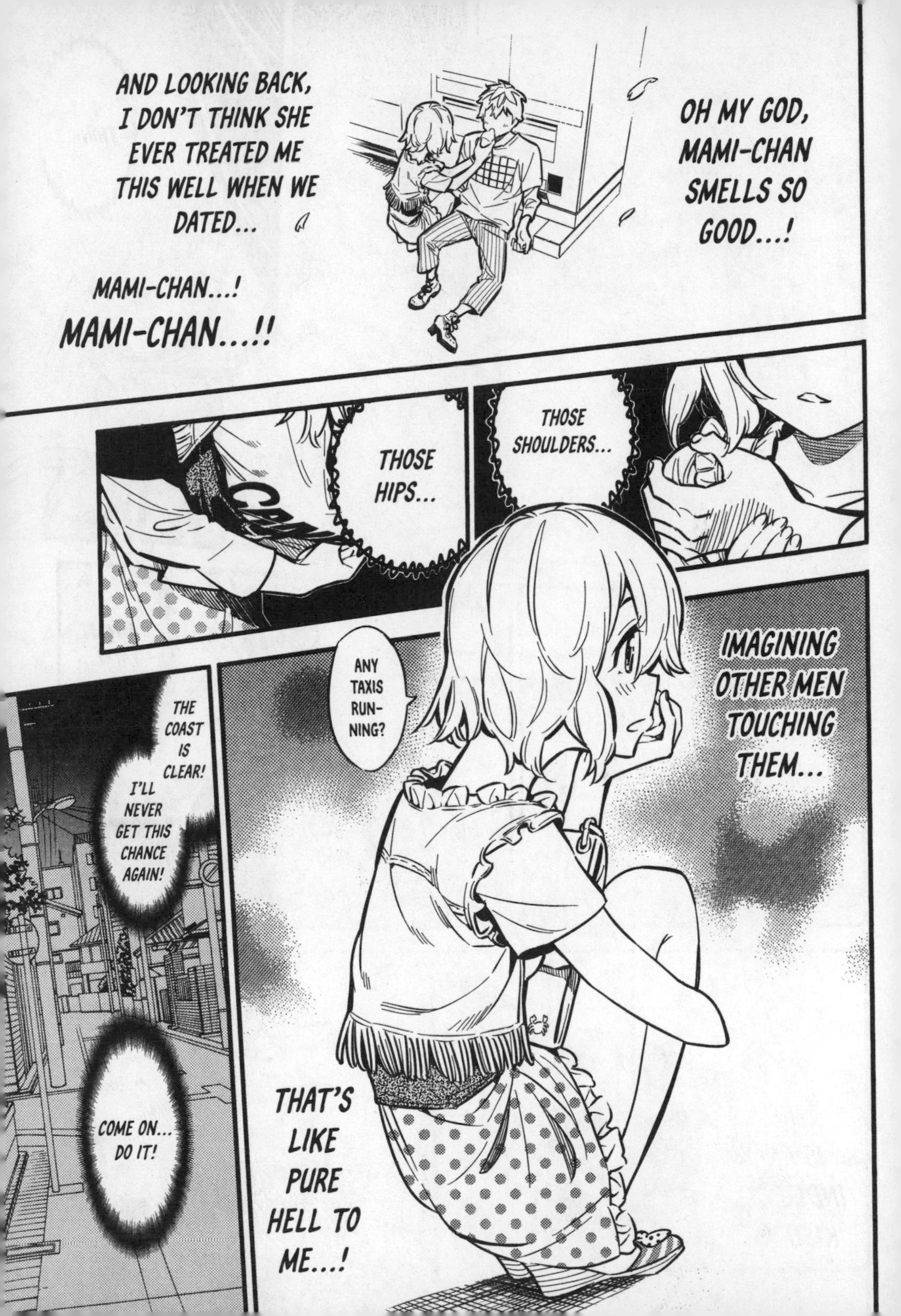
OH MY GOD, MAMI-CHAN SMELLS SO GOOD...!
AND LOOKING BACK, I DON'T THINK SHE EVER TREATED ME THIS WELL WHEN WE DATED...
MAMI-CHAN...!
MAMI-CHAN...!!
THOSE SHOULDERS...
THOSE HIPS...
IMAGINING OTHER MEN TOUCHING THEM...
ANY TAXIS RUN-NING?
THAT'S LIKE PURE HELL TO ME...!
THE COAST IS CLEAR!
I'LL NEVER GET THIS CHANCE AGAIN!
COME ON... DO IT!

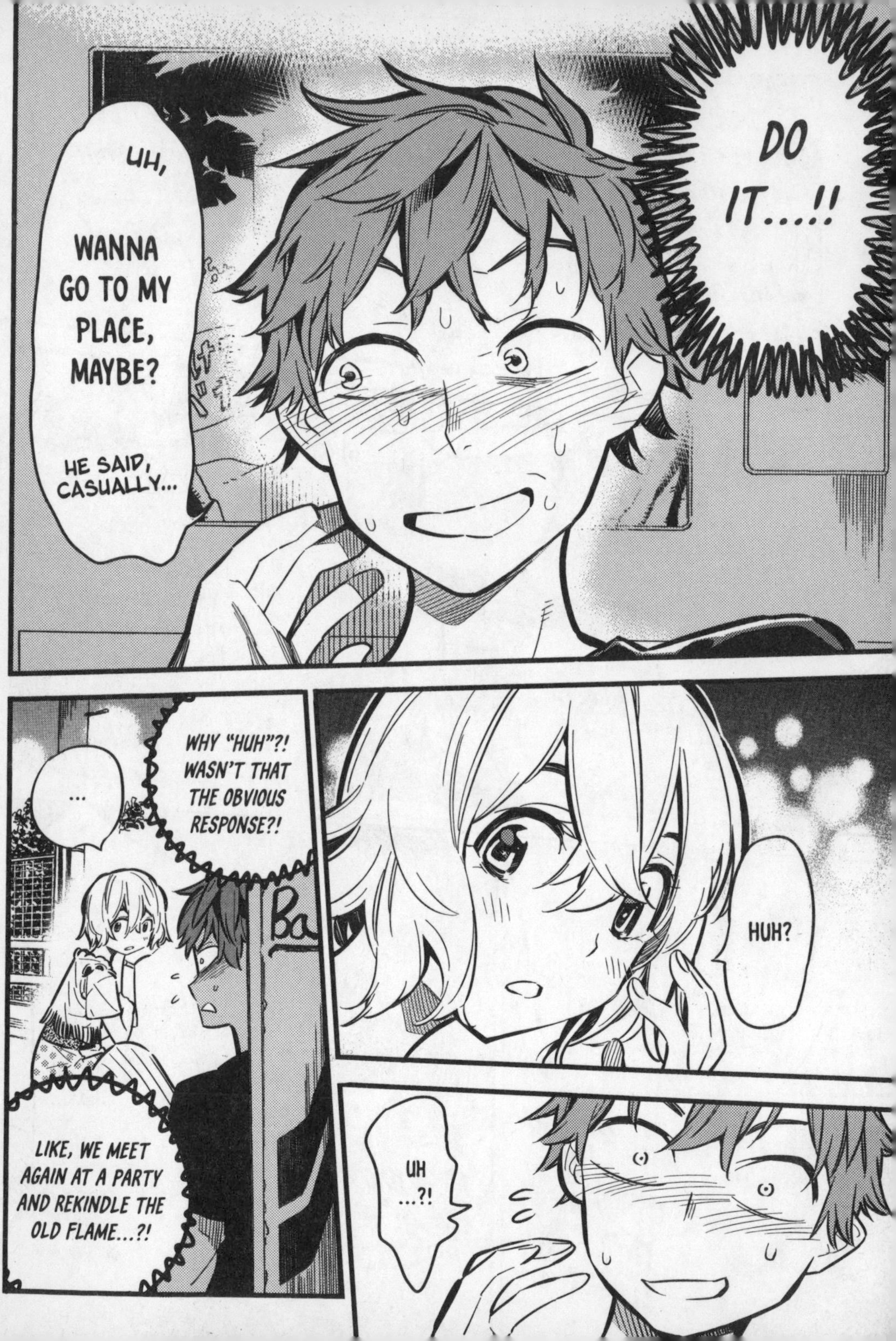
DO IT...!!
UH,
WANNA GO TO MY PLACE, MAYBE?
HE SAID, CASUALLY...
HUH?
UH ...?!
WHY "HUH"?! WASN'T THAT THE OBVIOUS RESPONSE?!
...
LIKE, WE MEET AGAIN AT A PARTY AND REKINDLE THE OLD FLAME...?!

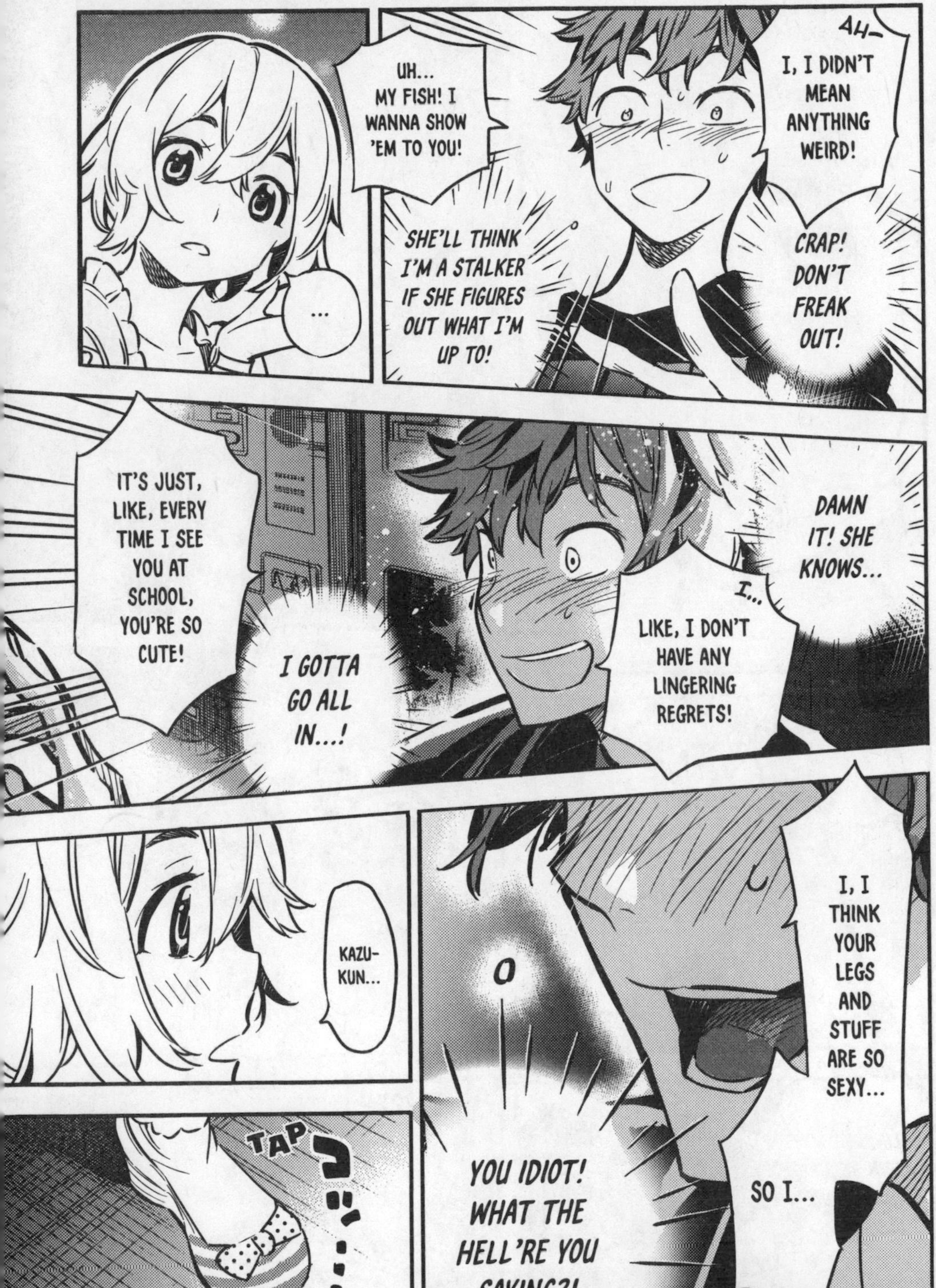
AH—
I, I DIDN'T MEAN ANYTHING WEIRD!
UH... MY FISH! I WANNA SHOW 'EM TO YOU!
CRAP! DON'T FREAK OUT!
SHE'LL THINK I'M A STALKER IF SHE FIGURES OUT WHAT I'M UP TO!
...
DAMN IT! SHE KNOWS...
I...
LIKE, I DON'T HAVE ANY LINGERING REGRETS!
IT'S JUST, LIKE, EVERY TIME I SEE YOU AT SCHOOL, YOU'RE SO CUTE!
I GOTTA GO ALL IN...!
I, I THINK YOUR LEGS AND STUFF ARE SO SEXY...
O
SO I...
YOU IDIOT! WHAT THE HELL'RE YOU SAYING?!
KAZU-KUN...
TAP

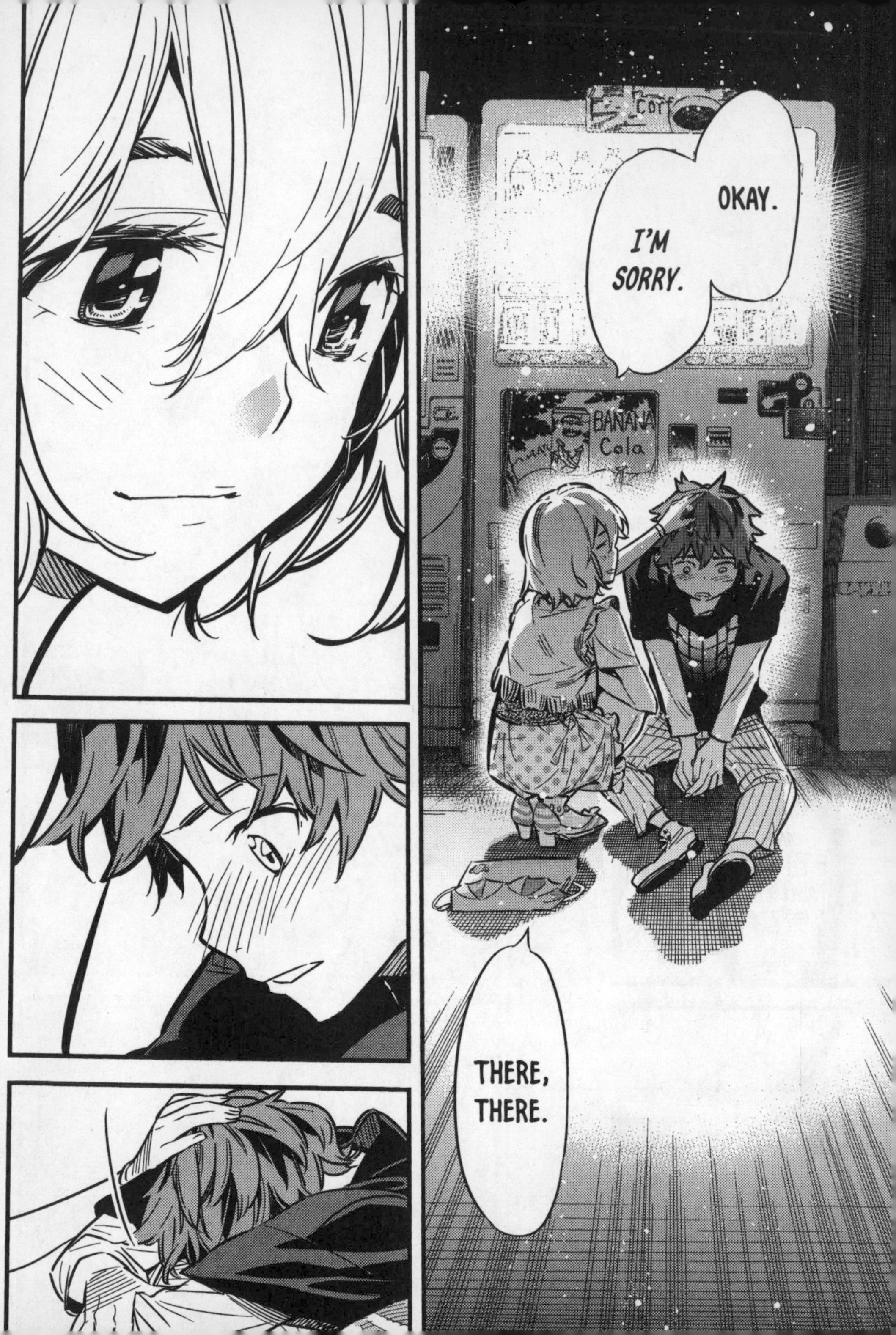
OKAY.
I'M SORRY.
BANANA Cola
THERE, THERE.

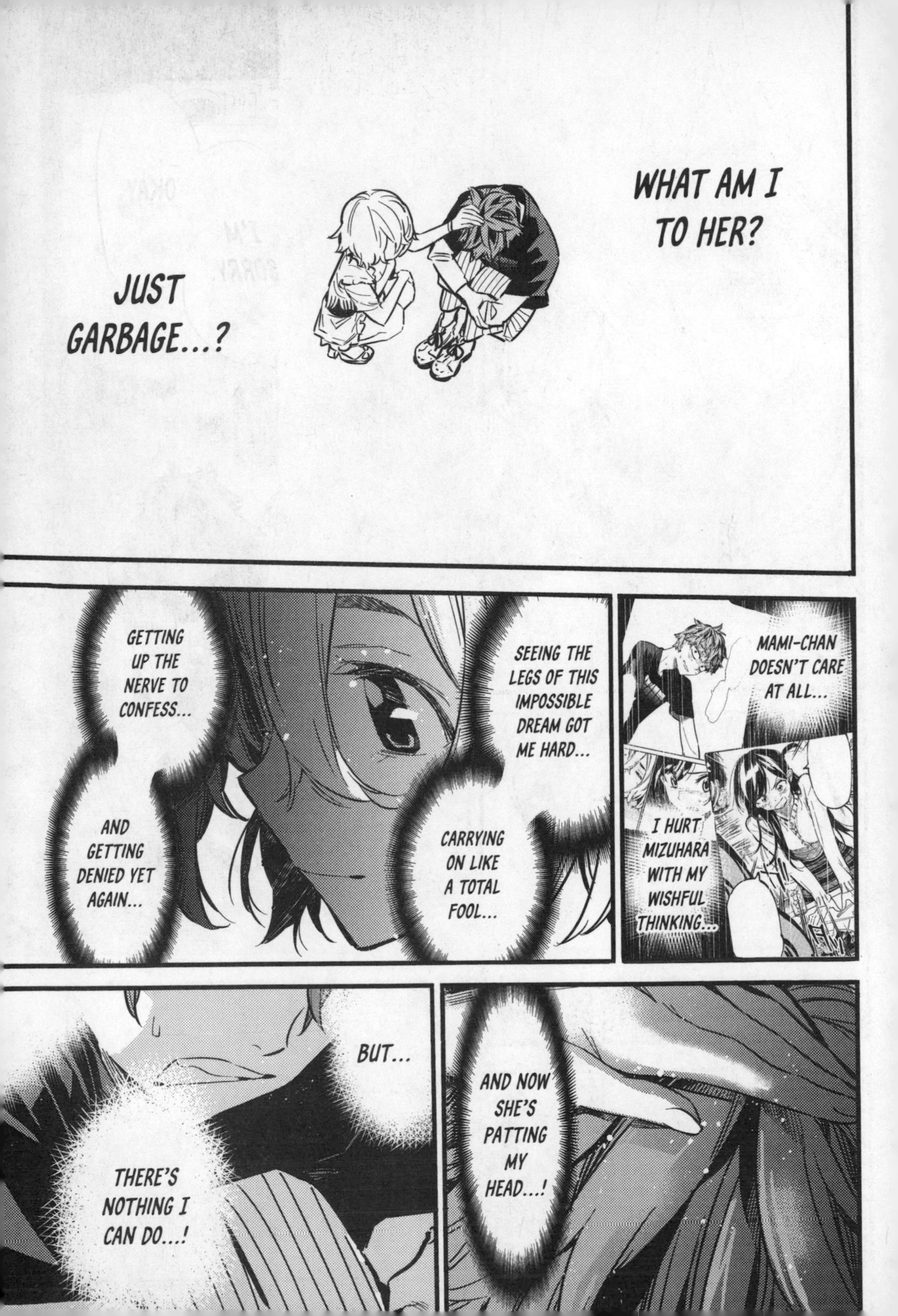
WHAT AM I TO HER?
JUST GARBAGE...?
MAMI-CHAN DOESN'T CARE AT ALL...
I HURT MIZUHARA WITH MY WISHFUL THINKING...
SEEING THE LEGS OF THIS IMPOSSIBLE DREAM GOT ME HARD...
GETTING UP THE NERVE TO CONFESS...
CARRYING ON LIKE A TOTAL FOOL...
AND GETTING DENIED YET AGAIN...
AND NOW SHE'S PATTING MY HEAD...!
BUT...
THERE'S NOTHING I CAN DO...!

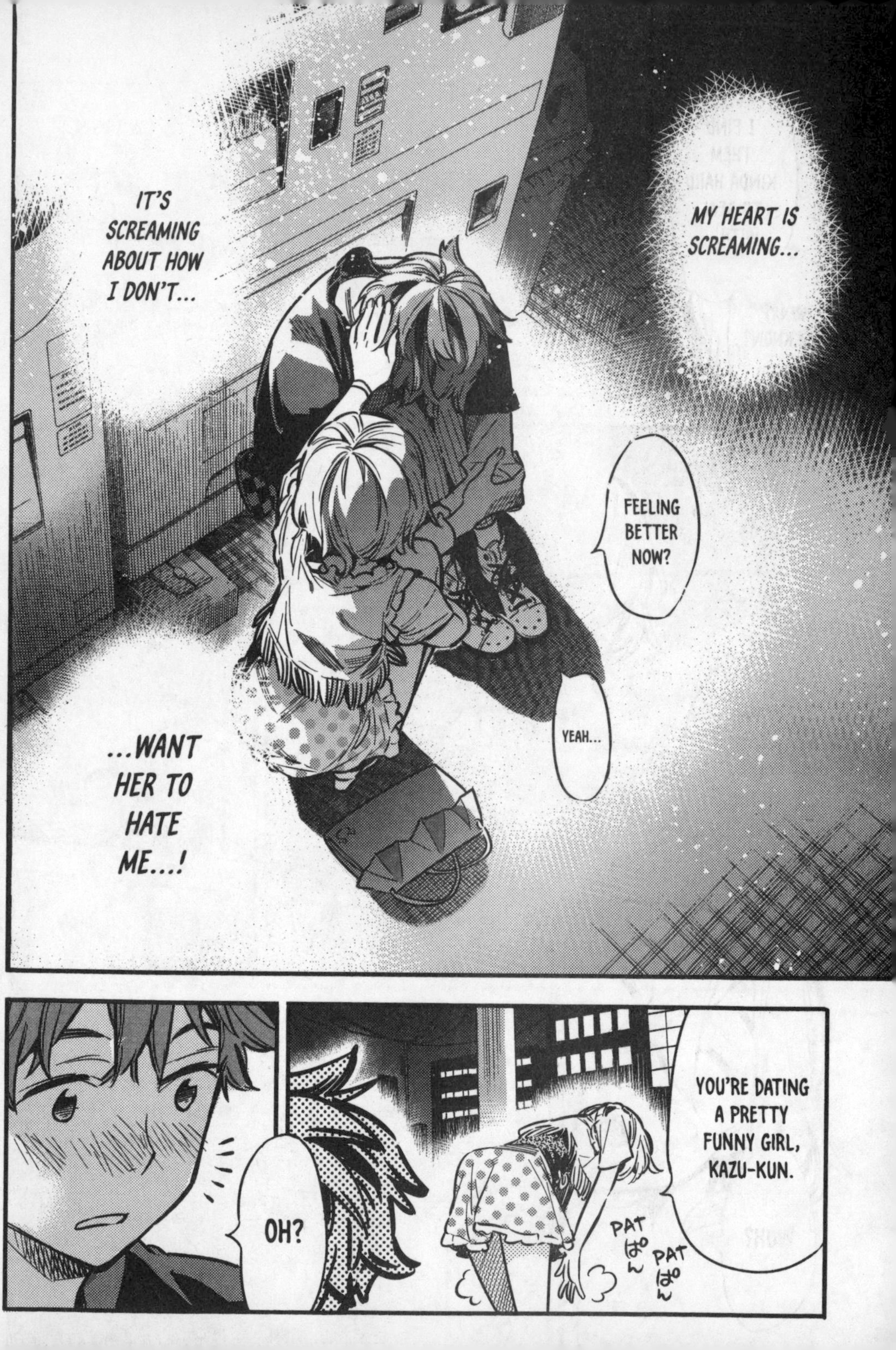
MY HEART IS SCREAMING...
IT'S SCREAMING ABOUT HOW I DON'T...
FEELING BETTER NOW?
YEAH...
...WANT HER TO HATE ME...!
YOU'RE DATING A PRETTY FUNNY GIRL, KAZU-KUN.
PAT ぱん
PAT ぱん
OH?

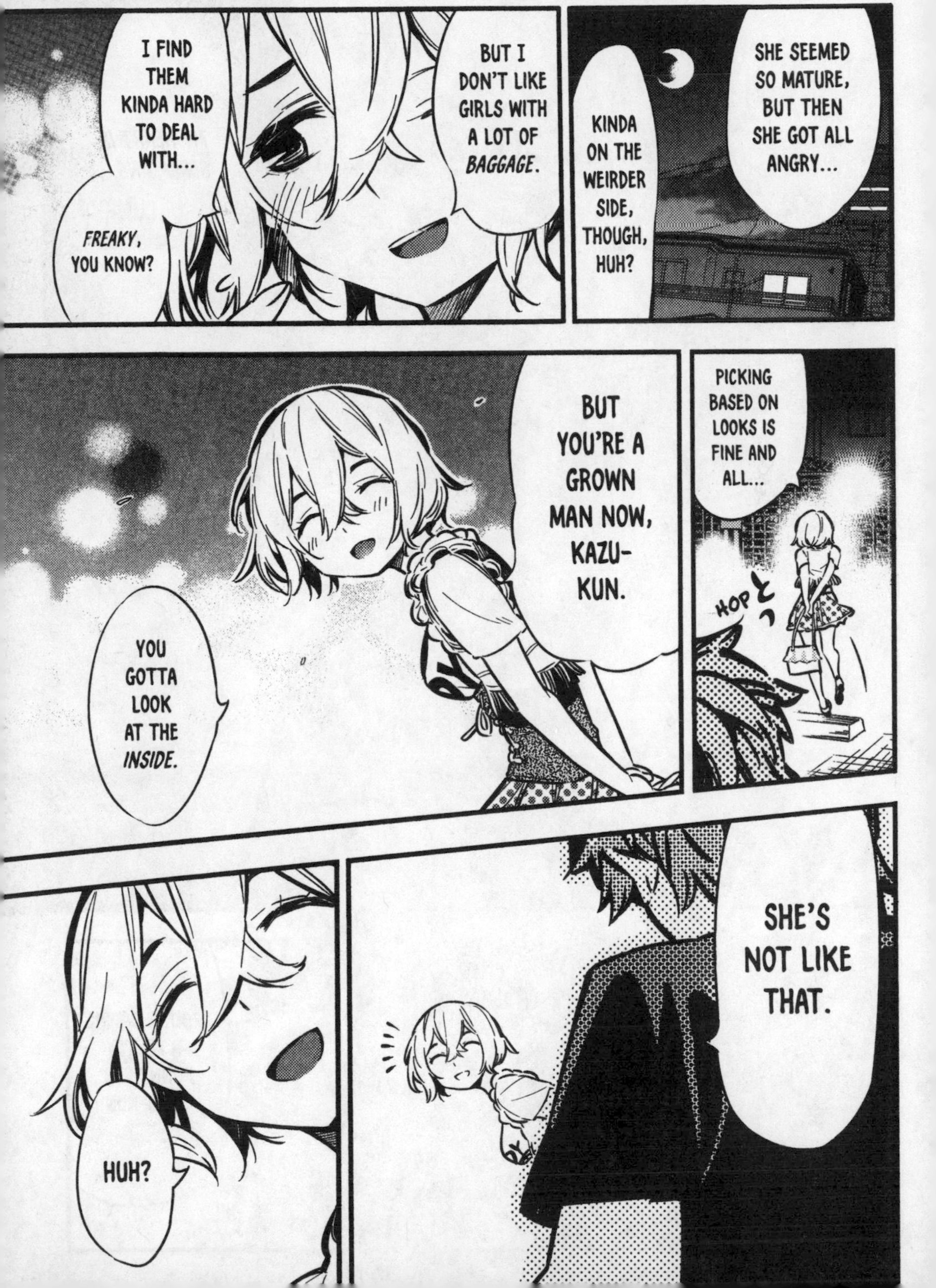
SHE SEEMED SO MATURE, BUT THEN SHE GOT ALL ANGRY...
KINDA ON THE WEIRDER SIDE, THOUGH, HUH?
BUT I DON'T LIKE GIRLS WITH A LOT OF *BAGGAGE*.
I FIND THEM KINDA HARD TO DEAL WITH...
FREAKY, YOU KNOW?
PICKING BASED ON LOOKS IS FINE AND ALL...
HOP
BUT YOU'RE A GROWN MAN NOW, KAZU-KUN.
YOU GOTTA LOOK AT THE *INSIDE*.
SHE'S NOT LIKE THAT.
HUH?

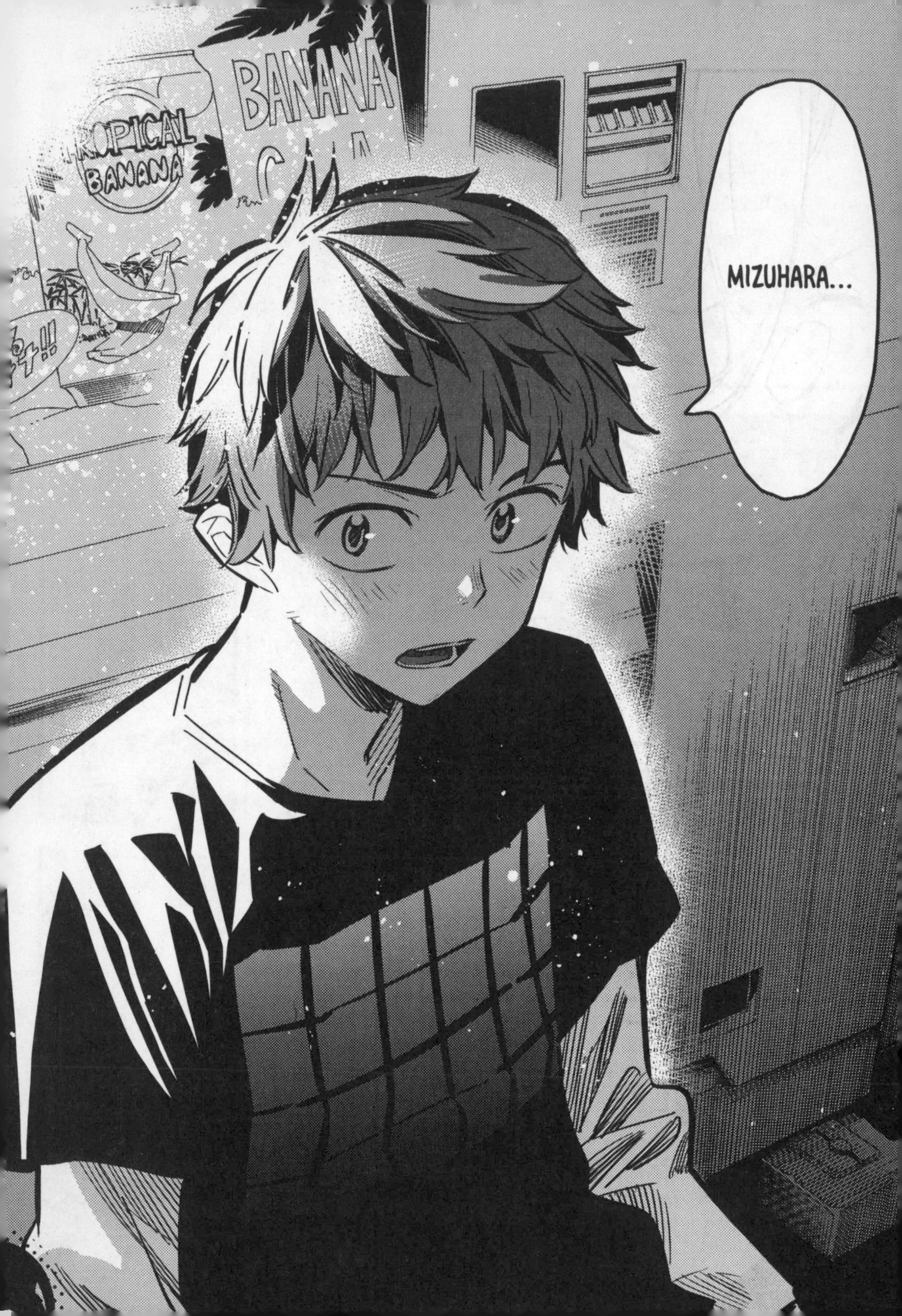
BANANA
ROPICAL
BANANA
MIZUHARA...

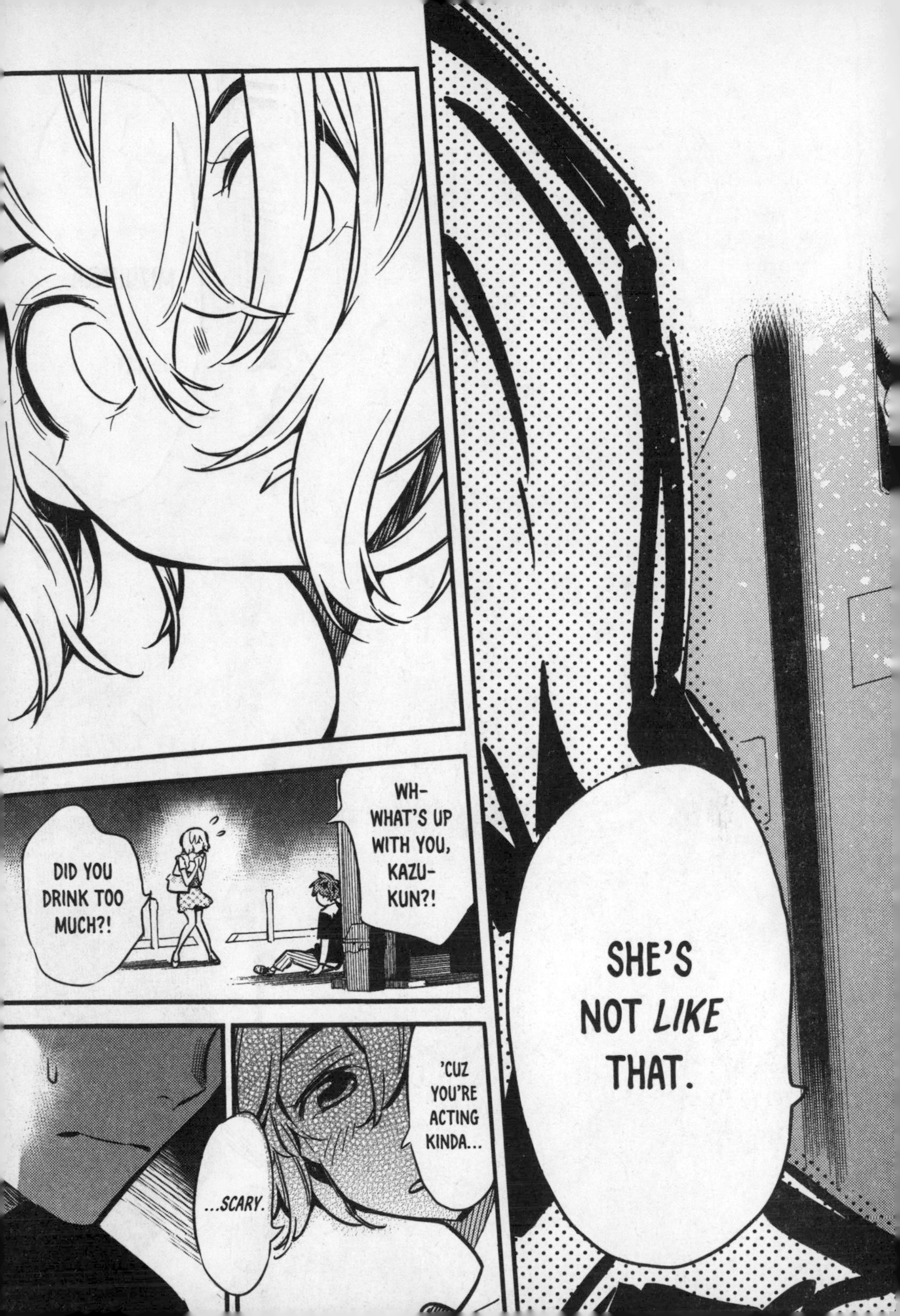
SHE'S NOT *LIKE* THAT.
WH- WHAT'S UP WITH YOU, KAZU-KUN?!
DID YOU DRINK TOO MUCH?!
'CUZ YOU'RE ACTING KINDA...
...SCARY.

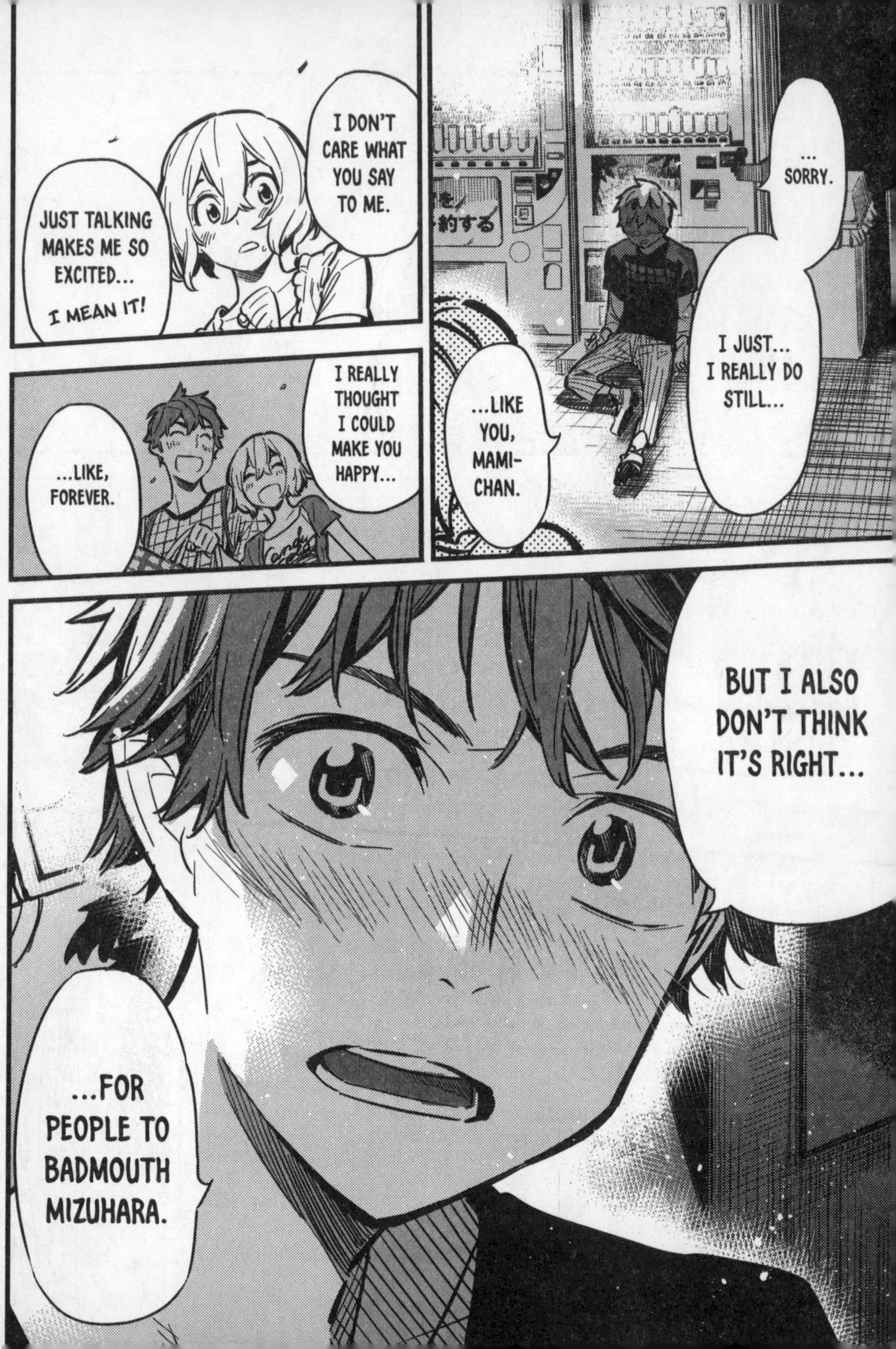
...SORRY.
I JUST... I REALLY DO STILL...
...LIKE YOU, MAMI-CHAN.
I DON'T CARE WHAT YOU SAY TO ME.
JUST TALKING MAKES ME SO EXCITED... I MEAN IT!
I REALLY THOUGHT I COULD MAKE YOU HAPPY...
...LIKE, FOREVER.
BUT I ALSO DON'T THINK IT'S RIGHT...
...FOR PEOPLE TO BADMOUTH MIZUHARA.

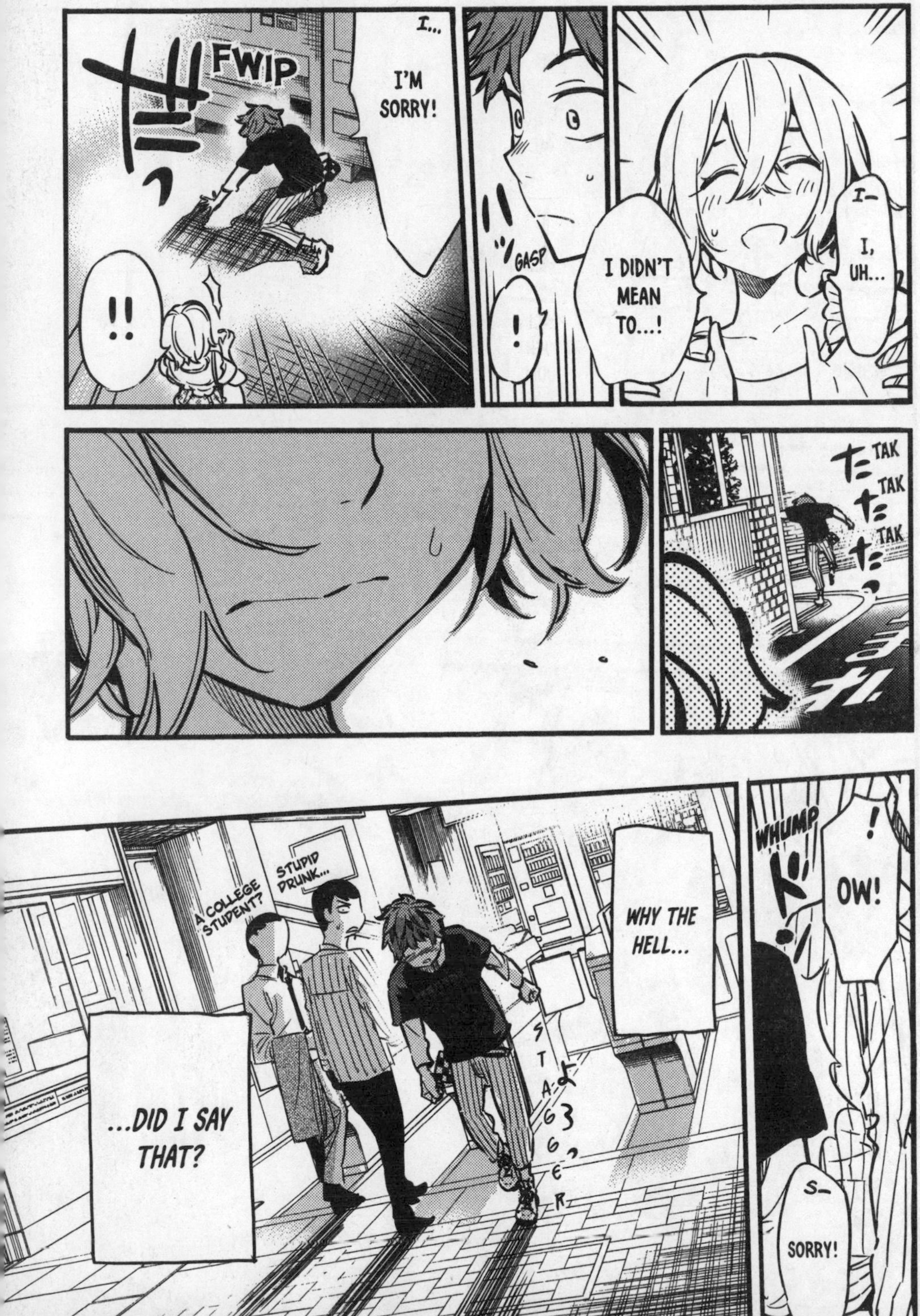
I— I, UH...
I DIDN'T MEAN TO...!
GASP
!
I... I'M SORRY!
FWIP
!!
TAK TAK TAK
!
WHUMP
OW!
S— SORRY!
WHY THE HELL...
STUPID DRUNK...
A COLLEGE STUDENT?
STAGGER
...DID I SAY THAT?

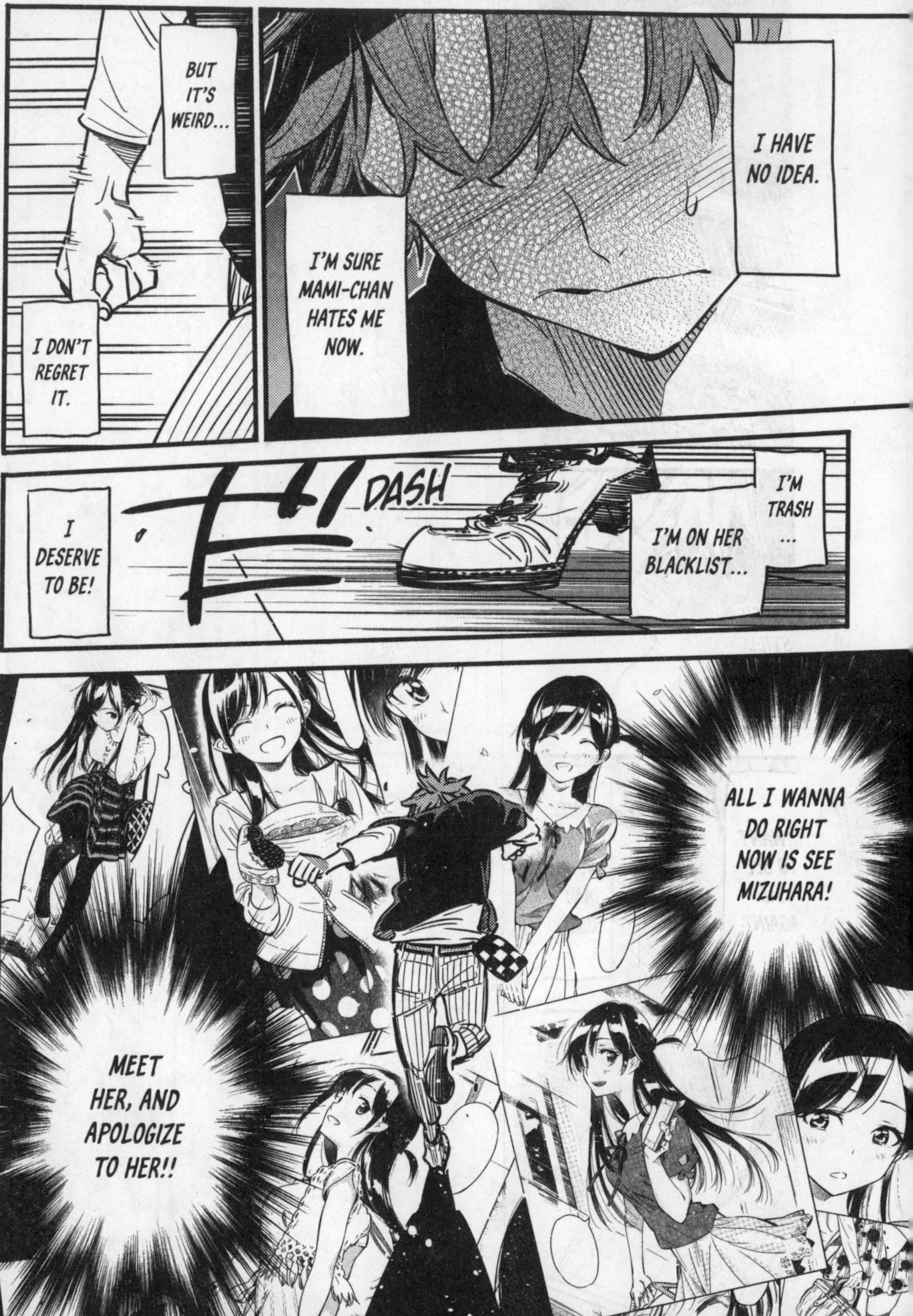
I HAVE NO IDEA.
I'M SURE MAMI-CHAN HATES ME NOW.
BUT IT'S WEIRD...
I DON'T REGRET IT.
I'M TRASH ...
I'M ON HER BLACKLIST...
DASH
I DESERVE TO BE!
ALL I WANNA DO RIGHT NOW IS SEE MIZUHARA!
MEET HER, AND APOLOGIZE TO HER!!

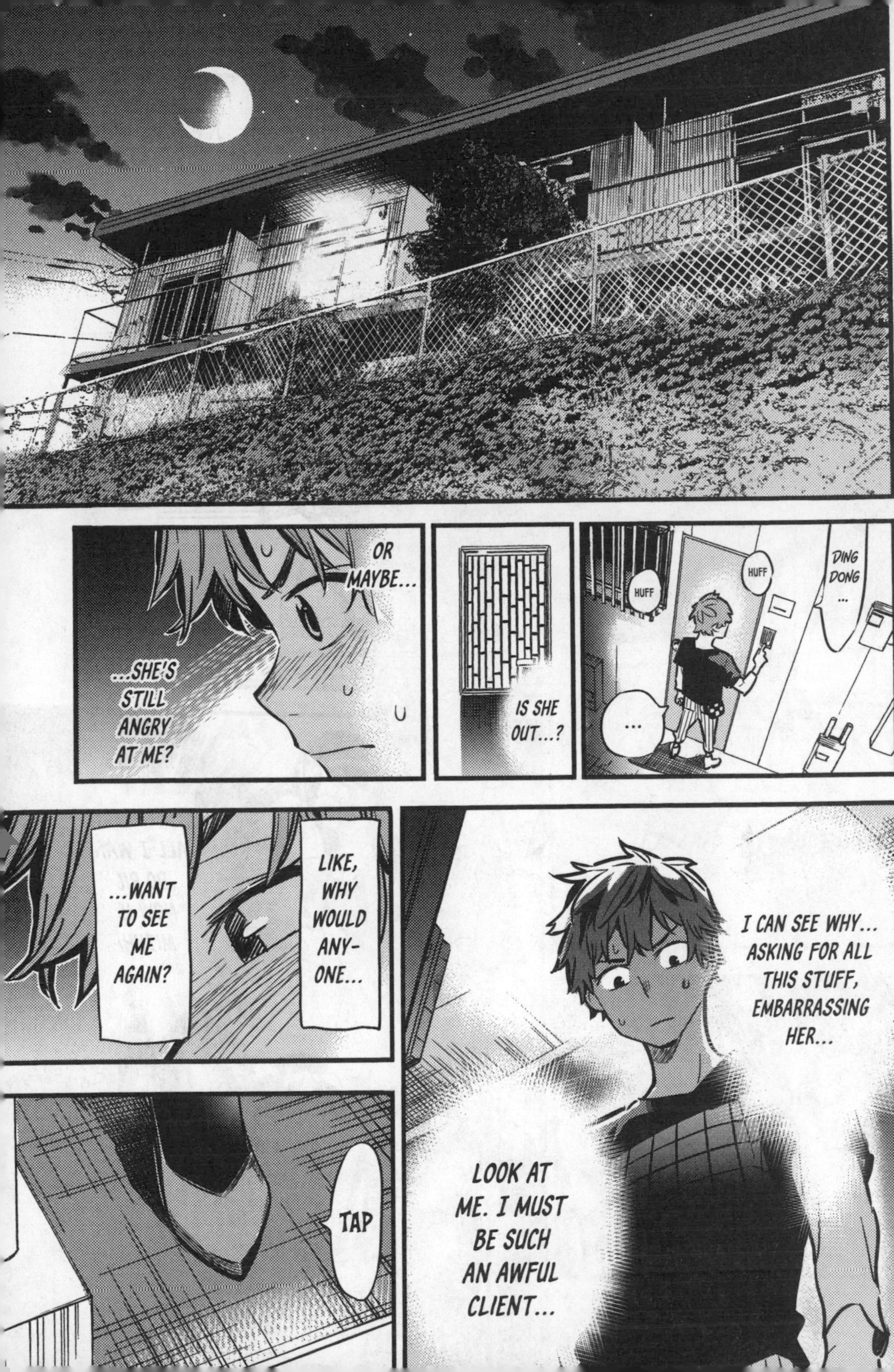
DING DONG ...
HUFF
HUFF
...
IS SHE OUT...?
OR MAYBE...
...SHE'S STILL ANGRY AT ME?
I CAN SEE WHY... ASKING FOR ALL THIS STUFF, EMBARRASSING HER...
LOOK AT ME. I MUST BE SUCH AN AWFUL CLIENT...
LIKE, WHY WOULD ANY-ONE...
...WANT TO SEE ME AGAIN?
TAP

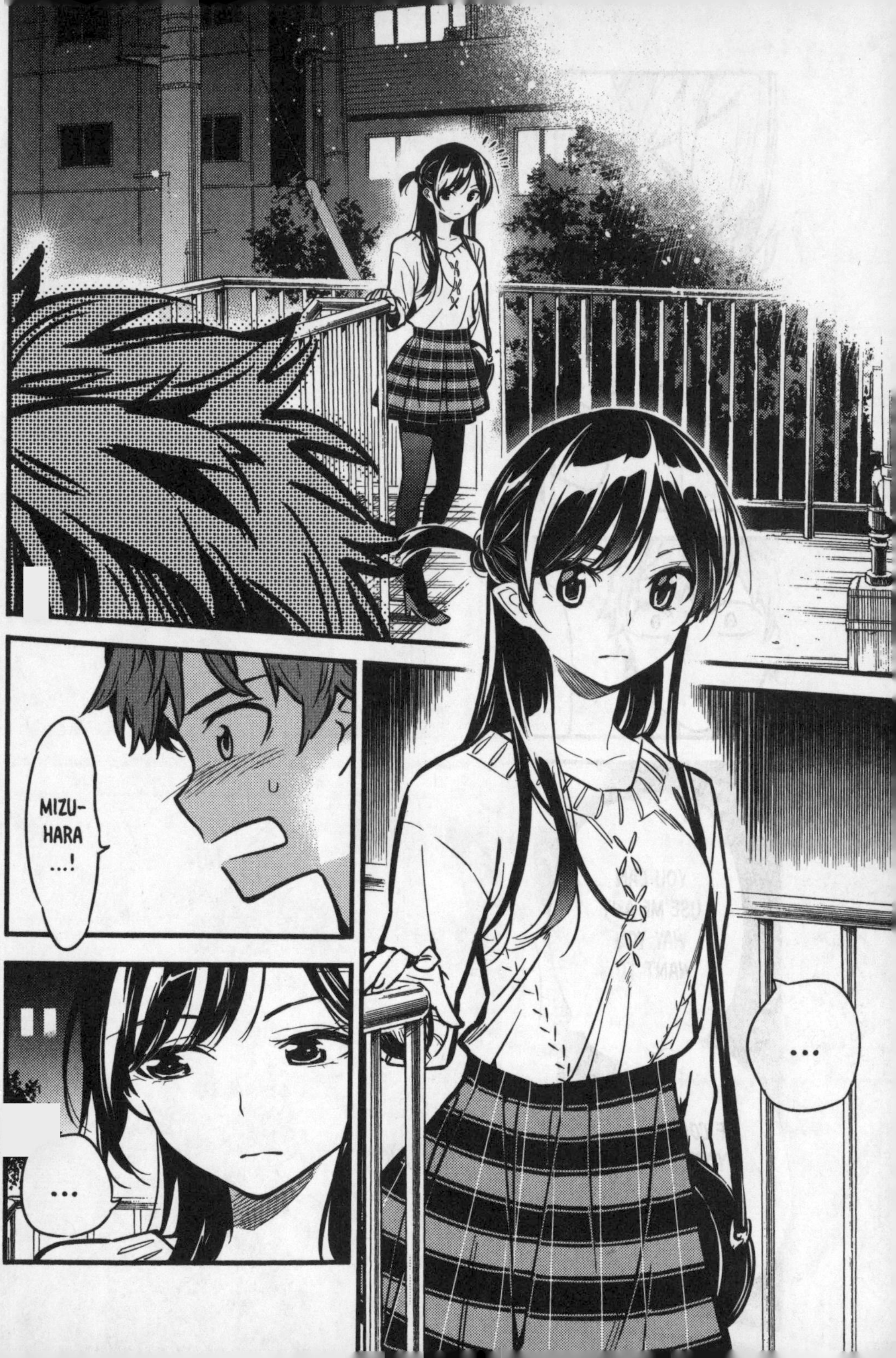
...
MIZU-HARA ...!
...

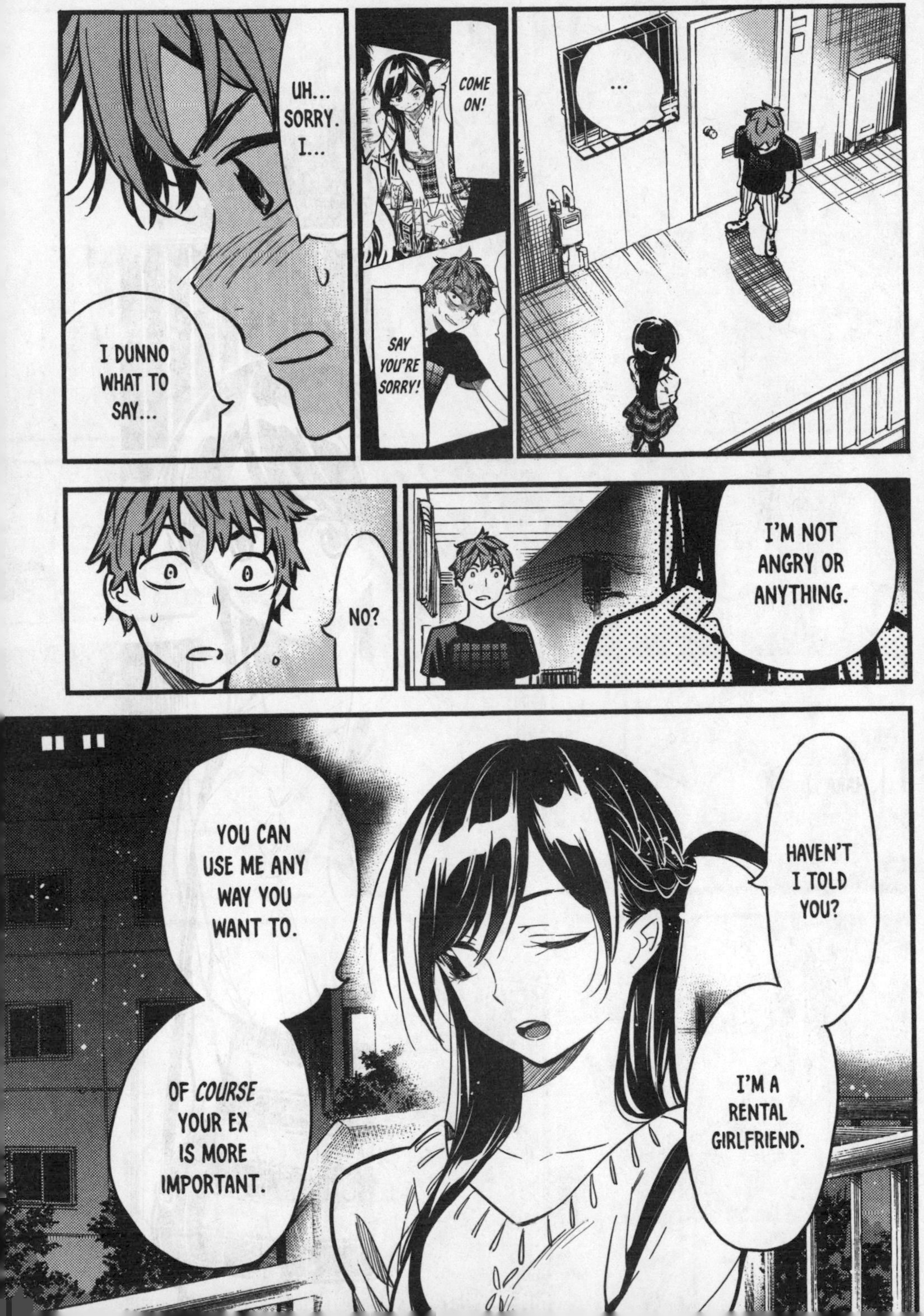
...
COME ON!
SAY YOU'RE SORRY!
UH... SORRY. I...
I DUNNO WHAT TO SAY...
I'M NOT ANGRY OR ANYTHING.
NO?
HAVEN'T I TOLD YOU?
I'M A RENTAL GIRLFRIEND.
YOU CAN USE ME ANY WAY YOU WANT TO.
OF *COURSE* YOUR EX IS MORE IMPORTANT.

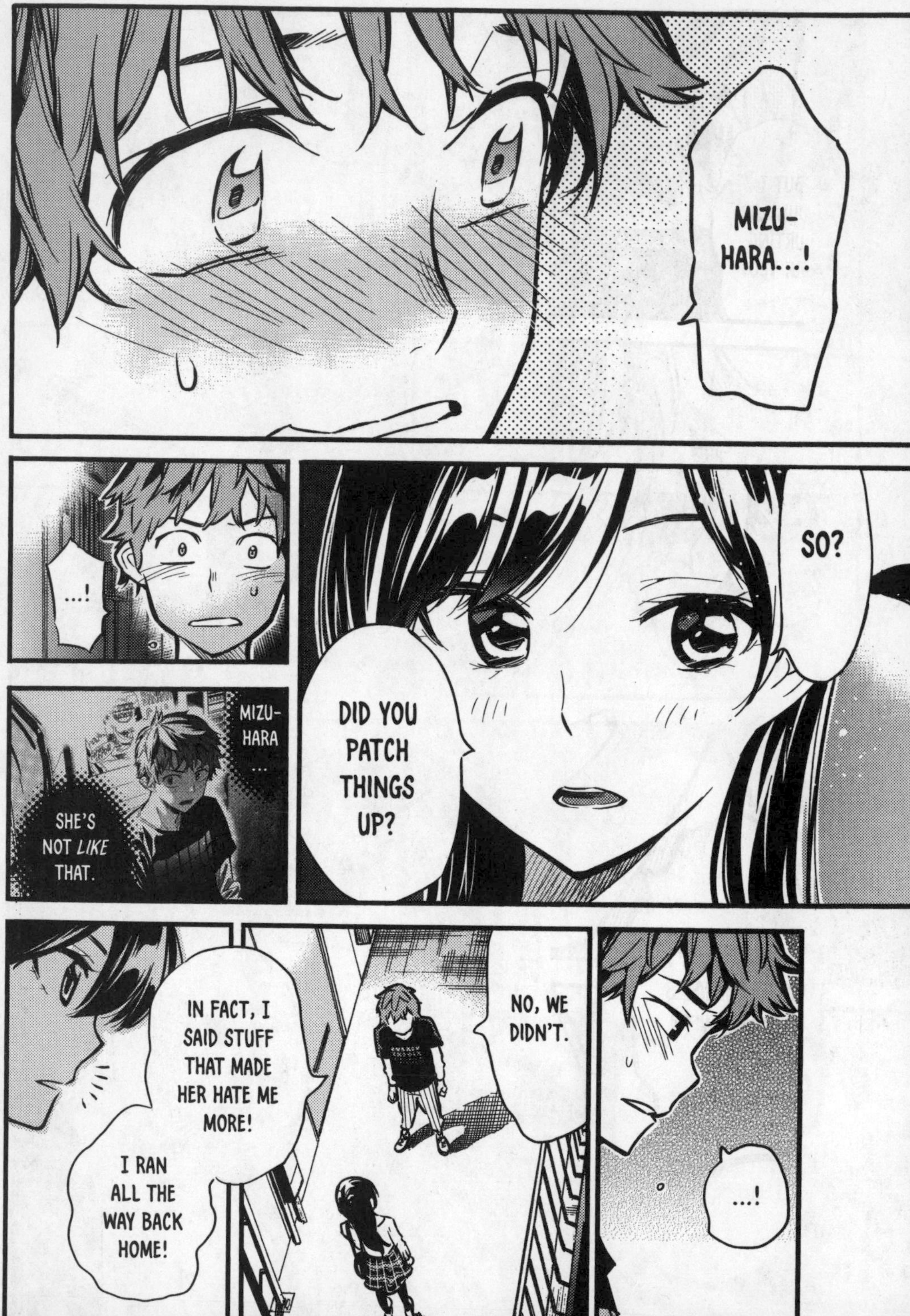
MIZU-HARA...!
SO?
DID YOU PATCH THINGS UP?
...!
MIZU-HARA...
SHE'S NOT *LIKE* THAT.
...!
NO, WE DIDN'T.
IN FACT, I SAID STUFF THAT MADE HER HATE ME MORE!
I RAN ALL THE WAY BACK HOME!

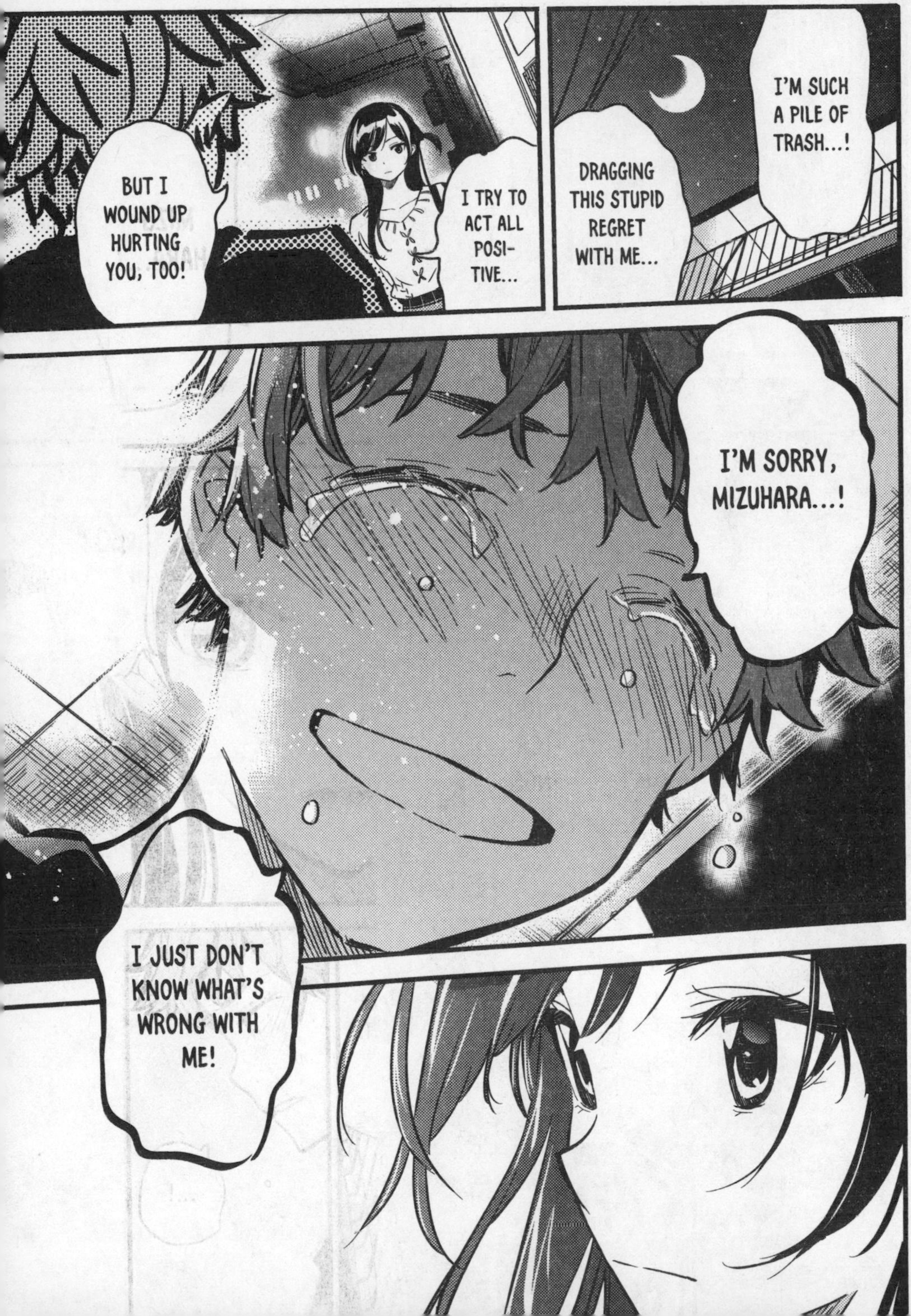
I'M SUCH A PILE OF TRASH...!
DRAGGING THIS STUPID REGRET WITH ME...
I TRY TO ACT ALL POSI-TIVE...
BUT I WOUND UP HURTING YOU, TOO!
I'M SORRY, MIZUHARA...!
I JUST DON'T KNOW WHAT'S WRONG WITH ME!

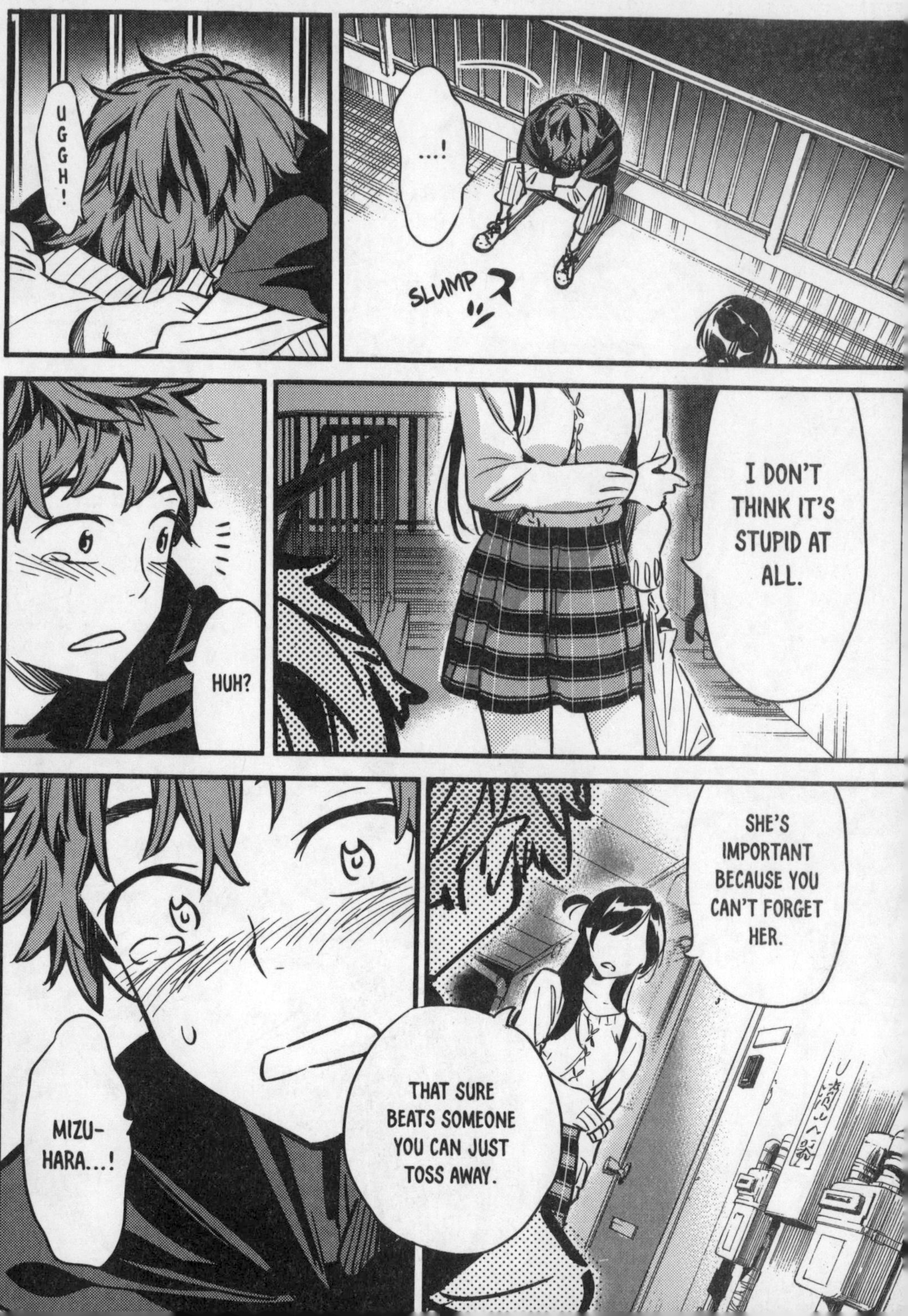
...!
SLUMP
UGGH!
I DON'T THINK IT'S STUPID AT ALL.
HUH?
SHE'S IMPORTANT BECAUSE YOU CAN'T FORGET HER.
THAT SURE BEATS SOMEONE YOU CAN JUST TOSS AWAY.
MIZU-HARA...!

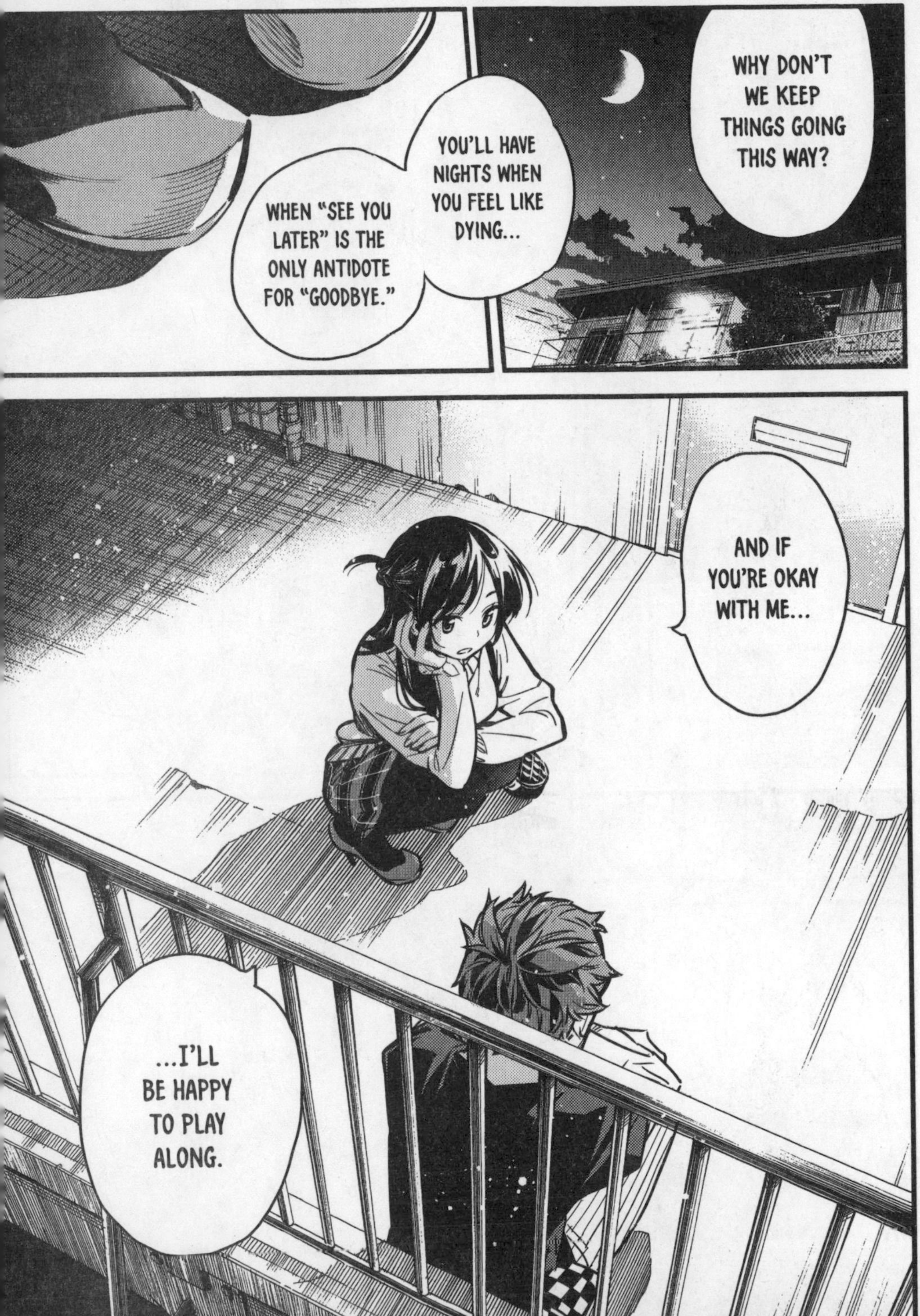
WHY DON'T WE KEEP THINGS GOING THIS WAY?
YOU'LL HAVE NIGHTS WHEN YOU FEEL LIKE DYING...
WHEN "SEE YOU LATER" IS THE ONLY ANTIDOTE FOR "GOODBYE."
AND IF YOU'RE OKAY WITH ME...
...I'LL BE HAPPY TO PLAY ALONG.

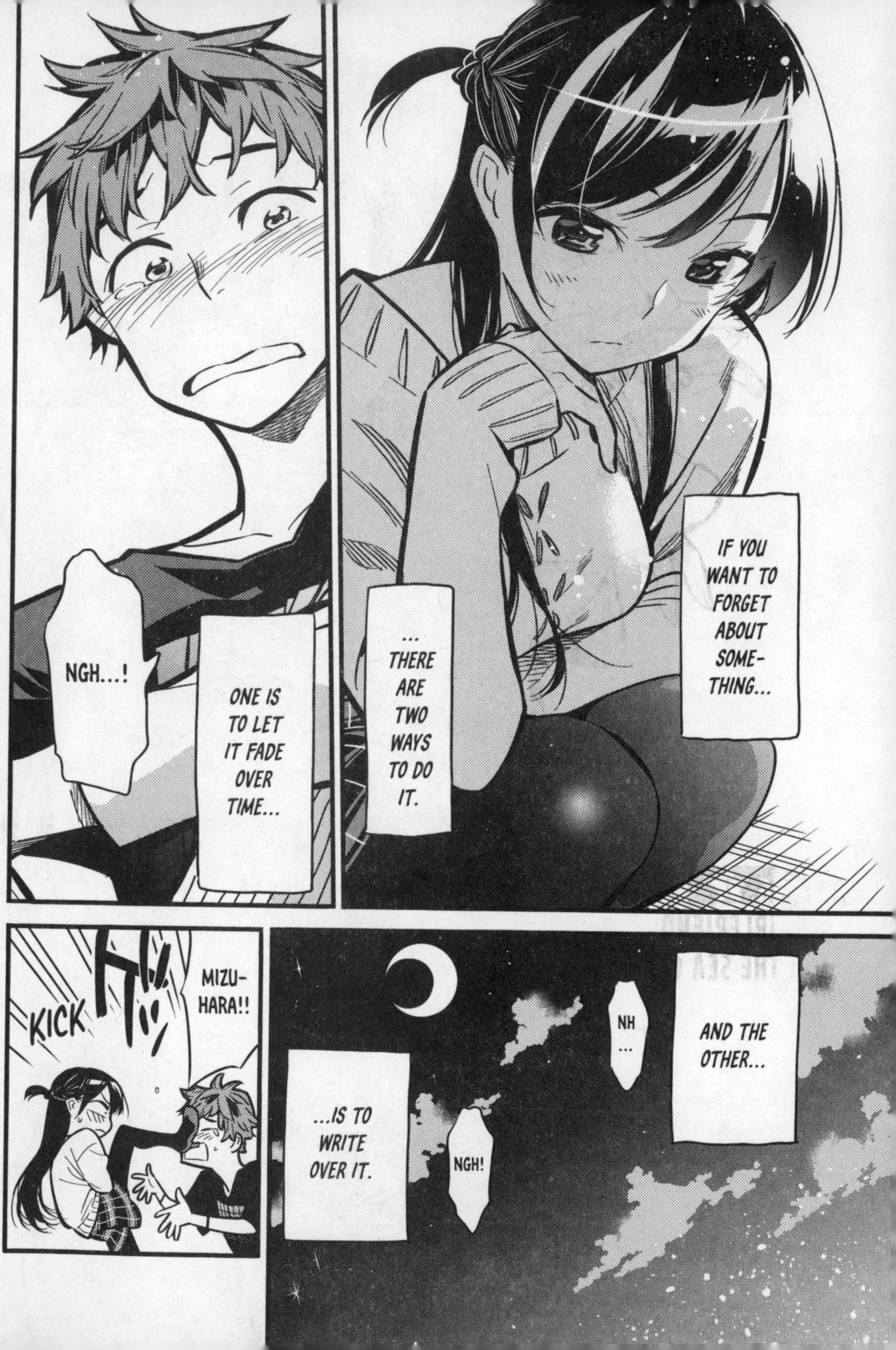
IF YOU WANT TO FORGET ABOUT SOME-THING...
... THERE ARE TWO WAYS TO DO IT.
ONE IS TO LET IT FADE OVER TIME...
NGH...!
AND THE OTHER...
NH ...
...IS TO WRITE OVER IT.
NGH!
MIZU-HARA!!
KICK

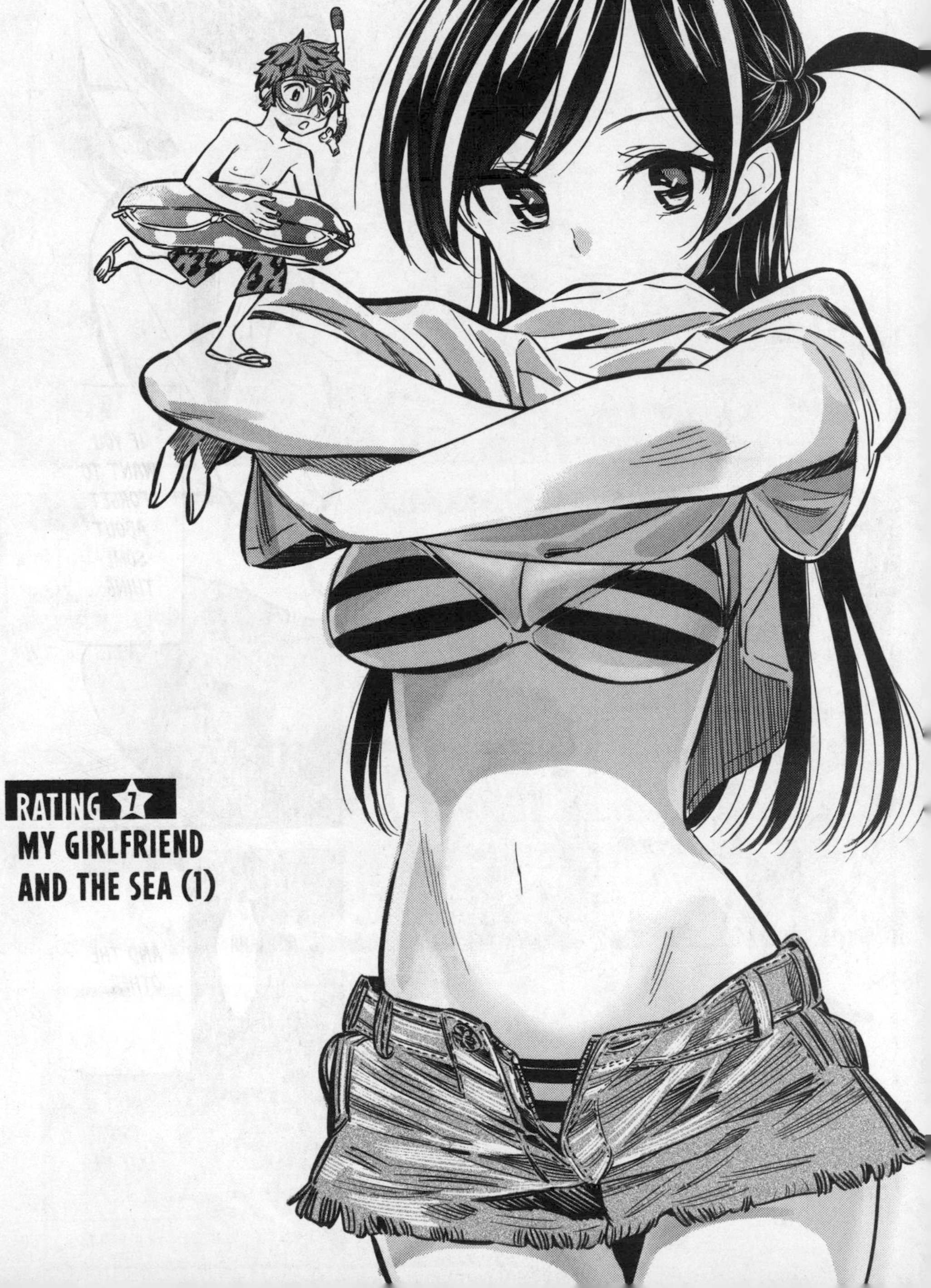
RATING 7
MY GIRLFRIEND AND THE SEA (1)

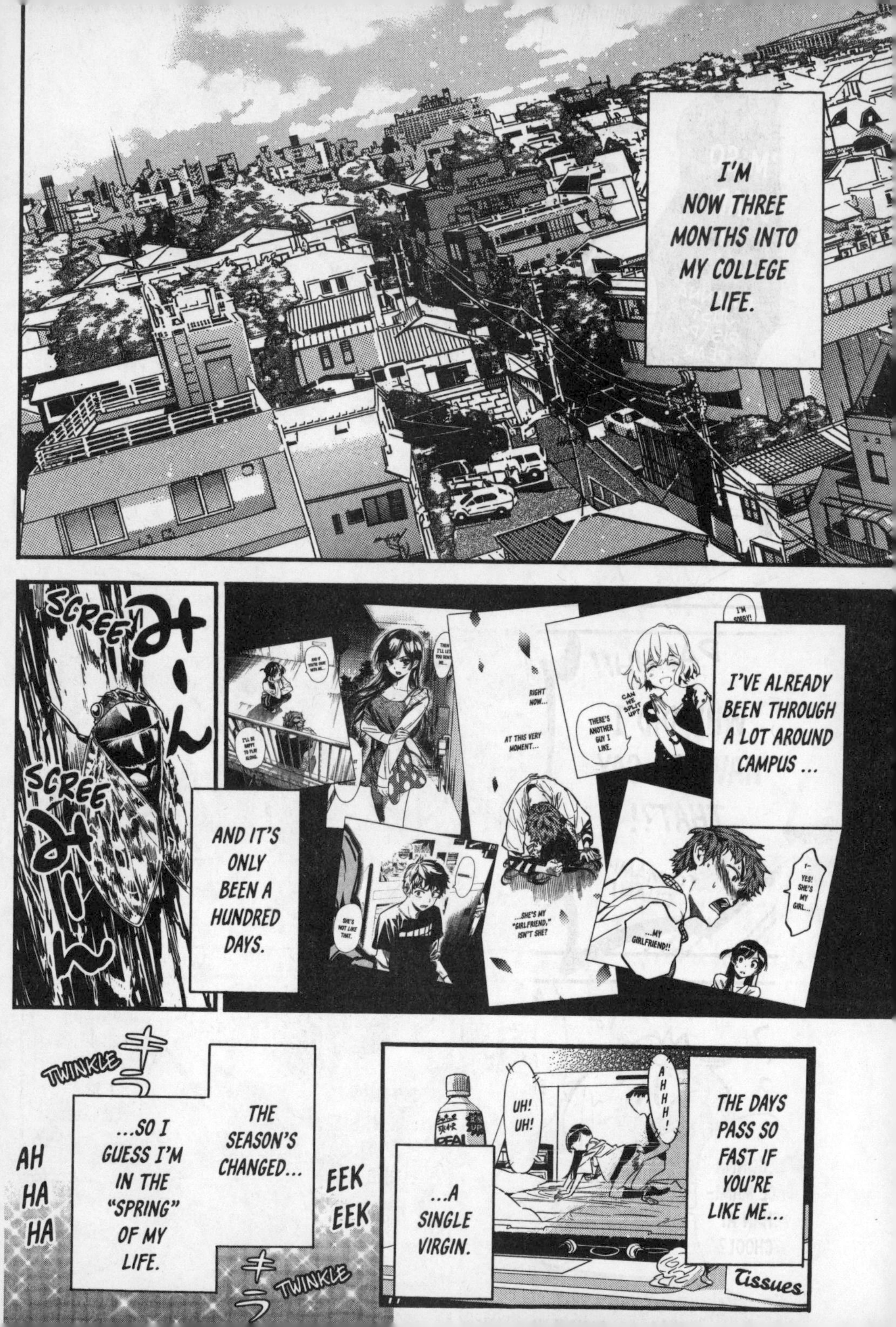
I'M NOW THREE MONTHS INTO MY COLLEGE LIFE.
I'VE ALREADY BEEN THROUGH A LOT AROUND CAMPUS ...
I'M SORRY!
CAN WE SPLIT UP?
THERE'S ANOTHER GUY I LIKE.
RIGHT NOW...
AT THIS VERY MOMENT...
I- YES! SHE'S MY GIRL...
...MY GIRLFRIEND!!
...SHE'S MY "GIRLFRIEND," ISN'T SHE?
I'LL BE HAPPY TO PLAY ALONG.
SHE'S NOT LIKE THAT.
SCREE
みーん
SCREE
みーん
AND IT'S ONLY BEEN A HUNDRED DAYS.
THE DAYS PASS SO FAST IF YOU'RE LIKE ME...
AHHH!
UH! UH!
...A SINGLE VIRGIN.
EEK
EEK
Tissues
TWINKLE
きら
THE SEASON'S CHANGED...
...SO I GUESS I'M IN THE "SPRING" OF MY LIFE.
AH
HA
HA
TWINKLE
きら

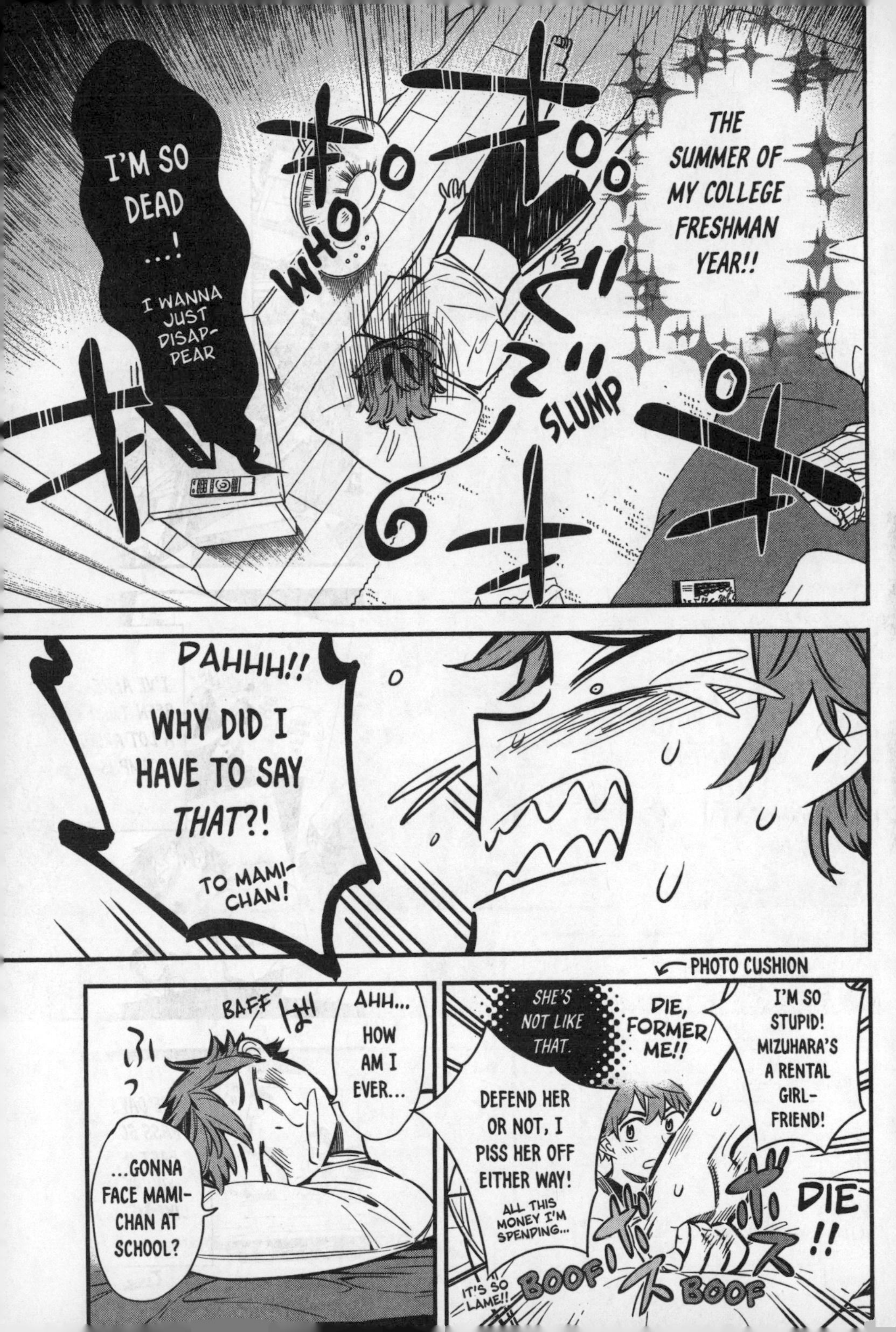
THE SUMMER OF MY COLLEGE FRESHMAN YEAR!!
WHOO
SLUMP
I'M SO DEAD ...!
I WANNA JUST DISAP-PEAR
DAHHH!!
WHY DID I HAVE TO SAY THAT?!
TO MAMI-CHAN!
PHOTO CUSHION
I'M SO STUPID! MIZUHARA'S A RENTAL GIRL-FRIEND!
DIE, FORMER ME!!
SHE'S NOT LIKE THAT.
DEFEND HER OR NOT, I PISS HER OFF EITHER WAY!
ALL THIS MONEY I'M SPENDING...
DIE!!
BOOF BOOF
IT'S SO LAME!!
AHH... HOW AM I EVER...
BAFF
...GONNA FACE MAMI-CHAN AT SCHOOL?

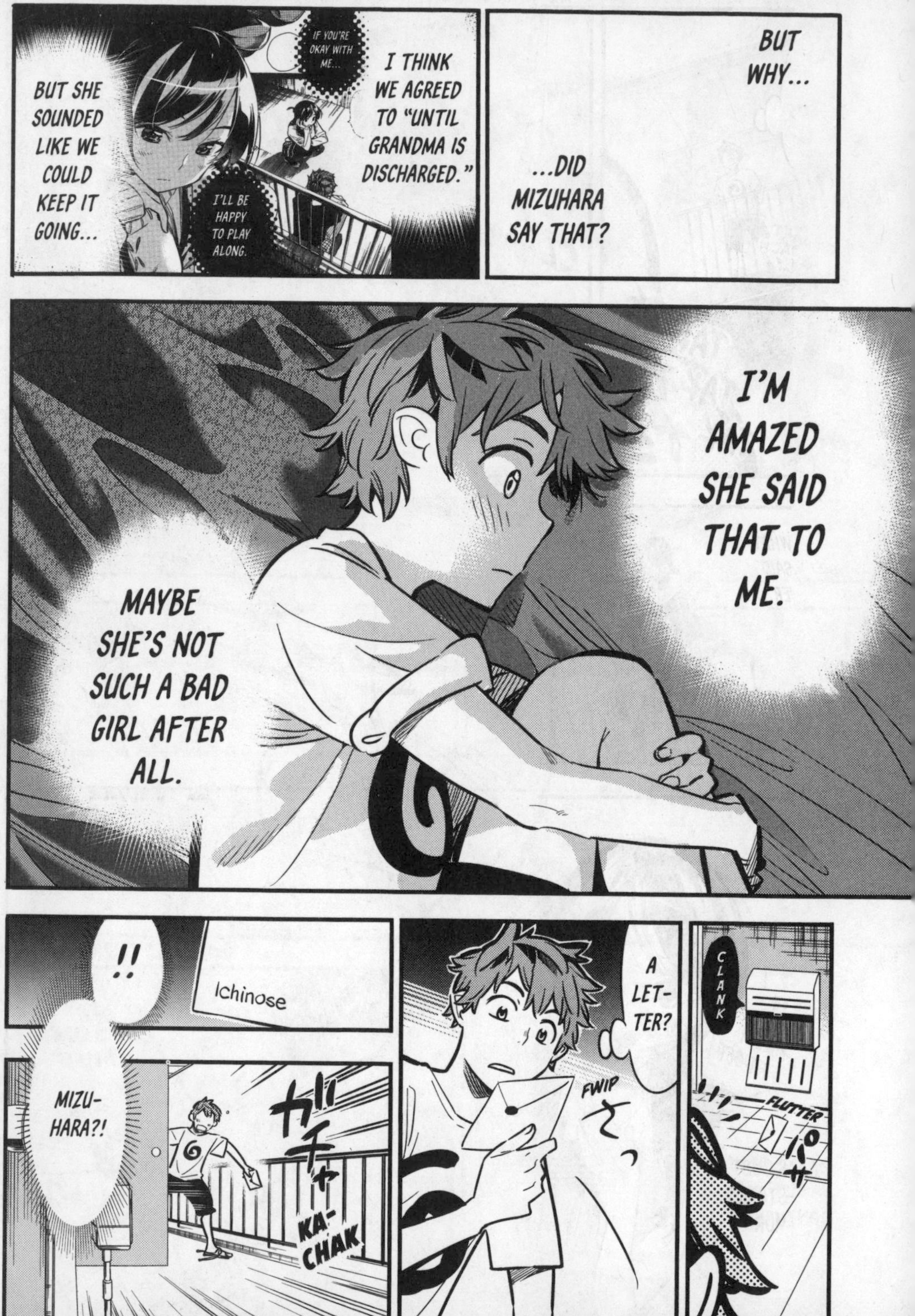
BUT WHY...
...DID MIZUHARA SAY THAT?
I THINK WE AGREED TO "UNTIL GRANDMA IS DISCHARGED."
IF YOU'RE OKAY WITH ME...
I'LL BE HAPPY TO PLAY ALONG.
BUT SHE SOUNDED LIKE WE COULD KEEP IT GOING...
I'M AMAZED SHE SAID THAT TO ME.
MAYBE SHE'S NOT SUCH A BAD GIRL AFTER ALL.
CLANK
FLUTTER
パサ
A LET-TER?
FWIP
!!
Ichinose
MIZU-HARA?!
ガチャ
KA-CHAK

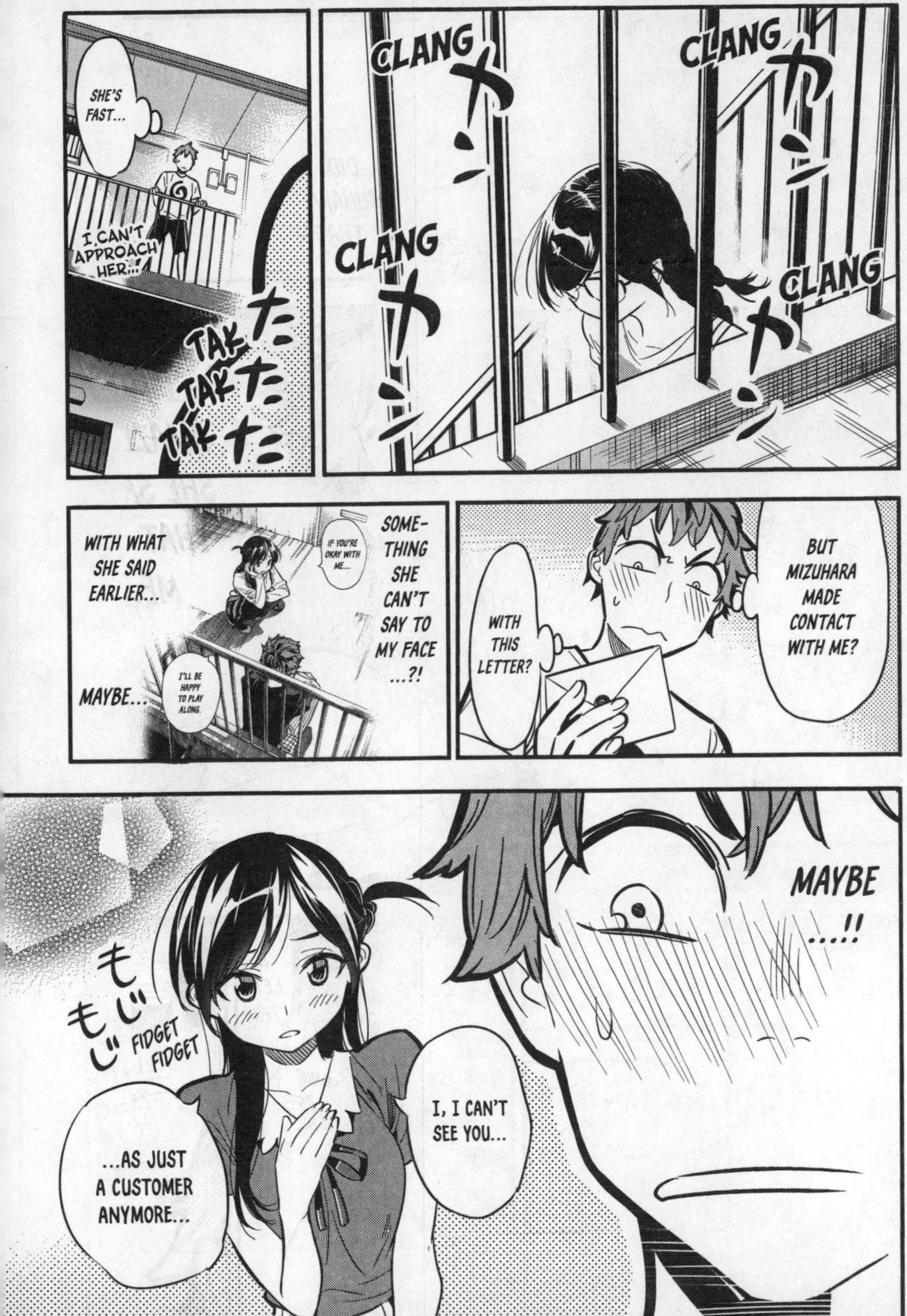
CLANG
CLANG
CLANG
CLANG
SHE'S FAST...
I CAN'T APPROACH HER...
TAK TAK TAK
BUT MIZUHARA MADE CONTACT WITH ME?
WITH THIS LETTER?
SOME-THING SHE CAN'T SAY TO MY FACE ...?!
IF YOU'RE OKAY WITH ME...
WITH WHAT SHE SAID EARLIER...
I'LL BE HAPPY TO PLAY ALONG.
MAYBE...
MAYBE ....!!
FIDGET FIDGET
I, I CAN'T SEE YOU...
...AS JUST A CUSTOMER ANYMORE...

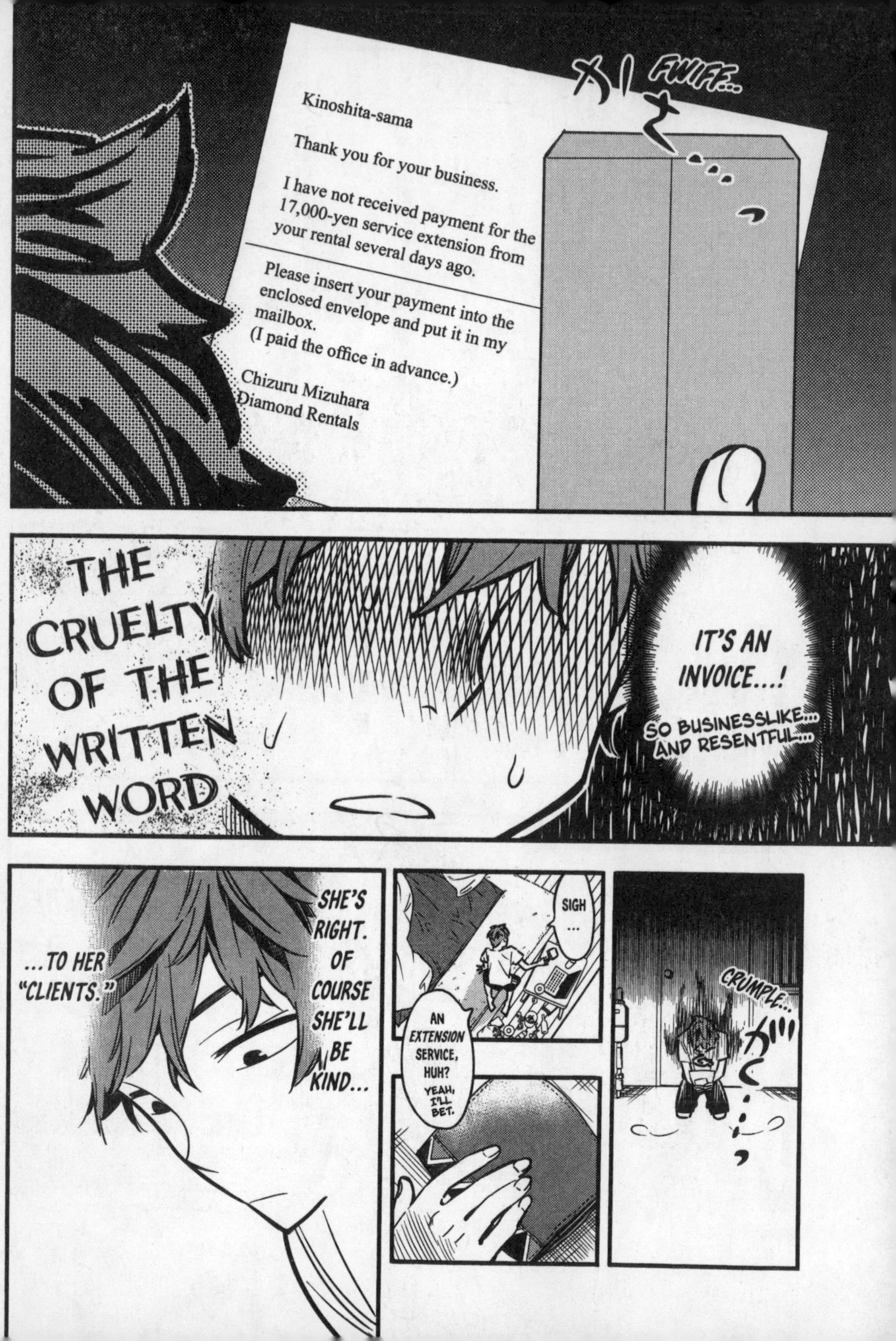
FWIFF...
Kinoshita-sama
Thank you for your business.
I have not received payment for the 17,000-yen service extension from your rental several days ago.
Please insert your payment into the enclosed envelope and put it in my mailbox.
(I paid the office in advance.)
Chizuru Mizuhara
Diamond Rentals
IT'S AN INVOICE...!
SO BUSINESSLIKE... AND RESENTFUL...
THE CRUELTY OF THE WRITTEN WORD
CRUMPLE...
SIGH ...
AN EXTENSION SERVICE, HUH?
YEAH, I'LL BET.
SHE'S RIGHT. OF COURSE SHE'LL BE KIND...
...TO HER "CLIENTS."

I MEAN, EITHER WAY, I CAN'T KEEP UP...

...THIS RENTAL STUFF FOREVER.

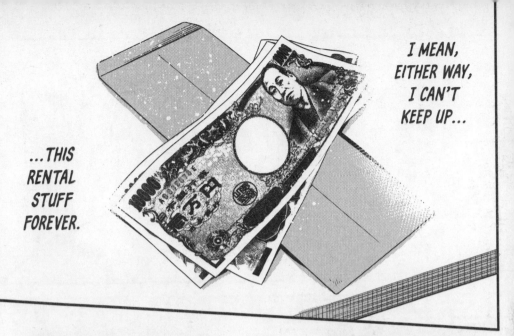

GEN-GEN-GEN-SE...

AH HA HA

EEK EEK EEK

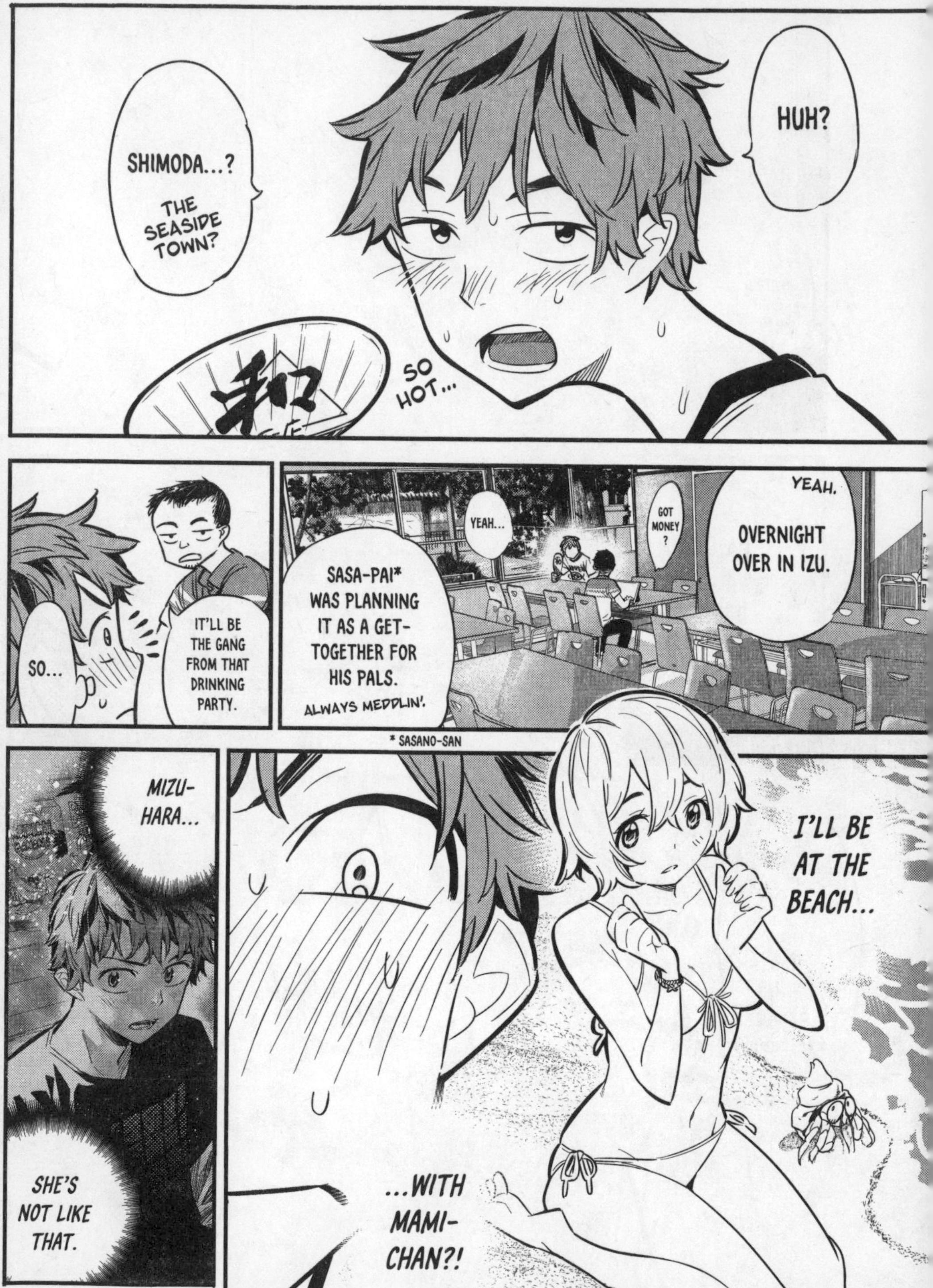
HUH?
SHIMODA...? THE SEASIDE TOWN?
SO HOT...
YEAH.
OVERNIGHT OVER IN IZU.
GOT MONEY ?
YEAH...
SASA-PAI* WAS PLANNING IT AS A GET-TOGETHER FOR HIS PALS.
ALWAYS MEDDLIN'.
IT'LL BE THE GANG FROM THAT DRINKING PARTY.
SO...
I'LL BE AT THE BEACH...
...WITH MAMI-CHAN?!
MIZU-HARA...
SHE'S NOT LIKE THAT.

* SASANO-SAN

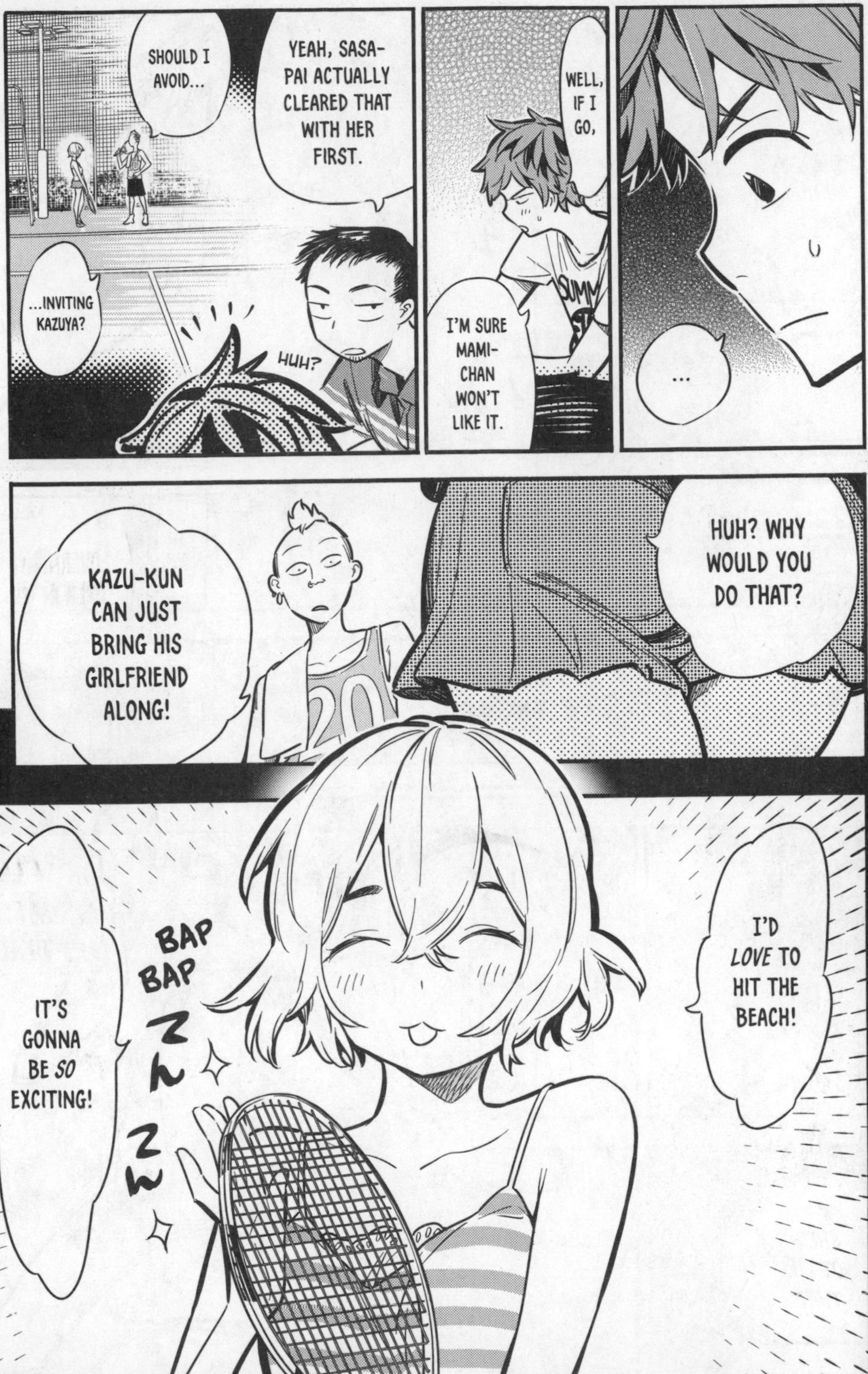
...
WELL, IF I GO,
I'M SURE MAMI-CHAN WON'T LIKE IT.
YEAH, SASA-PAI ACTUALLY CLEARED THAT WITH HER FIRST.
SHOULD I AVOID...
...INVITING KAZUYA?
HUH?
HUH? WHY WOULD YOU DO THAT?
KAZU-KUN CAN JUST BRING HIS GIRLFRIEND ALONG!
I'D *LOVE* TO HIT THE BEACH!
BAP BAP
IT'S GONNA BE *SO* EXCITING!

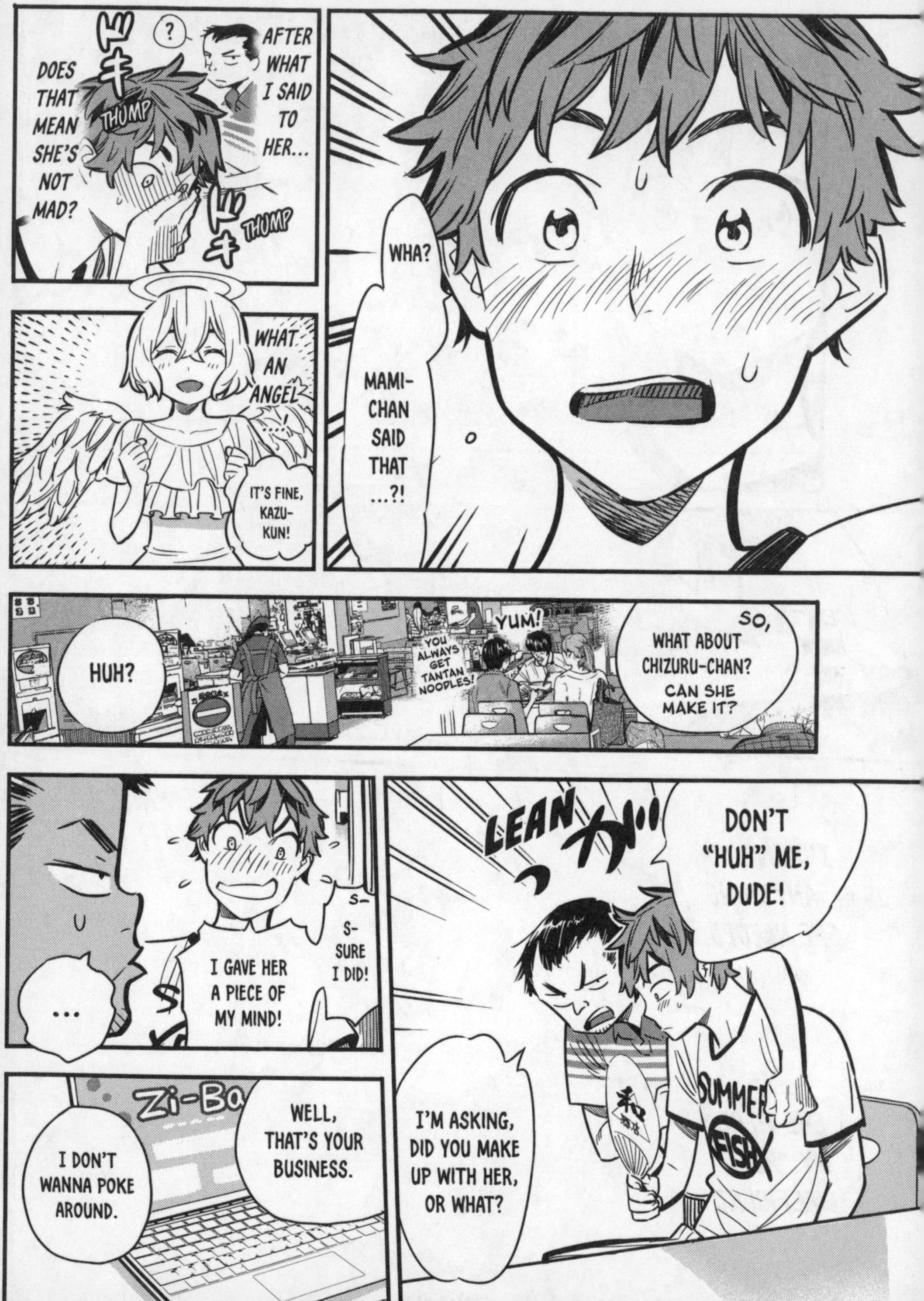
WHA?
MAMI-CHAN SAID THAT ...?!
AFTER WHAT I SAID TO HER...
?
ドキ THUMP
DOES THAT MEAN SHE'S NOT MAD?
ドキ THUMP
WHAT AN ANGEL...!
IT'S FINE, KAZU-KUN!
SO, WHAT ABOUT CHIZURU-CHAN? CAN SHE MAKE IT?
YUM!
YOU ALWAYS GET TANTAN NOODLES!
HUH?
DON'T "HUH" ME, DUDE!
LEAN
I'M ASKING, DID YOU MAKE UP WITH HER, OR WHAT?
SUMMER
FISH
S-S-SURE I DID!
I GAVE HER A PIECE OF MY MIND!
...
Zi-Bo
WELL, THAT'S YOUR BUSINESS.
I DON'T WANNA POKE AROUND.

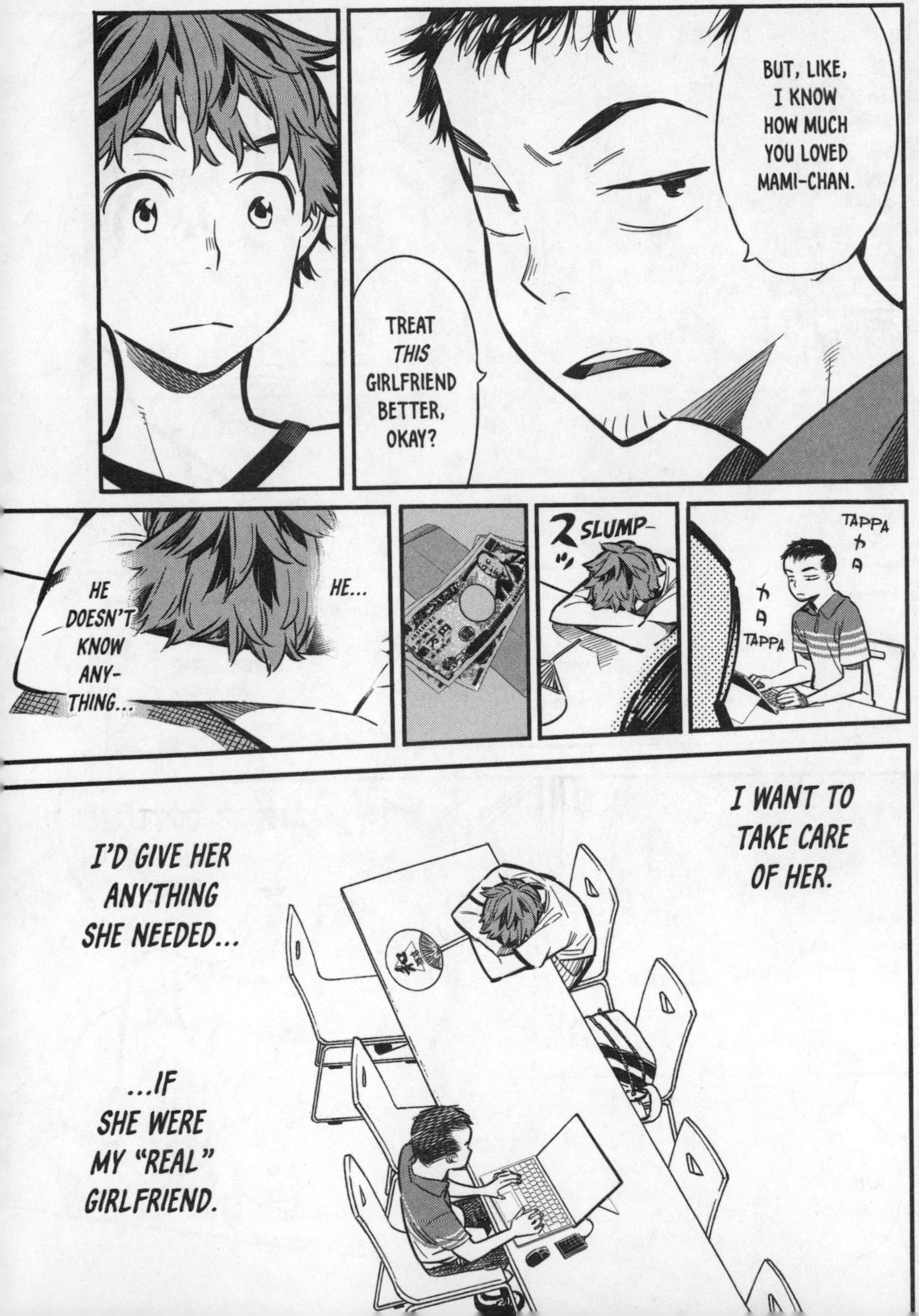
BUT, LIKE, I KNOW HOW MUCH YOU LOVED MAMI-CHAN.
TREAT *THIS* GIRLFRIEND BETTER, OKAY?
TAPPA
TAPPA
SLUMP-
HE...
HE DOESN'T KNOW ANY-THING...
I WANT TO TAKE CARE OF HER.
I'D GIVE HER ANYTHING SHE NEEDED...
...IF SHE WERE MY "REAL" GIRLFRIEND.

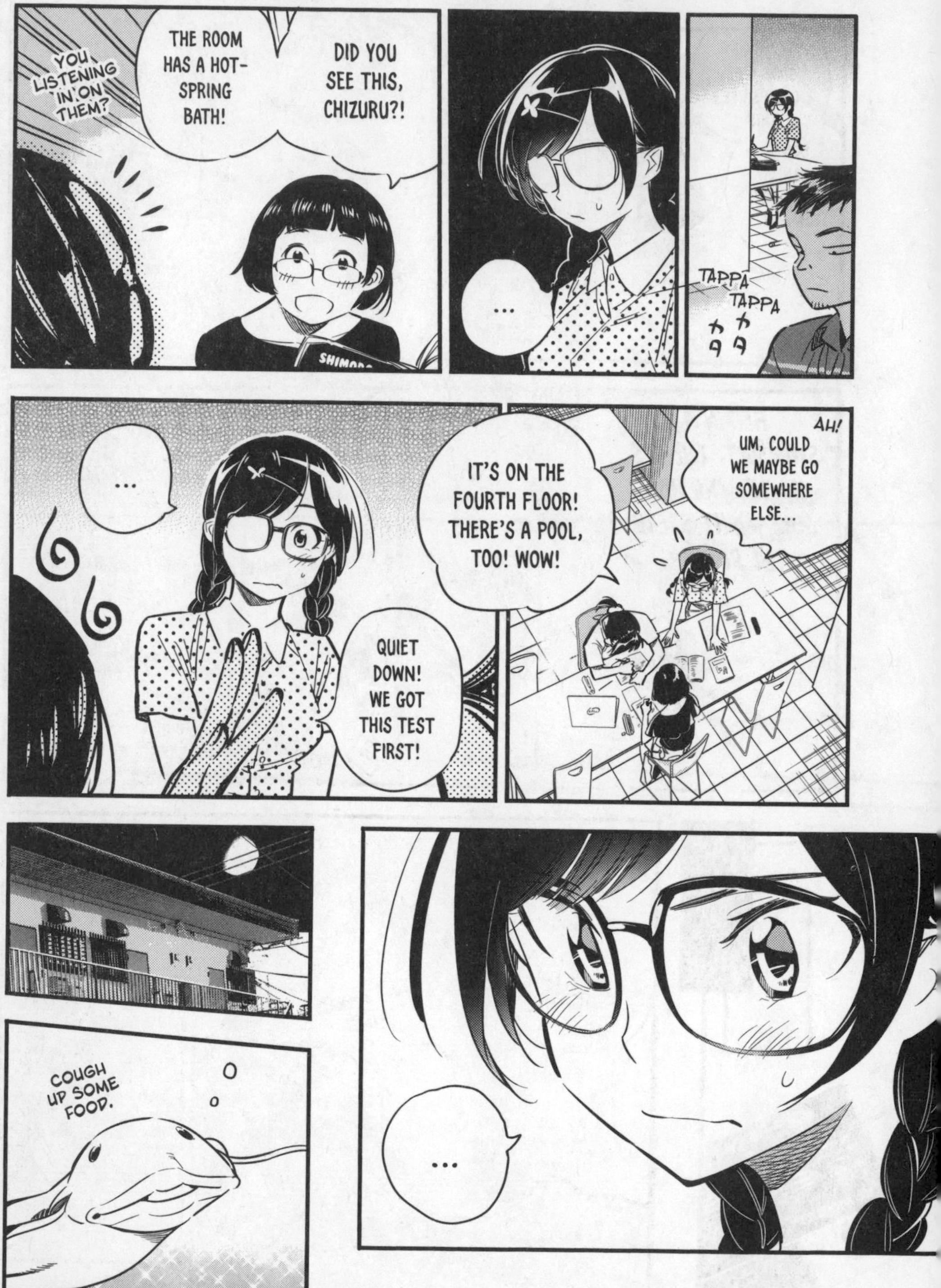
TAPPA TAPPA
カタ カタ
...
DID YOU SEE THIS, CHIZURU?!
THE ROOM HAS A HOT-SPRING BATH!
YOU LISTENING IN ON THEM?
SHIMODA
AH!
UM, COULD WE MAYBE GO SOMEWHERE ELSE...
IT'S ON THE FOURTH FLOOR! THERE'S A POOL, TOO! WOW!
QUIET DOWN! WE GOT THIS TEST FIRST!
...
...
COUGH UP SOME FOOD.

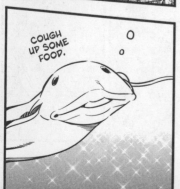

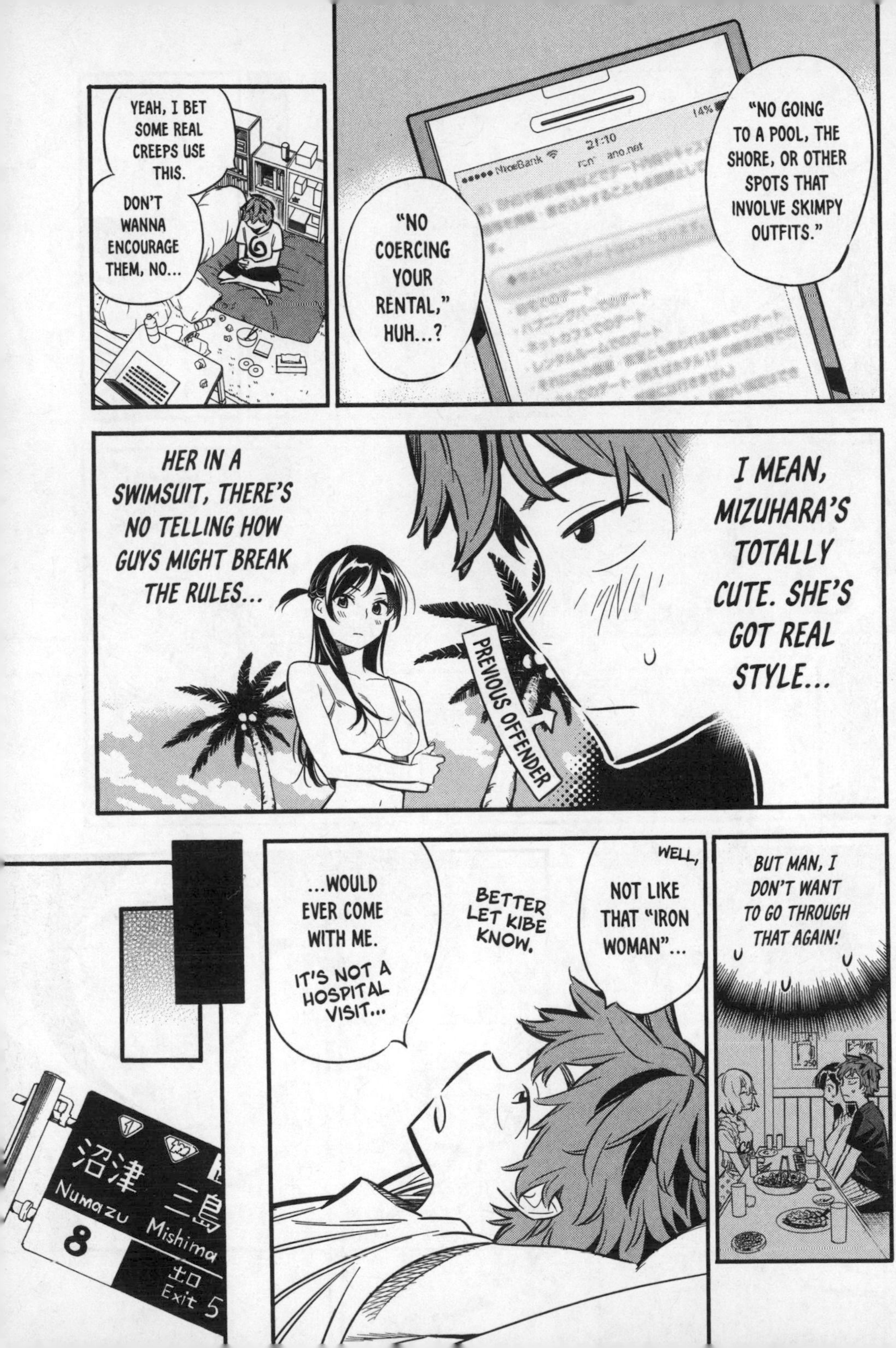
"NO GOING TO A POOL, THE SHORE, OR OTHER SPOTS THAT INVOLVE SKIMPY OUTFITS."
"NO COERCING YOUR RENTAL," HUH...?
YEAH, I BET SOME REAL CREEPS USE THIS.
DON'T WANNA ENCOURAGE THEM, NO...
I MEAN, MIZUHARA'S TOTALLY CUTE. SHE'S GOT REAL STYLE...
PREVIOUS OFFENDER
HER IN A SWIMSUIT, THERE'S NO TELLING HOW GUYS MIGHT BREAK THE RULES...
BUT MAN, I DON'T WANT TO GO THROUGH THAT AGAIN!
WELL,
NOT LIKE THAT "IRON WOMAN"...
BETTER LET KIBE KNOW.
...WOULD EVER COME WITH ME.
IT'S NOT A HOSPITAL VISIT...
沼津 三島
Numazu Mishima
8
出口
Exit 5

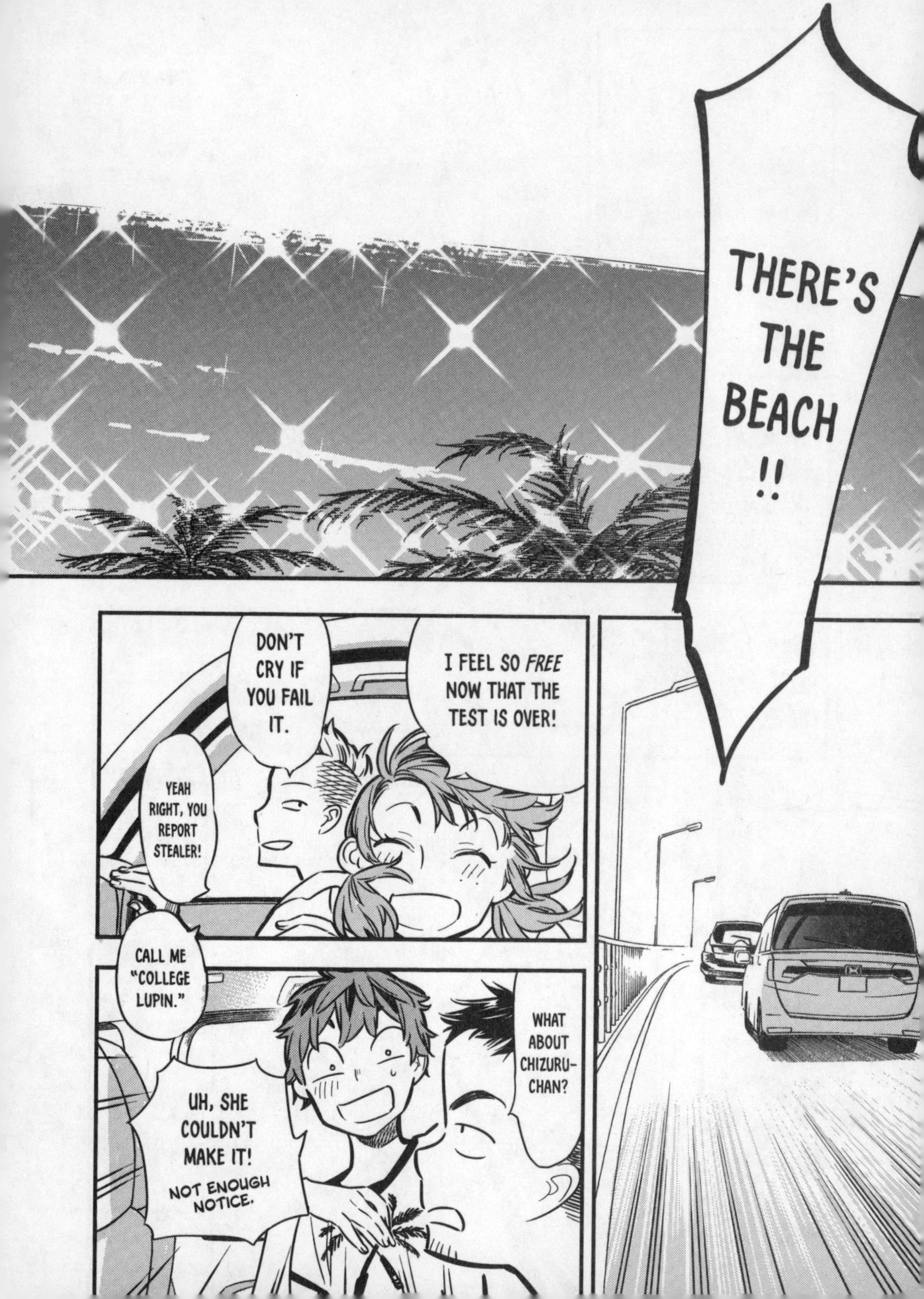
THERE'S THE BEACH!!
I FEEL SO *FREE* NOW THAT THE TEST IS OVER!
DON'T CRY IF YOU FAIL IT.
YEAH RIGHT, YOU REPORT STEALER!
CALL ME "COLLEGE LUPIN."
WHAT ABOUT CHIZURU-CHAN?
UH, SHE COULDN'T MAKE IT!
NOT ENOUGH NOTICE.

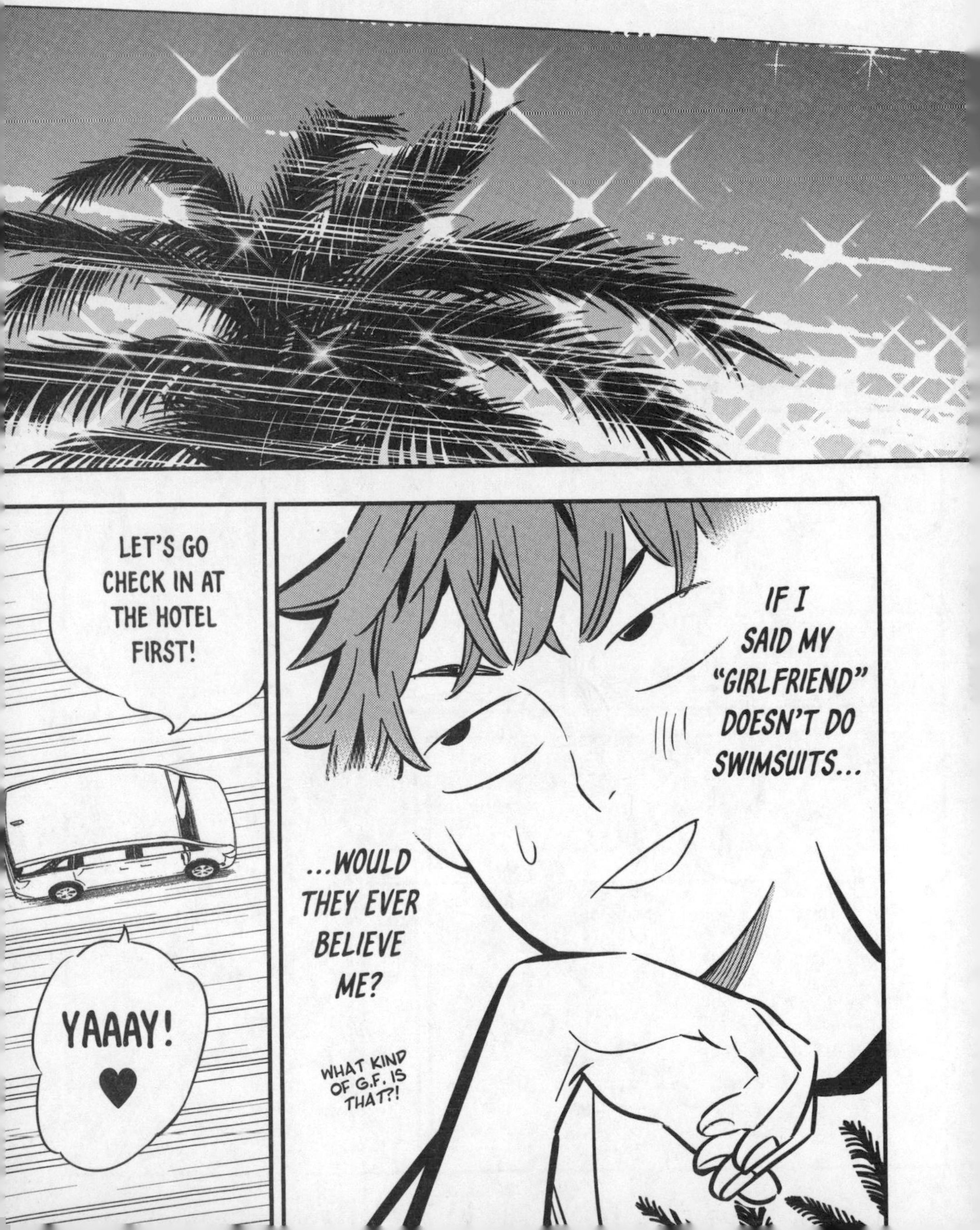
IF I SAID MY "GIRLFRIEND" DOESN'T DO SWIMSUITS...
...WOULD THEY EVER BELIEVE ME?
WHAT KIND OF G.F. IS THAT?!
LET'S GO CHECK IN AT THE HOTEL FIRST!
YAAAY! ♥

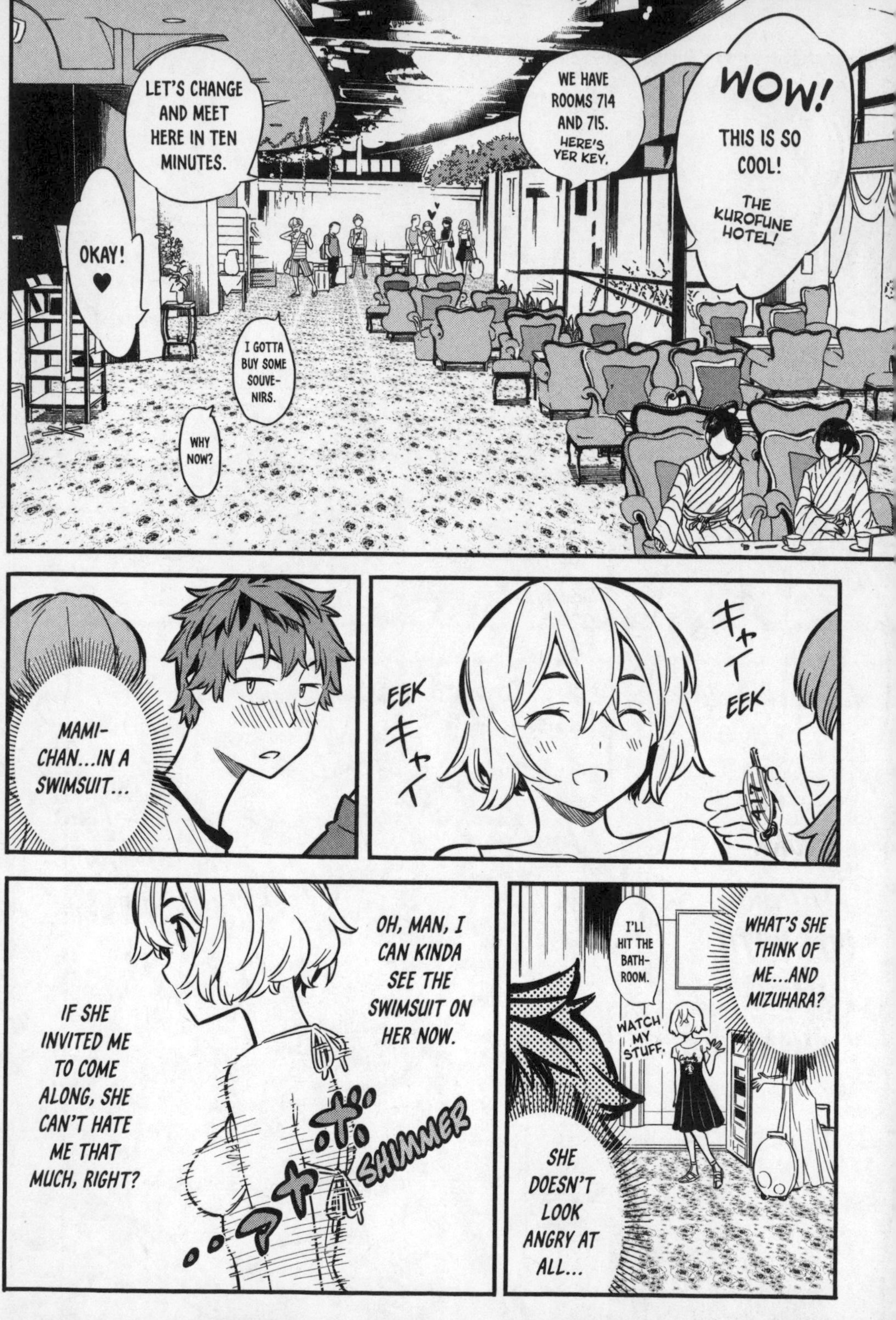
WOW! THIS IS SO COOL! THE KUROFUNE HOTEL!
WE HAVE ROOMS 714 AND 715. HERE'S YER KEY.
LET'S CHANGE AND MEET HERE IN TEN MINUTES.
OKAY! ♥
I GOTTA BUY SOME SOUVENIRS.
WHY NOW?
キャイ
EEK
EEK
キャイ
MAMI-CHAN...IN A SWIMSUIT...
WHAT'S SHE THINK OF ME...AND MIZUHARA?
I'LL HIT THE BATHROOM.
WATCH MY STUFF.
SHE DOESN'T LOOK ANGRY AT ALL...
OH, MAN, I CAN KINDA SEE THE SWIMSUIT ON HER NOW.
IF SHE INVITED ME TO COME ALONG, SHE CAN'T HATE ME THAT MUCH, RIGHT?
SHIMMER

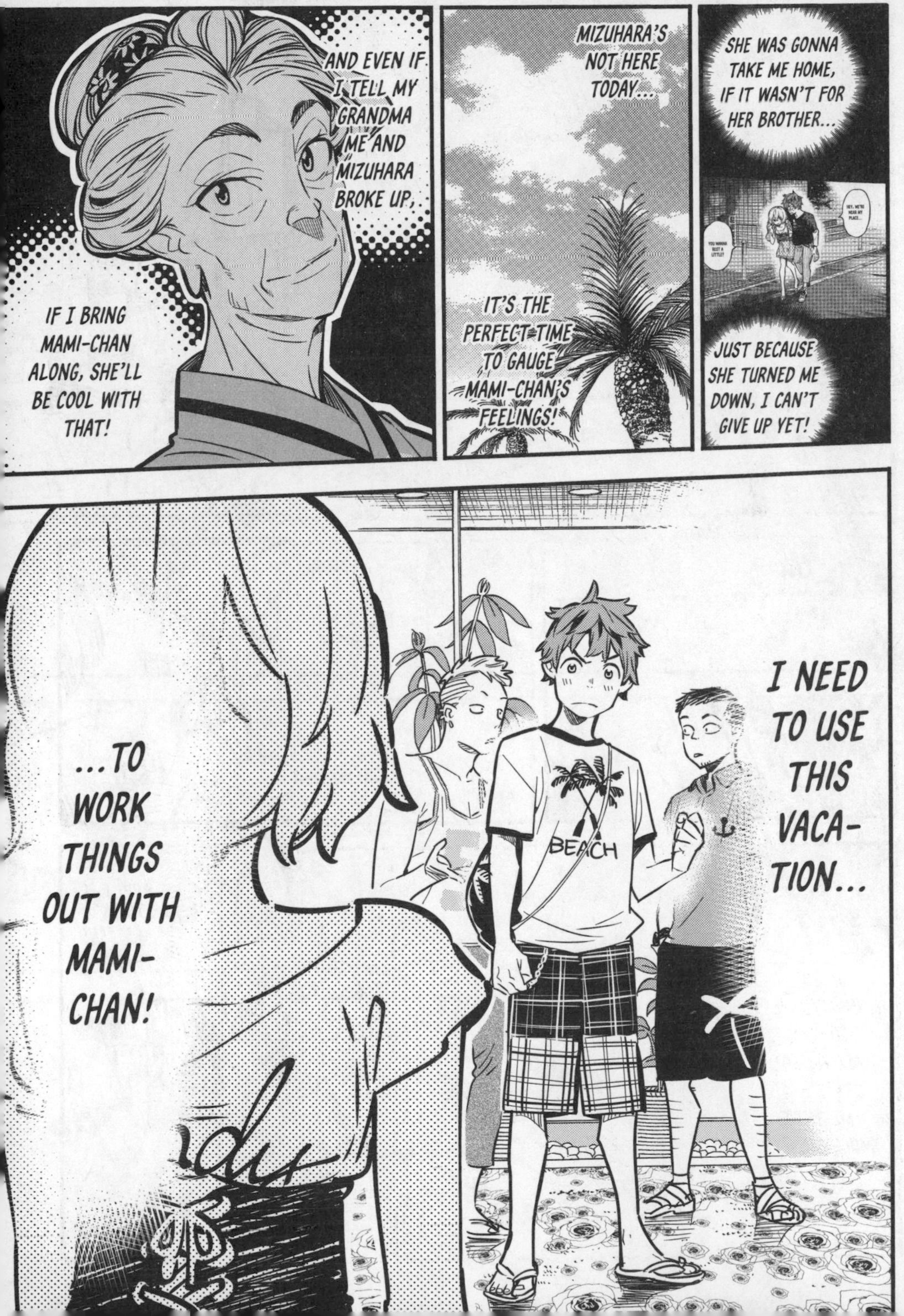
SHE WAS GONNA TAKE ME HOME, IF IT WASN'T FOR HER BROTHER...
HEY, WE'RE NEAR MY PLACE...
YOU WANNA REST A LITTLE?
JUST BECAUSE SHE TURNED ME DOWN, I CAN'T GIVE UP YET!
MIZUHARA'S NOT HERE TODAY...
IT'S THE PERFECT TIME TO GAUGE MAMI-CHAN'S FEELINGS!
AND EVEN IF I TELL MY GRANDMA ME AND MIZUHARA BROKE UP,
IF I BRING MAMI-CHAN ALONG, SHE'LL BE COOL WITH THAT!
I NEED TO USE THIS VACA-TION...
...TO WORK THINGS OUT WITH MAMI-CHAN!

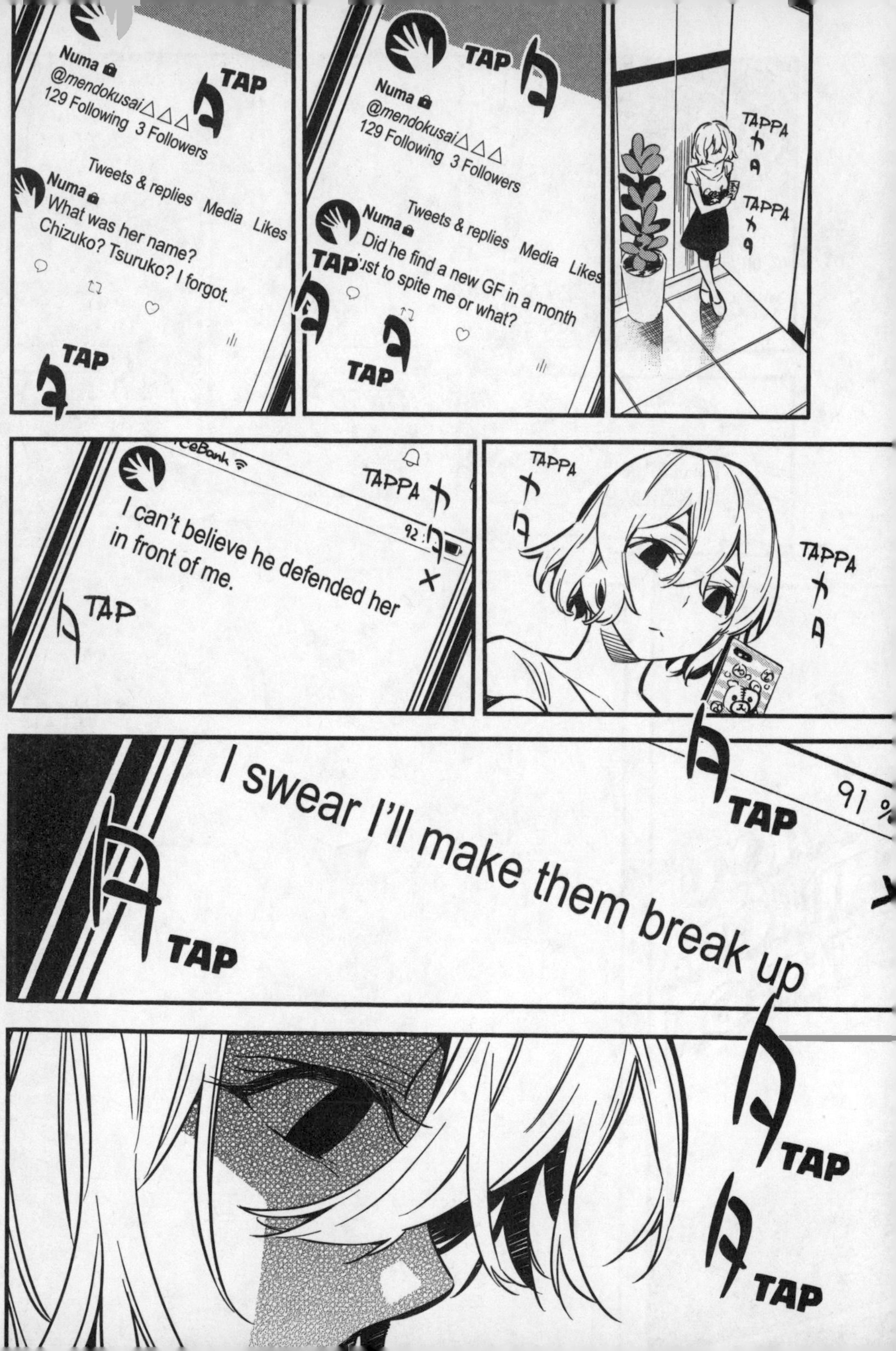
TAPPA
TAPPA
TAP
Numa
@mendokusai△△△
129 Following 3 Followers
Tweets & replies Media Likes
Numa
Did he find a new GF in a month just to spite me or what?
TAP
TAP
TAP
Numa
@mendokusai△△△
129 Following 3 Followers
Tweets & replies Media Likes
Numa
What was her name?
Chizuko? Tsuruko? I forgot.
TAP
TAPPA
TAPPA
TAPPA
I can't believe he defended her in front of me.
TAP
TAP
91%
I swear I'll make them break up
TAP
TAP
TAP

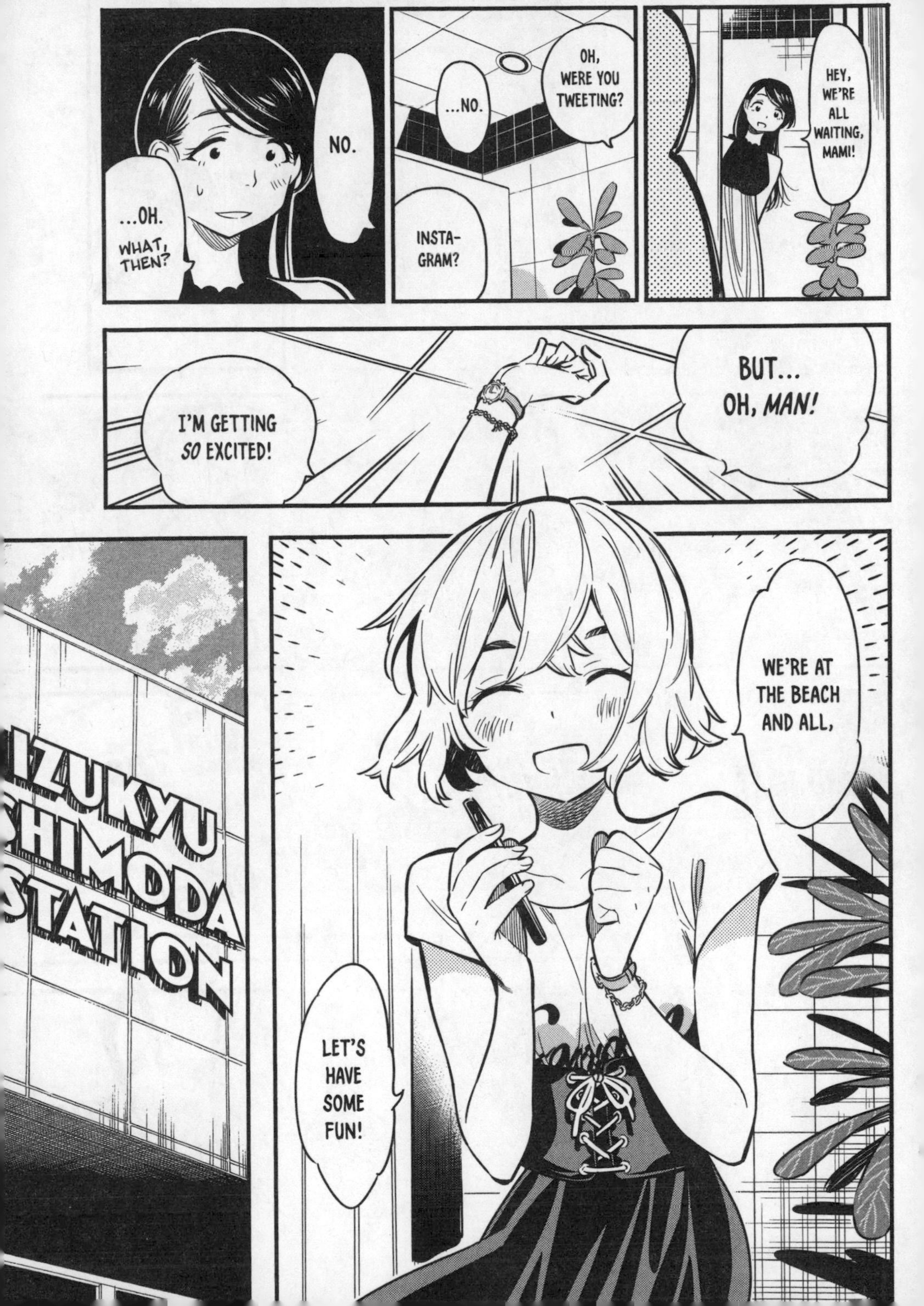
HEY, WE'RE ALL WAITING, MAMI!
OH, WERE YOU TWEETING?
...NO.
INSTA-GRAM?
NO.
...OH. WHAT, THEN?
BUT... OH, *MAN!*
I'M GETTING *SO* EXCITED!
WE'RE AT THE BEACH AND ALL,
LET'S HAVE SOME FUN!
IZUKYU SHIMODA STATION

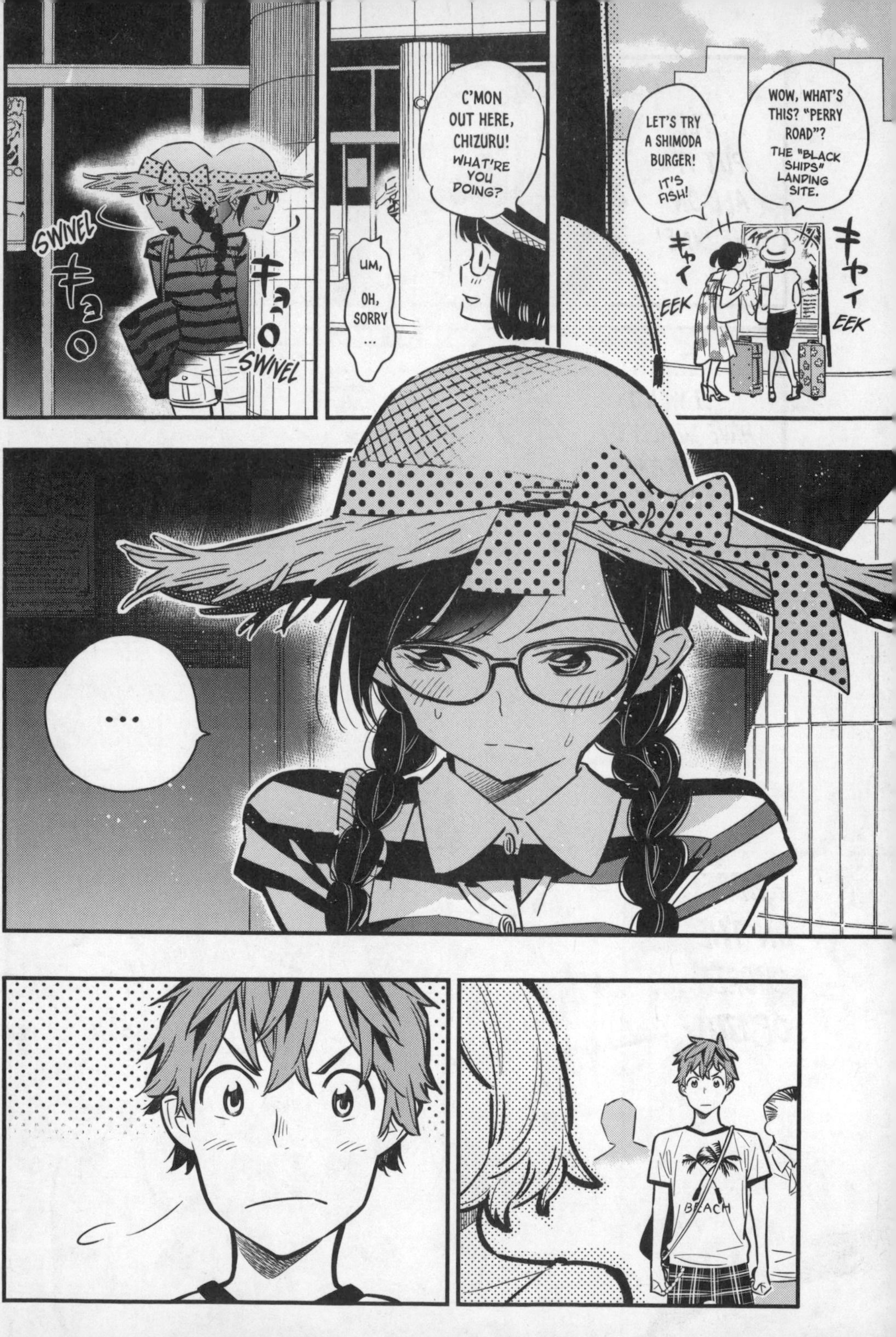
WOW, WHAT'S THIS? "PERRY ROAD"?
THE "BLACK SHIPS" LANDING SITE.
LET'S TRY A SHIMODA BURGER!
IT'S FISH!
キャイ
EEK
キャイ
EEK
C'MON OUT HERE, CHIZURU!
WHAT'RE YOU DOING?
UM, OH, SORRY ...
キョロ
SWIVEL
キョロ
SWIVEL
...
BEACH

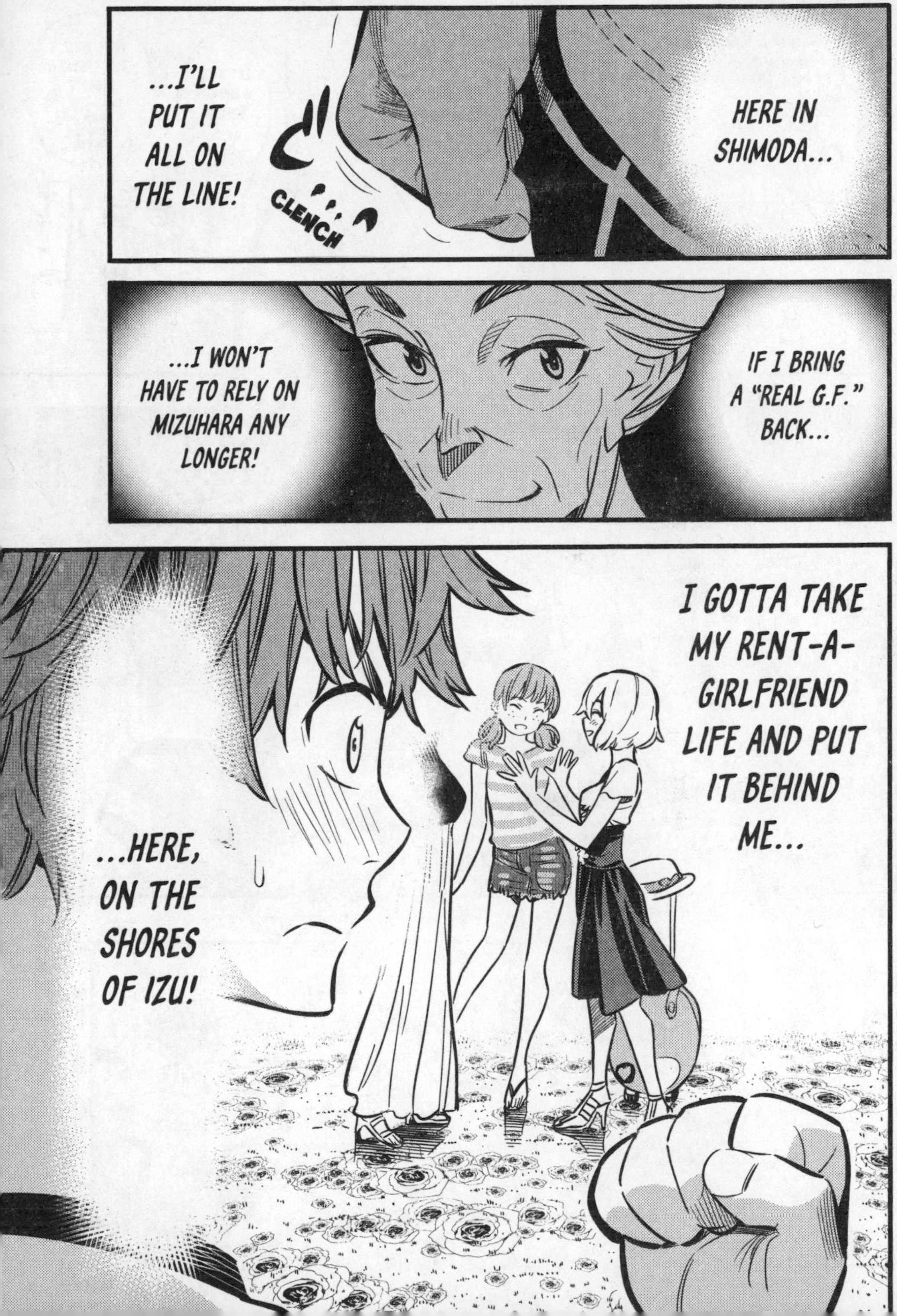
HERE IN SHIMODA...
...I'LL PUT IT ALL ON THE LINE!
CLENCH
IF I BRING A "REAL G.F." BACK...
...I WON'T HAVE TO RELY ON MIZUHARA ANY LONGER!
I GOTTA TAKE MY RENT-A-GIRLFRIEND LIFE AND PUT IT BEHIND ME...
...HERE, ON THE SHORES OF IZU!

RATING 8
MY GIRLFRIEND AND THE SEA (2)

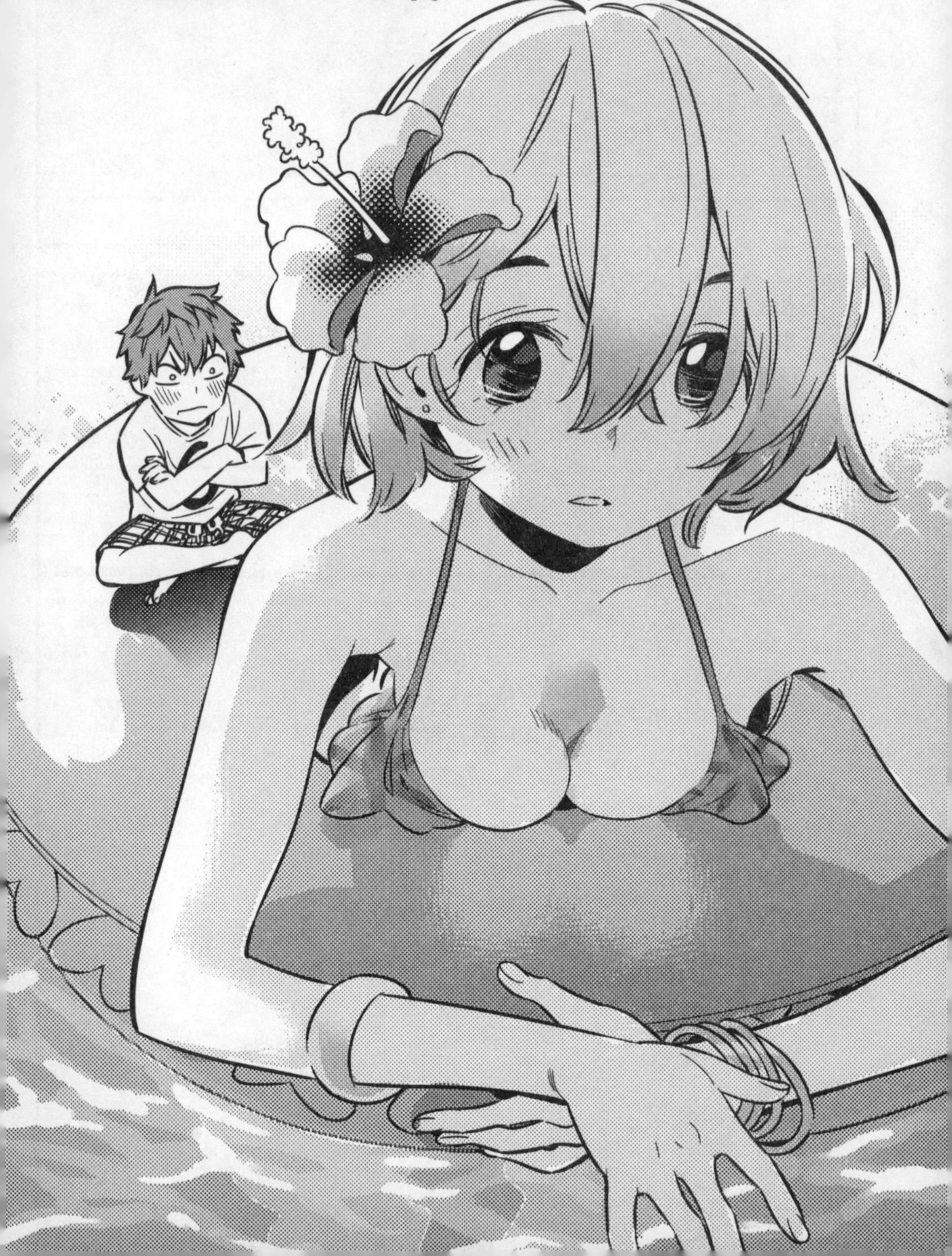

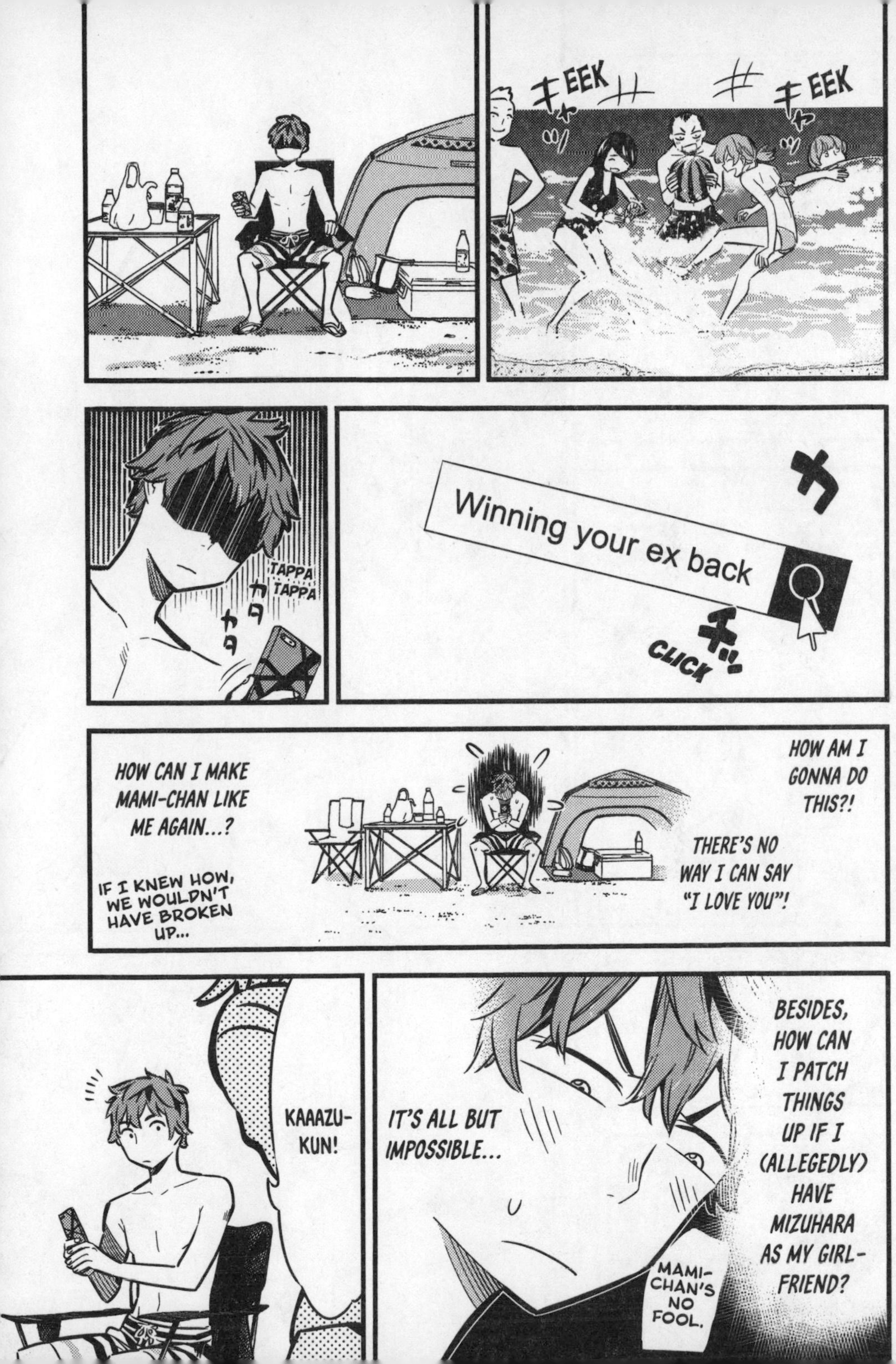
EEK
EEK
Winning your ex back
CLICK
TAPPA TAPPA
HOW AM I GONNA DO THIS?!
HOW CAN I MAKE MAMI-CHAN LIKE ME AGAIN...?
THERE'S NO WAY I CAN SAY "I LOVE YOU"!
IF I KNEW HOW, WE WOULDN'T HAVE BROKEN UP...
BESIDES, HOW CAN I PATCH THINGS UP IF I (ALLEGEDLY) HAVE MIZUHARA AS MY GIRL-FRIEND?
IT'S ALL BUT IMPOSSIBLE...
MAMI-CHAN'S NO FOOL.
KAAAZU-KUN!

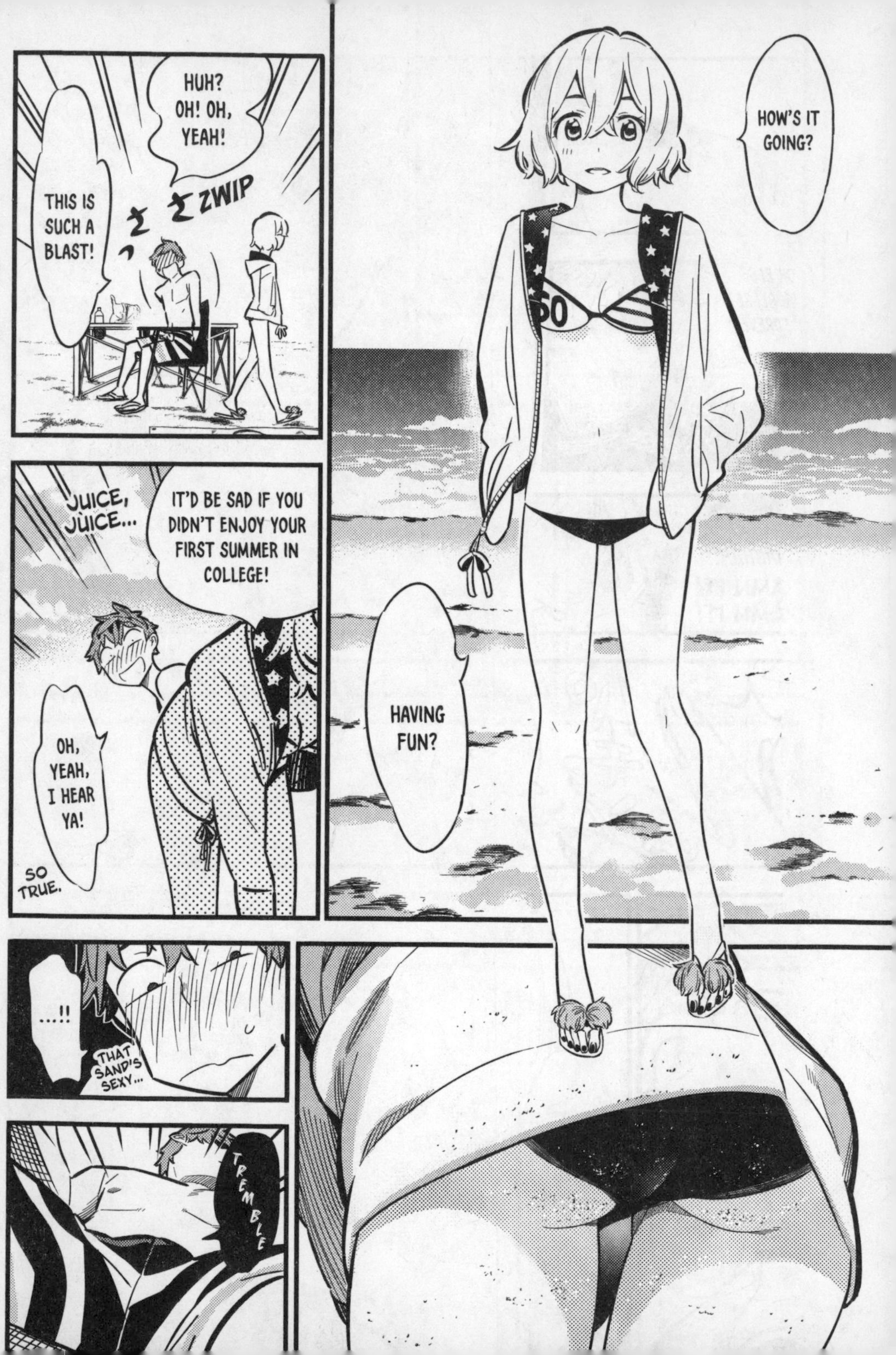
HOW'S IT GOING?
HAVING FUN?
HUH? OH! OH, YEAH!
THIS IS SUCH A BLAST!
ZWIP
IT'D BE SAD IF YOU DIDN'T ENJOY YOUR FIRST SUMMER IN COLLEGE!
JUICE, JUICE...
OH, YEAH, I HEAR YA!
SO TRUE.
...!!
THAT SAND'S SEXY...
TREMBLE

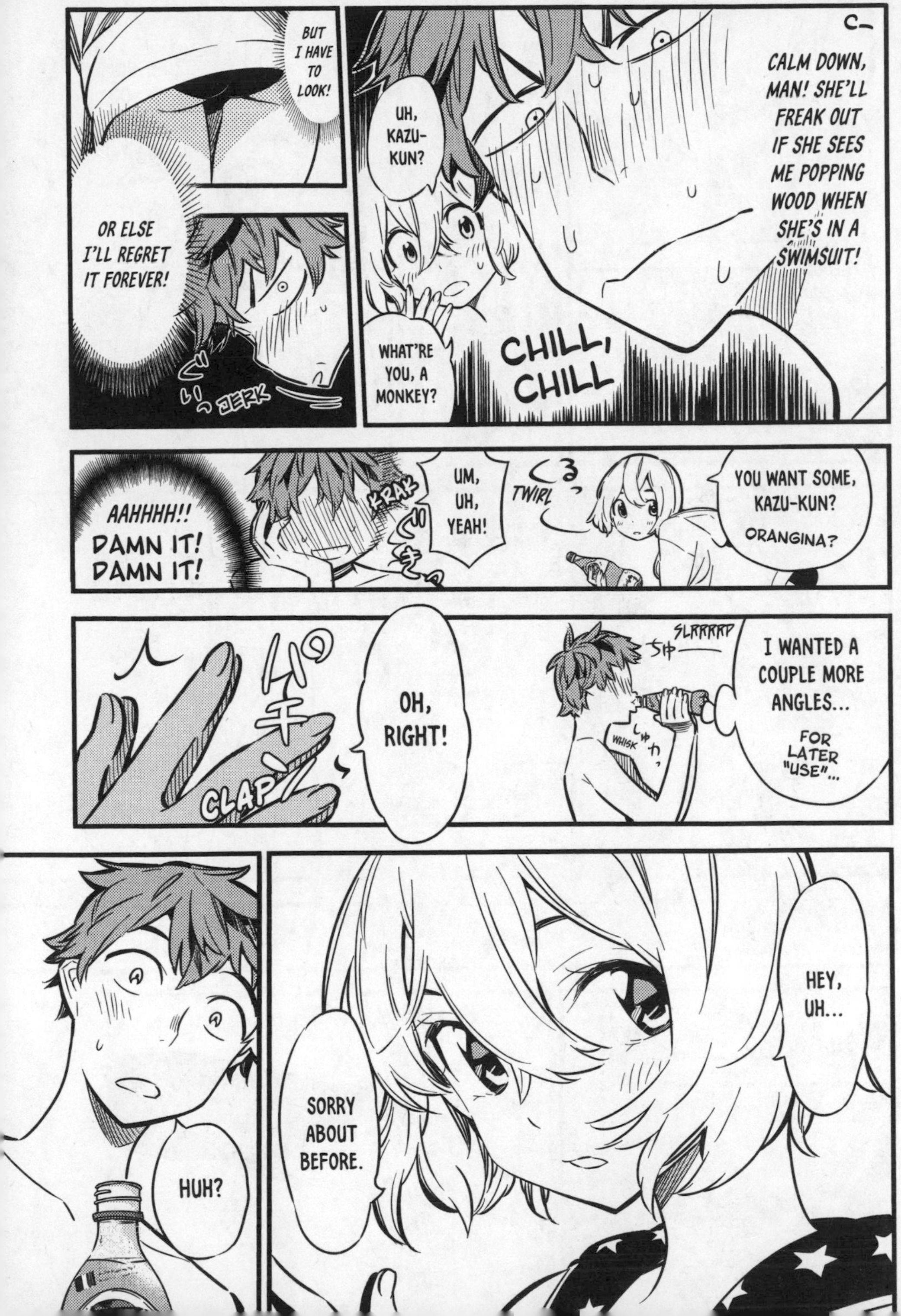
C—
CALM DOWN, MAN! SHE'LL FREAK OUT IF SHE SEES ME POPPING WOOD WHEN SHE'S IN A SWIMSUIT!
UH, KAZU-KUN?
CHILL, CHILL
WHAT'RE YOU, A MONKEY?
BUT I HAVE TO LOOK!
OR ELSE I'LL REGRET IT FOREVER!
JERK
YOU WANT SOME, KAZU-KUN?
ORANGINA?
TWIRL
UM, UH, YEAH!
KRAK
AAHHHH!! DAMN IT! DAMN IT!
I WANTED A COUPLE MORE ANGLES...
FOR LATER "USE"...
SLRRRRP
WHISK
OH, RIGHT!
CLAP
HEY, UH...
SORRY ABOUT BEFORE.
HUH?

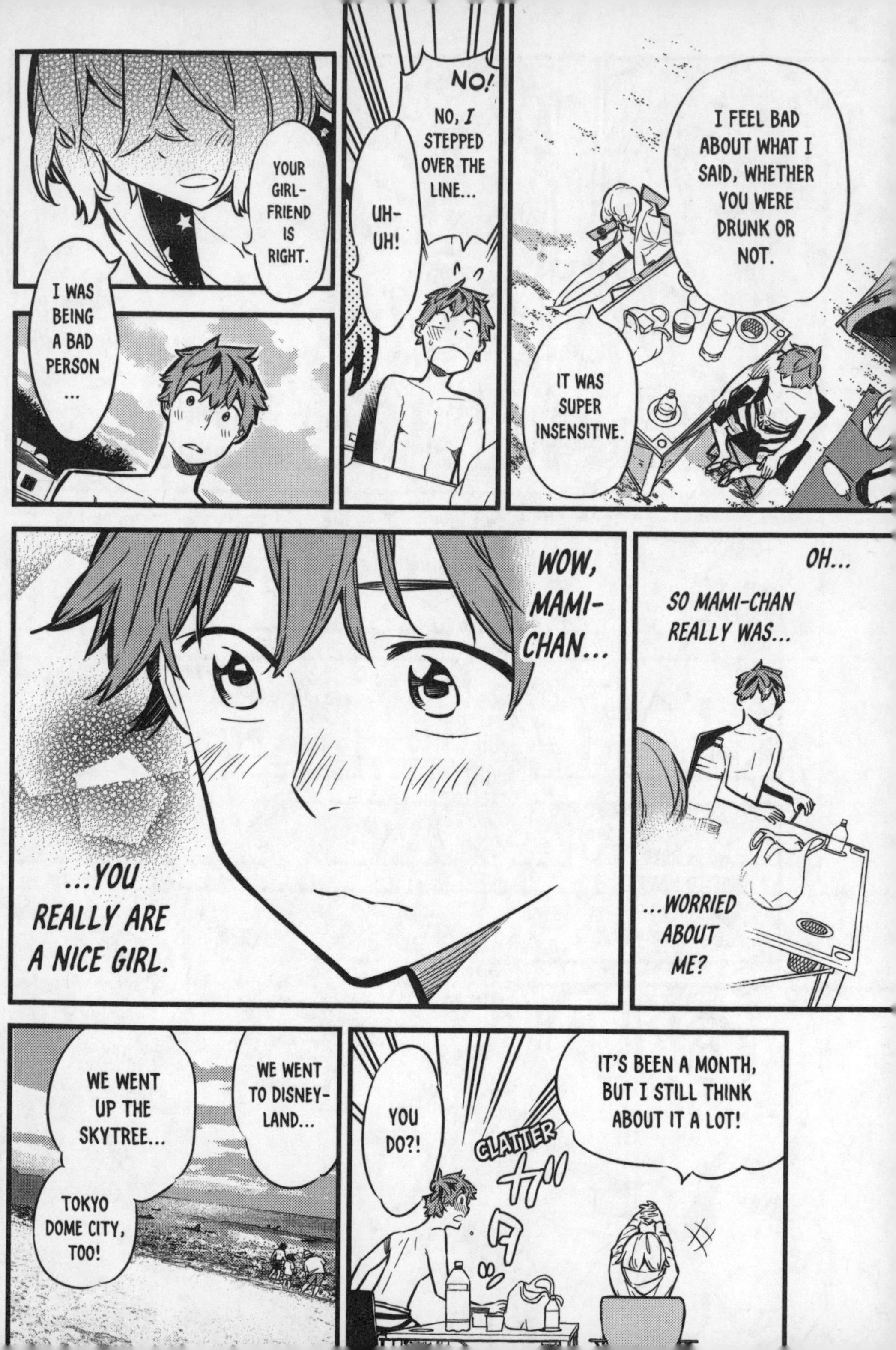
I FEEL BAD ABOUT WHAT I SAID, WHETHER YOU WERE DRUNK OR NOT.
IT WAS SUPER INSENSITIVE.
NO!
NO, *I* STEPPED OVER THE LINE...
UH-UH!
YOUR GIRL-FRIEND IS RIGHT.
I WAS BEING A BAD PERSON...
OH...
SO MAMI-CHAN REALLY WAS...
...WORRIED ABOUT ME?
WOW, MAMI-CHAN...
...YOU REALLY ARE A NICE GIRL.
IT'S BEEN A MONTH, BUT I STILL THINK ABOUT IT A LOT!
YOU DO?!
CLATTER
WE WENT TO DISNEY-LAND...
WE WENT UP THE SKYTREE...
TOKYO DOME CITY, TOO!

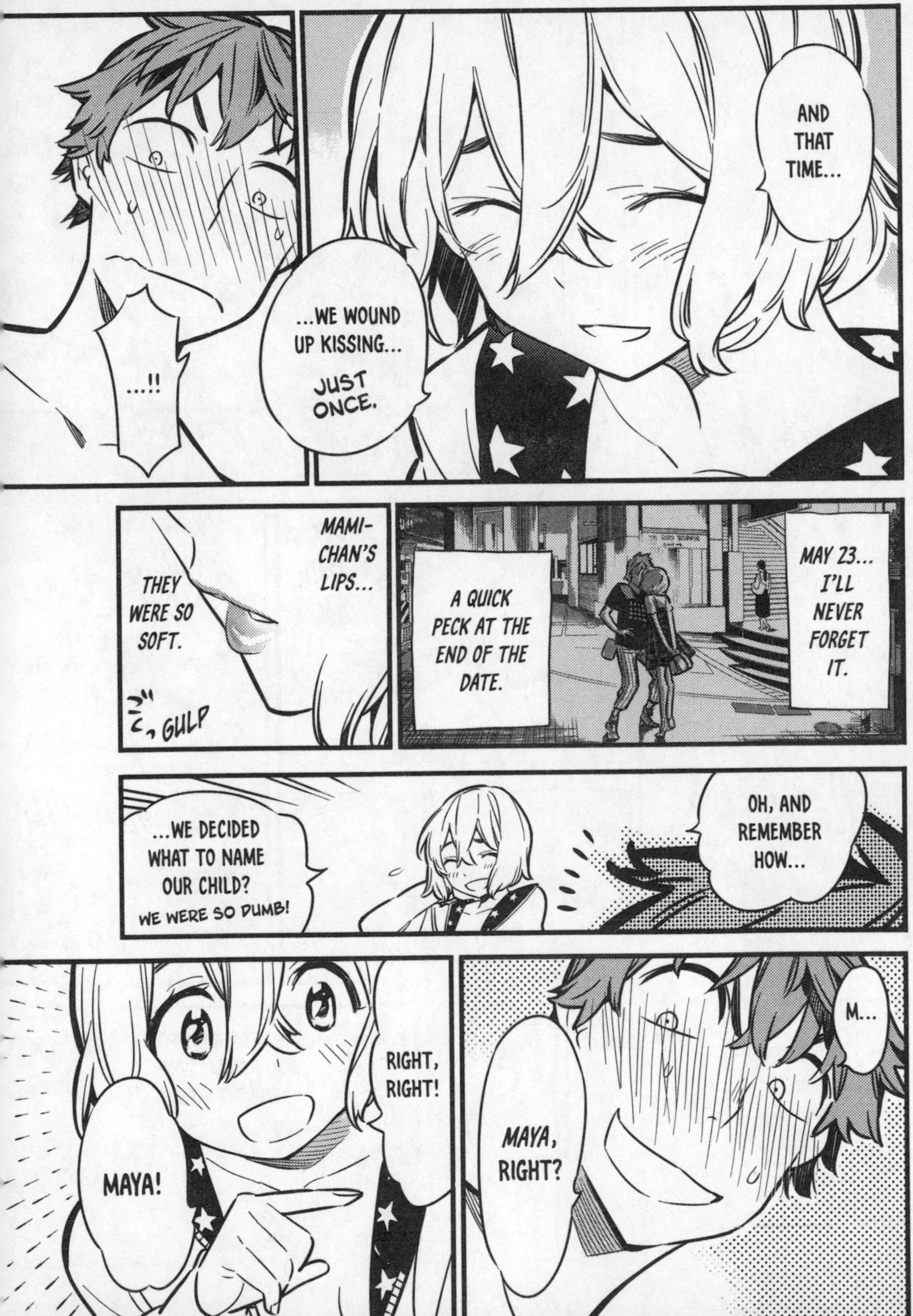
AND THAT TIME...
...WE WOUND UP KISSING... JUST ONCE.
...!!
MAY 23... I'LL NEVER FORGET IT.
A QUICK PECK AT THE END OF THE DATE.
MAMI-CHAN'S LIPS...
THEY WERE SO SOFT.
GULP
OH, AND REMEMBER HOW...
...WE DECIDED WHAT TO NAME OUR CHILD?
WE WERE SO DUMB!
M...
MAYA, RIGHT?
RIGHT, RIGHT!
MAYA!

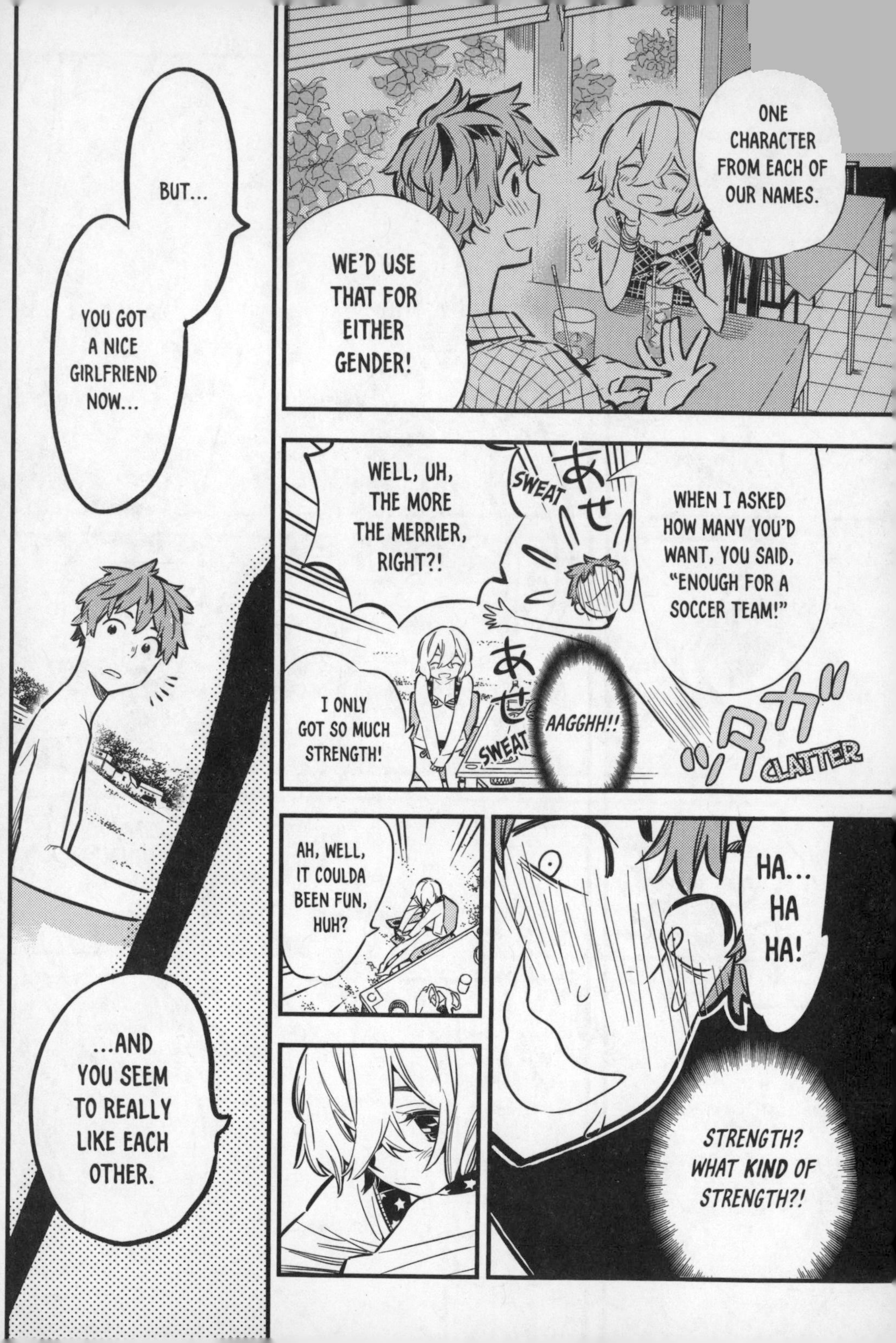
ONE CHARACTER FROM EACH OF OUR NAMES.
WE'D USE THAT FOR EITHER GENDER!
WHEN I ASKED HOW MANY YOU'D WANT, YOU SAID, "ENOUGH FOR A SOCCER TEAM!"
タガッ CLATTER
AAGGHH!!
あせ SWEAT
WELL, UH, THE MORE THE MERRIER, RIGHT?!
あせ SWEAT
I ONLY GOT SO MUCH STRENGTH!
HA... HA HA!
STRENGTH? WHAT KIND OF STRENGTH?!
AH, WELL, IT COULDA BEEN FUN, HUH?
BUT...
YOU GOT A NICE GIRLFRIEND NOW...
...AND YOU SEEM TO REALLY LIKE EACH OTHER.

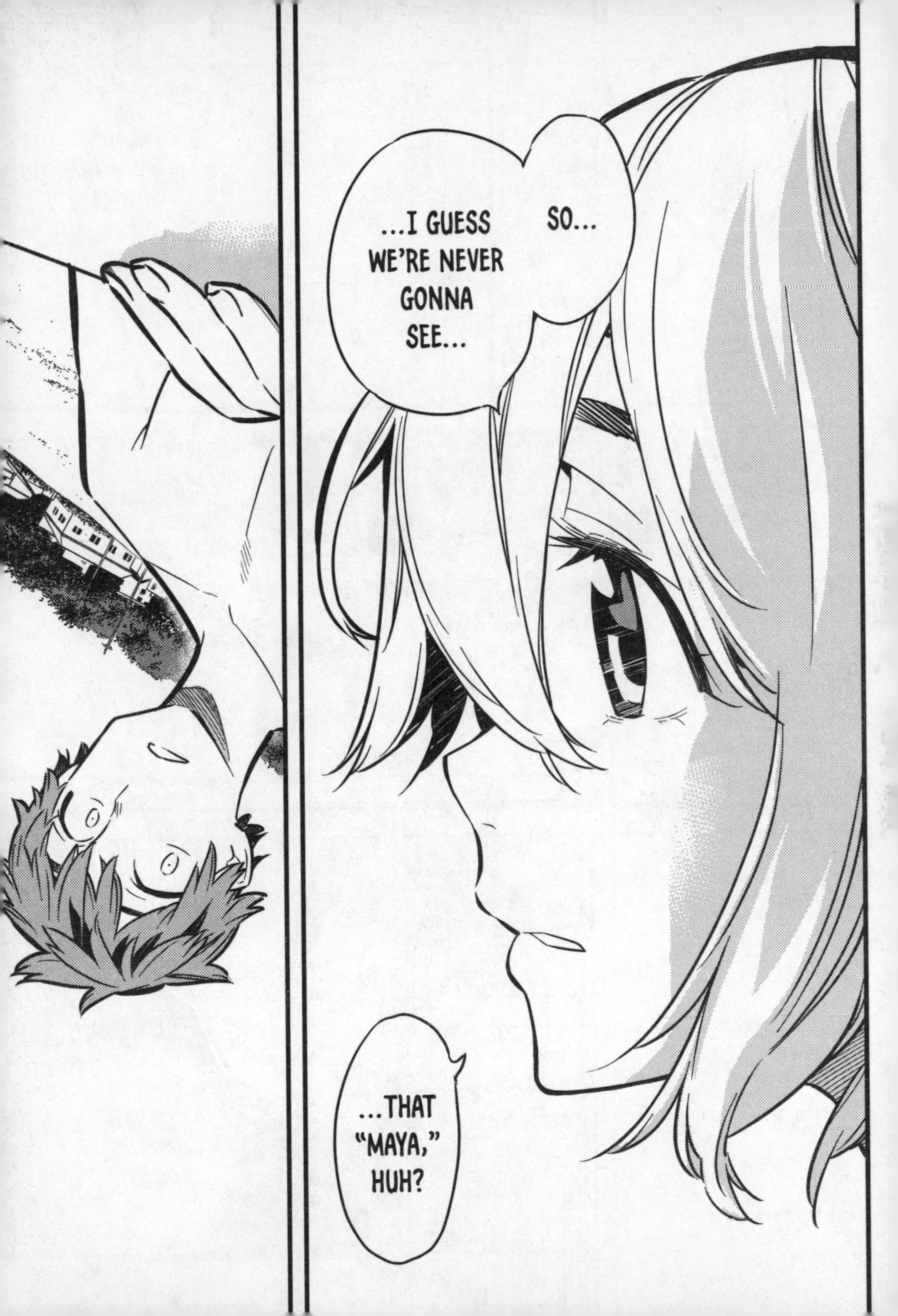
SO... ...I GUESS WE'RE NEVER GONNA SEE...
...THAT "MAYA," HUH?

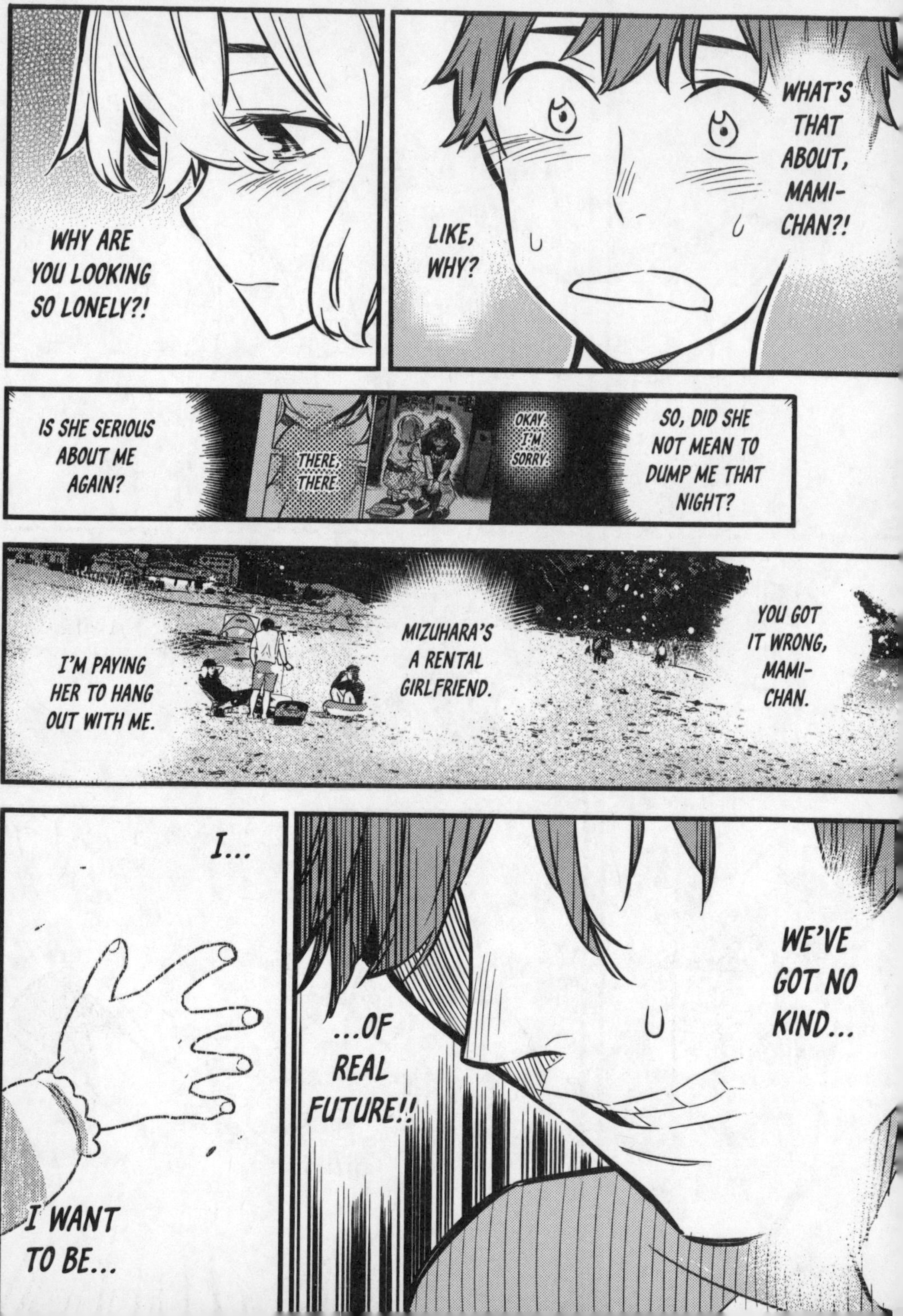
WHAT'S THAT ABOUT, MAMI-CHAN?!
LIKE, WHY?
WHY ARE YOU LOOKING SO LONELY?!
SO, DID SHE NOT MEAN TO DUMP ME THAT NIGHT?
OKAY. I'M SORRY.
THERE, THERE.
IS SHE SERIOUS ABOUT ME AGAIN?
YOU GOT IT WRONG, MAMI-CHAN.
MIZUHARA'S A RENTAL GIRLFRIEND.
I'M PAYING HER TO HANG OUT WITH ME.
WE'VE GOT NO KIND...
...OF REAL FUTURE!!
I...
I WANT TO BE...

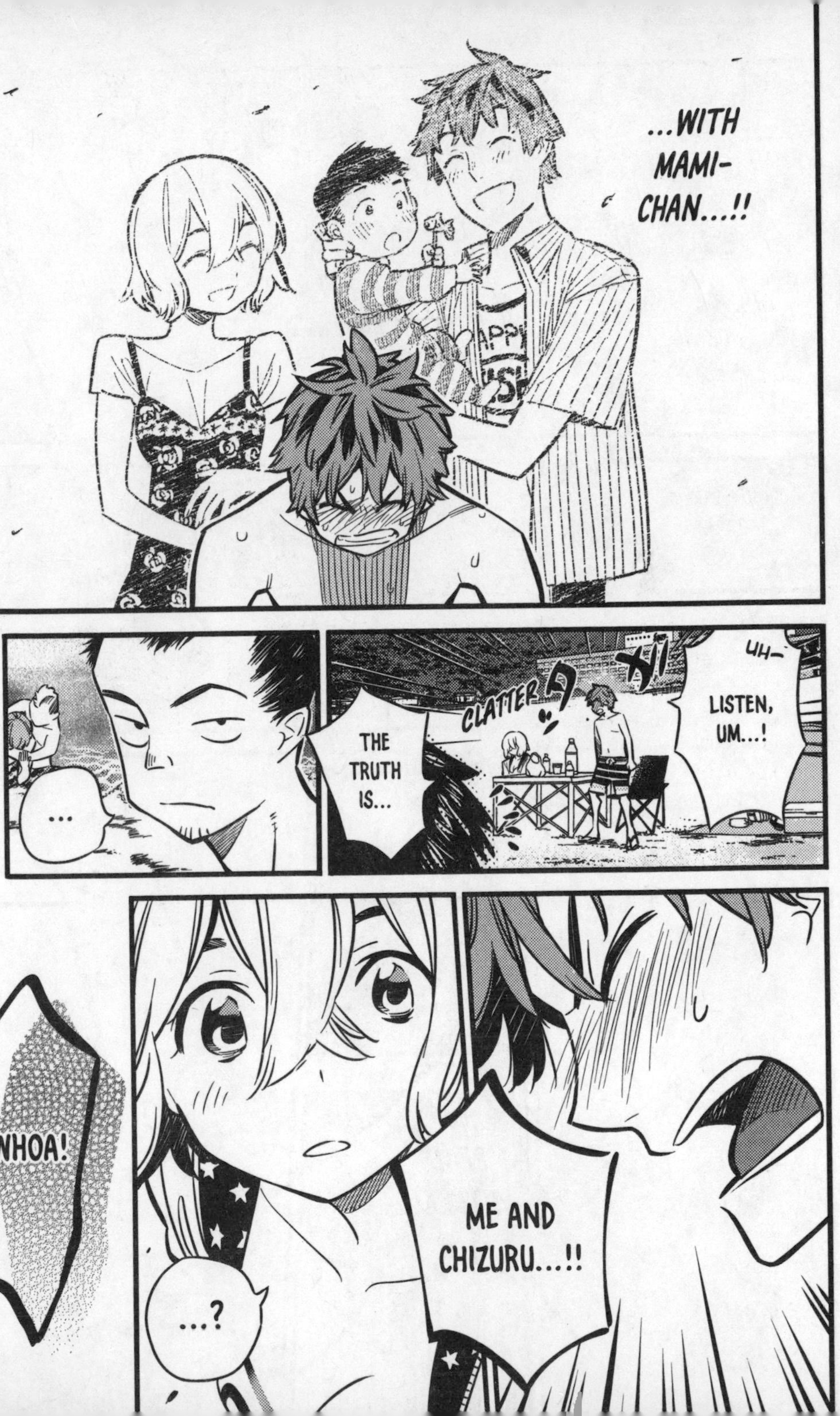

...WITH MAMI-CHAN...!!
UH—
LISTEN, UM...!
CLATTER
THE TRUTH IS...
...
ME AND CHIZURU...!!
WHOA!
...?

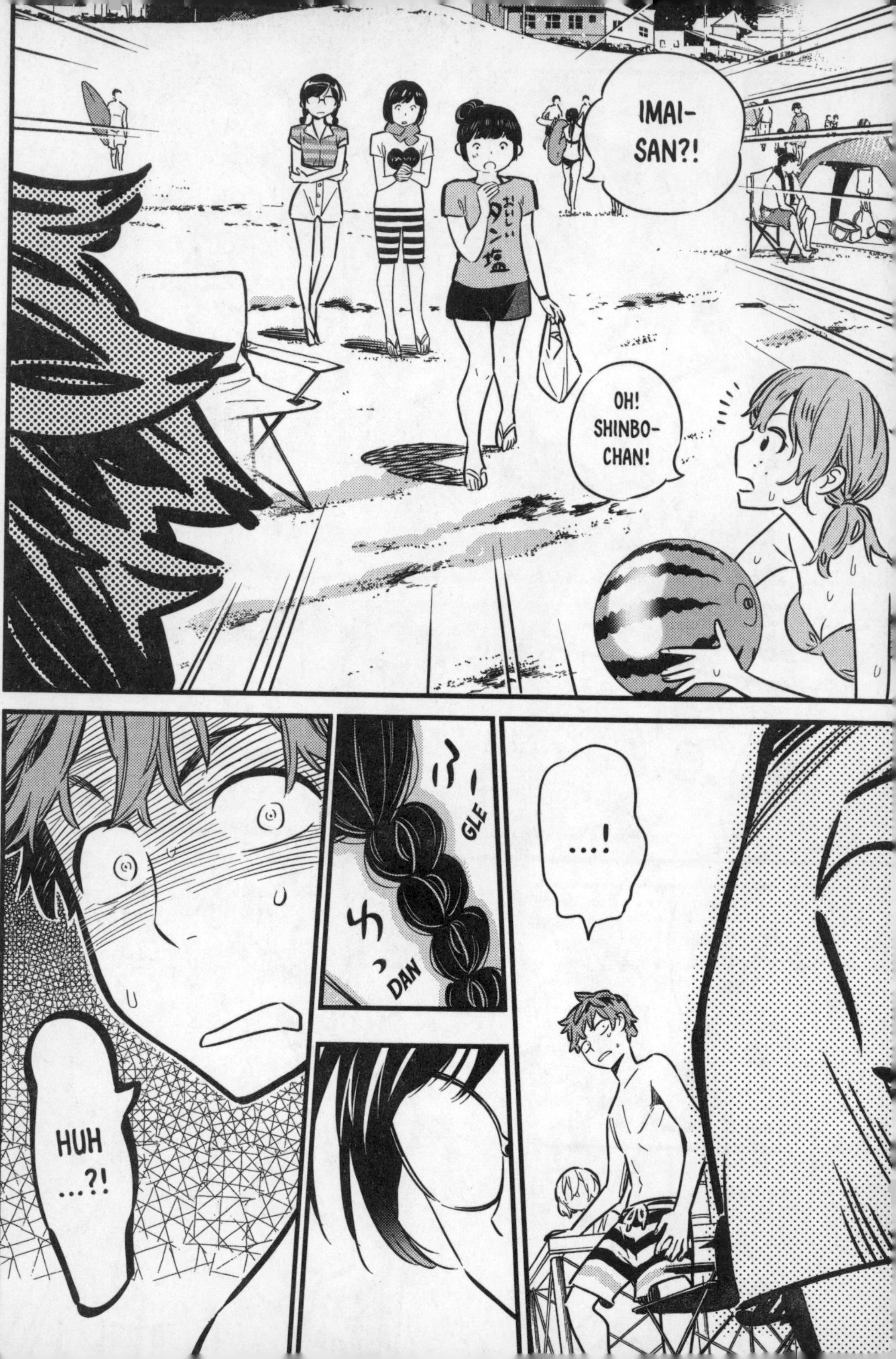
IMAI-SAN?!
OH! SHINBO-CHAN!
...!
GLE
DAN
HUH ...?!

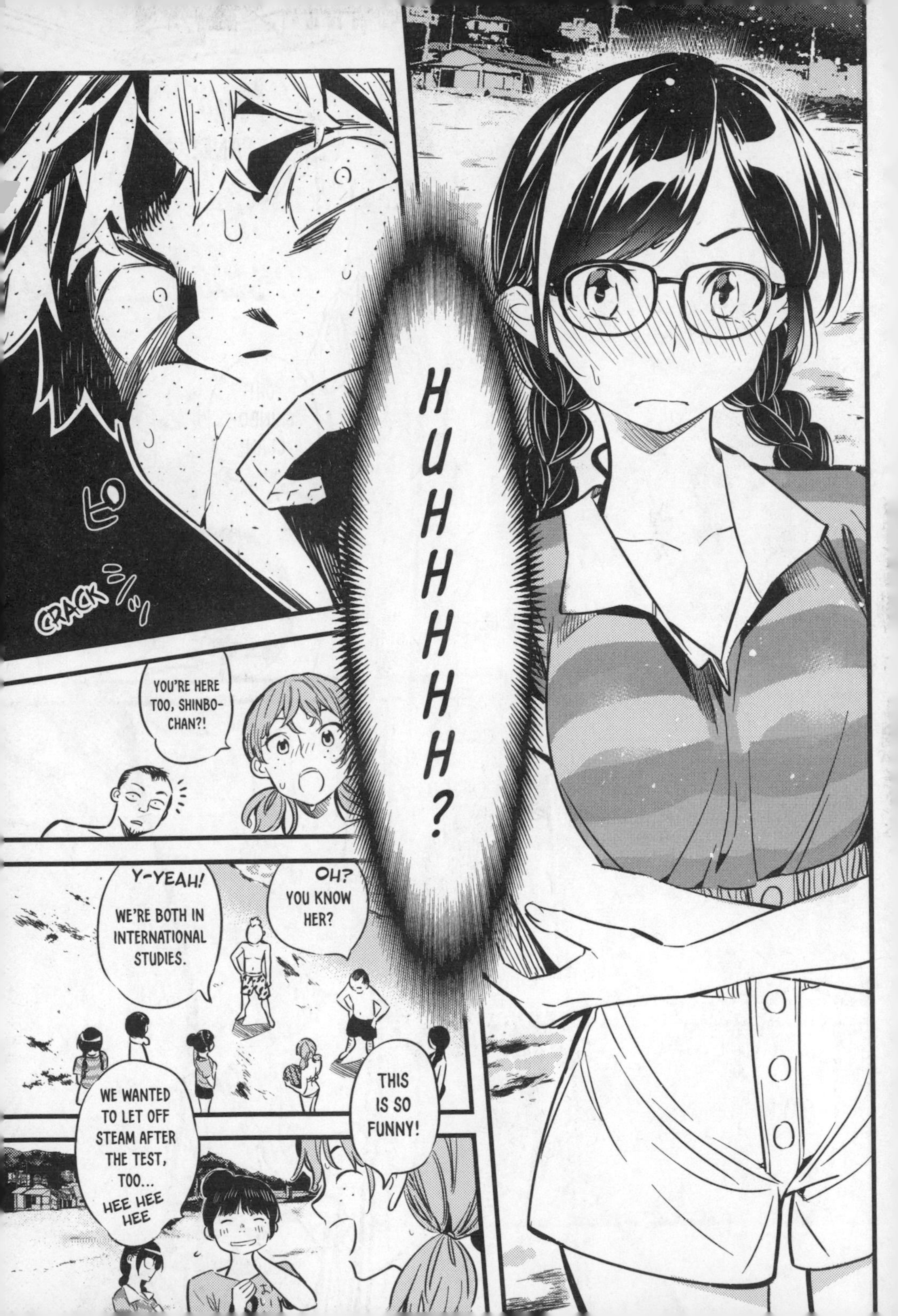
HUHHHHH?
CRACK
YOU'RE HERE TOO, SHINBO-CHAN?!
OH? YOU KNOW HER?
Y-YEAH! WE'RE BOTH IN INTERNATIONAL STUDIES.
THIS IS SO FUNNY!
WE WANTED TO LET OFF STEAM AFTER THE TEST, TOO... HEE HEE HEE

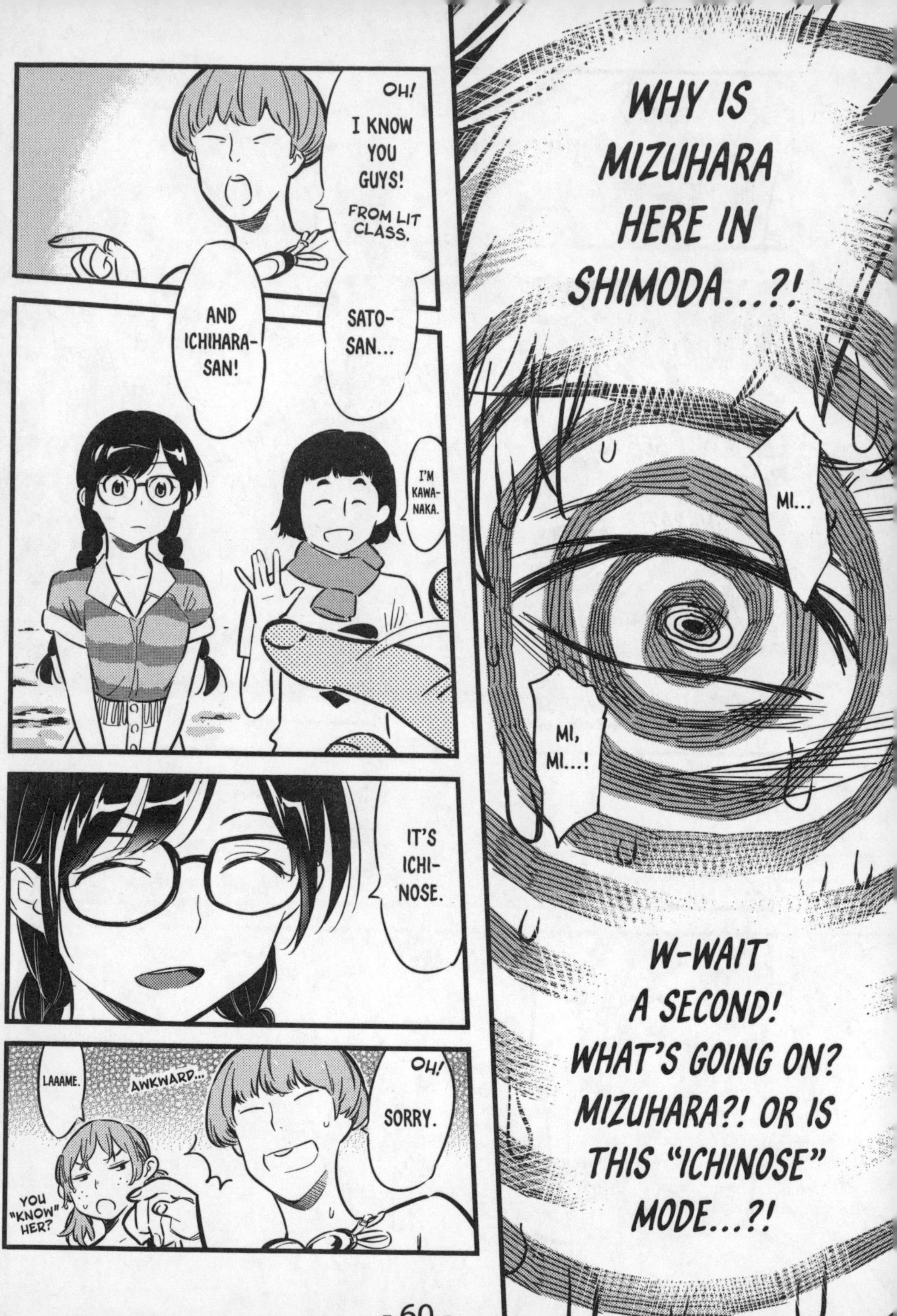
WHY IS MIZUHARA HERE IN SHIMODA...?!
MI...
MI, MI...!
W-WAIT A SECOND! WHAT'S GOING ON? MIZUHARA?! OR IS THIS "ICHINOSE" MODE...?!
OH! I KNOW YOU GUYS!
FROM LIT CLASS.
SATO-SAN...
AND ICHIHARA-SAN!
I'M KAWANAKA.
IT'S ICHINOSE.
OH!
SORRY.
AWKWARD...
LAAAME.
YOU "KNOW" HER?

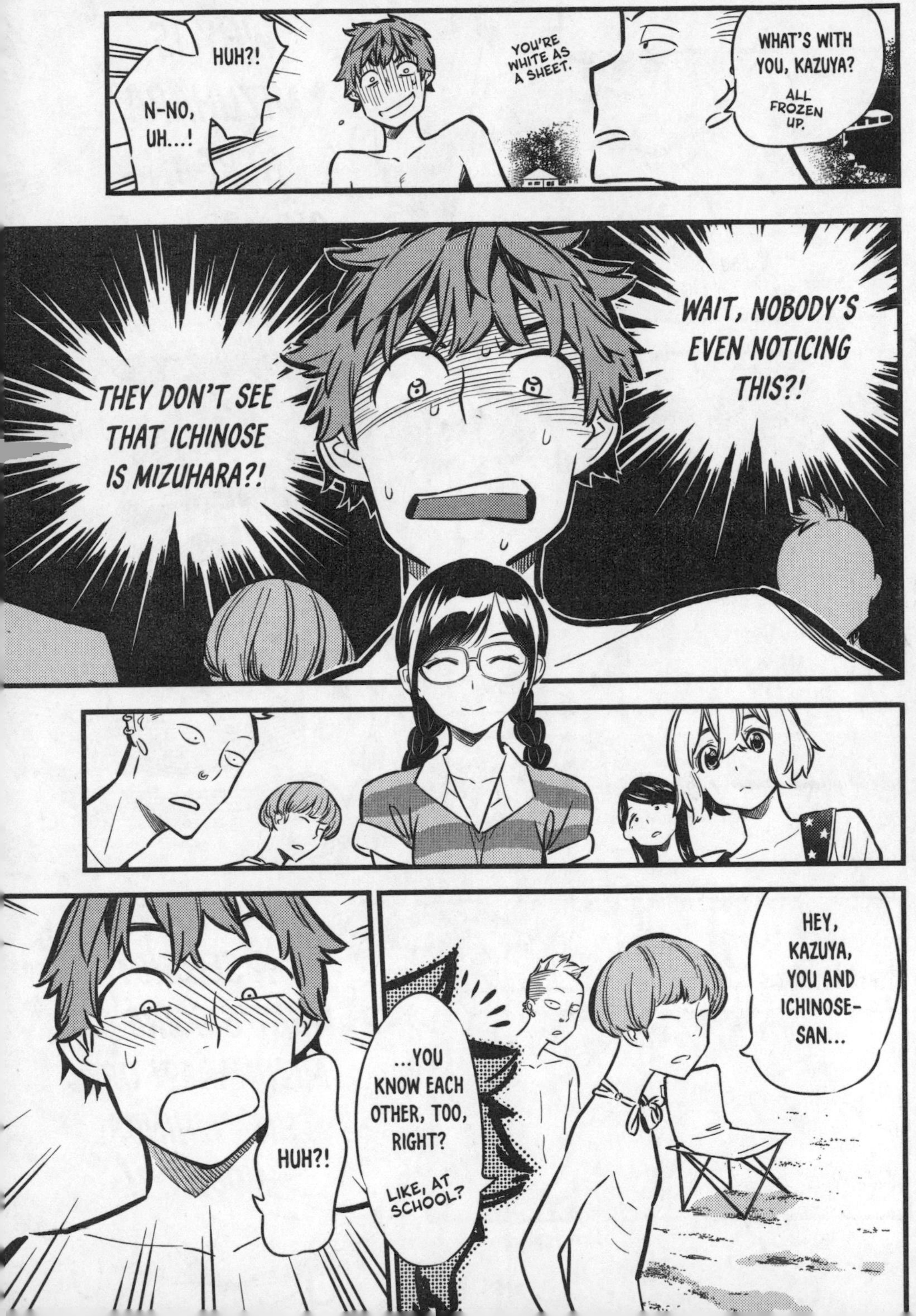
WHAT'S WITH YOU, KAZUYA?
ALL FROZEN UP.
YOU'RE WHITE AS A SHEET.
HUH?!
N-NO, UH...!
WAIT, NOBODY'S EVEN NOTICING THIS?!
THEY DON'T SEE THAT ICHINOSE IS MIZUHARA?!
HEY, KAZUYA, YOU AND ICHINOSE-SAN...
...YOU KNOW EACH OTHER, TOO, RIGHT?
LIKE, AT SCHOOL?
HUH?!

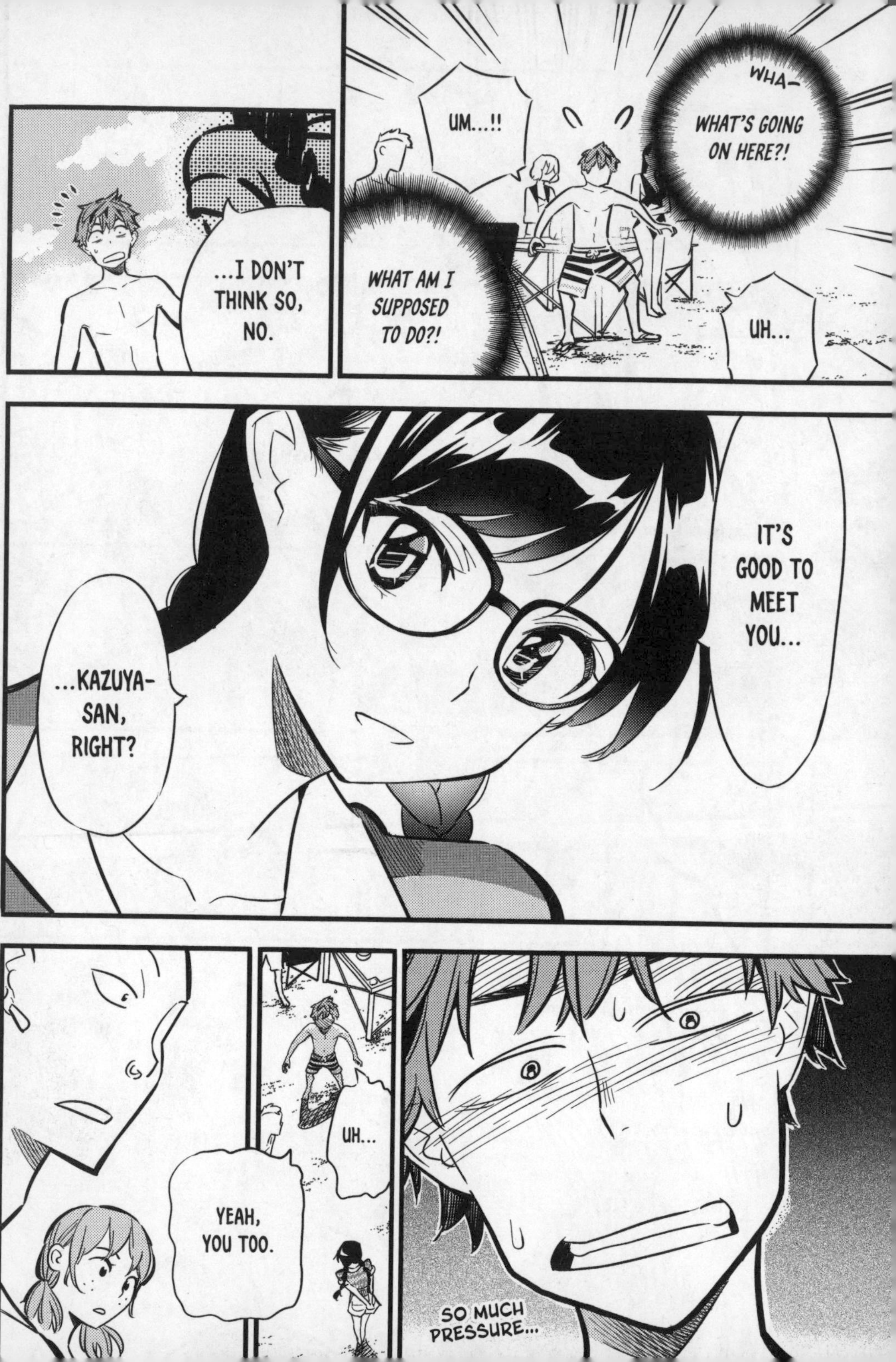
WHA—
WHAT'S GOING ON HERE?!
UM...!!
WHAT AM I SUPPOSED TO DO?!
UH...
...I DON'T THINK SO, NO.
IT'S GOOD TO MEET YOU...
...KAZUYA-SAN, RIGHT?
SO MUCH PRESSURE...
UH...
YEAH, YOU TOO.

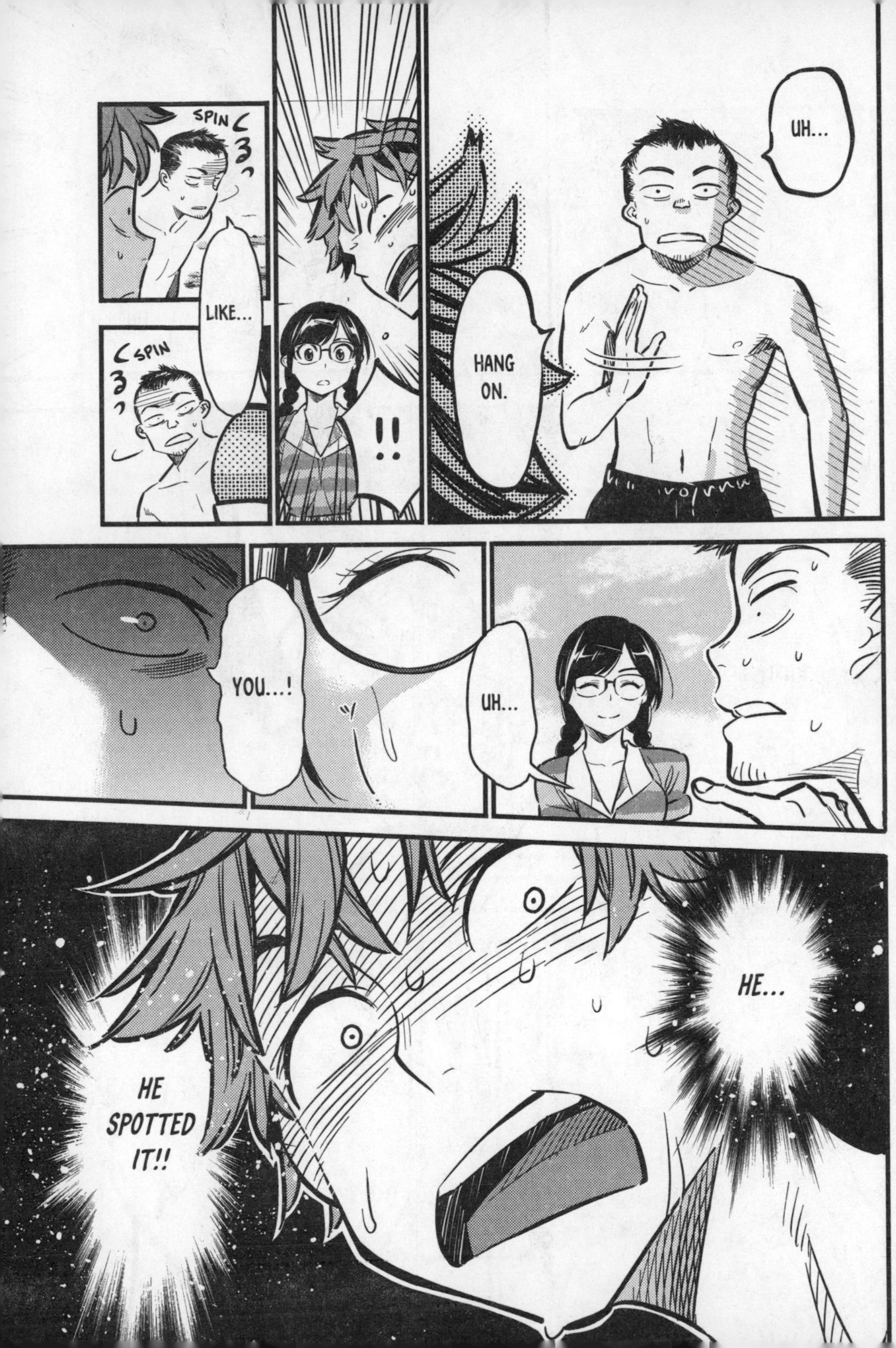
UH...
HANG ON.
!!
SPIN くるっ
LIKE...
SPIN くるっ
UH...
YOU...!
HE...
HE SPOTTED IT!!

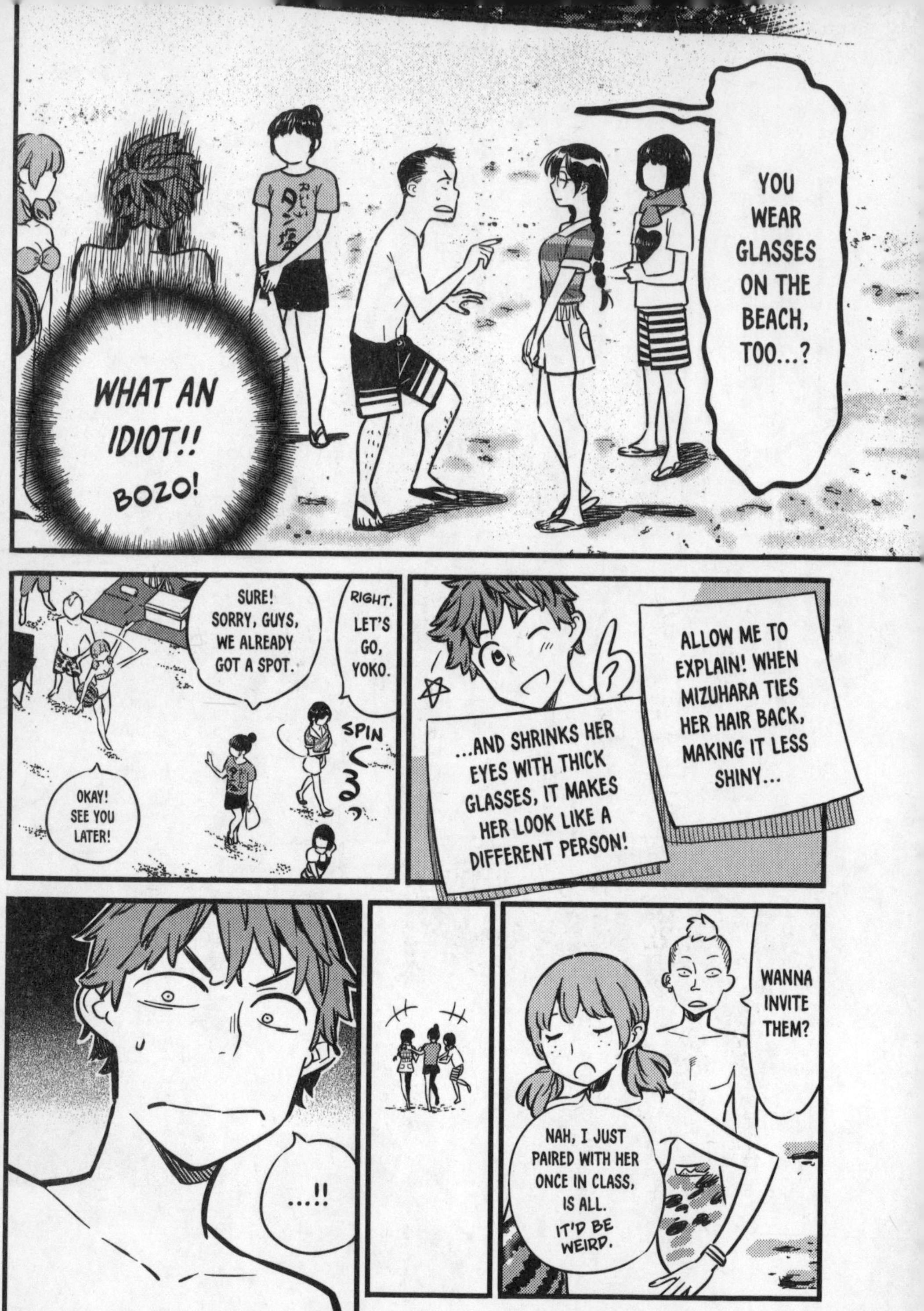
YOU WEAR GLASSES ON THE BEACH, TOO...?
WHAT AN IDIOT!!
BOZO!
ALLOW ME TO EXPLAIN! WHEN MIZUHARA TIES HER HAIR BACK, MAKING IT LESS SHINY...
...AND SHRINKS HER EYES WITH THICK GLASSES, IT MAKES HER LOOK LIKE A DIFFERENT PERSON!
RIGHT. LET'S GO, YOKO.
SURE! SORRY, GUYS, WE ALREADY GOT A SPOT.
SPIN
くるっ
OKAY! SEE YOU LATER!
WANNA INVITE THEM?
NAH, I JUST PAIRED WITH HER ONCE IN CLASS, IS ALL.
IT'D BE WEIRD.
...!!

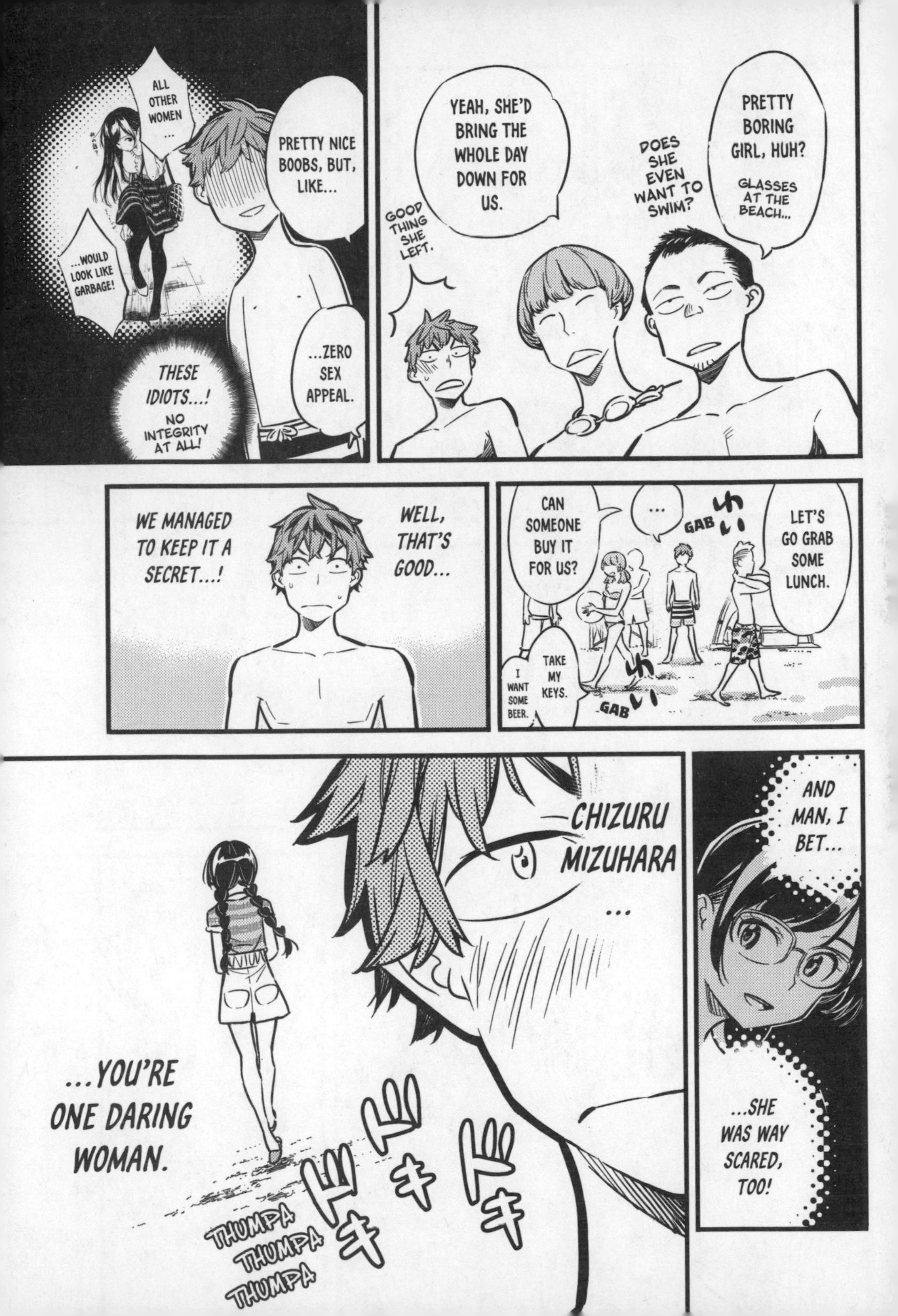
PRETTY BORING GIRL, HUH?
GLASSES AT THE BEACH...
DOES SHE EVEN WANT TO SWIM?
YEAH, SHE'D BRING THE WHOLE DAY DOWN FOR US.
GOOD THING SHE LEFT.
PRETTY NICE BOOBS, BUT, LIKE...
...ZERO SEX APPEAL.
ALL OTHER WOMEN ...
...WOULD LOOK LIKE GARBAGE!
THESE IDIOTS...!
NO INTEGRITY AT ALL!
LET'S GO GRAB SOME LUNCH.
GAB
...
CAN SOMEONE BUY IT FOR US?
TAKE MY KEYS.
I WANT SOME BEER.
GAB
WELL, THAT'S GOOD...
WE MANAGED TO KEEP IT A SECRET...!
AND MAN, I BET...
...SHE WAS WAY SCARED, TOO!
CHIZURU MIZUHARA
...
...YOU'RE ONE DARING WOMAN.
THUMPA THUMPA THUMPA

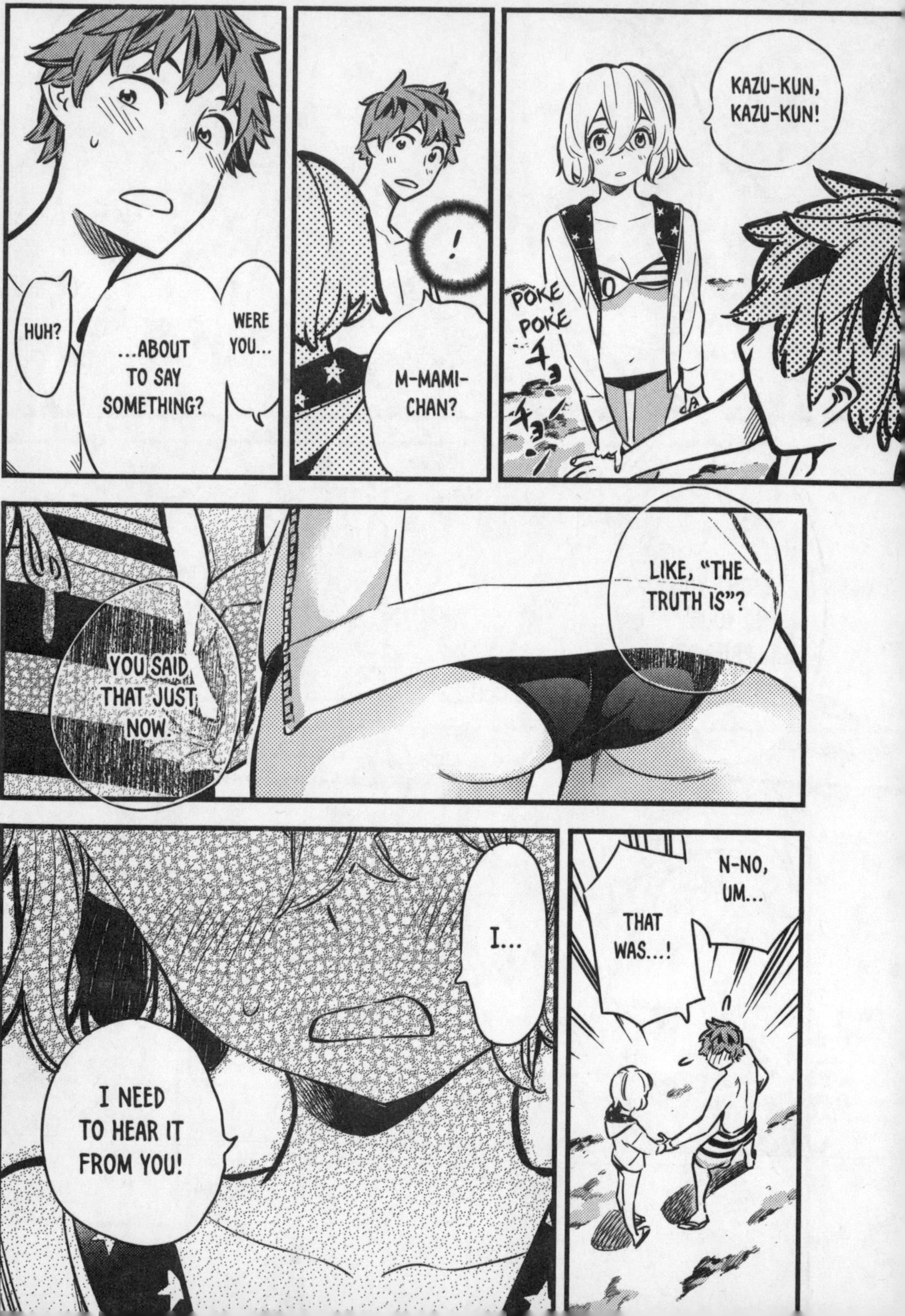
KAZU-KUN, KAZU-KUN!
POKE POKE
!
M-MAMI-CHAN?
WERE YOU...
...ABOUT TO SAY SOMETHING?
HUH?
LIKE, "THE TRUTH IS"?
YOU SAID THAT JUST NOW.
N-NO, UM...
THAT WAS...!
I...
I NEED TO HEAR IT FROM YOU!

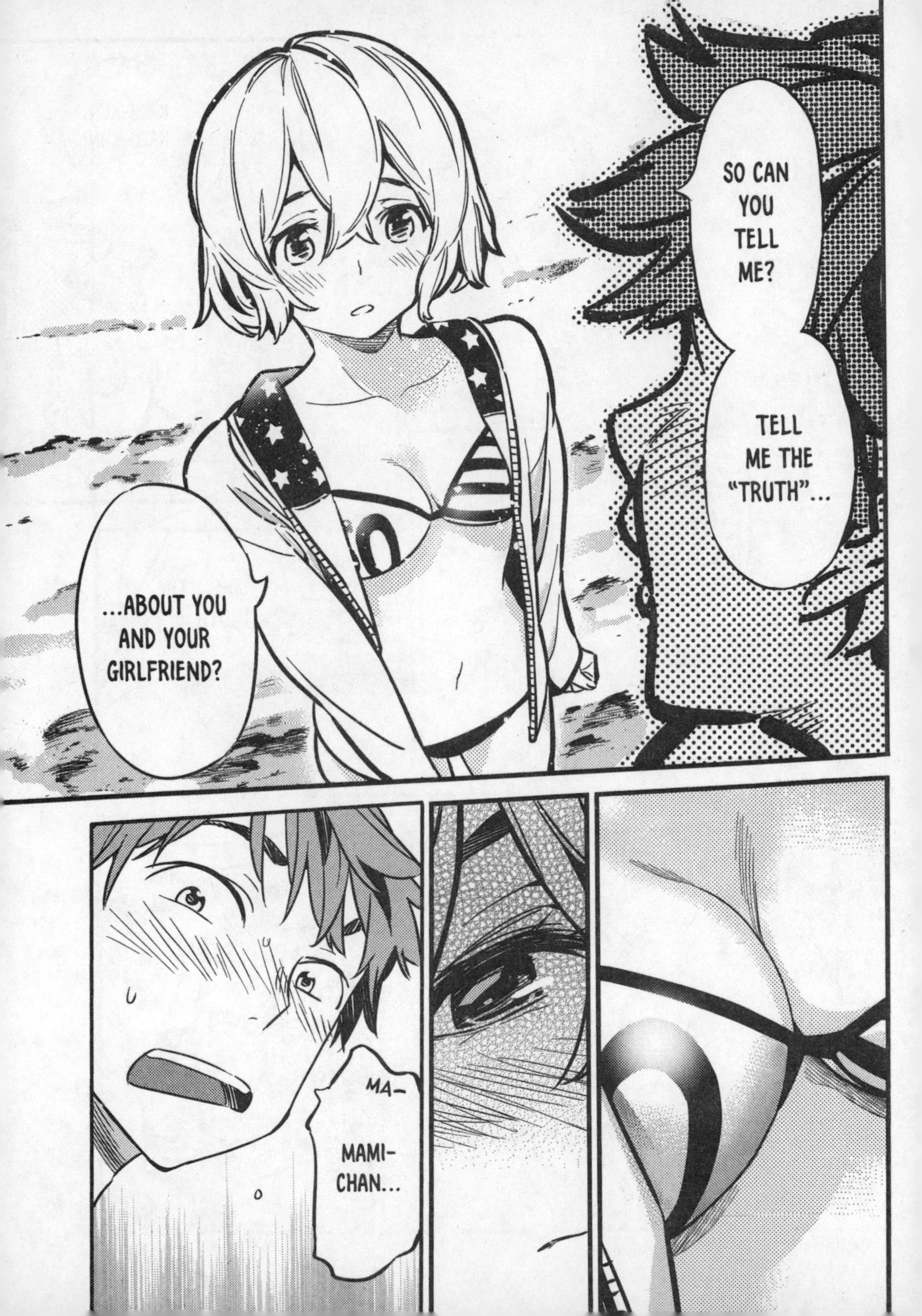
SO CAN YOU TELL ME?
TELL ME THE "TRUTH"...
...ABOUT YOU AND YOUR GIRLFRIEND?
MA-
MAMI-CHAN...

RATING 9
MY GIRLFRIEND-AND-THE-SEA (3)

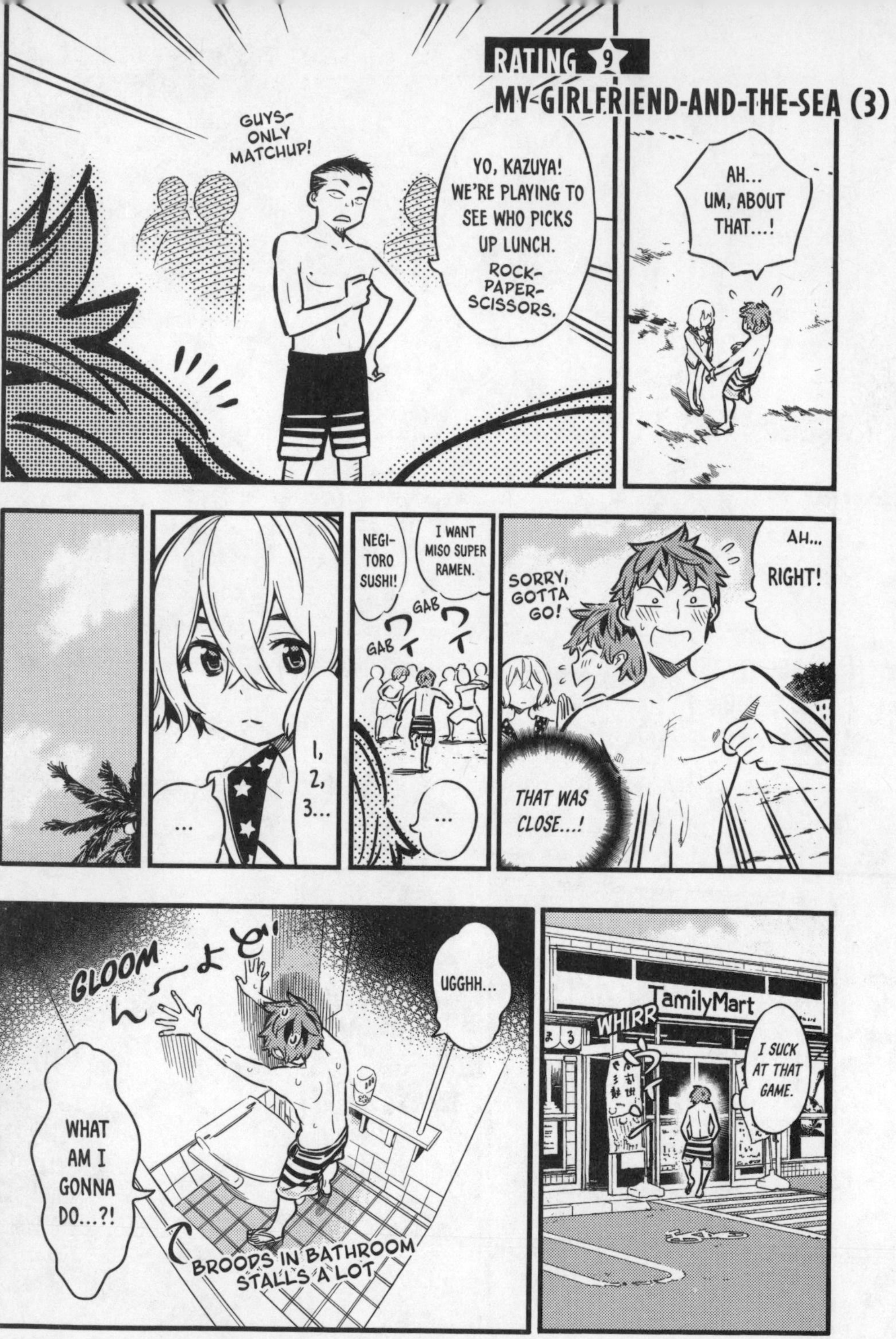
AH... UM, ABOUT THAT...!
YO, KAZUYA! WE'RE PLAYING TO SEE WHO PICKS UP LUNCH.
ROCK-PAPER-SCISSORS.
GUYS-ONLY MATCHUP!
AH... RIGHT!
SORRY, GOTTA GO!
THAT WAS CLOSE...!
I WANT MISO SUPER RAMEN.
NEGI-TORO SUSHI!
GAB
GAB
...
1, 2, 3...
...
WHIRR
TamilyMart
I SUCK AT THAT GAME.
UGGHH...
GLOOM
WHAT AM I GONNA DO...?!
BROODS IN BATHROOM STALLS A LOT

KAZUYA TRIES TO GRASP THE SITUATION

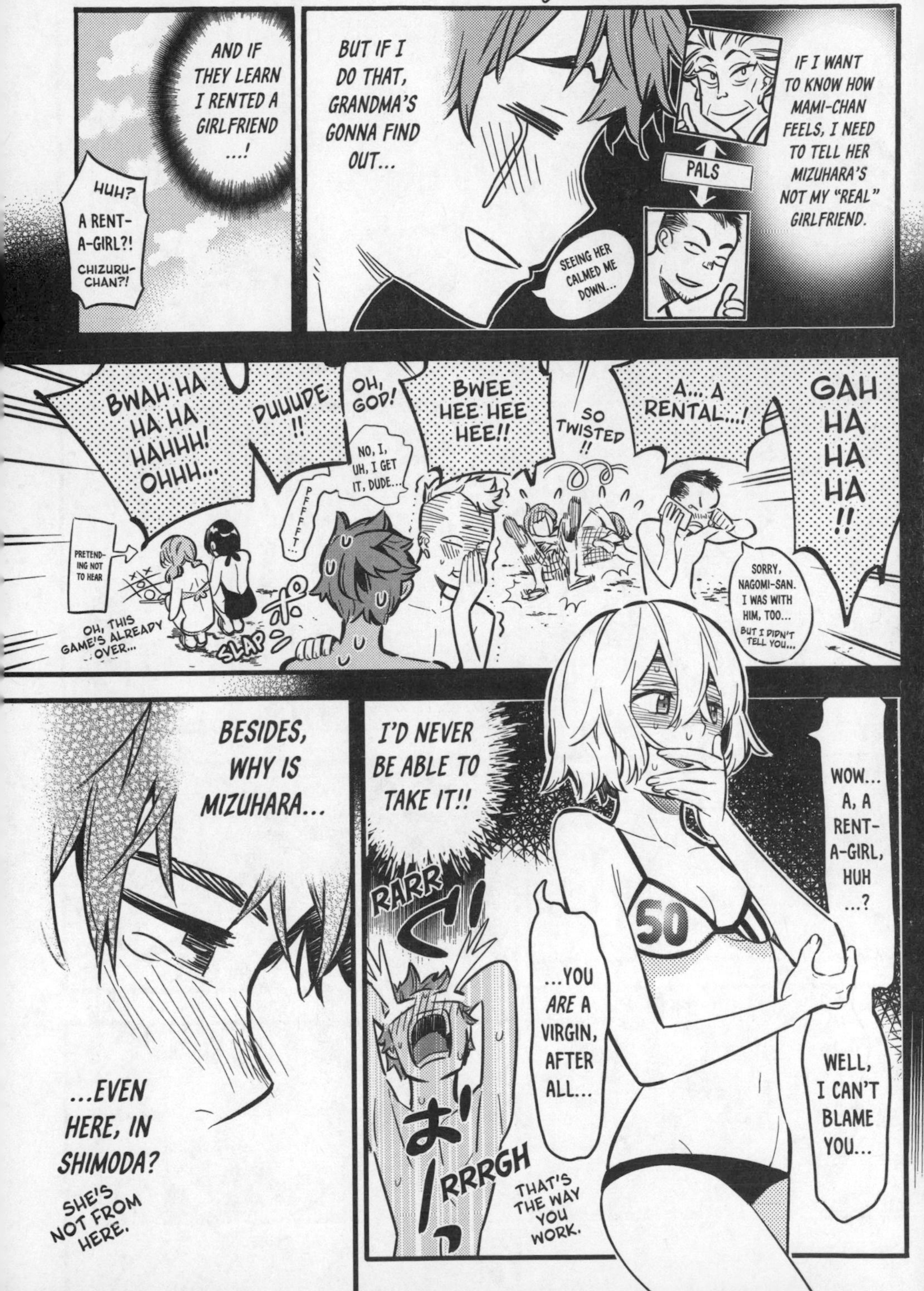
IF I WANT TO KNOW HOW MAMI-CHAN FEELS, I NEED TO TELL HER MIZUHARA'S NOT MY "REAL" GIRLFRIEND.
PALS
SEEING HER CALMED ME DOWN...
BUT IF I DO THAT, GRANDMA'S GONNA FIND OUT...
AND IF THEY LEARN I RENTED A GIRLFRIEND ...!
HUH? A RENT-A-GIRL?!
CHIZURU-CHAN?!
GAH HA HA HA!!
A... A RENTAL...!
SO TWISTED!!
BWEE HEE HEE HEE!!
OH, GOD!
DUUUDE!!
BWAH HA HA HA HAHHH! OHHH...
NO, I, UH, I GET IT, DUDE...
PFFFFT...
SORRY, NAGOMI-SAN. I WAS WITH HIM, TOO...
BUT I DIDN'T TELL YOU...
SLAP
PRETENDING NOT TO HEAR
OH, THIS GAME'S ALREADY OVER...
WOW... A, A RENT-A-GIRL, HUH ...?
WELL, I CAN'T BLAME YOU...
...YOU ARE A VIRGIN, AFTER ALL...
I'D NEVER BE ABLE TO TAKE IT!!
RARR
RRRGH
THAT'S THE WAY YOU WORK.
BESIDES, WHY IS MIZUHARA...
...EVEN HERE, IN SHIMODA?
SHE'S NOT FROM HERE.

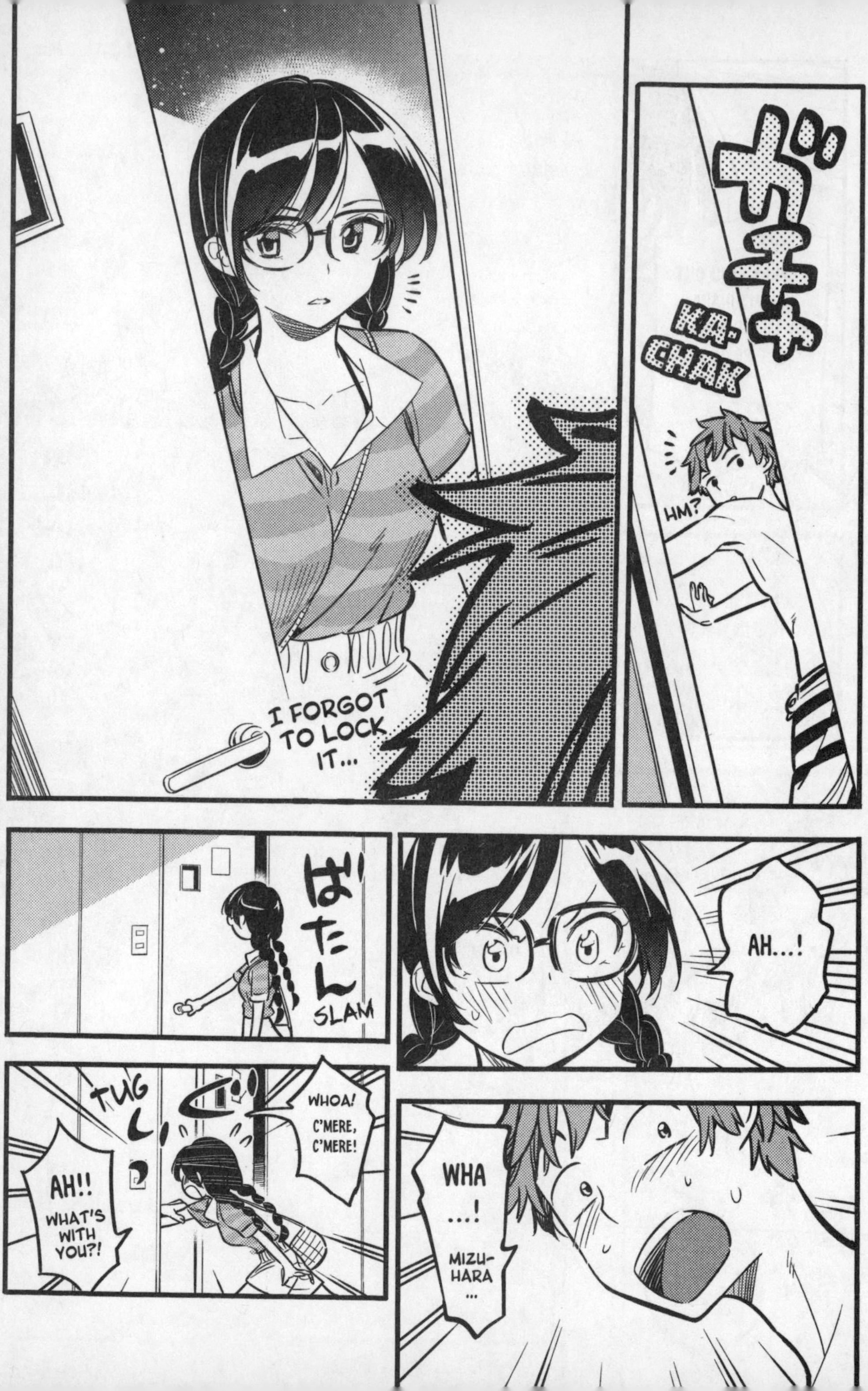
ガチャ
KA-CHAK
HM?
I FORGOT TO LOCK IT...
AH...!
ばたん
SLAM
WHA...!
MIZUHARA...
WHOA! C'MERE, C'MERE!
TUG
AH!! WHAT'S WITH YOU?!

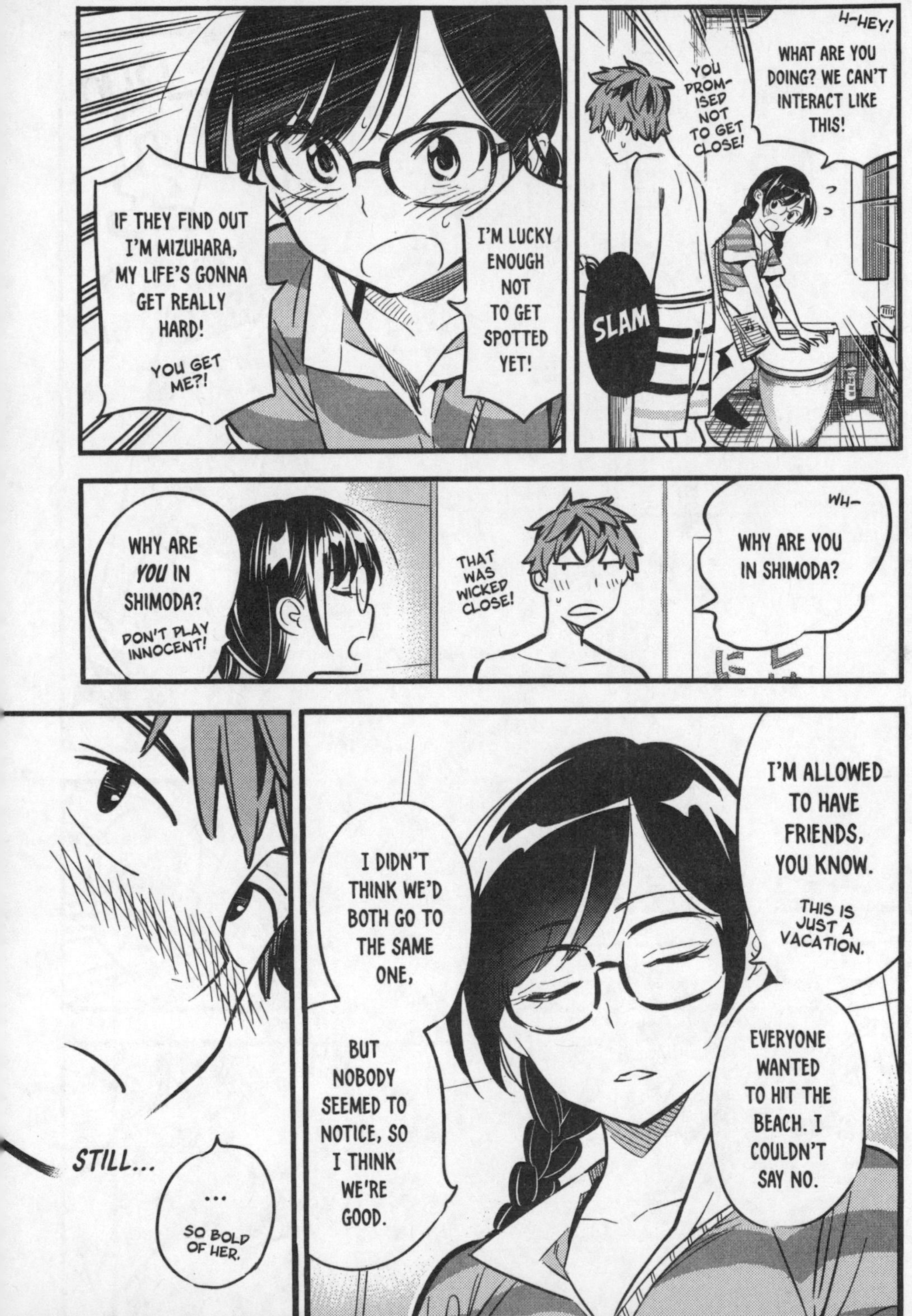
H-HEY!
WHAT ARE YOU DOING? WE CAN'T INTERACT LIKE THIS!
YOU PROMISED NOT TO GET CLOSE!
SLAM
I'M LUCKY ENOUGH NOT TO GET SPOTTED YET!
IF THEY FIND OUT I'M MIZUHARA, MY LIFE'S GONNA GET REALLY HARD!
YOU GET ME?!
WH-
WHY ARE YOU IN SHIMODA?
THAT WAS WICKED CLOSE!
WHY ARE *YOU* IN SHIMODA?
DON'T PLAY INNOCENT!
I'M ALLOWED TO HAVE FRIENDS, YOU KNOW.
THIS IS JUST A VACATION.
EVERYONE WANTED TO HIT THE BEACH. I COULDN'T SAY NO.
I DIDN'T THINK WE'D BOTH GO TO THE SAME ONE,
BUT NOBODY SEEMED TO NOTICE, SO I THINK WE'RE GOOD.
STILL...
...
SO BOLD OF HER.

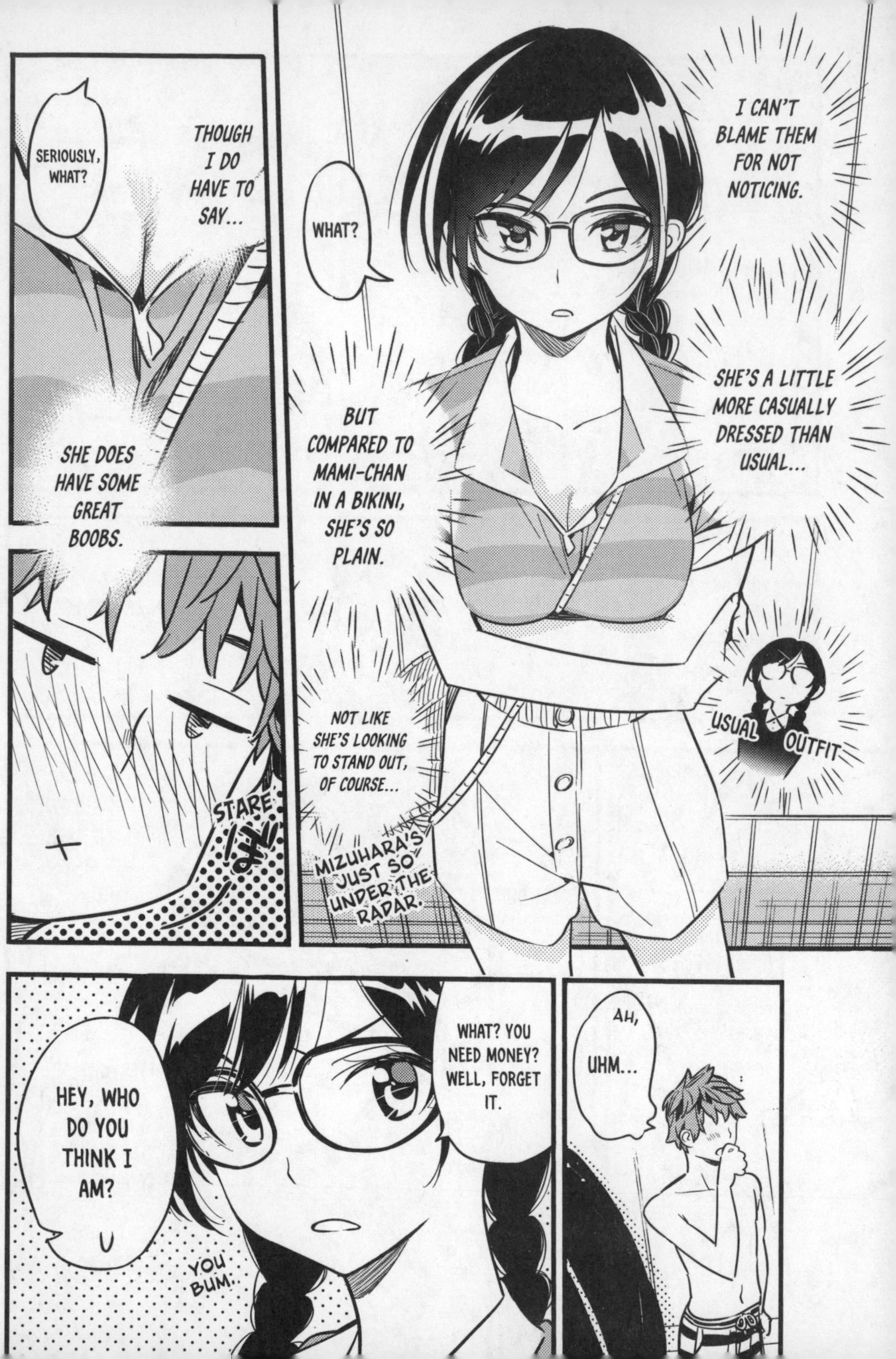
I CAN'T BLAME THEM FOR NOT NOTICING.
WHAT?
SHE'S A LITTLE MORE CASUALLY DRESSED THAN USUAL...
USUAL OUTFIT
BUT COMPARED TO MAMI-CHAN IN A BIKINI, SHE'S SO PLAIN.
NOT LIKE SHE'S LOOKING TO STAND OUT, OF COURSE...
MIZUHARA'S JUST SO UNDER THE RADAR.
SERIOUSLY, WHAT?
THOUGH I DO HAVE TO SAY...
SHE DOES HAVE SOME GREAT BOOBS.
STARE
AH, UHM...
WHAT? YOU NEED MONEY? WELL, FORGET IT.
HEY, WHO DO YOU THINK I AM?
YOU BUM.

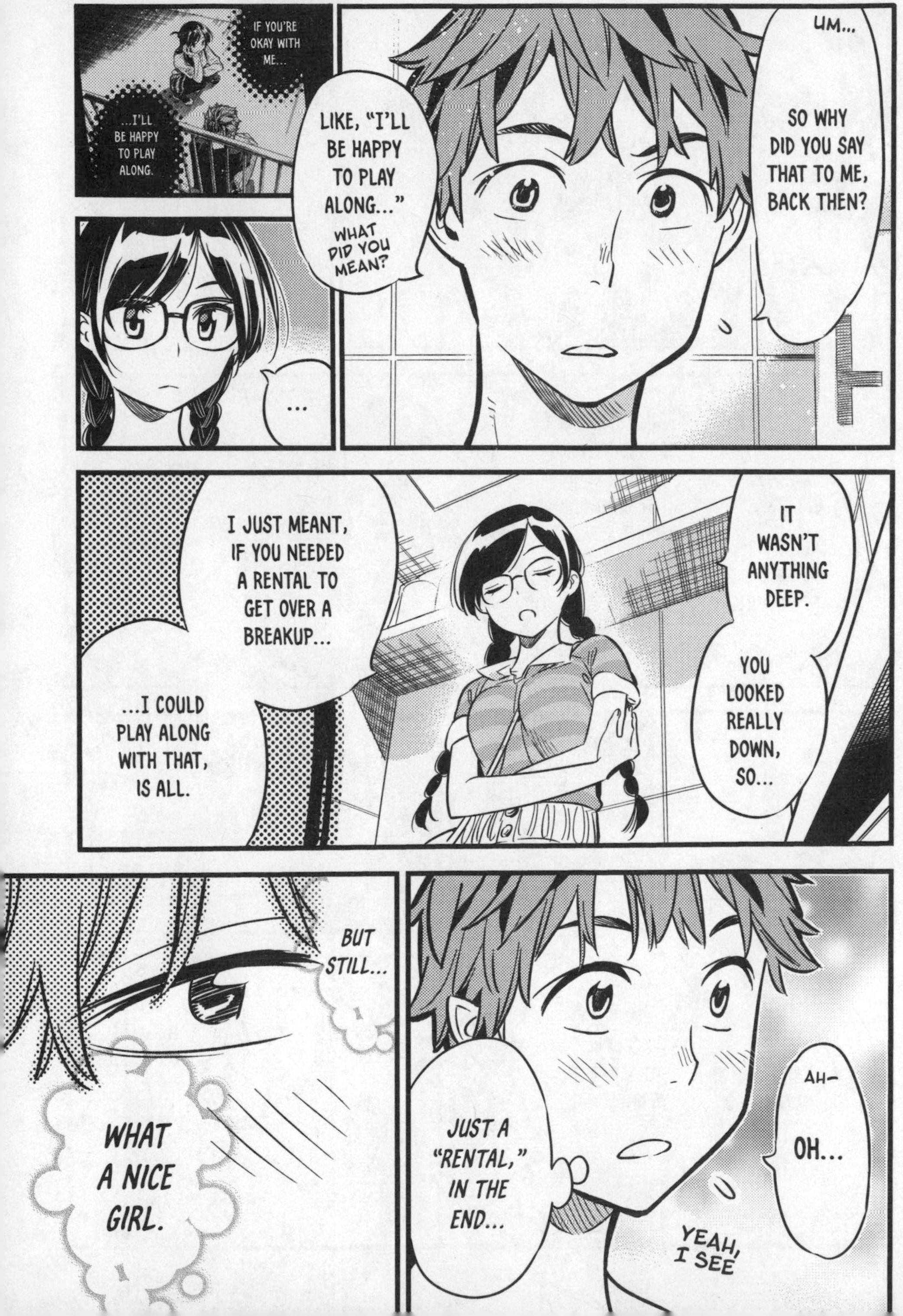
UM...
SO WHY DID YOU SAY THAT TO ME, BACK THEN?
LIKE, "I'LL BE HAPPY TO PLAY ALONG..." WHAT DID YOU MEAN?
IF YOU'RE OKAY WITH ME...
...I'LL BE HAPPY TO PLAY ALONG.
...
IT WASN'T ANYTHING DEEP.
YOU LOOKED REALLY DOWN, SO...
I JUST MEANT, IF YOU NEEDED A RENTAL TO GET OVER A BREAKUP...
...I COULD PLAY ALONG WITH THAT, IS ALL.
AH—
OH...
YEAH, I SEE
JUST A "RENTAL," IN THE END...
BUT STILL...
WHAT A NICE GIRL.

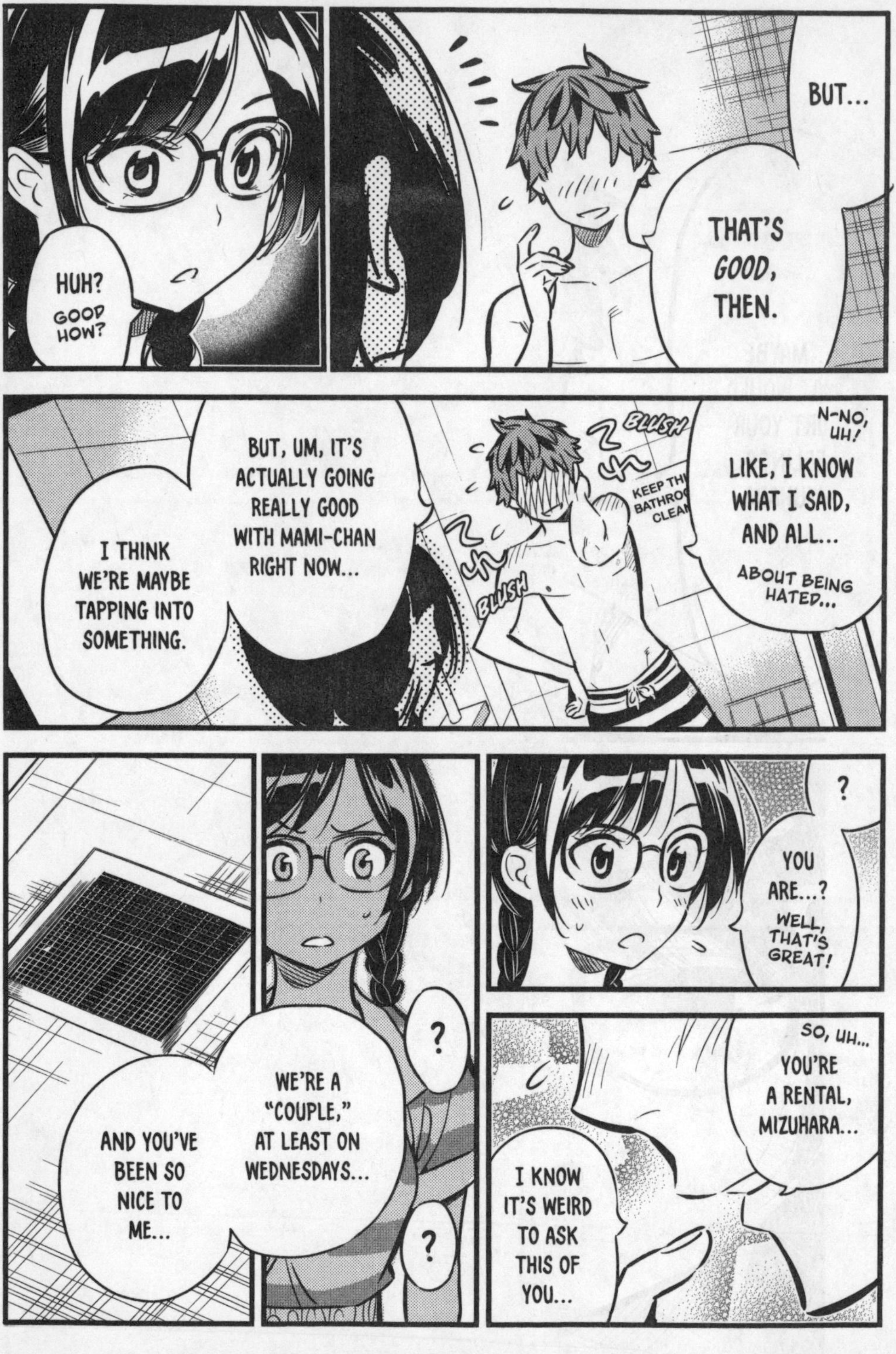
BUT...
THAT'S GOOD, THEN.
HUH? GOOD HOW?
N-NO, UH!
LIKE, I KNOW WHAT I SAID, AND ALL...
ABOUT BEING HATED...
BLUSH
BLUSH
BUT, UM, IT'S ACTUALLY GOING REALLY GOOD WITH MAMI-CHAN RIGHT NOW...
I THINK WE'RE MAYBE TAPPING INTO SOMETHING.
?
YOU ARE...?
WELL, THAT'S GREAT!
SO, UH...
YOU'RE A RENTAL, MIZUHARA...
I KNOW IT'S WEIRD TO ASK THIS OF YOU...
?
WE'RE A "COUPLE," AT LEAST ON WEDNESDAYS...
AND YOU'VE BEEN SO NICE TO ME...
?

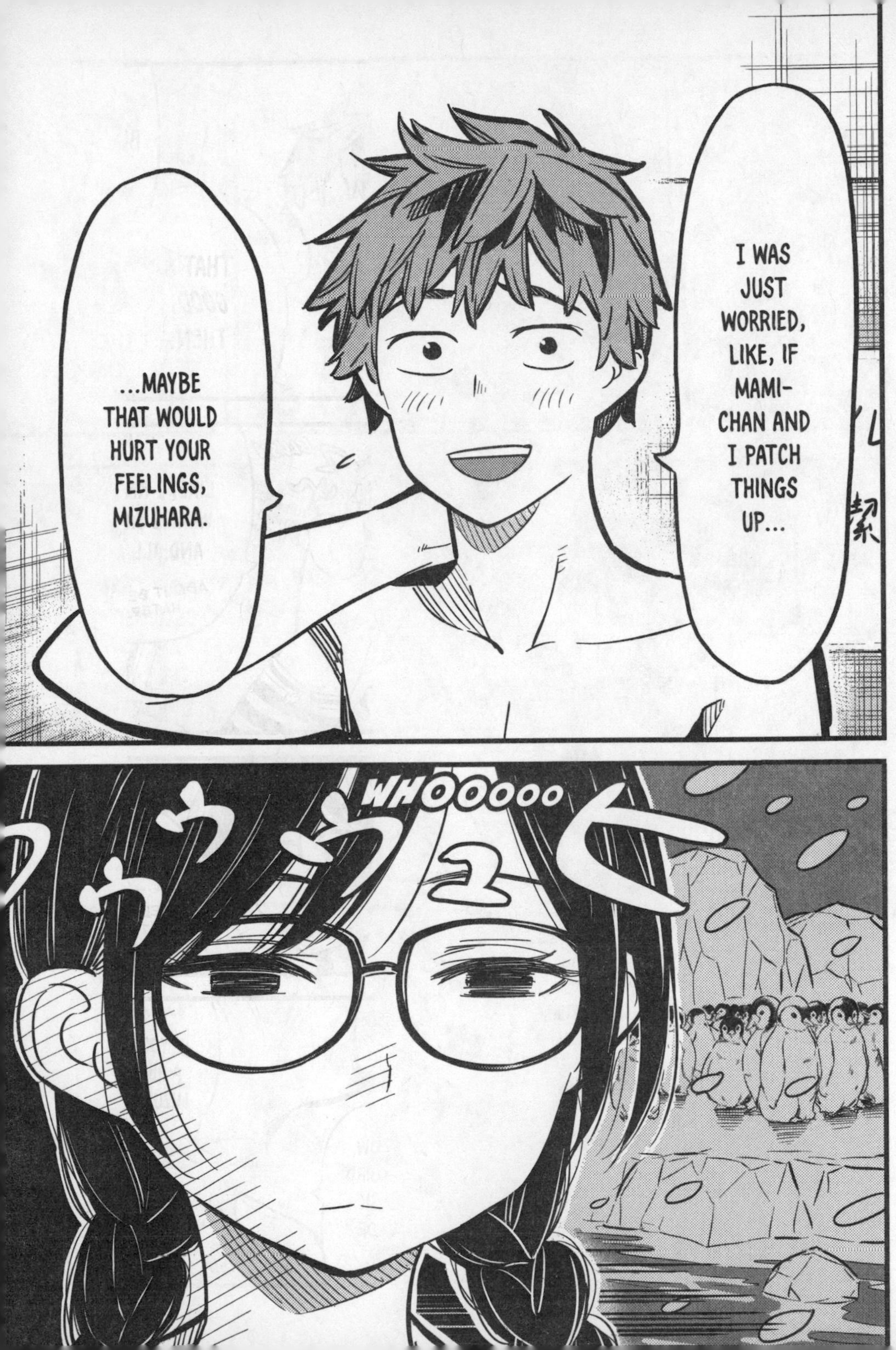
I WAS JUST WORRIED, LIKE, IF MAMI-CHAN AND I PATCH THINGS UP...
...MAYBE THAT WOULD HURT YOUR FEELINGS, MIZUHARA.
WHOOOOOO

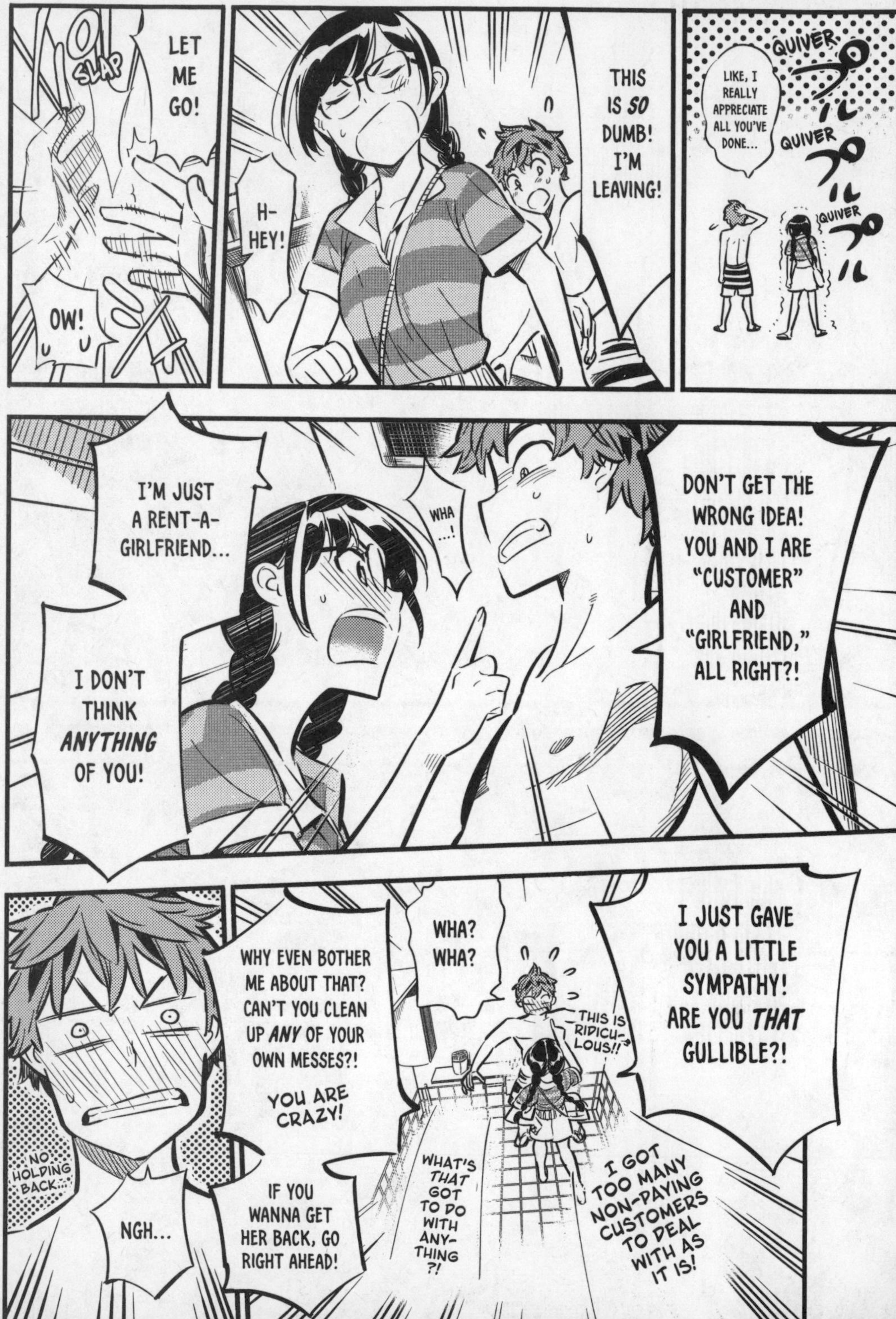
QUIVER プル
QUIVER プル
QUIVER プル
LIKE, I REALLY APPRECIATE ALL YOU'VE DONE...
THIS IS SO DUMB! I'M LEAVING!
H-HEY!
LET ME GO!
SLAP
OW!
DON'T GET THE WRONG IDEA! YOU AND I ARE "CUSTOMER" AND "GIRLFRIEND," ALL RIGHT?!
WHA...!
I'M JUST A RENT-A-GIRLFRIEND...
I DON'T THINK ANYTHING OF YOU!
I JUST GAVE YOU A LITTLE SYMPATHY! ARE YOU THAT GULLIBLE?!
WHA? WHA?
THIS IS RIDICULOUS!!
WHY EVEN BOTHER ME ABOUT THAT? CAN'T YOU CLEAN UP ANY OF YOUR OWN MESSES?!
YOU ARE CRAZY!
I GOT TOO MANY NON-PAYING CUSTOMERS TO DEAL WITH AS IT IS!
WHAT'S THAT GOT TO DO WITH ANYTHING?!
IF YOU WANNA GET HER BACK, GO RIGHT AHEAD!
NO HOLDING BACK...
NGH...

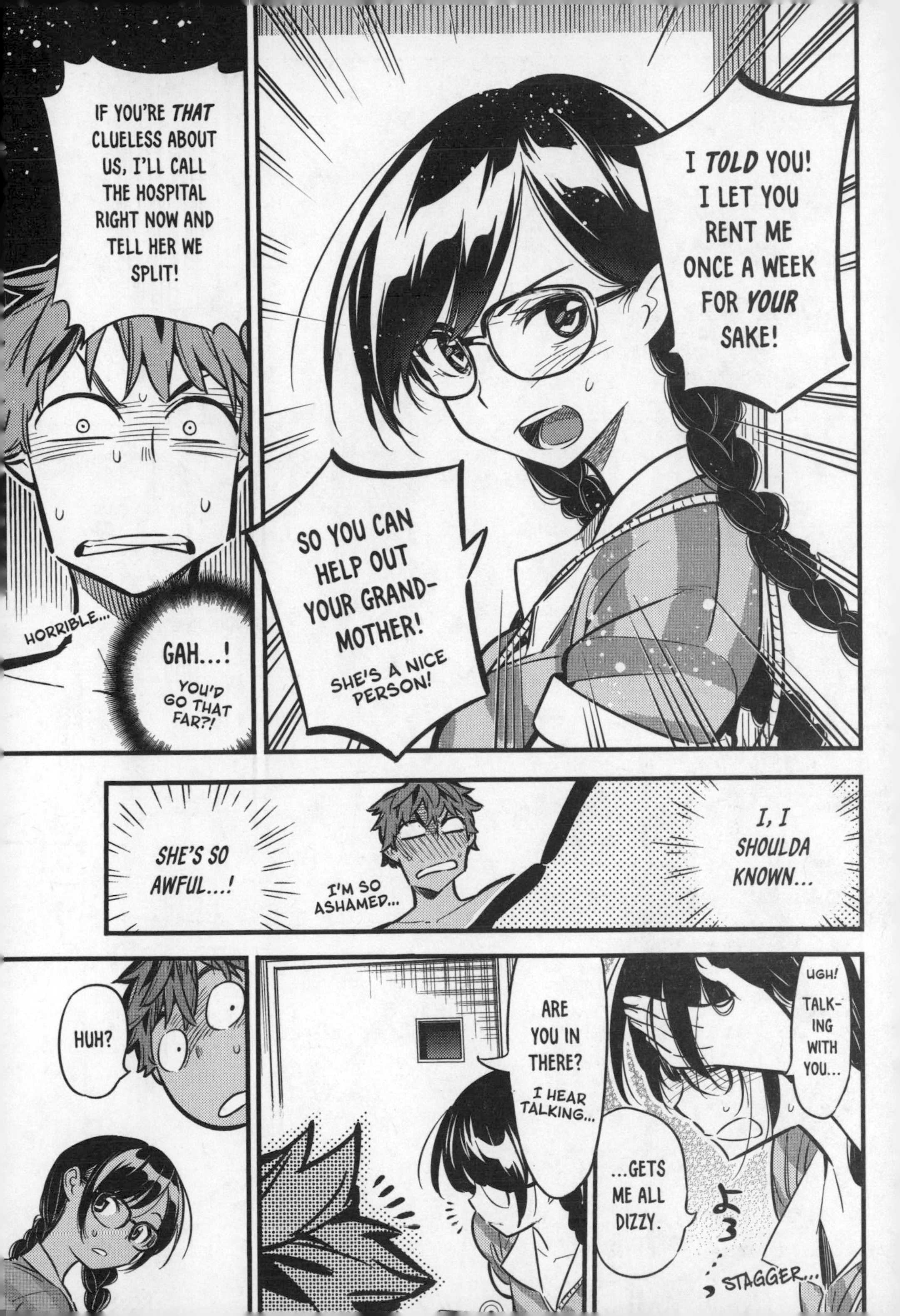
I TOLD YOU! I LET YOU RENT ME ONCE A WEEK FOR YOUR SAKE!
SO YOU CAN HELP OUT YOUR GRAND-MOTHER!
SHE'S A NICE PERSON!
IF YOU'RE THAT CLUELESS ABOUT US, I'LL CALL THE HOSPITAL RIGHT NOW AND TELL HER WE SPLIT!
GAH...!
YOU'D GO THAT FAR?!
HORRIBLE...
I, I SHOULDA KNOWN...
I'M SO ASHAMED...
SHE'S SO AWFUL...!
UGH! TALK-ING WITH YOU...
...GETS ME ALL DIZZY.
よろ
STAGGER...
ARE YOU IN THERE?
I HEAR TALKING...
HUH?

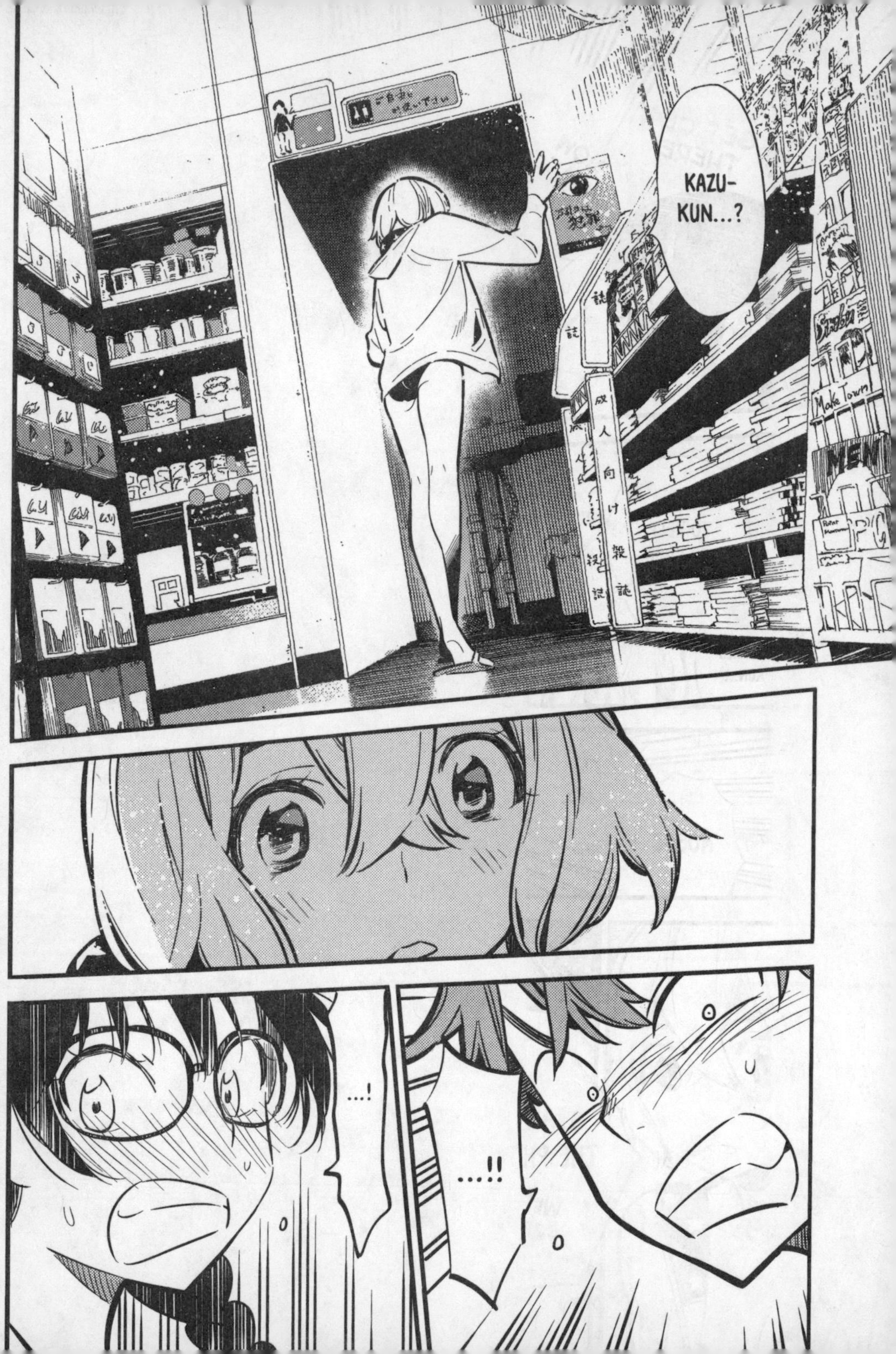
KAZU-KUN...?
成人向け雑誌
...!
...!!

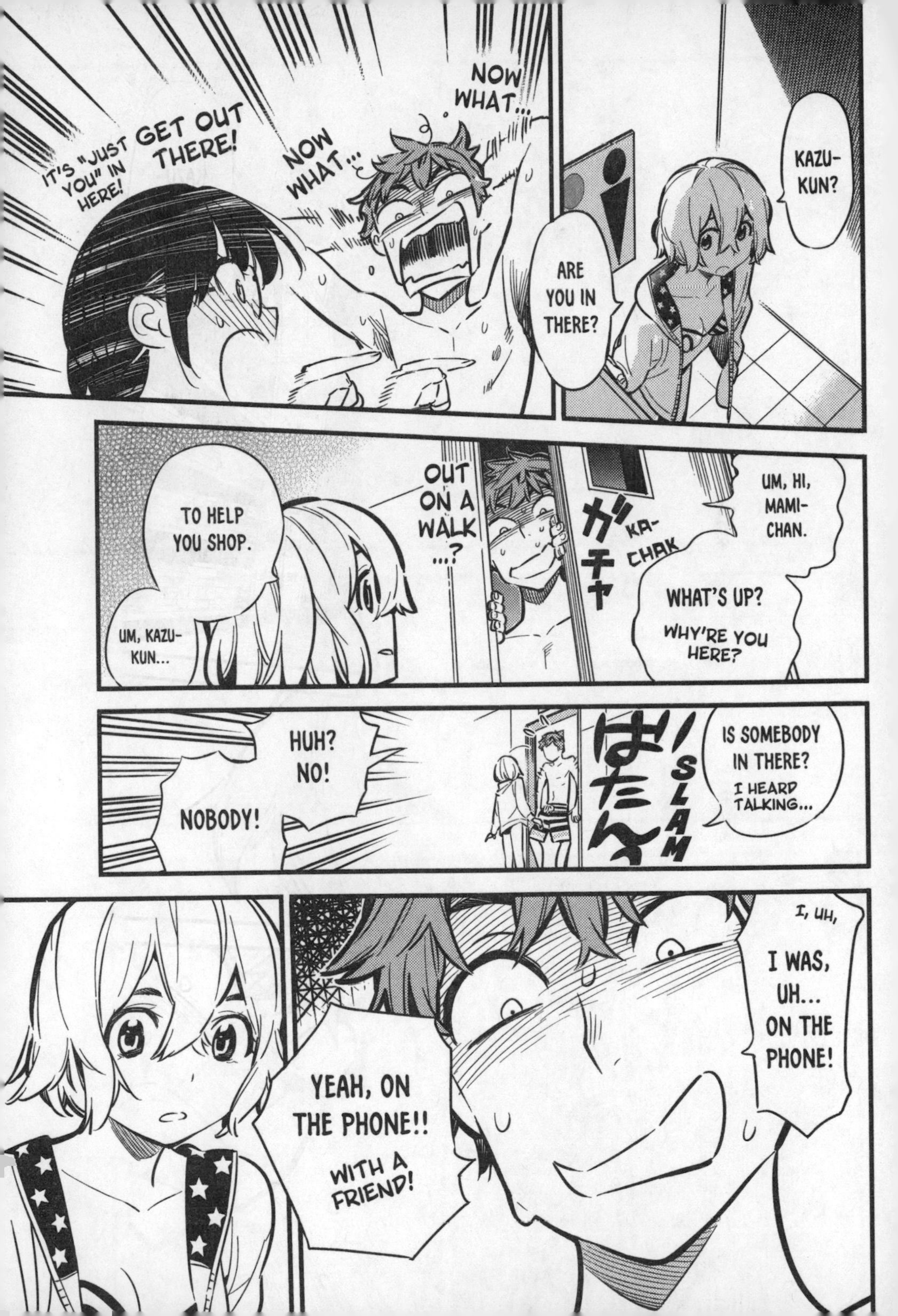
KAZU-KUN?
ARE YOU IN THERE?
NOW WHAT...
NOW WHAT...
GET OUT THERE!
IT'S "JUST YOU" IN HERE!
UM, HI, MAMI-CHAN.
WHAT'S UP?
WHY'RE YOU HERE?
ガチャ
KA-CHAK
OUT ON A WALK...?
TO HELP YOU SHOP.
UM, KAZU-KUN...
IS SOMEBODY IN THERE?
I HEARD TALKING...
ばたん
SLAM
HUH? NO!
NOBODY!
I, UH,
I WAS, UH... ON THE PHONE!
YEAH, ON THE PHONE!!
WITH A FRIEND!

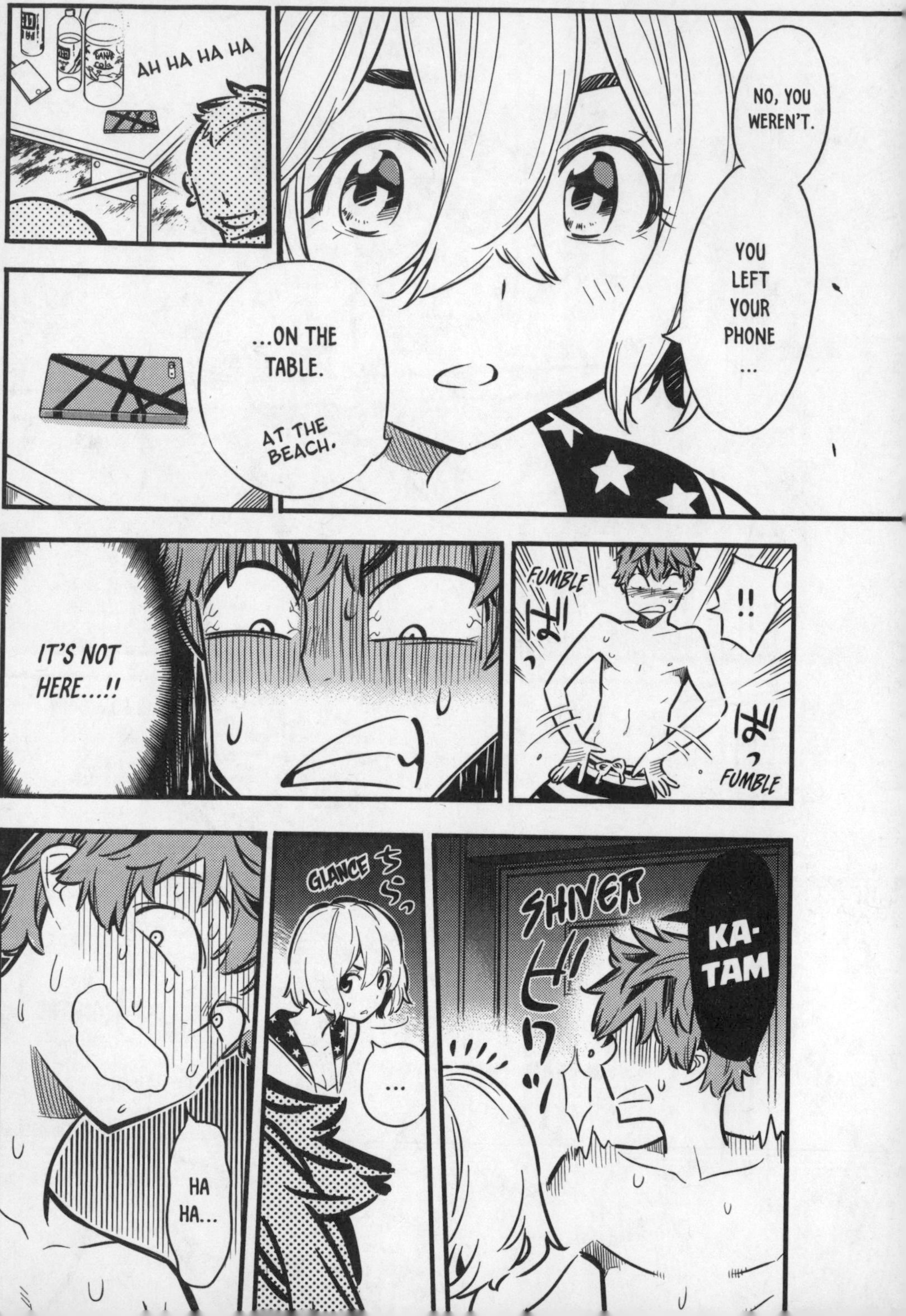
NO, YOU WEREN'T.
YOU LEFT YOUR PHONE ...
...ON THE TABLE.
AT THE BEACH.
AH HA HA HA
FUMBLE
!!
FUMBLE
IT'S NOT HERE...!!
SHIVER
KA-TAM
GLANCE
...
HA HA...

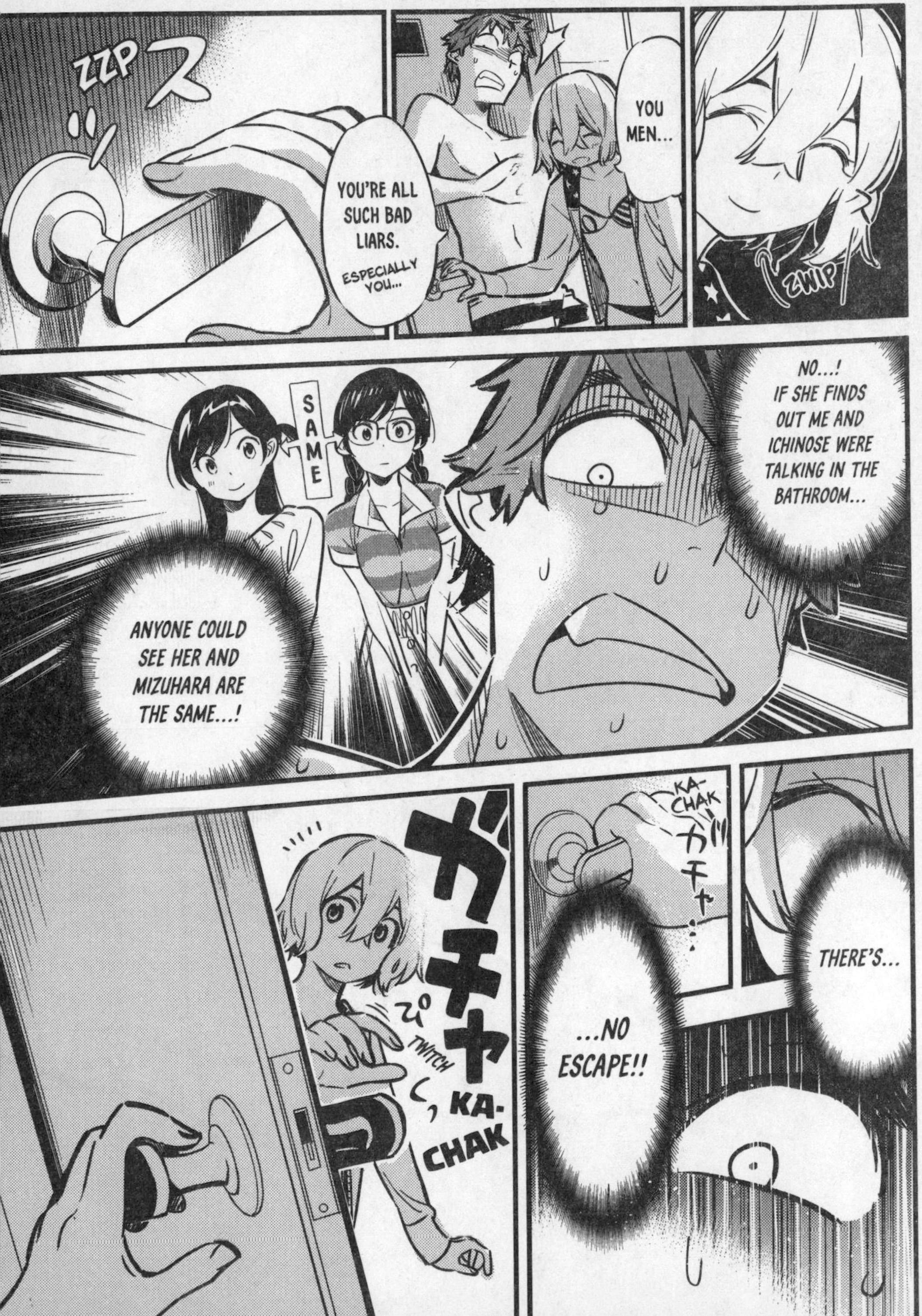
ZWIP
YOU MEN...
YOU'RE ALL SUCH BAD LIARS.
ESPECIALLY YOU...
ZZP
ス
NO...! IF SHE FINDS OUT ME AND ICHINOSE WERE TALKING IN THE BATHROOM...
SAME
SAME
ANYONE COULD SEE HER AND MIZUHARA ARE THE SAME...!
THERE'S...
...NO ESCAPE!!
KA-CHAK
ガチャ
ガチャ
ぴく
TWITCH
KA-CHAK

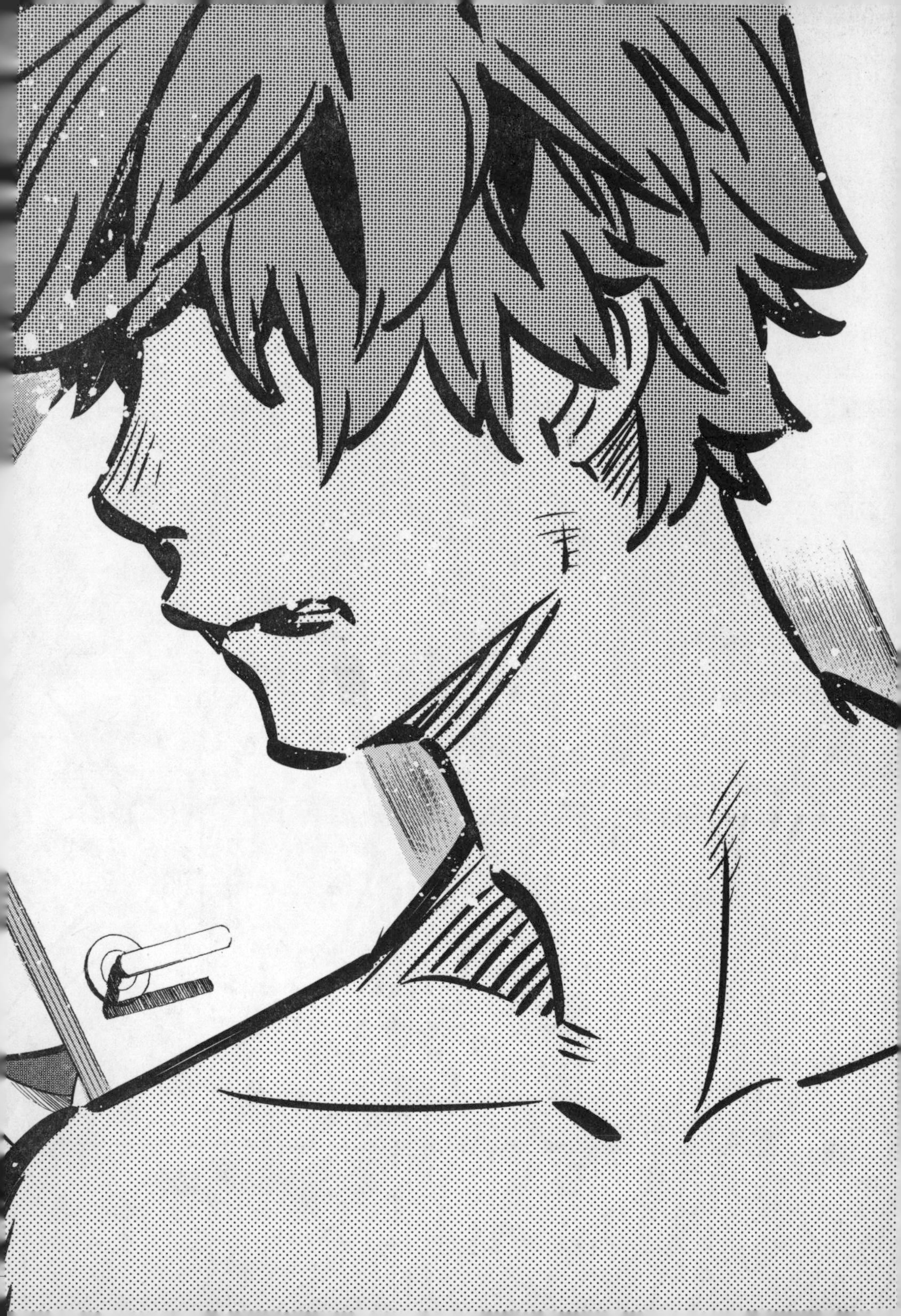

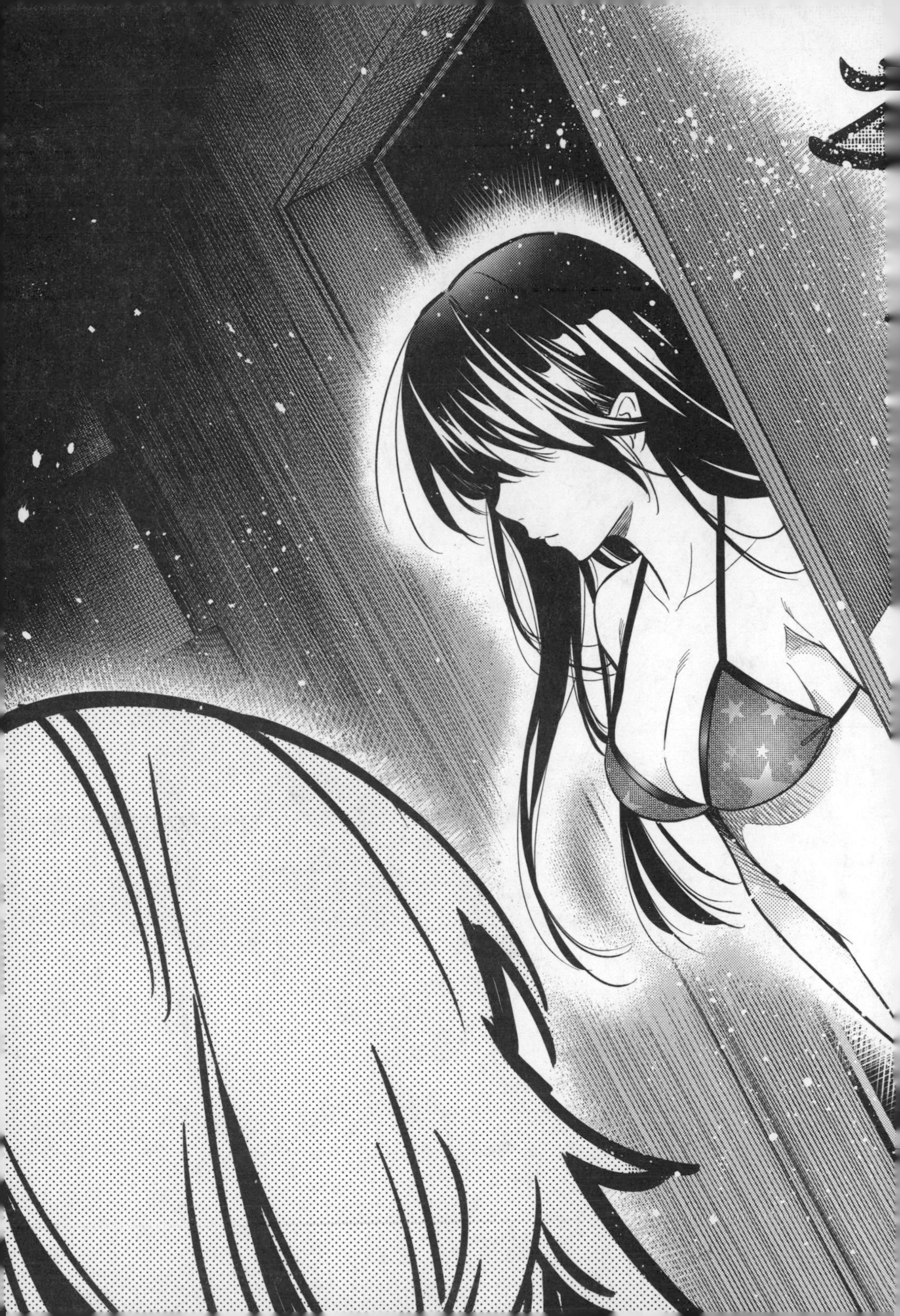

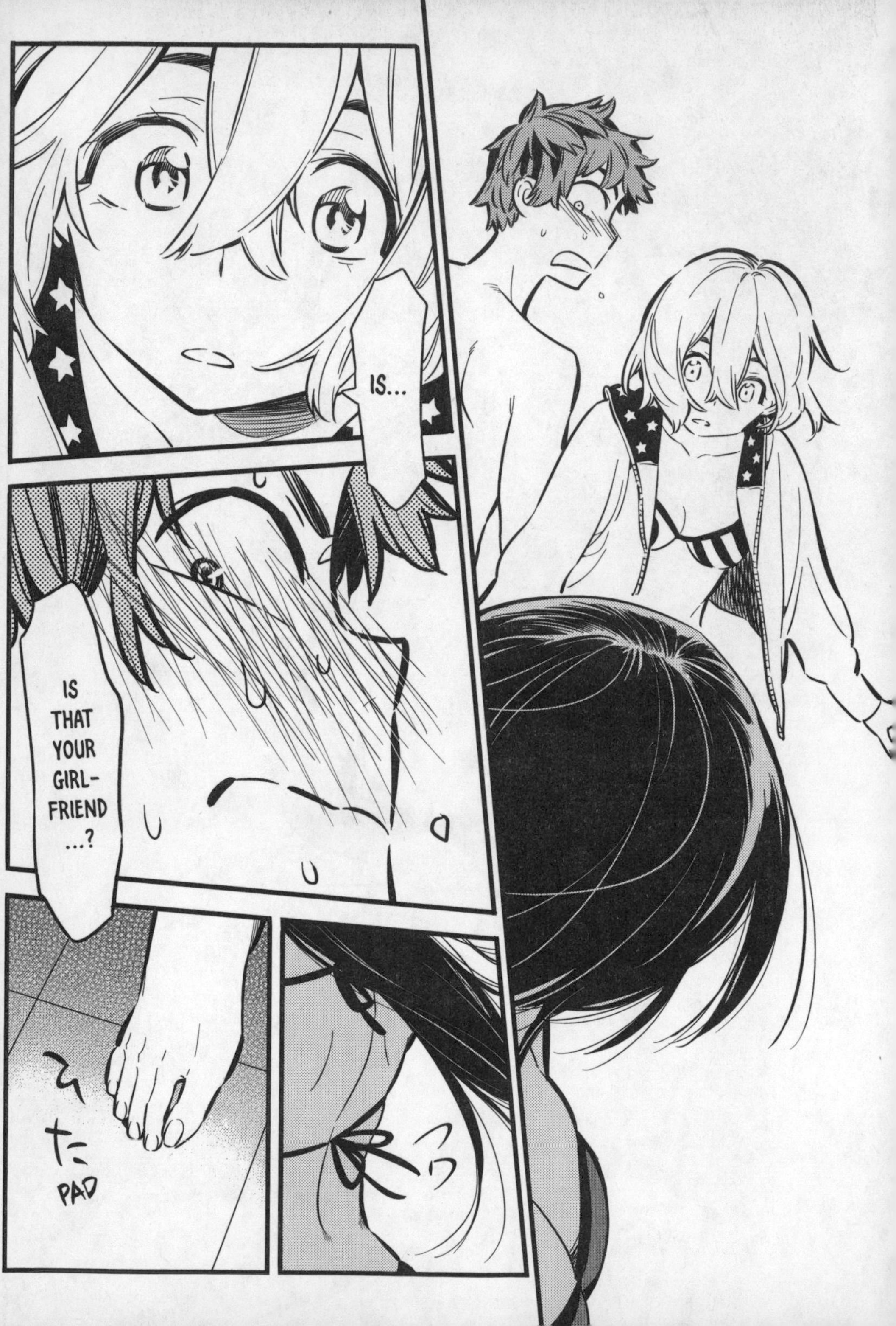
IS...
IS THAT YOUR GIRL-FRIEND ...?
PAD

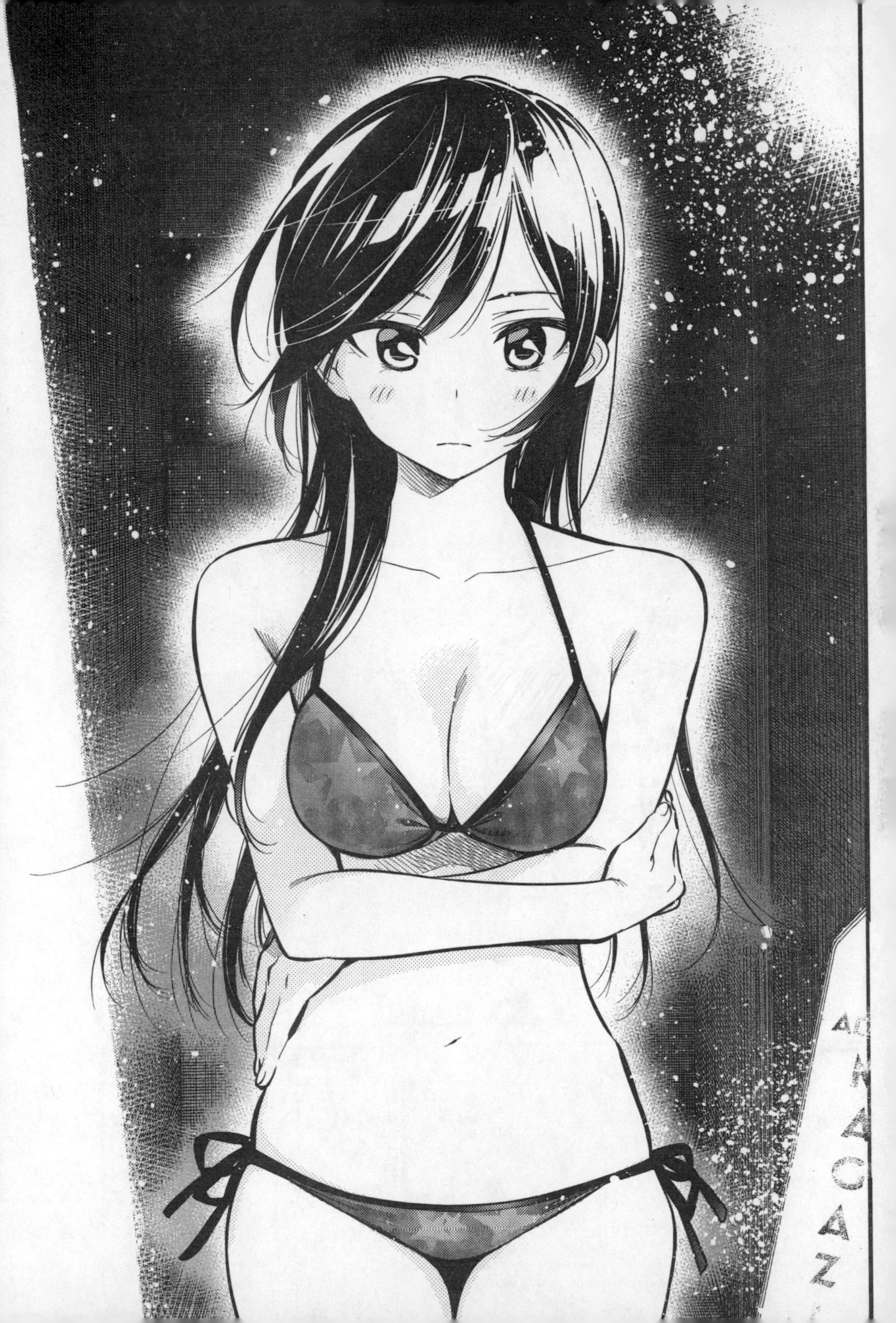

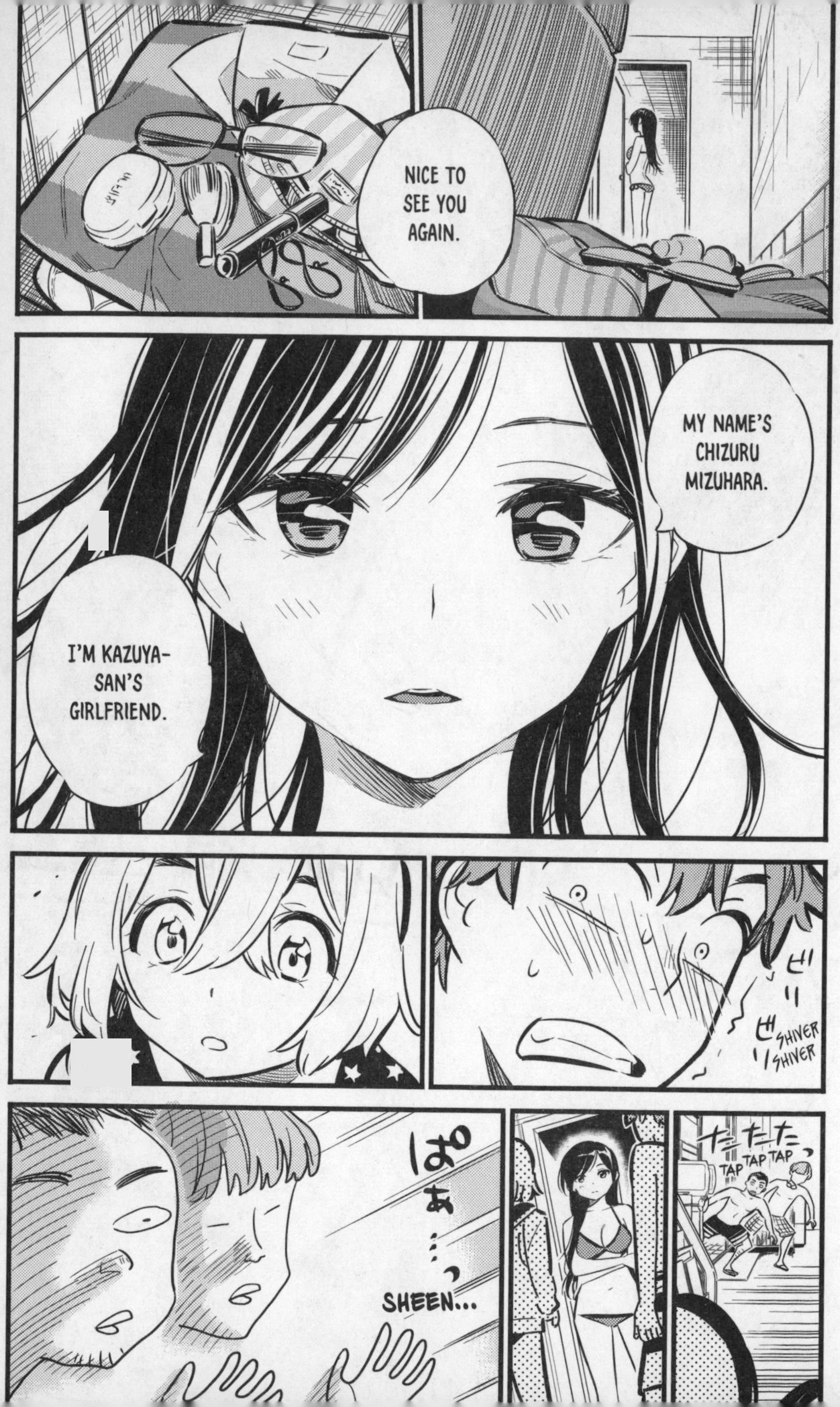
NICE TO SEE YOU AGAIN.
MY NAME'S CHIZURU MIZUHARA.
I'M KAZUYA-SAN'S GIRLFRIEND.
ビリビリ
SHIVER SHIVER
たたたっ
TAP TAP TAP
ぱぁ…っ
SHEEN...

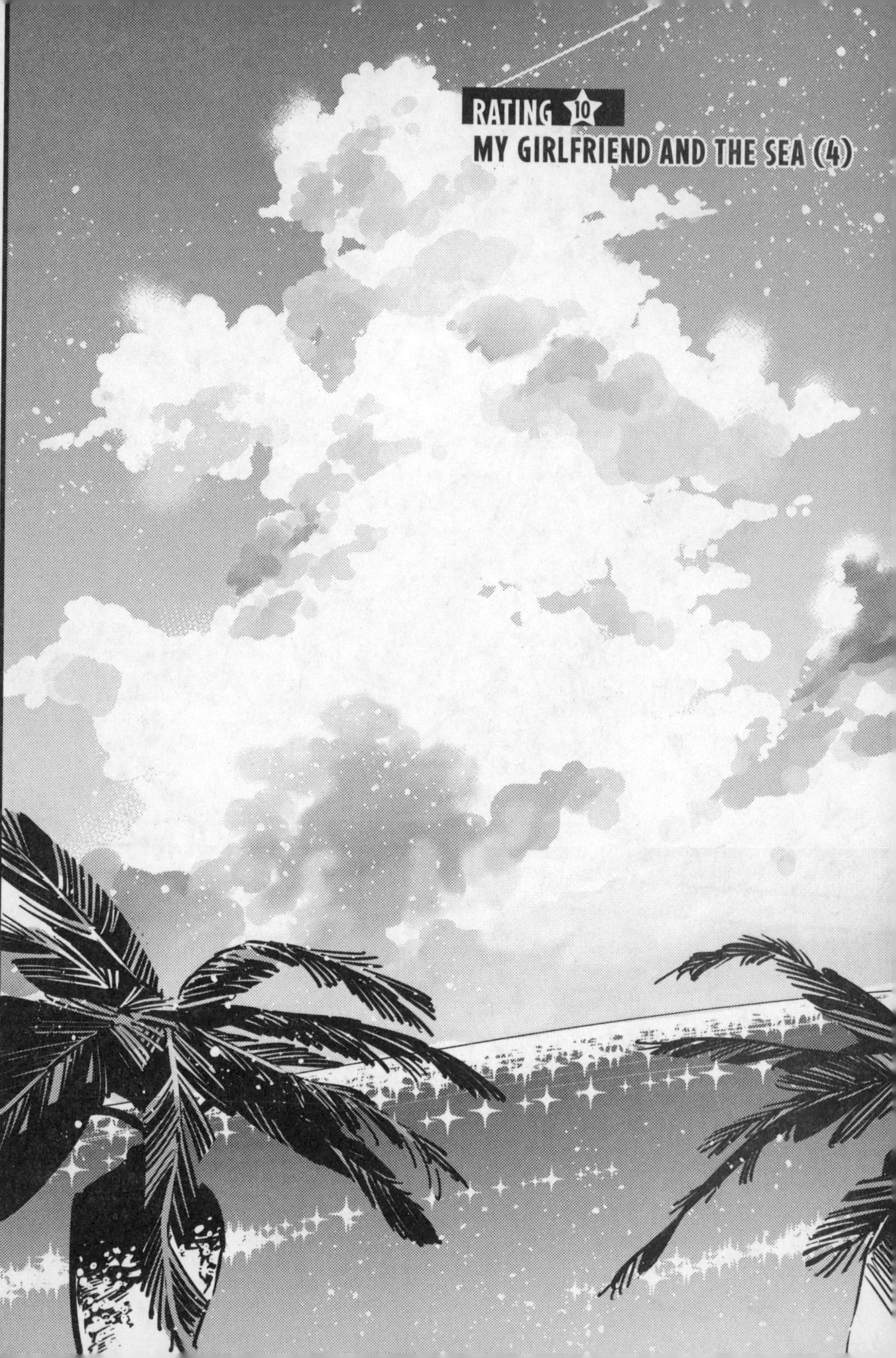
RATING 10
MY GIRLFRIEND AND THE SEA (4)

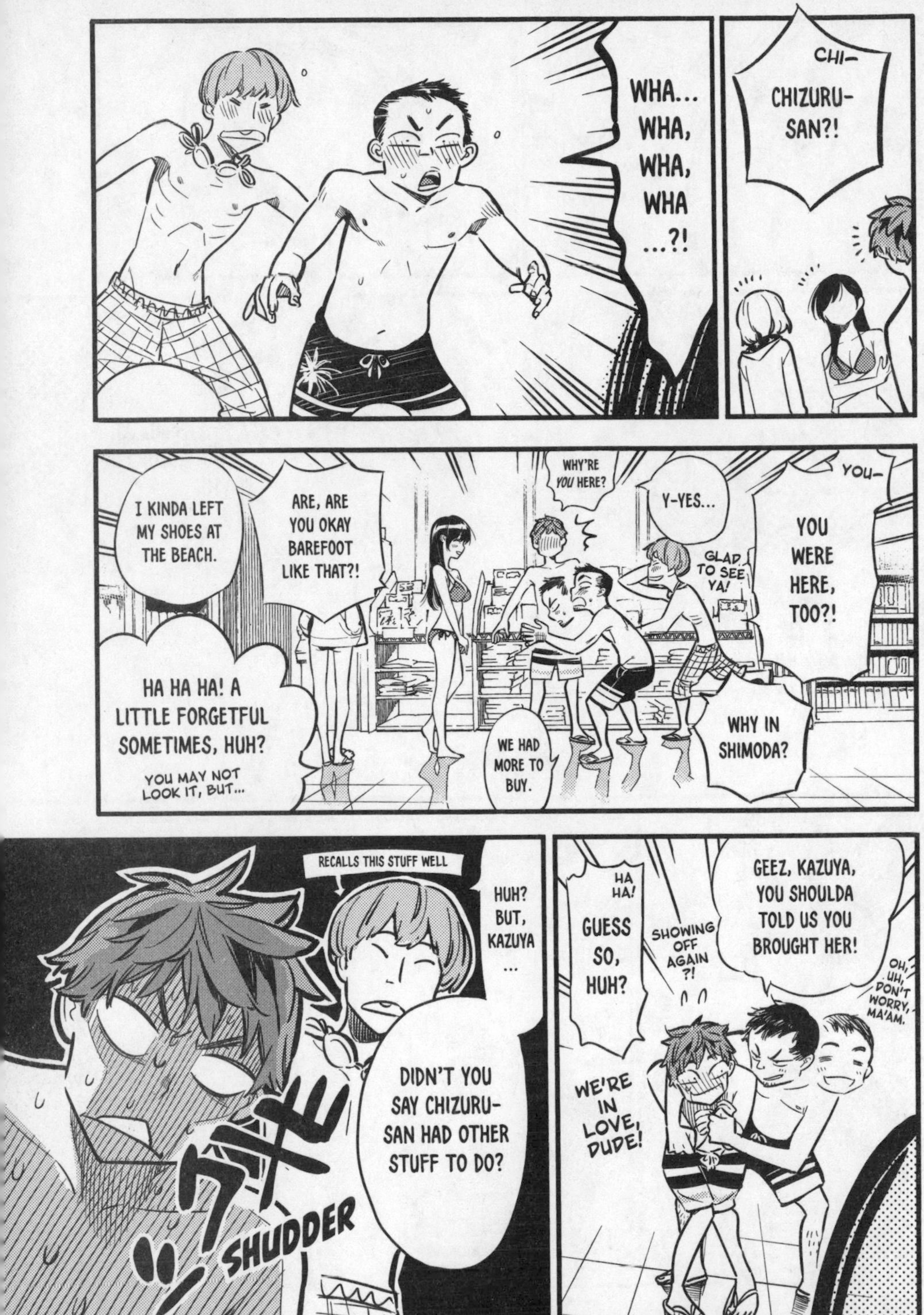
CHI-
CHIZURU-SAN?!
WHA... WHA, WHA, WHA ...?!
YOU—
YOU WERE HERE, TOO?!
Y-YES...
WHY'RE *YOU* HERE?
GLAD TO SEE YA!
WHY IN SHIMODA?
WE HAD MORE TO BUY.
ARE, ARE YOU OKAY BAREFOOT LIKE THAT?!
I KINDA LEFT MY SHOES AT THE BEACH.
HA HA HA! A LITTLE FORGETFUL SOMETIMES, HUH?
YOU MAY NOT LOOK IT, BUT...
GEEZ, KAZUYA, YOU SHOULDA TOLD US YOU BROUGHT HER!
OH, UH, DON'T WORRY, MA'AM.
SHOWING OFF AGAIN?!
HA HA!
GUESS SO, HUH?
WE'RE IN LOVE, DUDE!
RECALLS THIS STUFF WELL
HUH? BUT, KAZUYA ...
DIDN'T YOU SAY CHIZURU-SAN HAD OTHER STUFF TO DO?
SHUDDER

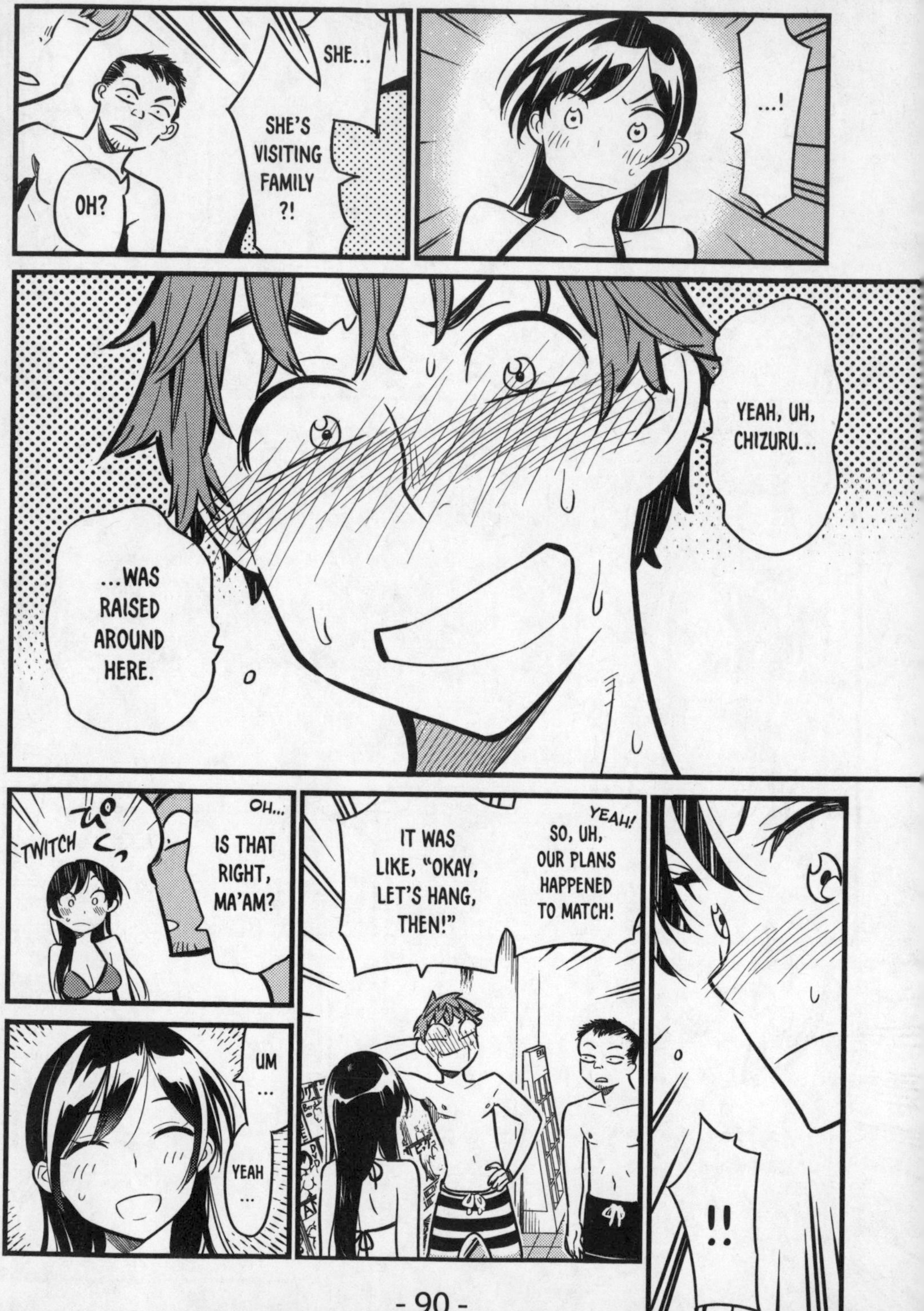
...!
SHE...
SHE'S VISITING FAMILY ?!
OH?
YEAH, UH, CHIZURU...
...WAS RAISED AROUND HERE.
!!
YEAH!
SO, UH, OUR PLANS HAPPENED TO MATCH!
IT WAS LIKE, "OKAY, LET'S HANG, THEN!"
OH...
IS THAT RIGHT, MA'AM?
TWITCH
UM ...
YEAH ...

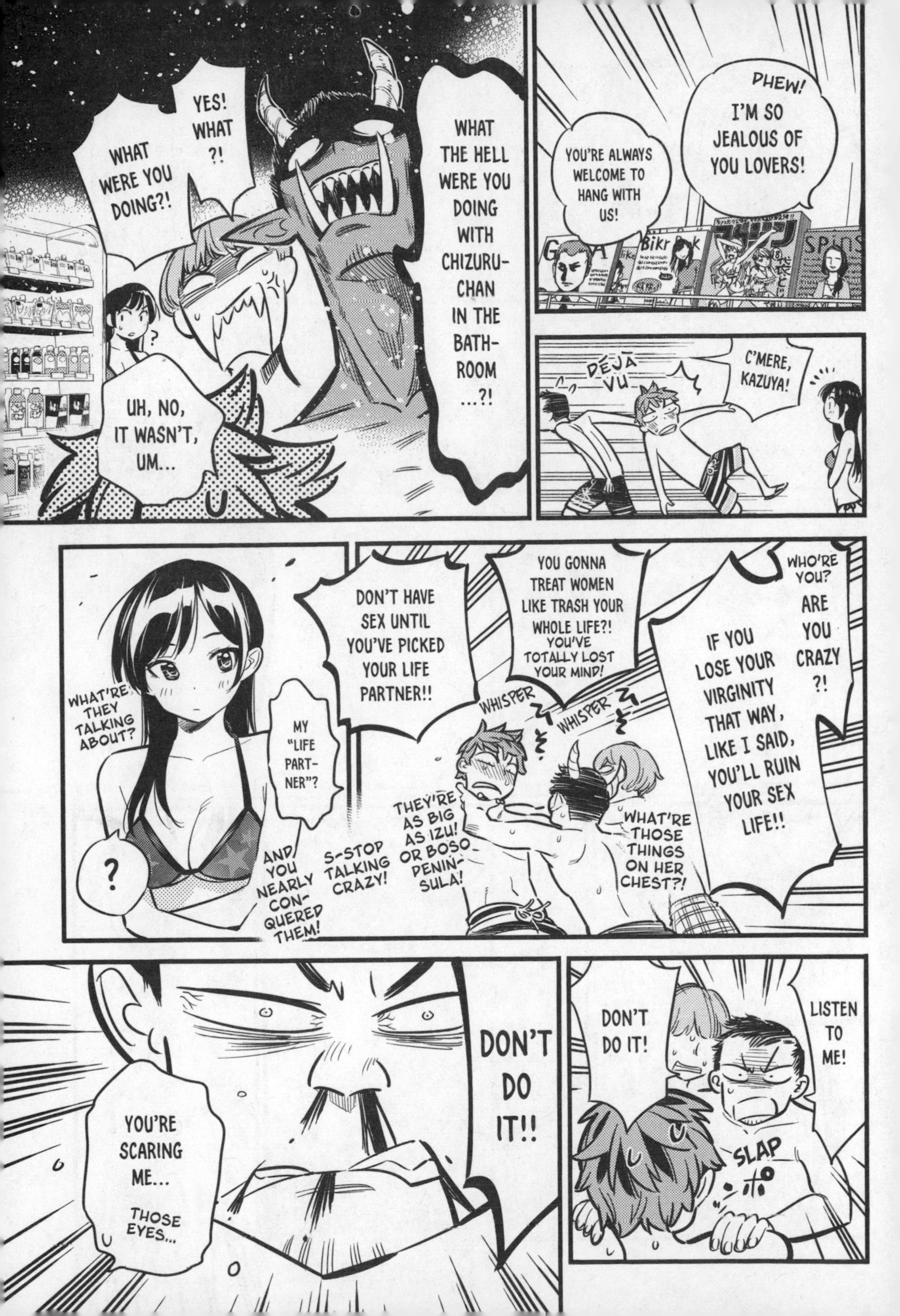
PHEW! I'M SO JEALOUS OF YOU LOVERS!
YOU'RE ALWAYS WELCOME TO HANG WITH US!
C'MERE, KAZUYA!
DÉJÀ VU
WHAT THE HELL WERE YOU DOING WITH CHIZURU-CHAN IN THE BATH-ROOM ...?!
YES! WHAT ?!
WHAT WERE YOU DOING?!
UH, NO, IT WASN'T, UM...
WHO'RE YOU? ARE YOU CRAZY ?!
IF YOU LOSE YOUR VIRGINITY THAT WAY, LIKE I SAID, YOU'LL RUIN YOUR SEX LIFE!!
YOU GONNA TREAT WOMEN LIKE TRASH YOUR WHOLE LIFE?! YOU'VE TOTALLY LOST YOUR MIND!
DON'T HAVE SEX UNTIL YOU'VE PICKED YOUR LIFE PARTNER!!
WHISPER
WHISPER
WHAT'RE THOSE THINGS ON HER CHEST?!
THEY'RE AS BIG AS IZU OR BOSO PENIN-SULA!
S-STOP TALKING CRAZY!
AND YOU NEARLY CON-QUERED THEM!
MY "LIFE PART-NER"?
WHAT'RE THEY TALKING ABOUT?
?
LISTEN TO ME!
DON'T DO IT!
SLAP
DON'T DO IT!!
YOU'RE SCARING ME...
THOSE EYES...

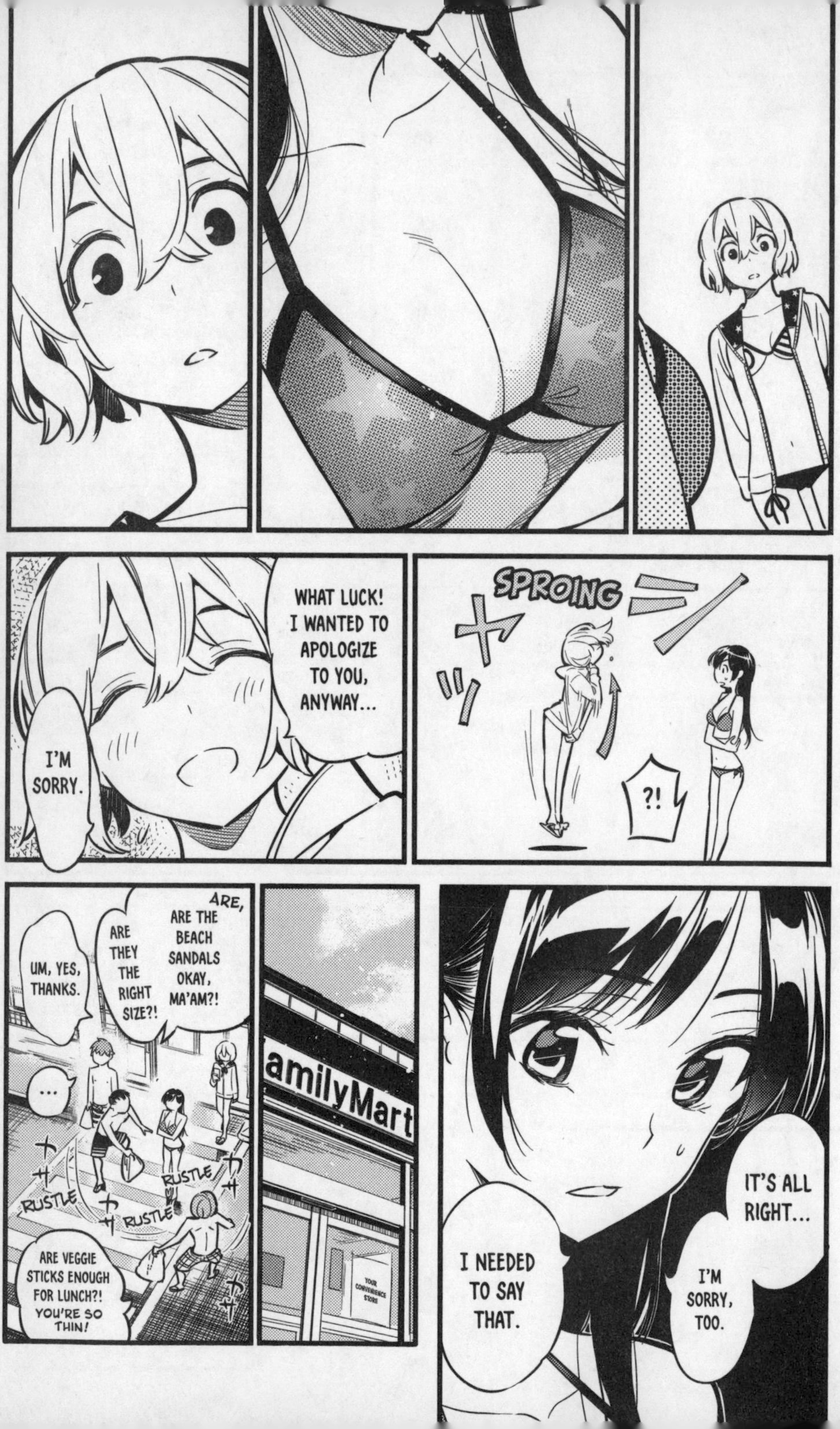
SPROING
?!
WHAT LUCK! I WANTED TO APOLOGIZE TO YOU, ANYWAY...
I'M SORRY.
IT'S ALL RIGHT...
I'M SORRY, TOO.
I NEEDED TO SAY THAT.
amilyMart
YOUR CONVENIENCE STORE
ARE, ARE THE BEACH SANDALS OKAY, MA'AM?!
ARE THEY THE RIGHT SIZE?!
UM, YES, THANKS.
...
RUSTLE
RUSTLE
RUSTLE
ARE VEGGIE STICKS ENOUGH FOR LUNCH?! YOU'RE SO THIN!

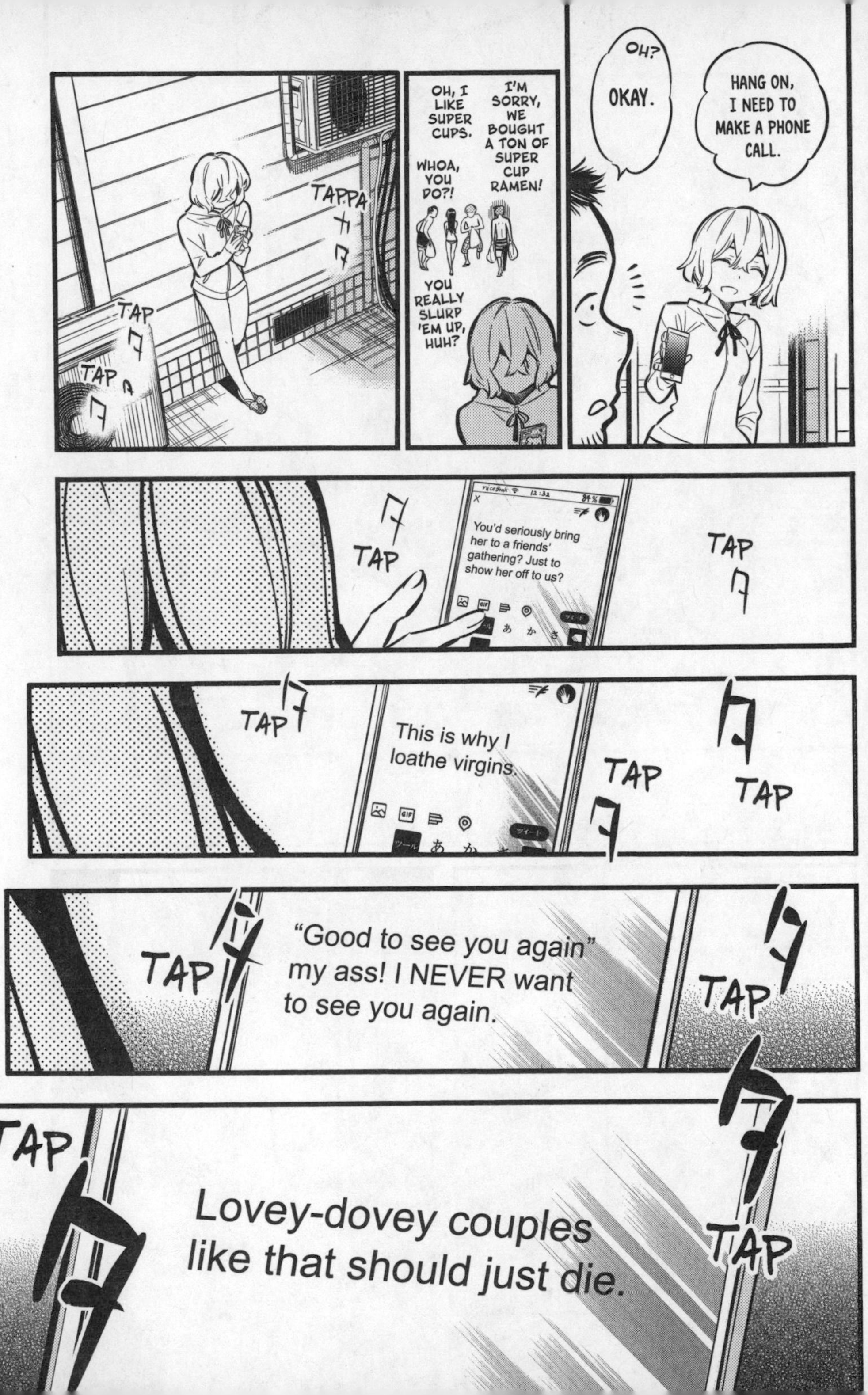
HANG ON, I NEED TO MAKE A PHONE CALL.
OH? OKAY.
I'M SORRY, WE BOUGHT A TON OF SUPER CUP RAMEN!
OH, I LIKE SUPER CUPS.
WHOA, YOU DO?!
YOU REALLY SLURP 'EM UP, HUH?
TAPPA
TAP
TAP
TAP
TAP
You'd seriously bring her to a friends' gathering? Just to show her off to us?
TAP
TAP
TAP
This is why I loathe virgins.
TAP
TAP
"Good to see you again" my ass! I NEVER want to see you again.
TAP
TAP
Lovey-dovey couples like that should just die.
TAP

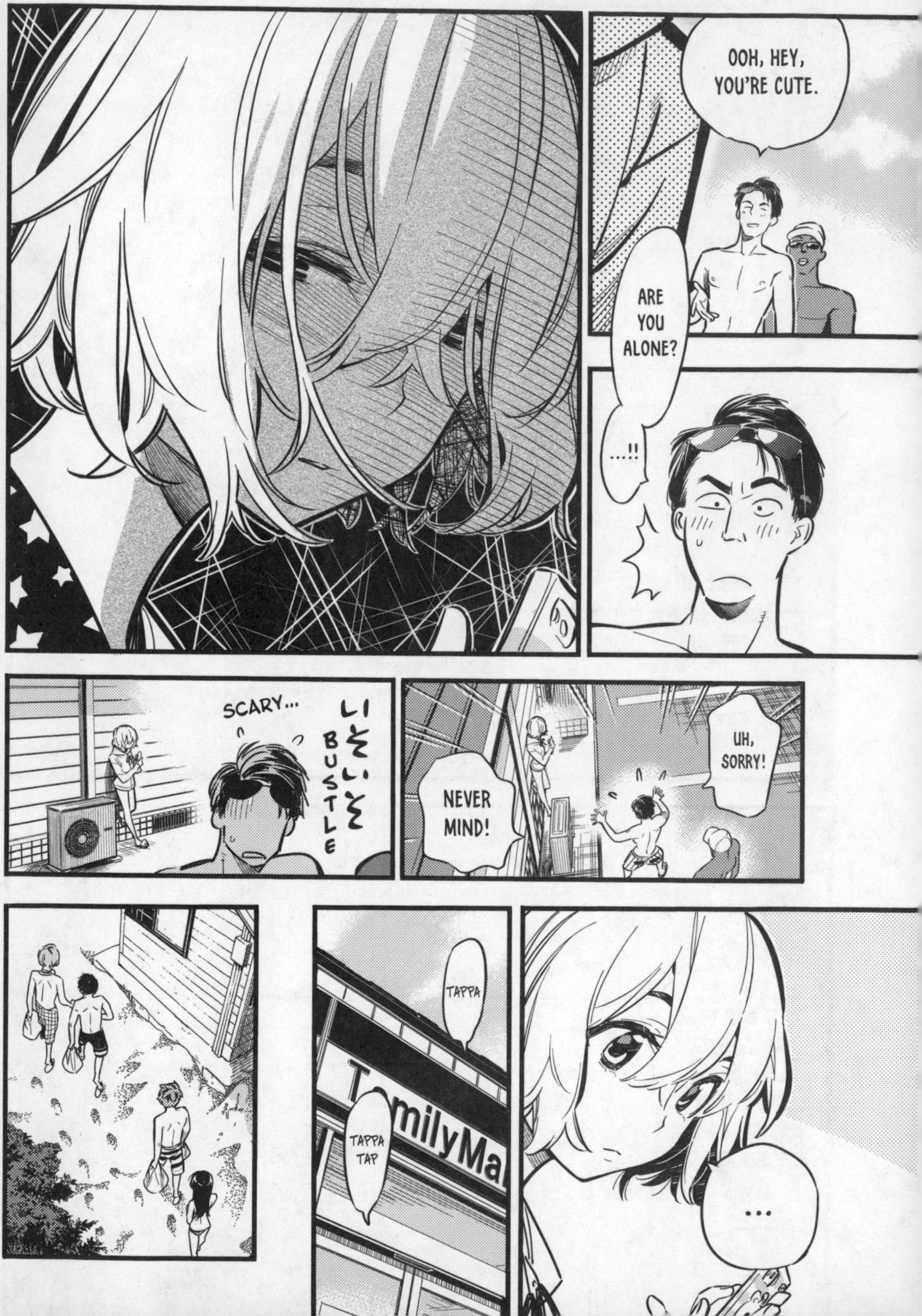
OOH, HEY, YOU'RE CUTE.
ARE YOU ALONE?
...!!
UH, SORRY!
NEVER MIND!
SCARY...
BUSTLE
...
TAPPA
TAPPA TAP

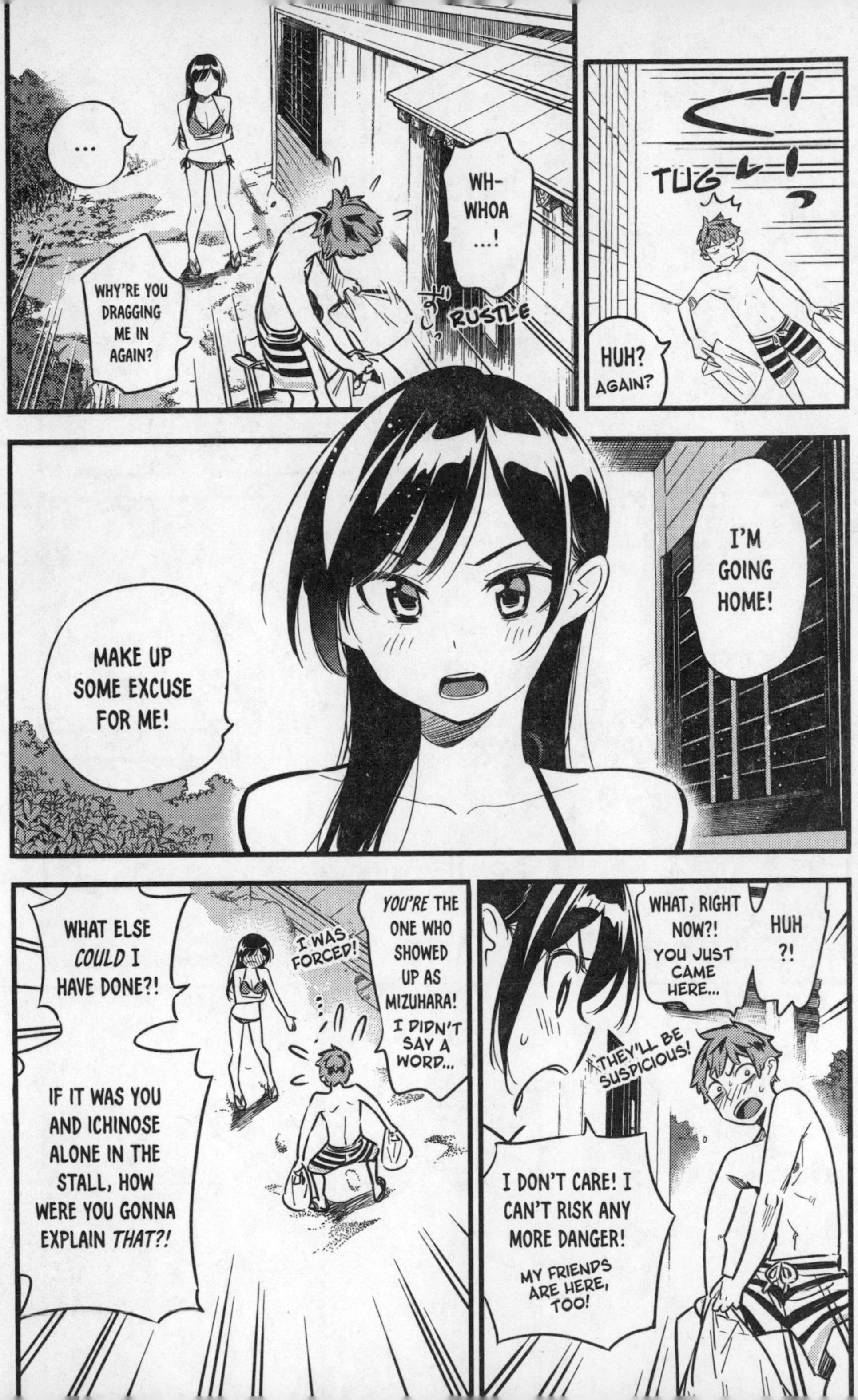
TUG
HUH? AGAIN?
WH- WHOA ...!
...
RUSTLE
WHY'RE YOU DRAGGING ME IN AGAIN?
I'M GOING HOME!
MAKE UP SOME EXCUSE FOR ME!
HUH ?!
WHAT, RIGHT NOW?! YOU JUST CAME HERE...
THEY'LL BE SUSPICIOUS!
I DON'T CARE! I CAN'T RISK ANY MORE DANGER!
MY FRIENDS ARE HERE, TOO!
YOU'RE THE ONE WHO SHOWED UP AS MIZUHARA! I DIDN'T SAY A WORD...
I WAS FORCED!
WHAT ELSE *COULD* I HAVE DONE?!
IF IT WAS YOU AND ICHINOSE ALONE IN THE STALL, HOW WERE YOU GONNA EXPLAIN *THAT*?!

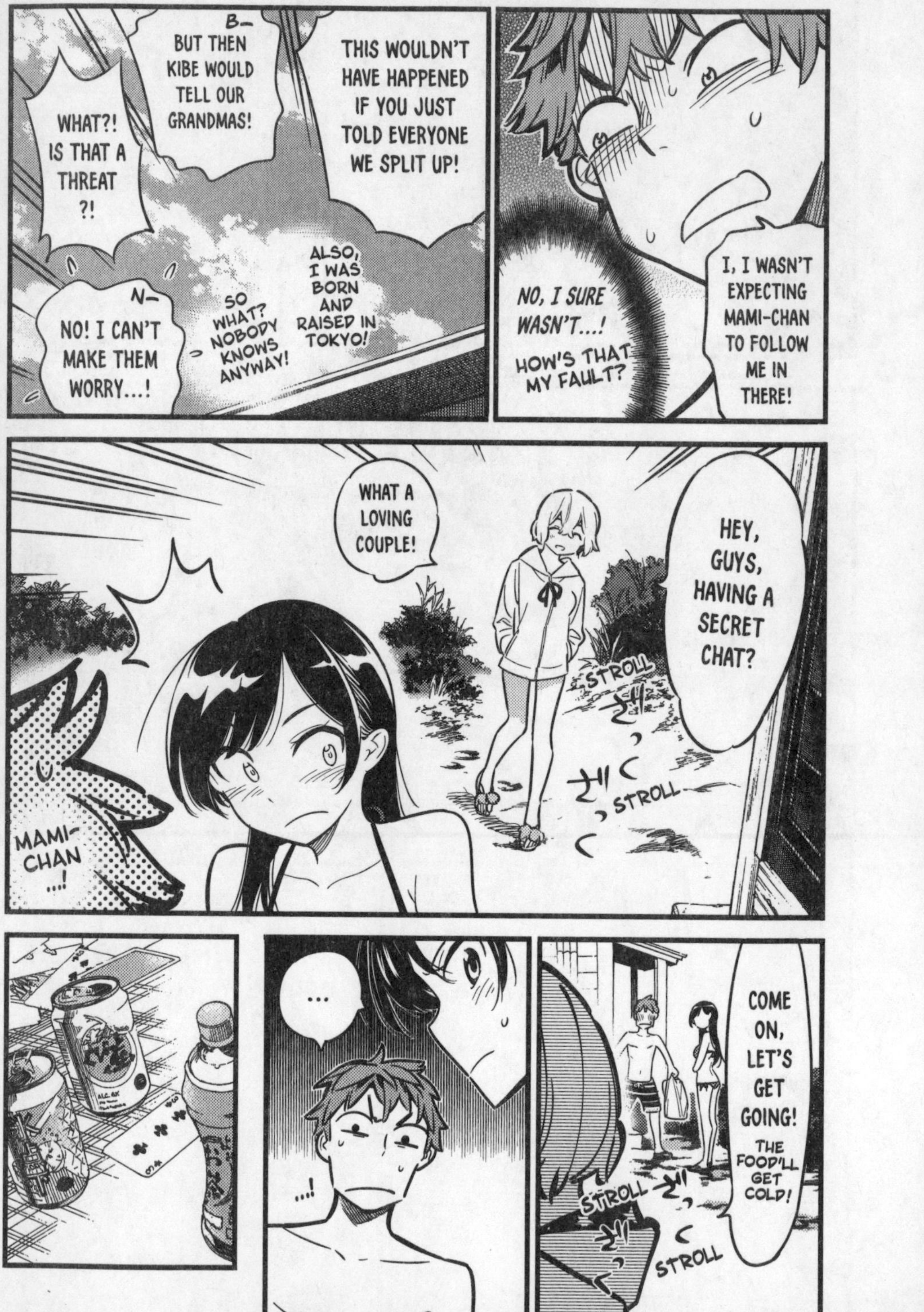
I, I WASN'T EXPECTING MAMI-CHAN TO FOLLOW ME IN THERE!
NO, I SURE WASN'T...!
HOW'S THAT MY FAULT?
THIS WOULDN'T HAVE HAPPENED IF YOU JUST TOLD EVERYONE WE SPLIT UP!
B— BUT THEN KIBE WOULD TELL OUR GRANDMAS!
WHAT?! IS THAT A THREAT ?!
ALSO, I WAS BORN AND RAISED IN TOKYO!
SO WHAT? NOBODY KNOWS ANYWAY!
N— NO! I CAN'T MAKE THEM WORRY...!
HEY, GUYS, HAVING A SECRET CHAT?
WHAT A LOVING COUPLE!
STROLL
STROLL
MAMI-CHAN ...!
COME ON, LET'S GET GOING!
THE FOOD'LL GET COLD!
STROLL
STROLL
...
...!

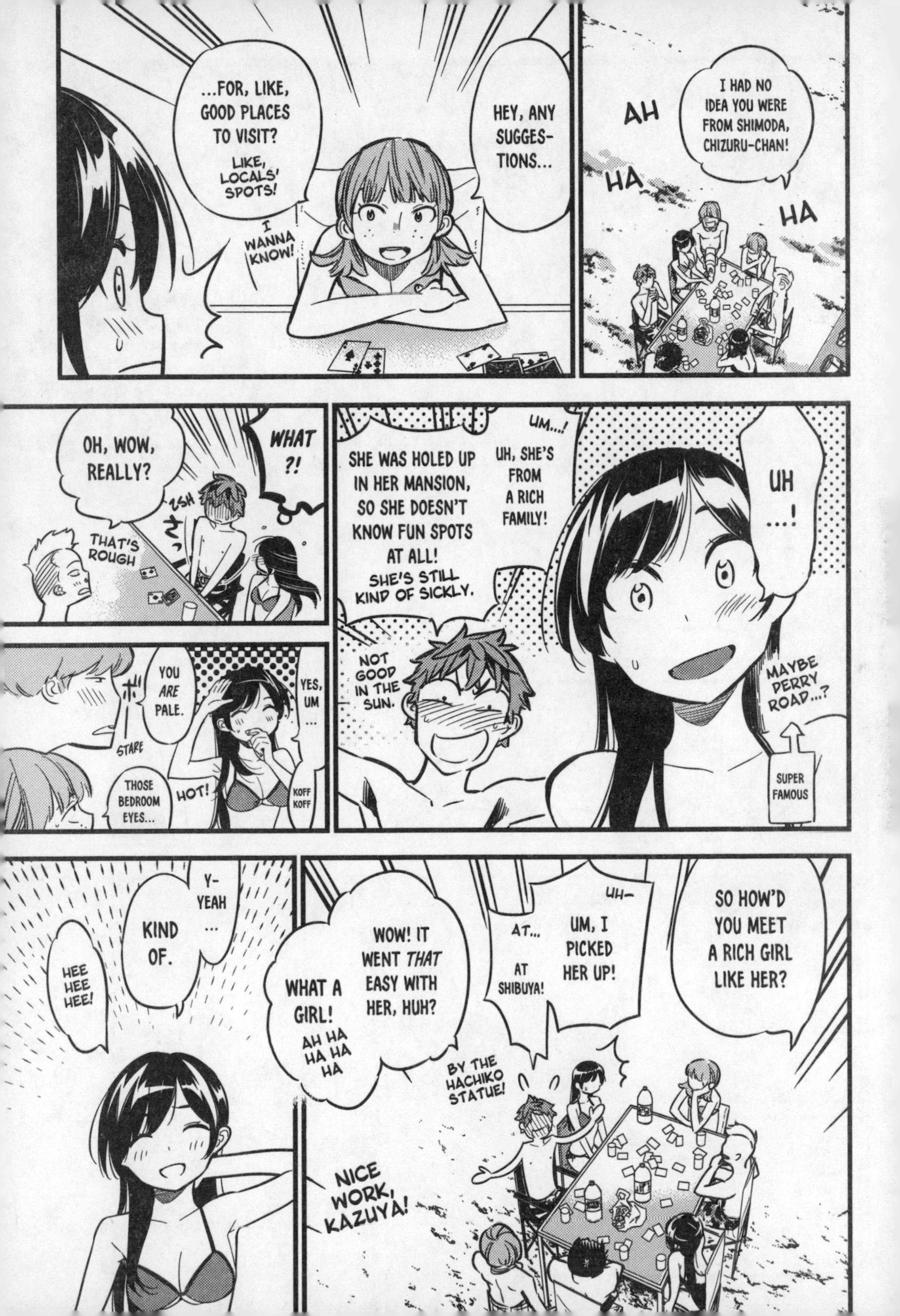

AH
HA
HA
I HAD NO IDEA YOU WERE FROM SHIMODA, CHIZURU-CHAN!
HEY, ANY SUGGES-TIONS...
...FOR, LIKE, GOOD PLACES TO VISIT?
LIKE, LOCALS' SPOTS!
I WANNA KNOW!
UH ...!
MAYBE PERRY ROAD...?
SUPER FAMOUS
UM...!
UH, SHE'S FROM A RICH FAMILY!
SHE WAS HOLED UP IN HER MANSION, SO SHE DOESN'T KNOW FUN SPOTS AT ALL!
SHE'S STILL KIND OF SICKLY.
NOT GOOD IN THE SUN.
WHAT ?!
OH, WOW, REALLY?
ZSH
THAT'S ROUGH
YES, UM ...
KOFF KOFF
YOU *ARE* PALE.
STARE
HOT!
THOSE BEDROOM EYES...
SO HOW'D YOU MEET A RICH GIRL LIKE HER?
UH—
UM, I PICKED HER UP!
AT...
AT SHIBUYA!
BY THE HACHIKO STATUE!
WOW! IT WENT *THAT* EASY WITH HER, HUH?
WHAT A GIRL!
AH HA HA HA HA
NICE WORK, KAZUYA!
Y-YEAH ...
KIND OF.
HEE HEE HEE!

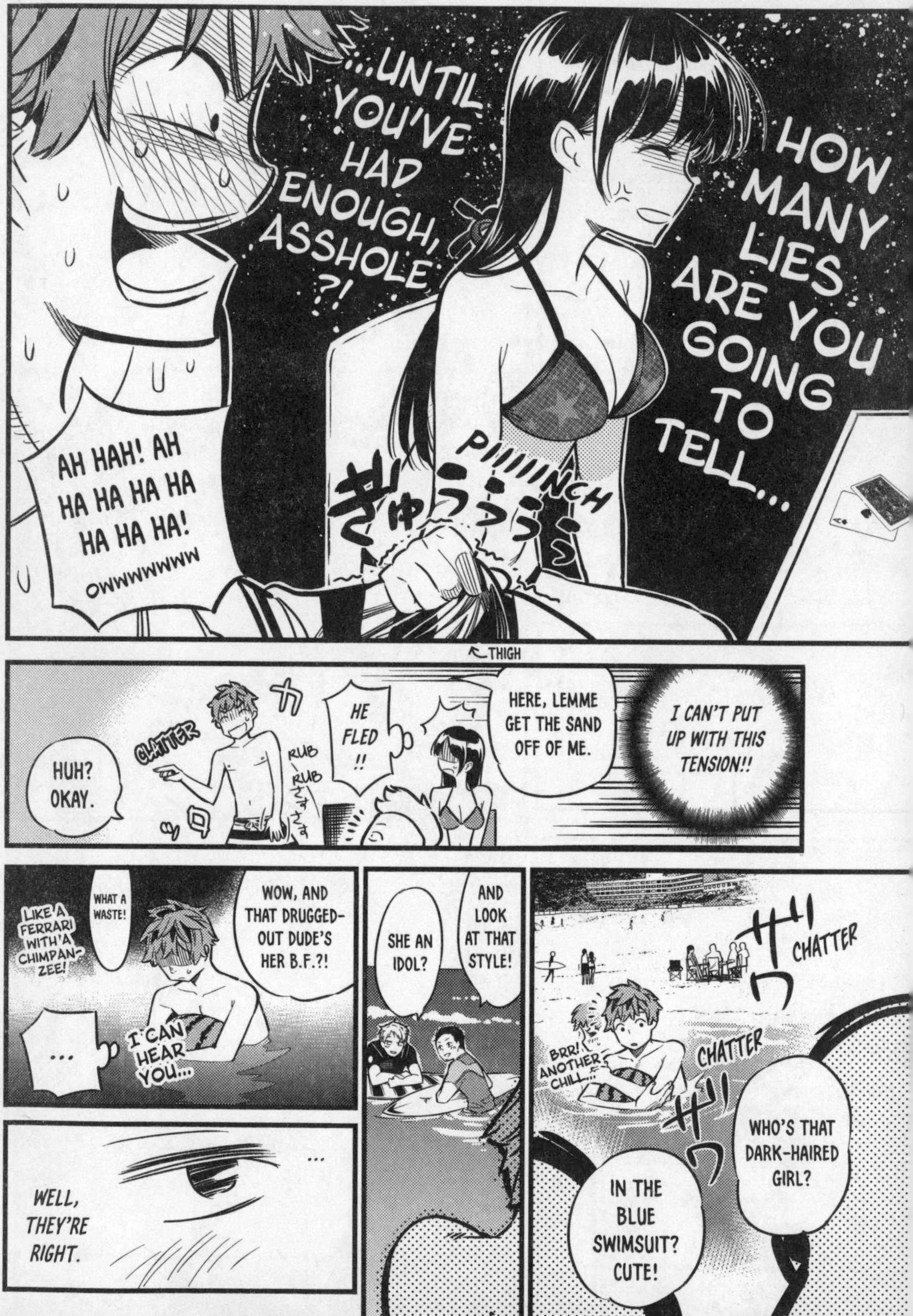
HOW MANY LIES ARE YOU GOING TO TELL...
...UNTIL YOU'VE HAD ENOUGH, ASSHOLE?!
PIIIIINCH
ぎゅううう
AH HAH! AH HA HA HA HA HA HA HA!
OWWWWWWW
THIGH
I CAN'T PUT UP WITH THIS TENSION!!
HERE, LEMME GET THE SAND OFF OF ME.
HE FLED !!
RUB RUB
さすさす
CHATTER
HUH? OKAY.
ザワ
CHATTER
BRR! ANOTHER CHILL...
CHATTER
ザワ
WHO'S THAT DARK-HAIRED GIRL?
IN THE BLUE SWIMSUIT? CUTE!
AND LOOK AT THAT STYLE!
SHE AN IDOL?
WOW, AND THAT DRUGGED-OUT DUDE'S HER B.F.?!
WHAT A WASTE!
LIKE A FERRARI WITH A CHIMPANZEE!
...
I CAN HEAR YOU...
...
WELL, THEY'RE RIGHT.

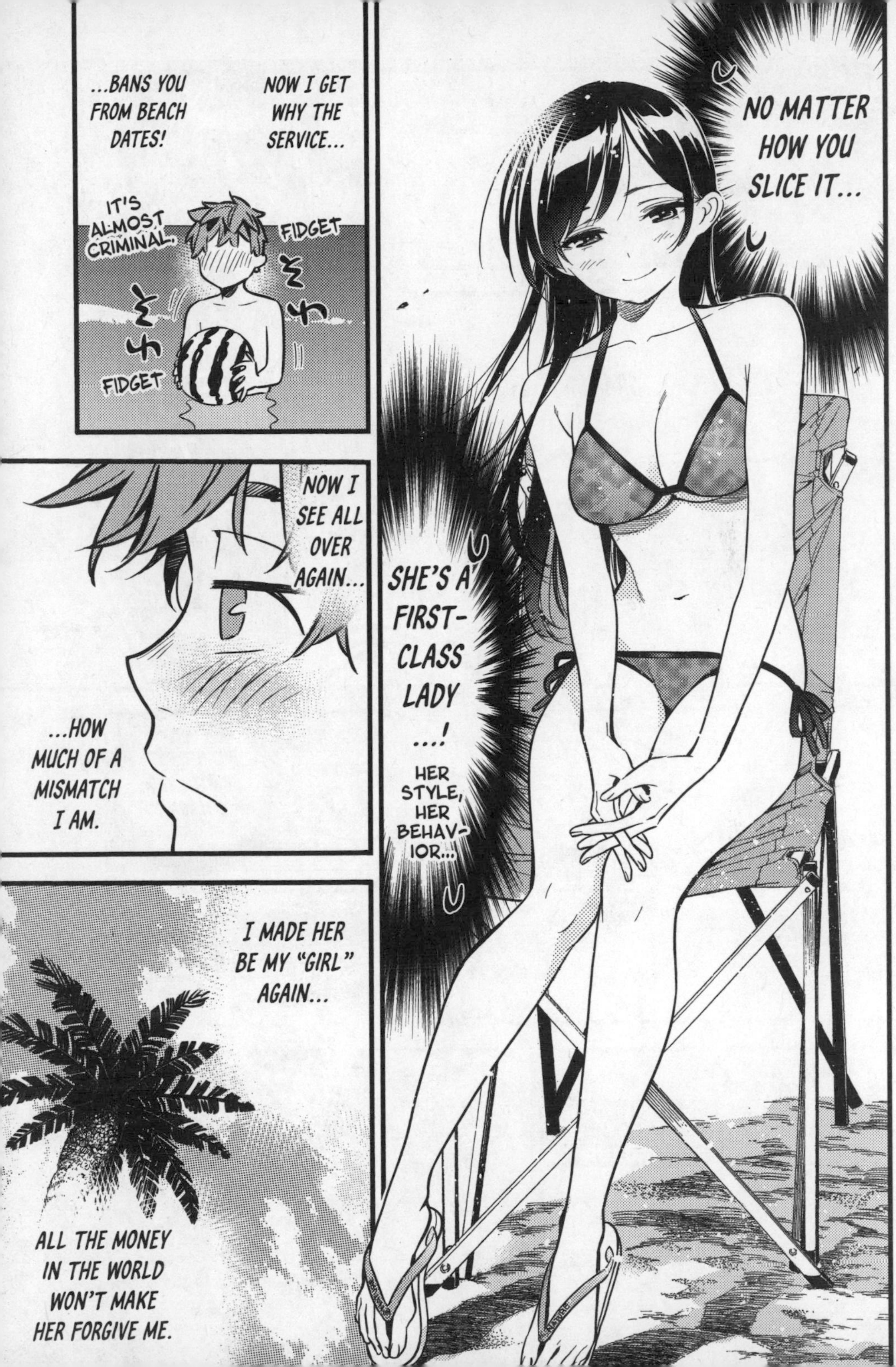
NO MATTER HOW YOU SLICE IT...
SHE'S A FIRST-CLASS LADY ...!
HER STYLE, HER BEHAVIOR...
NOW I GET WHY THE SERVICE...
...BANS YOU FROM BEACH DATES!
IT'S ALMOST CRIMINAL.
FIDGET
FIDGET
NOW I SEE ALL OVER AGAIN...
...HOW MUCH OF A MISMATCH I AM.
I MADE HER BE MY "GIRL" AGAIN...
ALL THE MONEY IN THE WORLD WON'T MAKE HER FORGIVE ME.

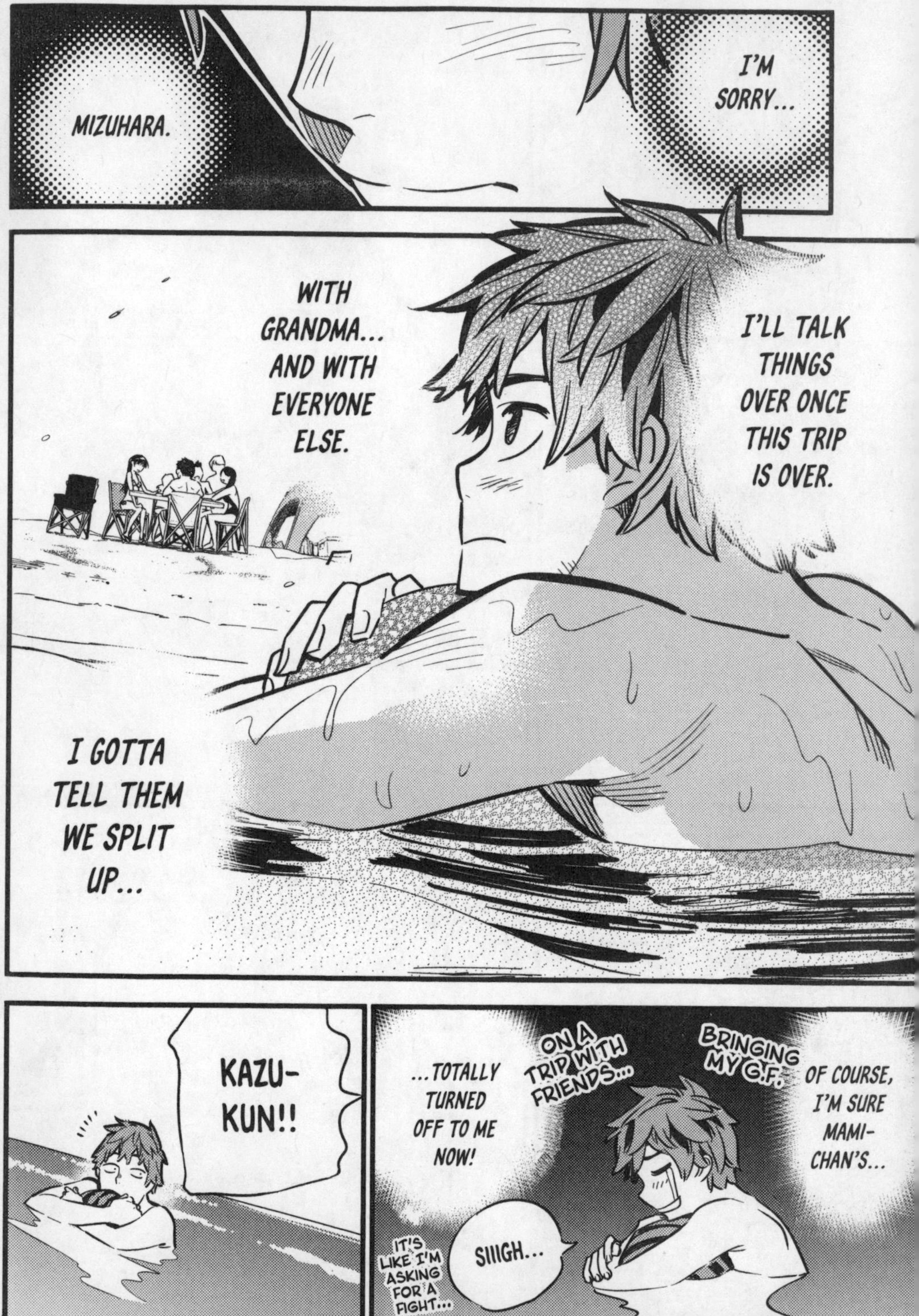
I'M SORRY...
MIZUHARA.
I'LL TALK THINGS OVER ONCE THIS TRIP IS OVER.
WITH GRANDMA... AND WITH EVERYONE ELSE.
I GOTTA TELL THEM WE SPLIT UP...
OF COURSE, I'M SURE MAMI-CHAN'S...
BRINGING MY G.F.
ON A TRIP WITH FRIENDS...
...TOTALLY TURNED OFF TO ME NOW!
SIIIGH...
IT'S LIKE I'M ASKING FOR A FIGHT...
KAZU-KUN!!

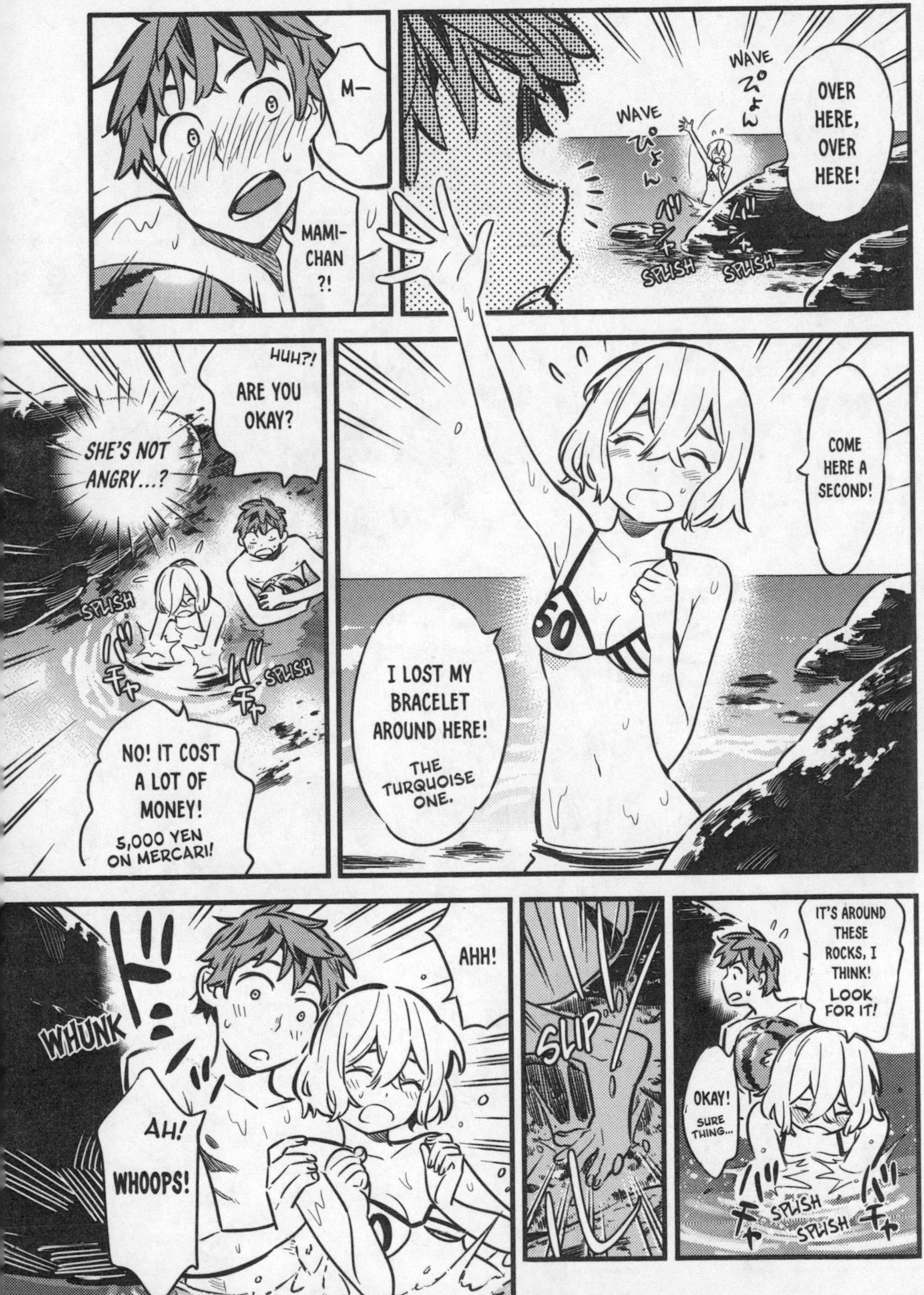
WAVE ぴょん
OVER HERE, OVER HERE!
WAVE ぴょん
SPLISH
SPLISH
M—
MAMI-CHAN?!
COME HERE A SECOND!
I LOST MY BRACELET AROUND HERE!
THE TURQUOISE ONE.
HUH?!
ARE YOU OKAY?
SHE'S NOT ANGRY...?
SPLISH
SPLISH
NO! IT COST A LOT OF MONEY!
5,000 YEN ON MERCARI!
IT'S AROUND THESE ROCKS, I THINK!
LOOK FOR IT!
OKAY!
SURE THING...
SPLISH
SPLISH
SLIP
AHH!
WHUNK
AH!
WHOOPS!

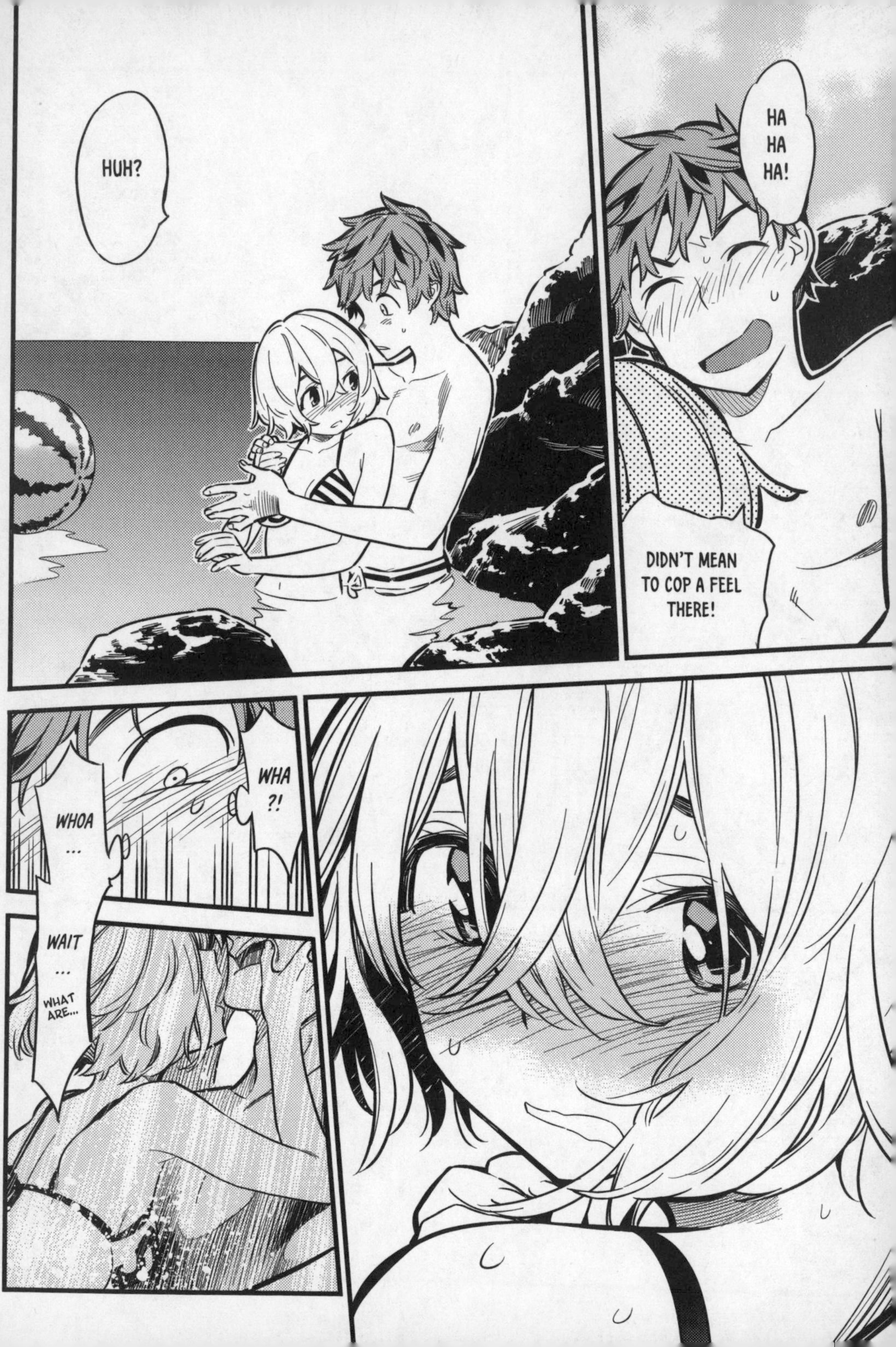
HA HA HA!
DIDN'T MEAN TO COP A FEEL THERE!
HUH?
WHA ?!
WHOA ...
WAIT ...
WHAT ARE...

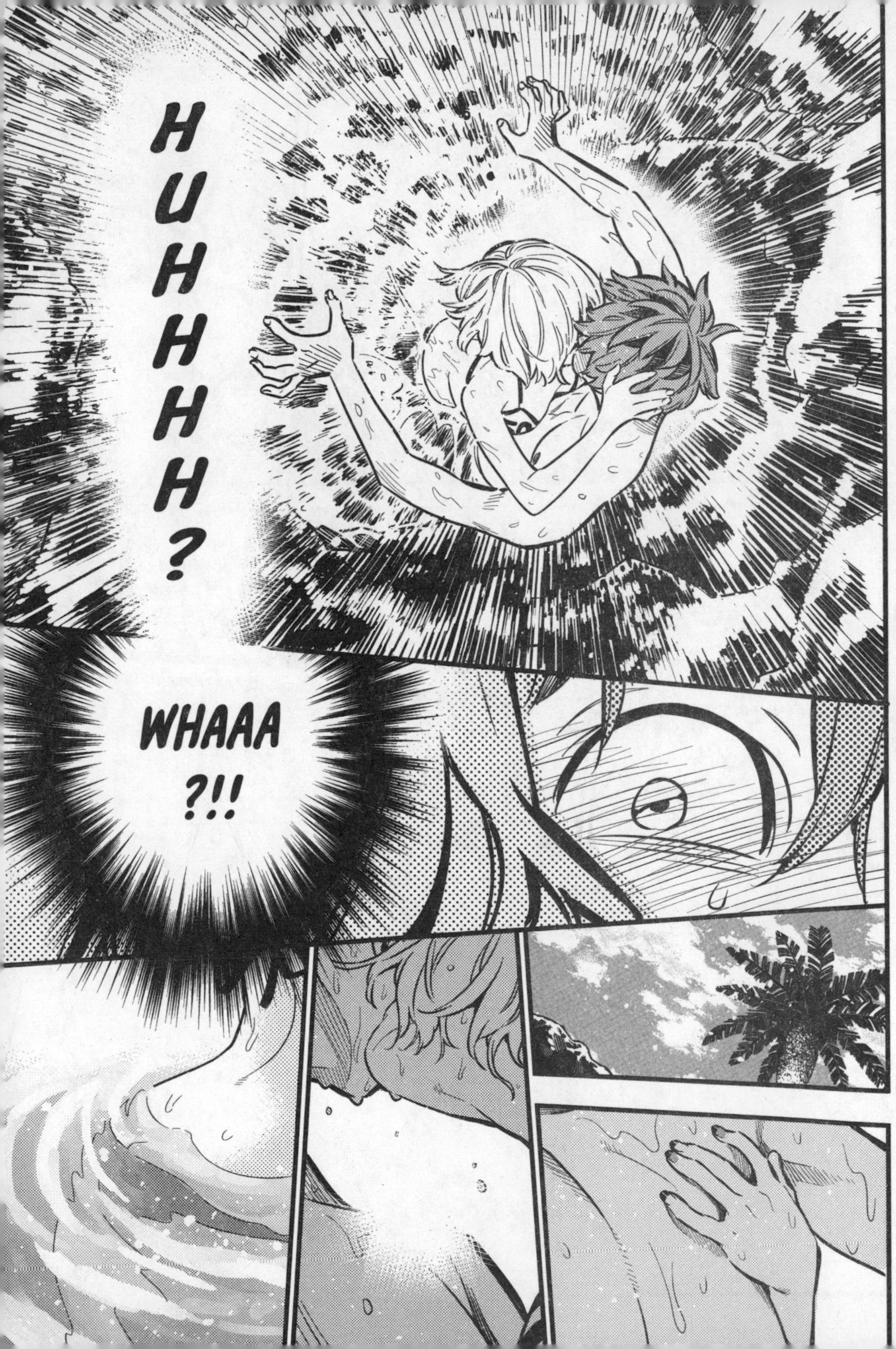
HUHHHHH?
WHAAA ?!!

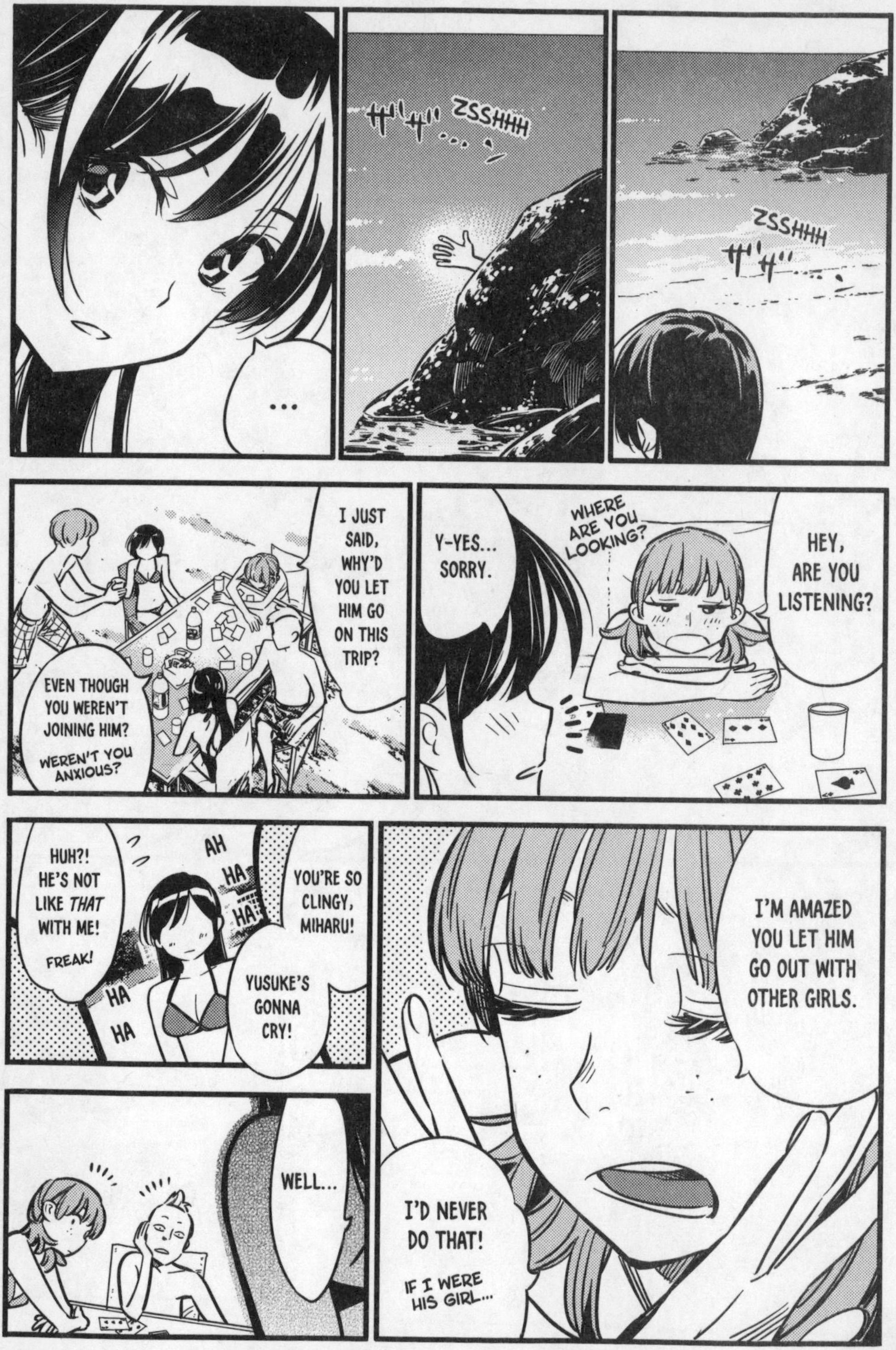
ZSSHHH
ZSSHHH
...
HEY, ARE YOU LISTENING?
WHERE ARE YOU LOOKING?
Y-YES... SORRY.
I JUST SAID, WHY'D YOU LET HIM GO ON THIS TRIP?
EVEN THOUGH YOU WEREN'T JOINING HIM?
WEREN'T YOU ANXIOUS?
I'M AMAZED YOU LET HIM GO OUT WITH OTHER GIRLS.
I'D NEVER DO THAT!
IF I WERE HIS GIRL...
YOU'RE SO CLINGY, MIHARU!
YUSUKE'S GONNA CRY!
AH HA HA
HUH?! HE'S NOT LIKE *THAT* WITH ME!
FREAK!
HA HA
WELL...

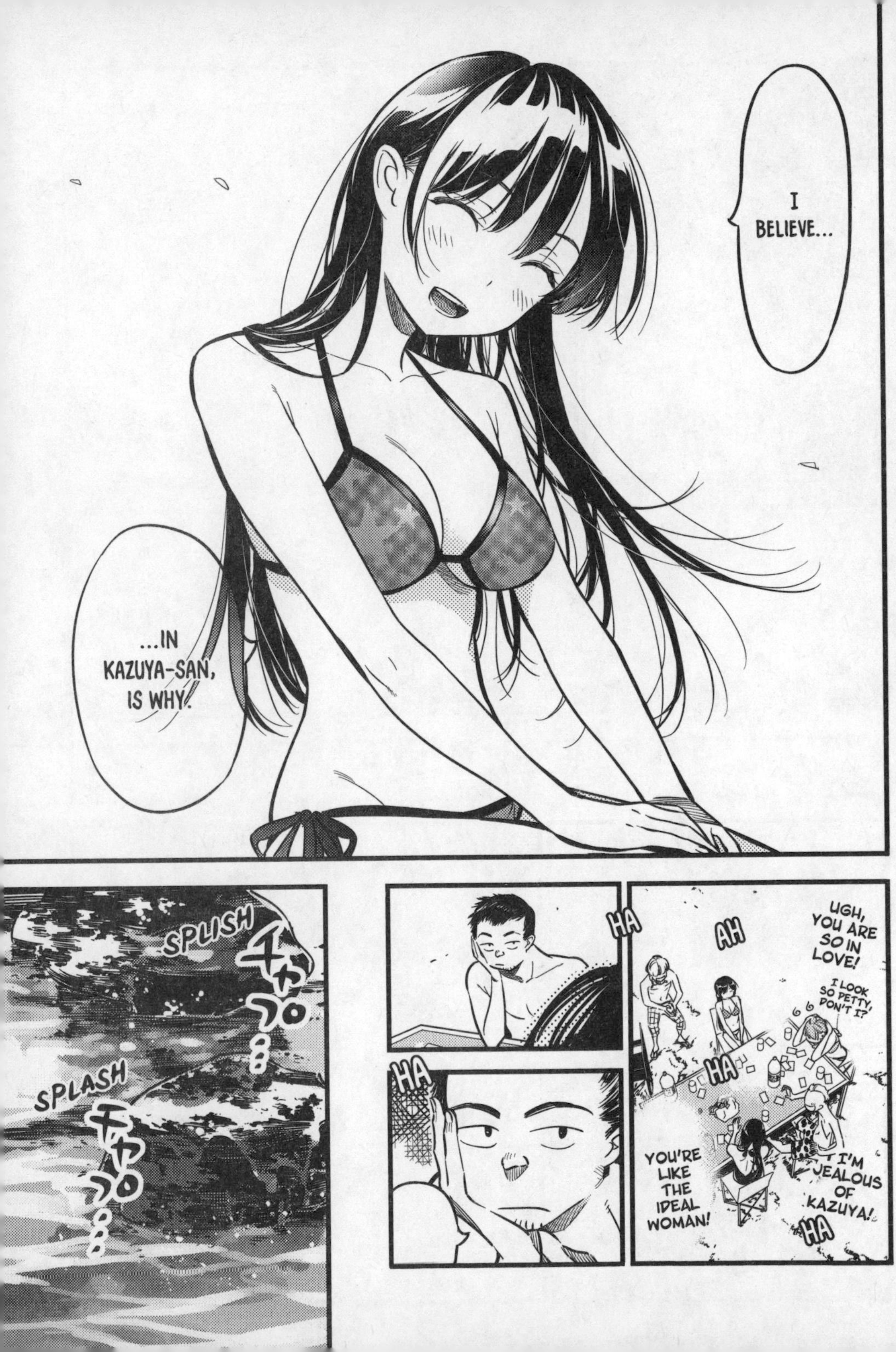
I BELIEVE...
...IN KAZUYA-SAN, IS WHY.
UGH, YOU ARE SO IN LOVE!
AH
I LOOK SO PETTY, DON'T I?
HA
I'M JEALOUS OF KAZUYA!
YOU'RE LIKE THE IDEAL WOMAN!
HA
HA
HA
SPLISH
SPLASH

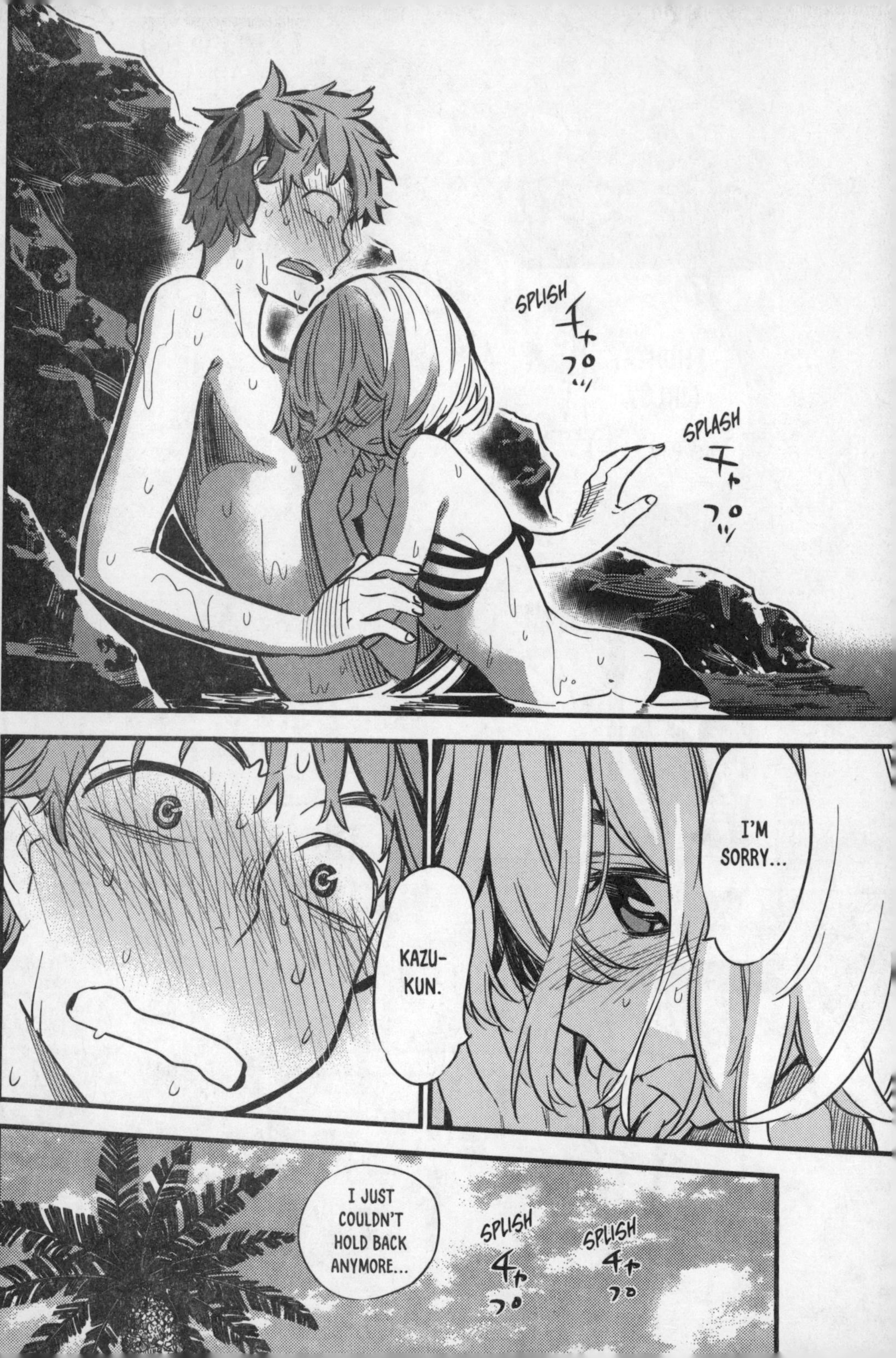
SPLISH
チャプッ
SPLASH
チャプッ
I'M SORRY...
KAZU-KUN.
I JUST COULDN'T HOLD BACK ANYMORE...
SPLISH
チャプ
SPLISH
チャプ

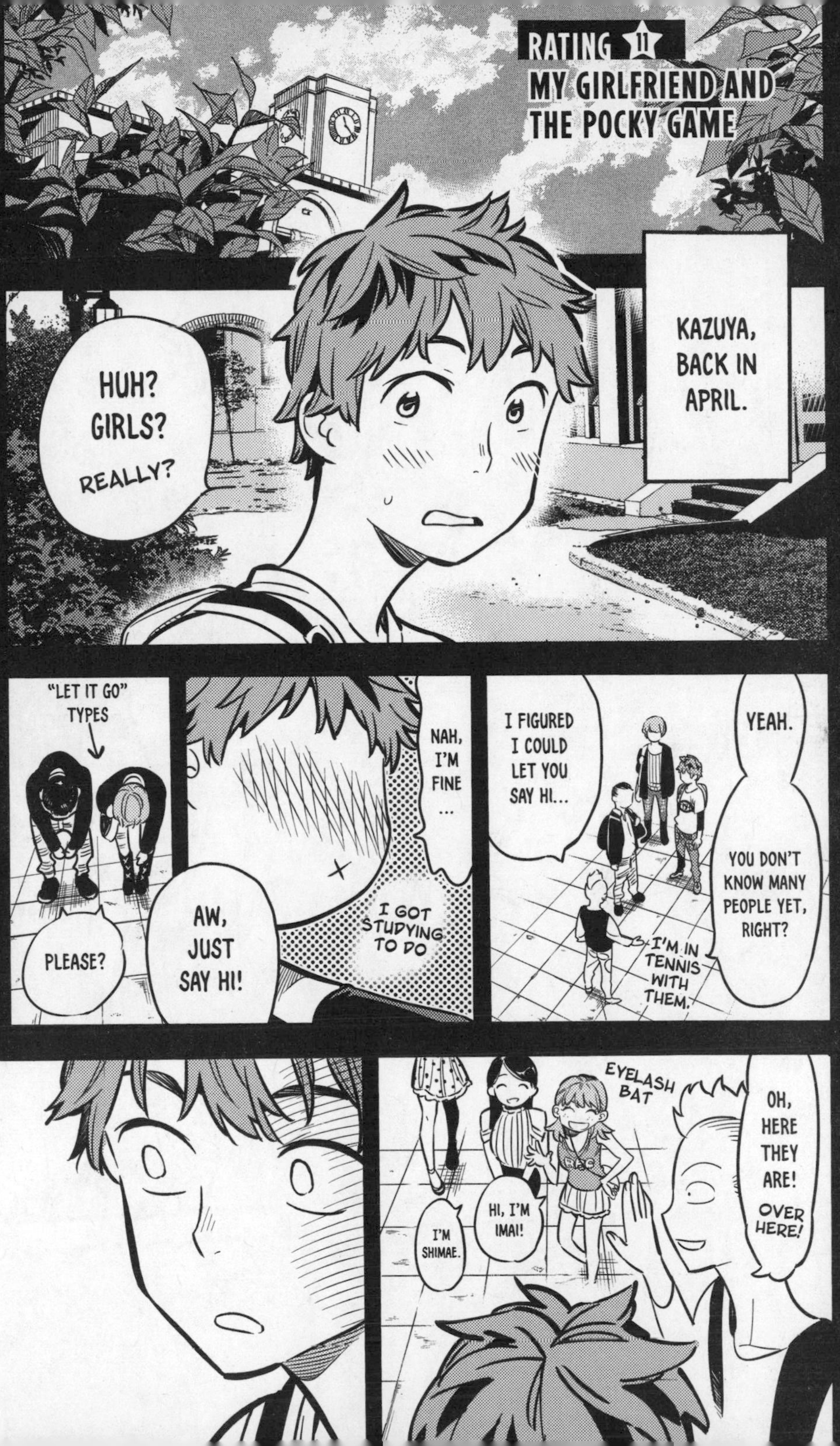
RATING 11
MY GIRLFRIEND AND THE POCKY GAME
KAZUYA, BACK IN APRIL.
HUH? GIRLS? REALLY?
YEAH.
YOU DON'T KNOW MANY PEOPLE YET, RIGHT?
I FIGURED I COULD LET YOU SAY HI...
I'M IN TENNIS WITH THEM.
NAH, I'M FINE ...
I GOT STUDYING TO DO
AW, JUST SAY HI!
"LET IT GO" TYPES
PLEASE?
OH, HERE THEY ARE!
OVER HERE!
EYELASH BAT
HI, I'M IMAI!
I'M SHIMAE.

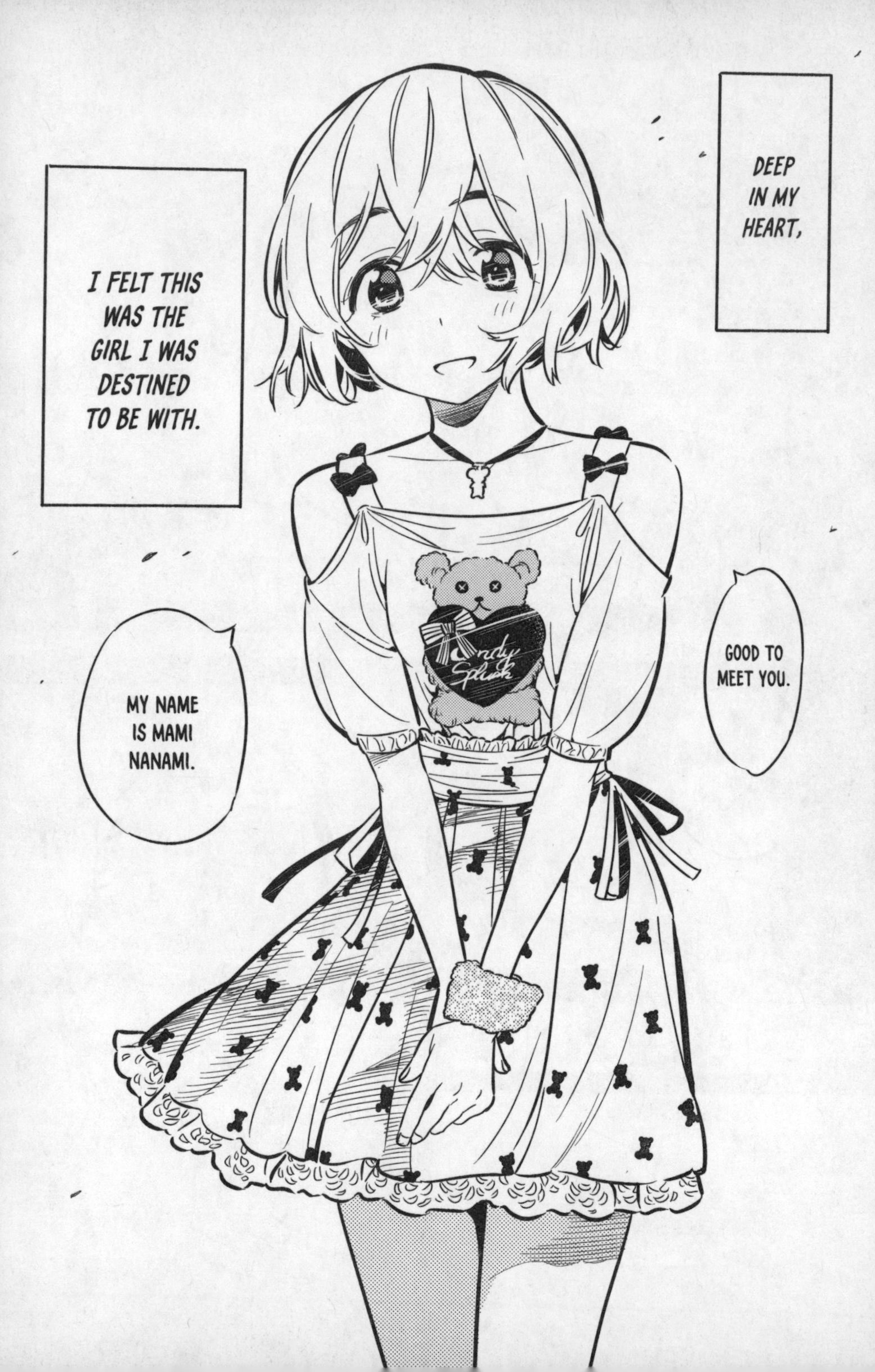
DEEP IN MY HEART,
I FELT THIS WAS THE GIRL I WAS DESTINED TO BE WITH.
GOOD TO MEET YOU.
MY NAME IS MAMI NANAMI.

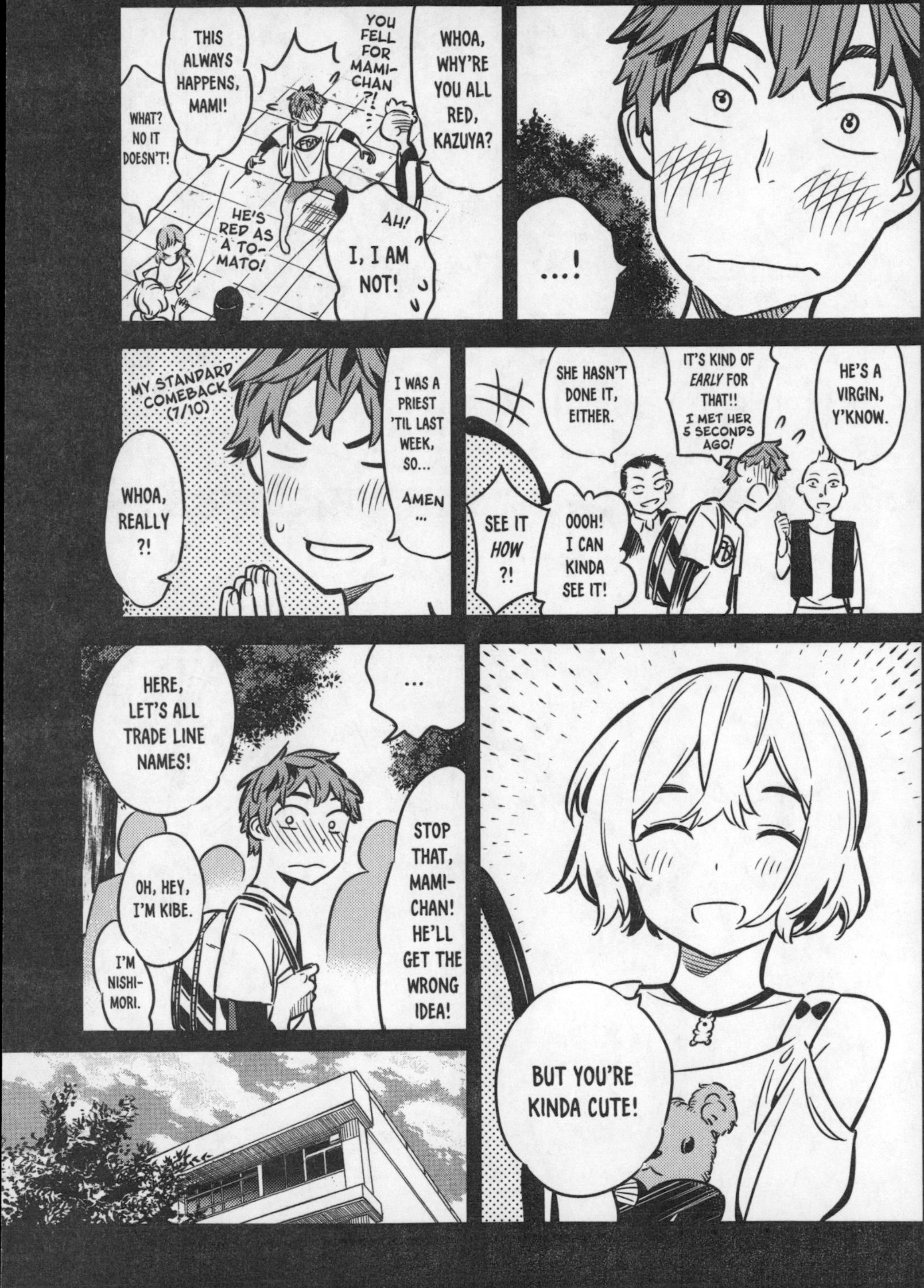
...!
WHOA, WHY'RE YOU ALL RED, KAZUYA?
YOU FELL FOR MAMI-CHAN?!
THIS ALWAYS HAPPENS, MAMI!
WHAT? NO IT DOESN'T!
AH! I, I AM NOT!
HE'S RED AS A TO-MATO!
HE'S A VIRGIN, Y'KNOW.
IT'S KIND OF *EARLY* FOR THAT!! I MET HER 5 SECONDS AGO!
SHE HASN'T DONE IT, EITHER.
OOOH! I CAN KINDA SEE IT!
SEE IT *HOW*?!
I WAS A PRIEST 'TIL LAST WEEK, SO... AMEN...
MY STANDARD COMEBACK (7/10)
WHOA, REALLY?!
BUT YOU'RE KINDA CUTE!
...
HERE, LET'S ALL TRADE LINE NAMES!
STOP THAT, MAMI-CHAN! HE'LL GET THE WRONG IDEA!
OH, HEY, I'M KIBE.
I'M NISHI-MORI.

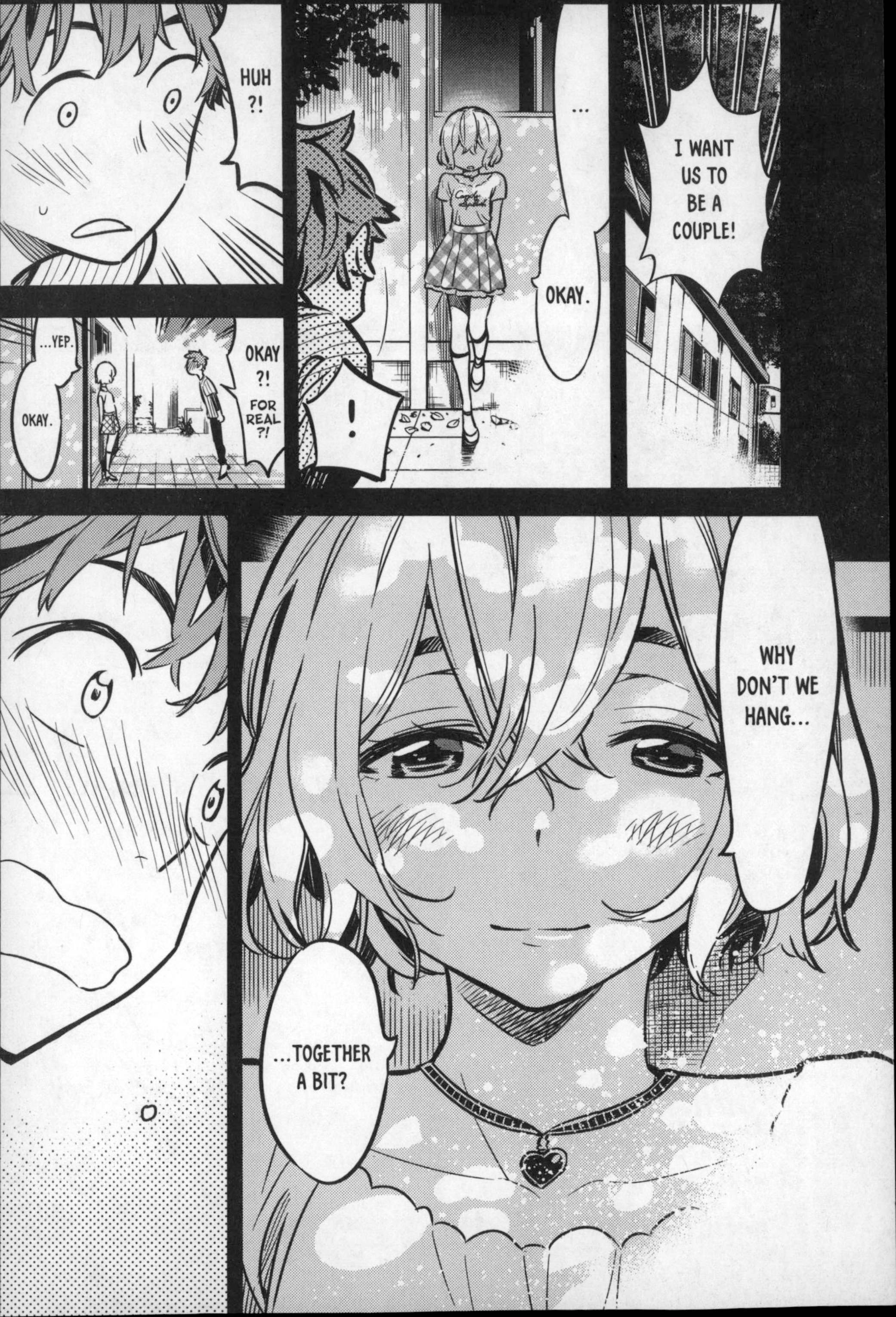
I WANT US TO BE A COUPLE!
...
OKAY.
!
HUH ?!
OKAY ?! FOR REAL ?!
...YEP.
OKAY.
WHY DON'T WE HANG...
...TOGETHER A BIT?

BUT HOW SHOULD I CLOSE THE DISTANCE?
TAPPA TAPPA
I MAY TURN HER OFF IF I GO TOO HARD.
BUT I CAN'T HOLD BACK ANY LONGER...
JUST DO IT!
BIP
BA-DING
Mami
I'm free on Sunday! Let's go to Disney!
BIP
BIP
BIP BIP
AH...
MY MIND'S...
...PIN-BALLING LIKE MAD...
ROLL
ROLL
AHHHH...

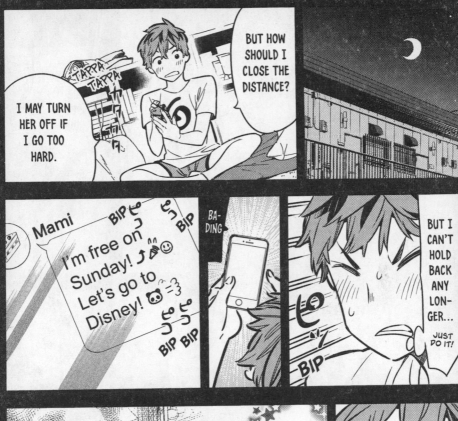

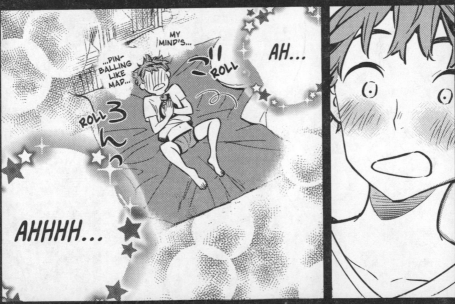

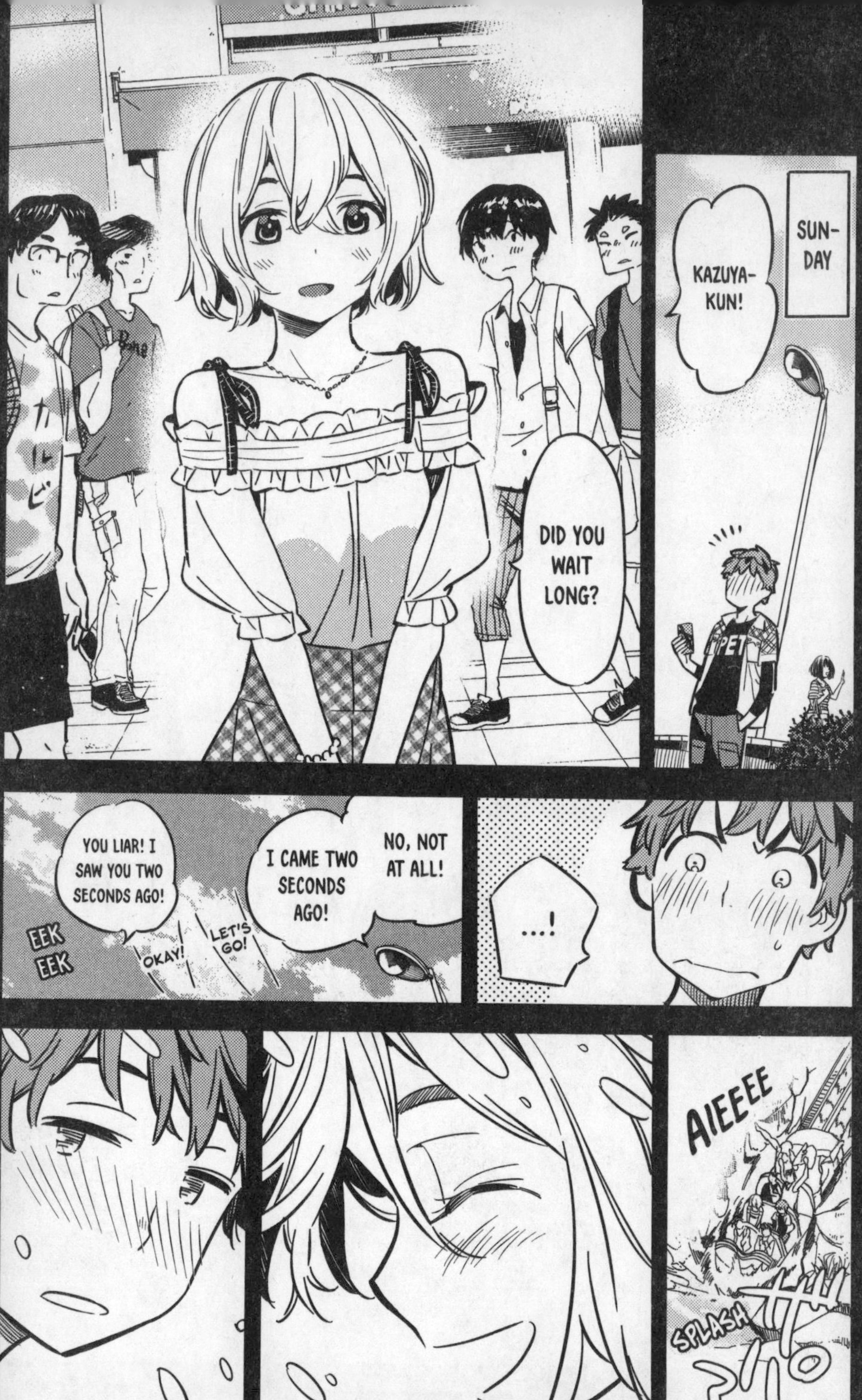
SUNDAY
KAZUYA-KUN!
DID YOU WAIT LONG?
...!
NO, NOT AT ALL!
I CAME TWO SECONDS AGO!
YOU LIAR! I SAW YOU TWO SECONDS AGO!
LET'S GO!
OKAY!
EEK EEK
AIEEEE
SPLASH

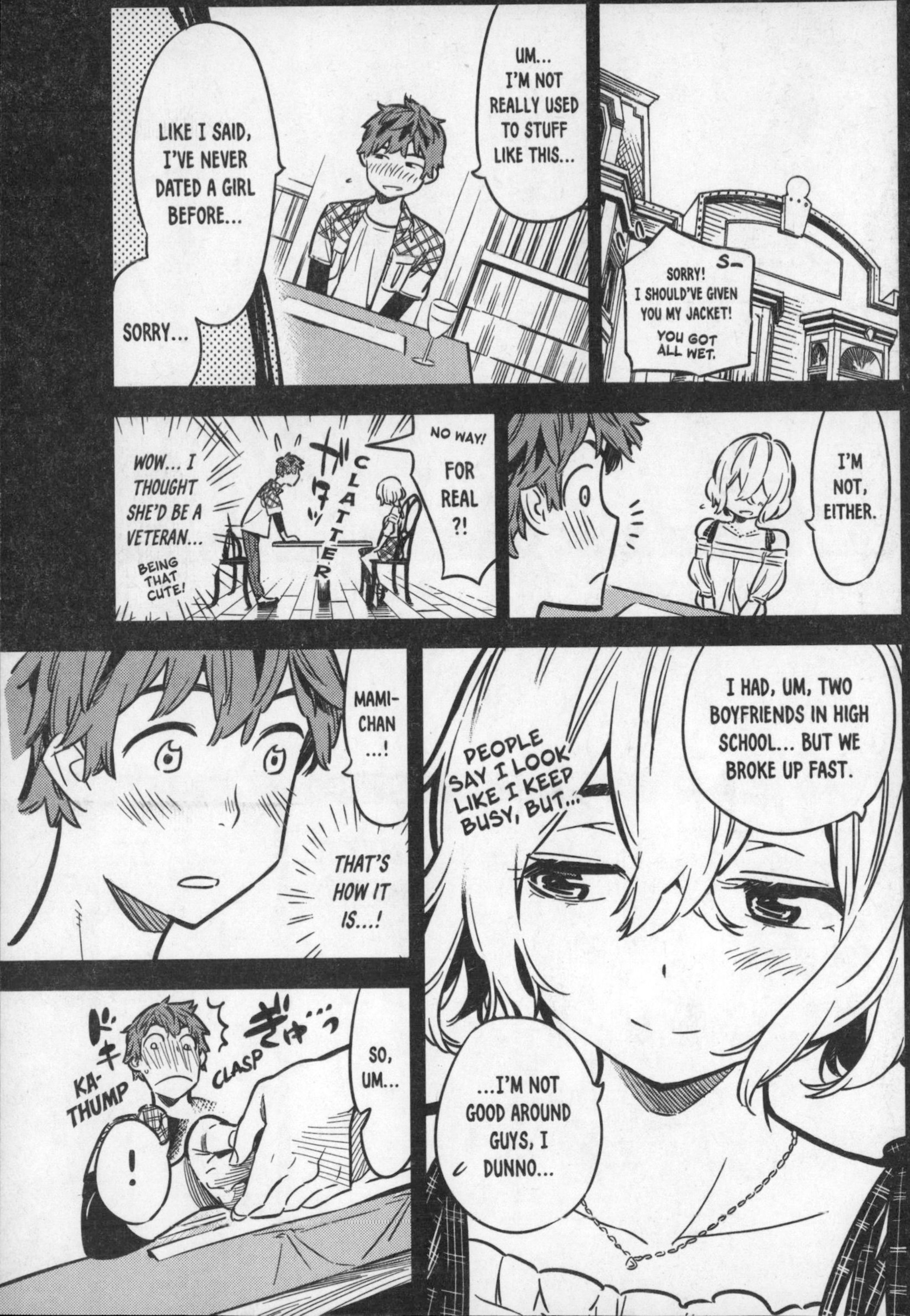
S–
SORRY! I SHOULD'VE GIVEN YOU MY JACKET!
YOU GOT ALL WET.
UM... I'M NOT REALLY USED TO STUFF LIKE THIS...
LIKE I SAID, I'VE NEVER DATED A GIRL BEFORE...
SORRY...
I'M NOT, EITHER.
NO WAY!
FOR REAL ?!
CLATTER
WOW... I THOUGHT SHE'D BE A VETERAN...
BEING THAT CUTE!
I HAD, UM, TWO BOYFRIENDS IN HIGH SCHOOL... BUT WE BROKE UP FAST.
PEOPLE SAY I LOOK LIKE I KEEP BUSY, BUT...
...I'M NOT GOOD AROUND GUYS, I DUNNO...
MAMI-CHAN ...!
THAT'S HOW IT IS...!
SO, UM...
CLASP
KA-THUMP
!

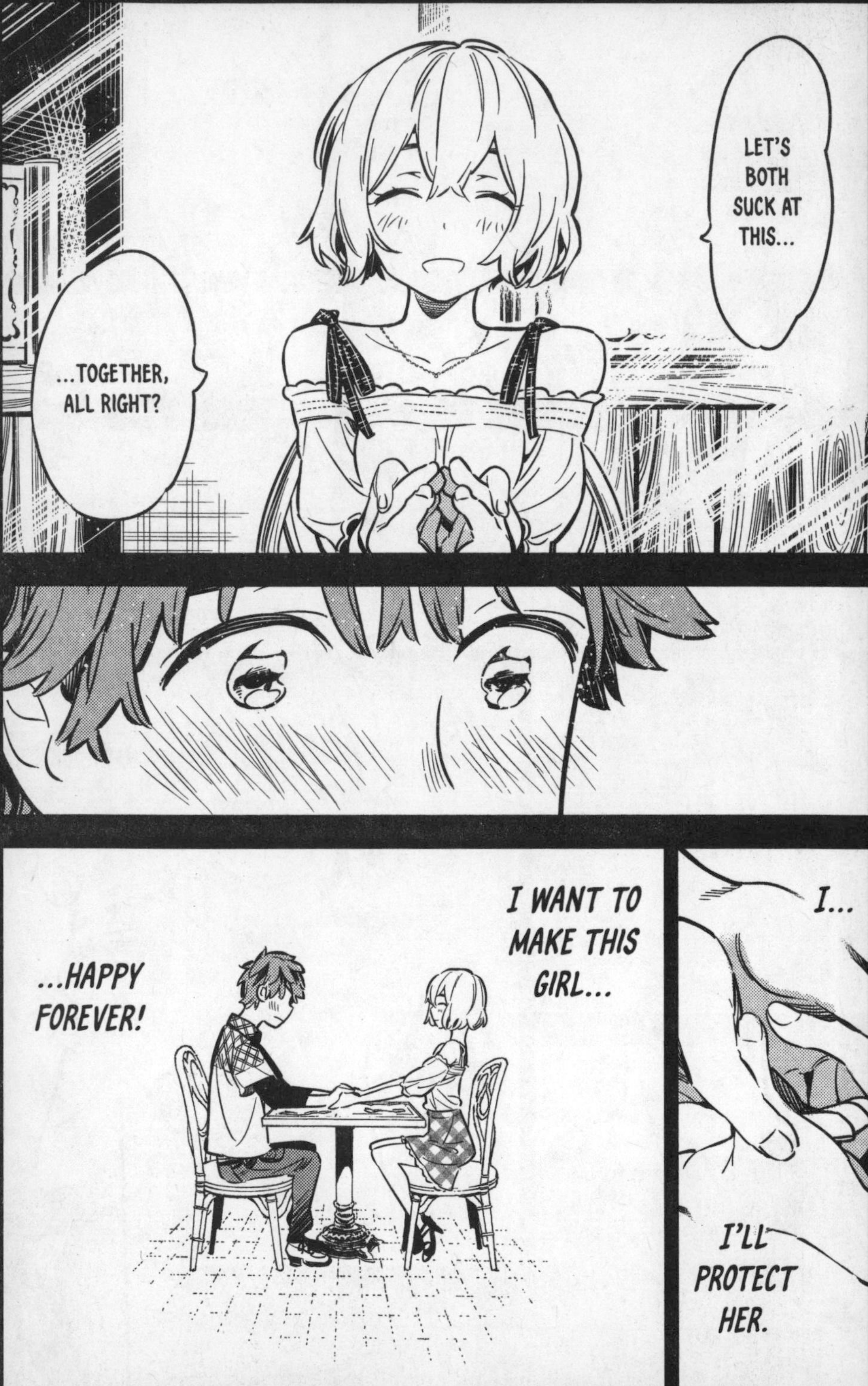
LET'S BOTH SUCK AT THIS...
...TOGETHER, ALL RIGHT?
I...
I'LL PROTECT HER.
I WANT TO MAKE THIS GIRL...
...HAPPY FOREVER!

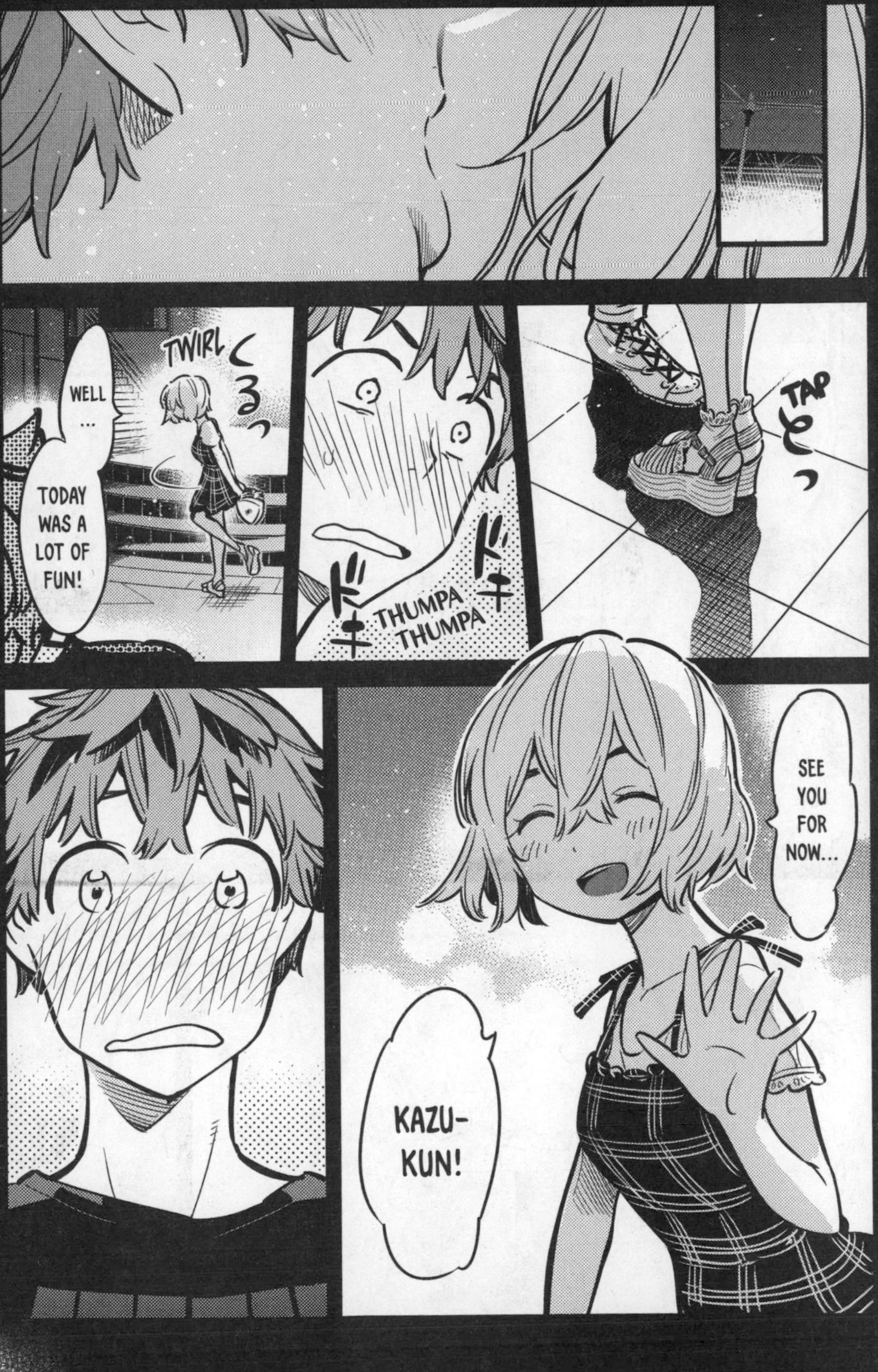
TAP
とっ
ドキ
ドキ
THUMPA THUMPA
TWIRL
くるっ
WELL...
TODAY WAS A LOT OF FUN!
SEE YOU FOR NOW...
KAZU-KUN!

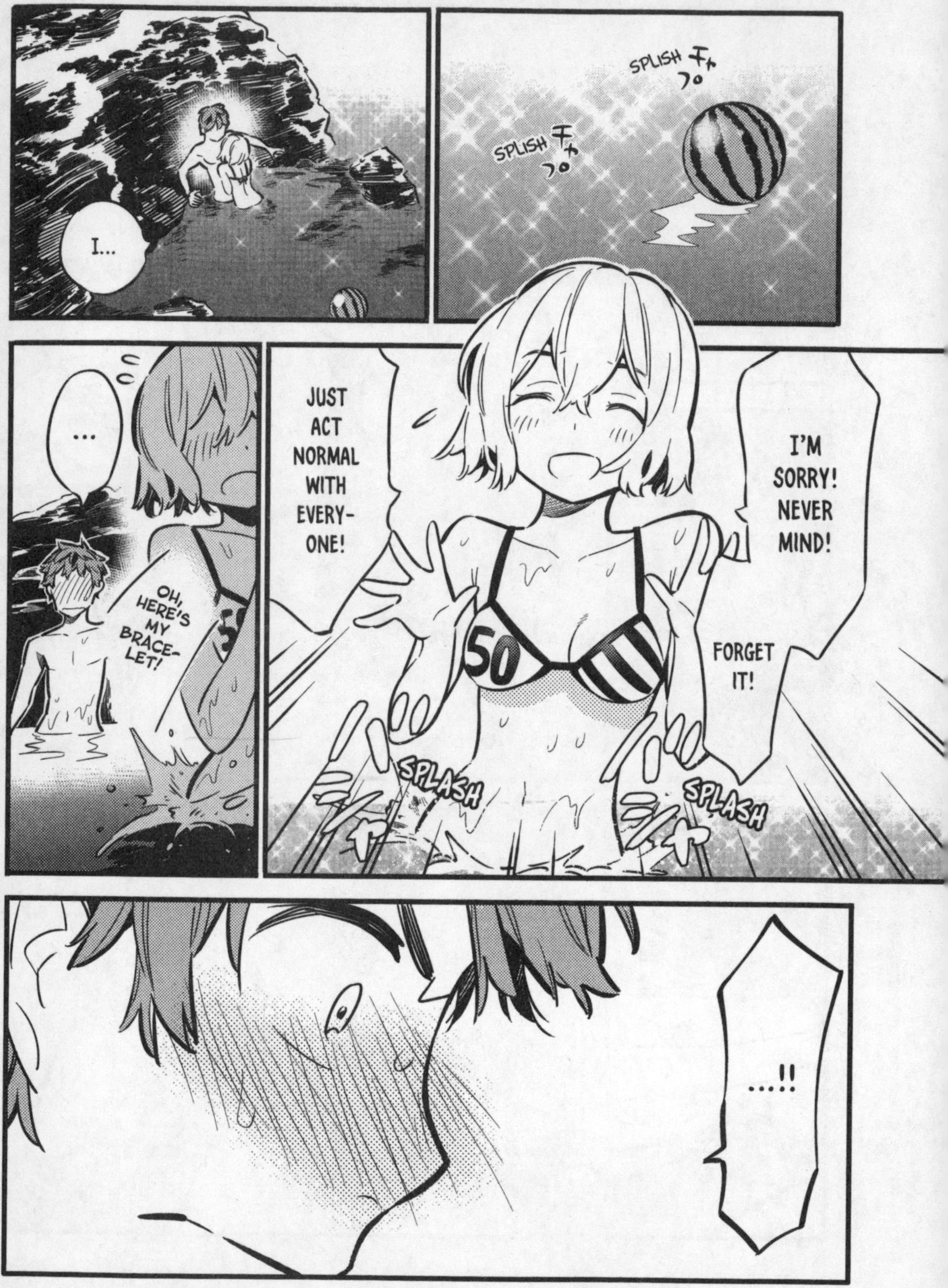
SPLISH チャプ
SPLISH チャプ
I...
I'M SORRY! NEVER MIND!
JUST ACT NORMAL WITH EVERY-ONE!
FORGET IT!
SPLASH
SPLASH
...
OH, HERE'S MY BRACE-LET!
...!!

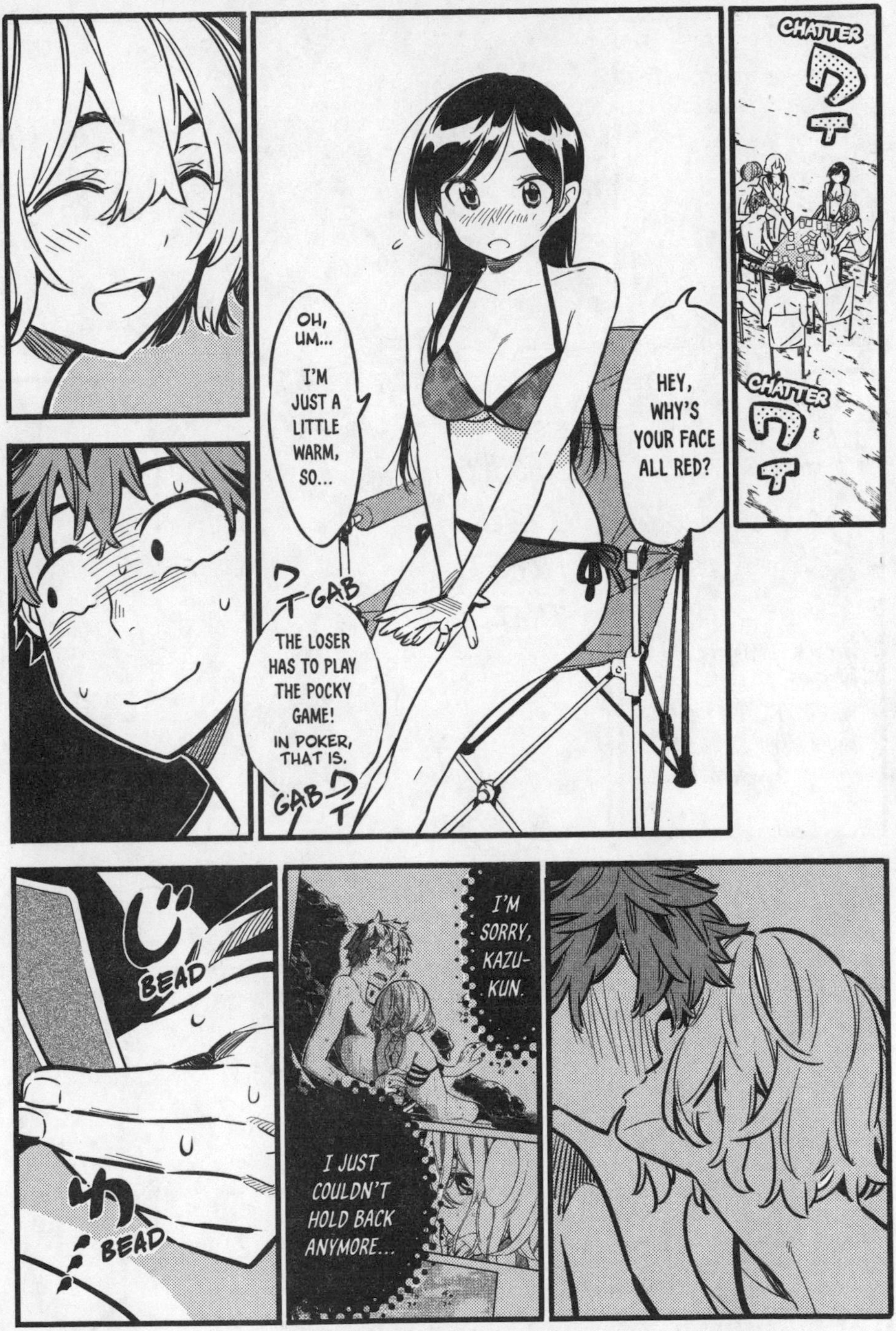
CHATTER
CHATTER
HEY, WHY'S YOUR FACE ALL RED?
OH, UM... I'M JUST A LITTLE WARM, SO...
GAB
THE LOSER HAS TO PLAY THE POCKY GAME! IN POKER, THAT IS.
GAB
I'M SORRY, KAZU-KUN.
I JUST COULDN'T HOLD BACK ANYMORE...
BEAD
BEAD

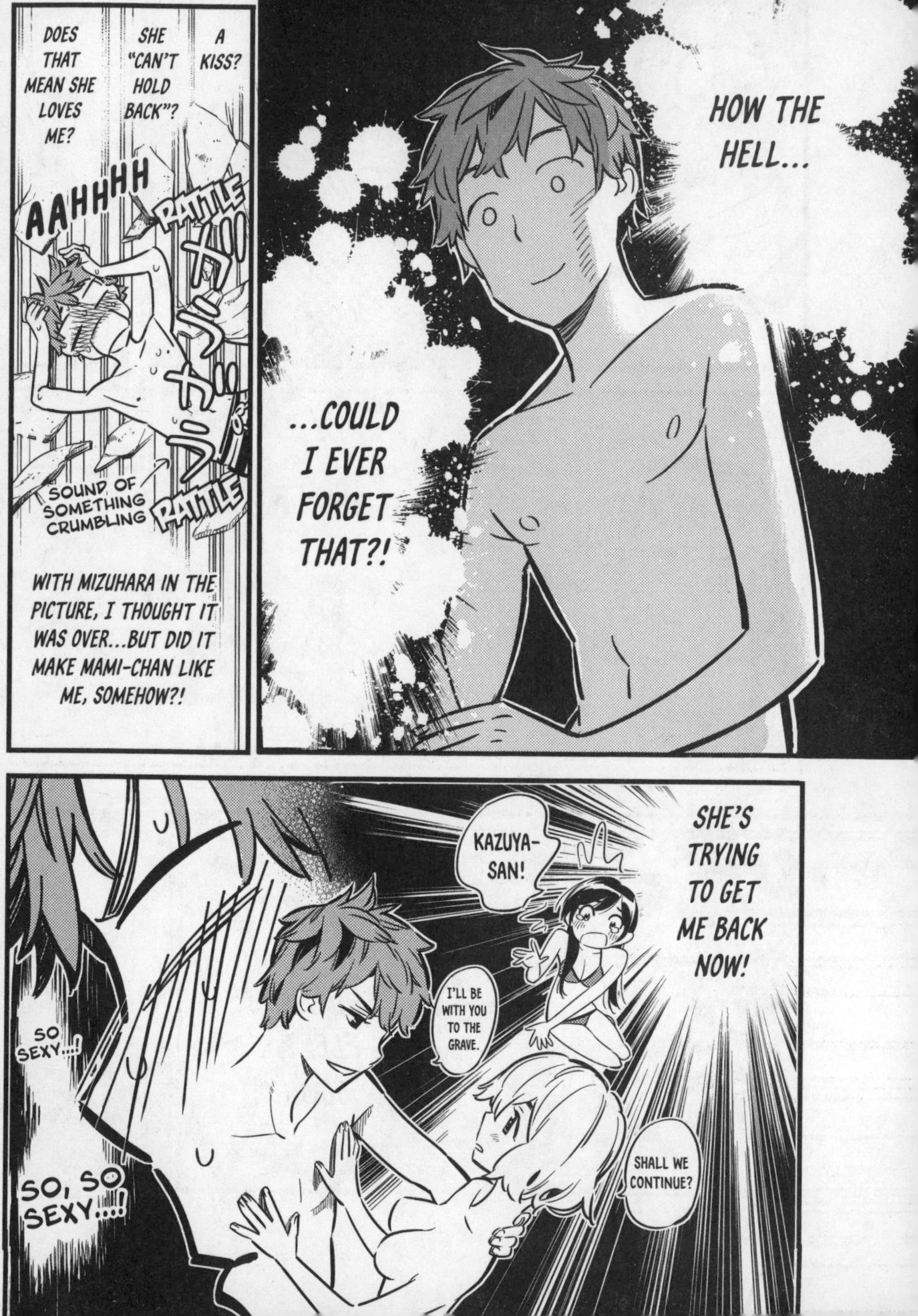
HOW THE HELL...
...COULD I EVER FORGET THAT?!
A KISS?
SHE "CAN'T HOLD BACK"?
DOES THAT MEAN SHE LOVES ME?
AAHHHH
RATTLE
SOUND OF SOMETHING CRUMBLING
RATTLE
WITH MIZUHARA IN THE PICTURE, I THOUGHT IT WAS OVER...BUT DID IT MAKE MAMI-CHAN LIKE ME, SOMEHOW?!
SHE'S TRYING TO GET ME BACK NOW!
KAZUYA-SAN!
I'LL BE WITH YOU TO THE GRAVE.
SHALL WE CONTINUE?
SO SEXY...!
SO, SO SEXY...!

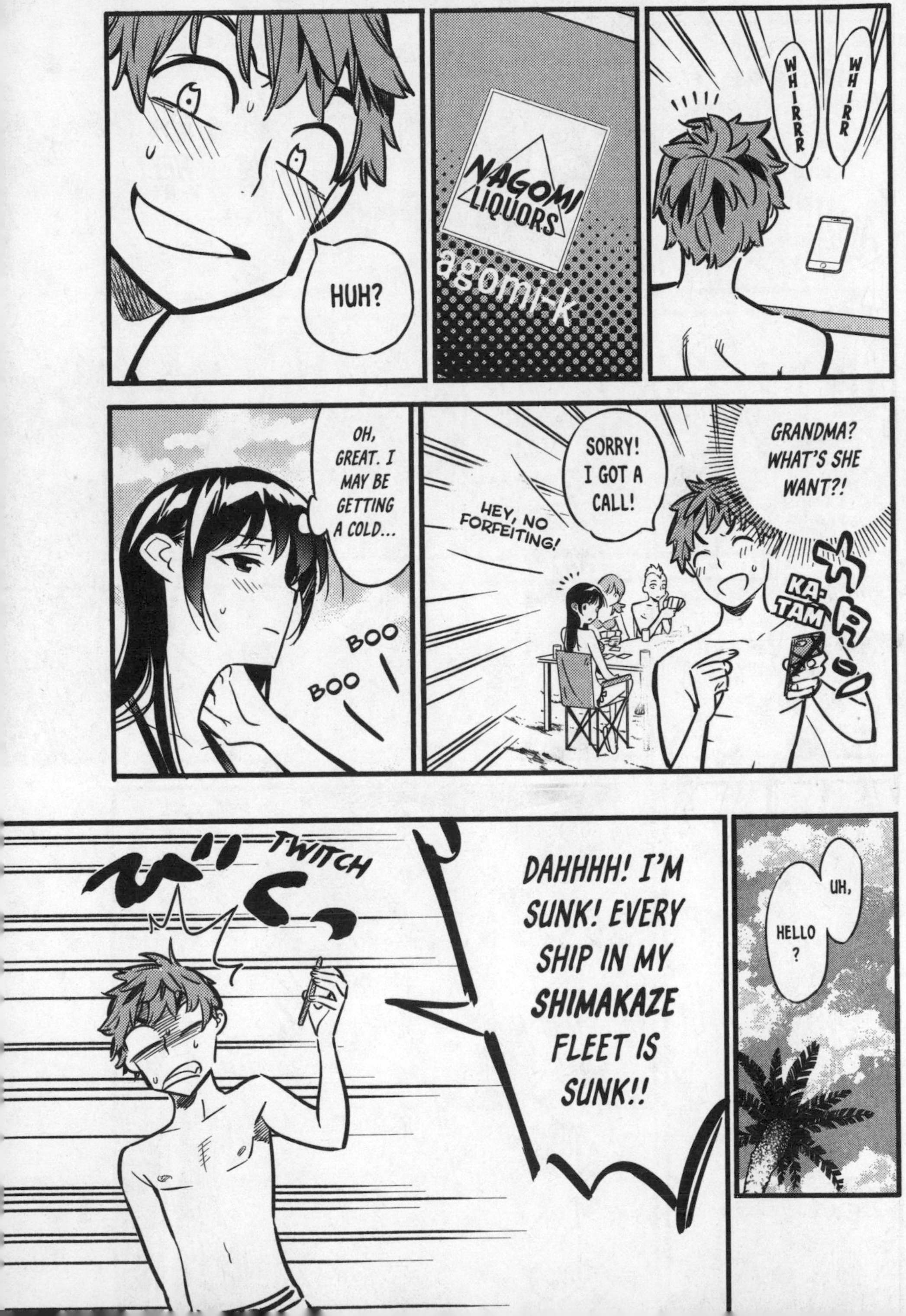
WHIRR
WHIRRR
NAGOMI LIQUORS
agomi-k
HUH?
GRANDMA? WHAT'S SHE WANT?!
KA-TAM
SORRY! I GOT A CALL!
HEY, NO FORFEITING!
OH, GREAT. I MAY BE GETTING A COLD...
BOO
BOO
UH, HELLO?
DAHHHH! I'M SUNK! EVERY SHIP IN MY SHIMAKAZE FLEET IS SUNK!!
TWITCH

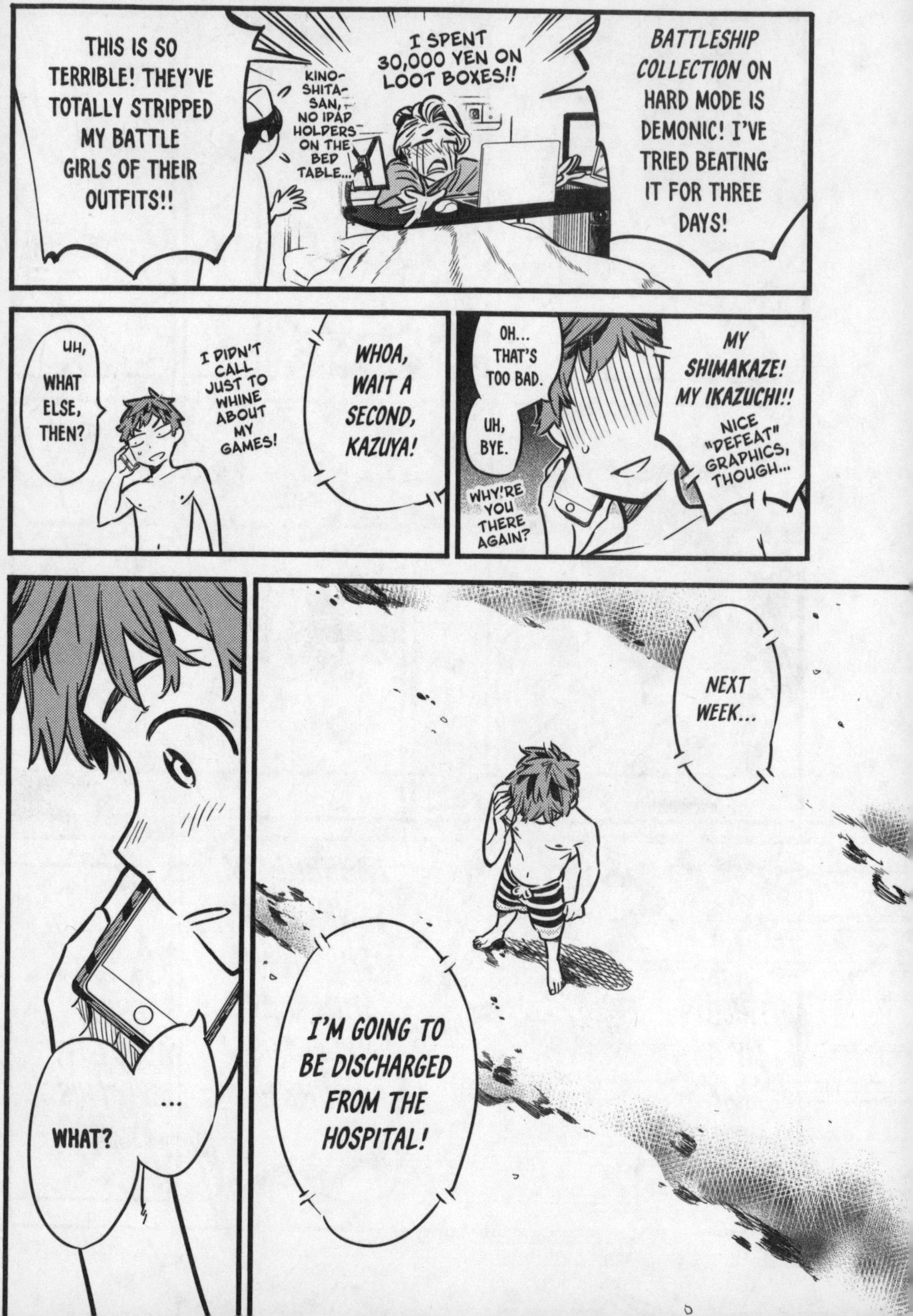
BATTLESHIP COLLECTION ON HARD MODE IS DEMONIC! I'VE TRIED BEATING IT FOR THREE DAYS!
I SPENT 30,000 YEN ON LOOT BOXES!!
KINO-SHITA-SAN, NO IPAD HOLDERS ON THE BED TABLE...
THIS IS SO TERRIBLE! THEY'VE TOTALLY STRIPPED MY BATTLE GIRLS OF THEIR OUTFITS!!
MY SHIMAKAZE! MY IKAZUCHI!!
NICE "DEFEAT" GRAPHICS, THOUGH...
OH... THAT'S TOO BAD.
UH, BYE.
WHY'RE YOU THERE AGAIN?
WHOA, WAIT A SECOND, KAZUYA!
I DIDN'T CALL JUST TO WHINE ABOUT MY GAMES!
UH, WHAT ELSE, THEN?
NEXT WEEK...
I'M GOING TO BE DISCHARGED FROM THE HOSPITAL!
... WHAT?

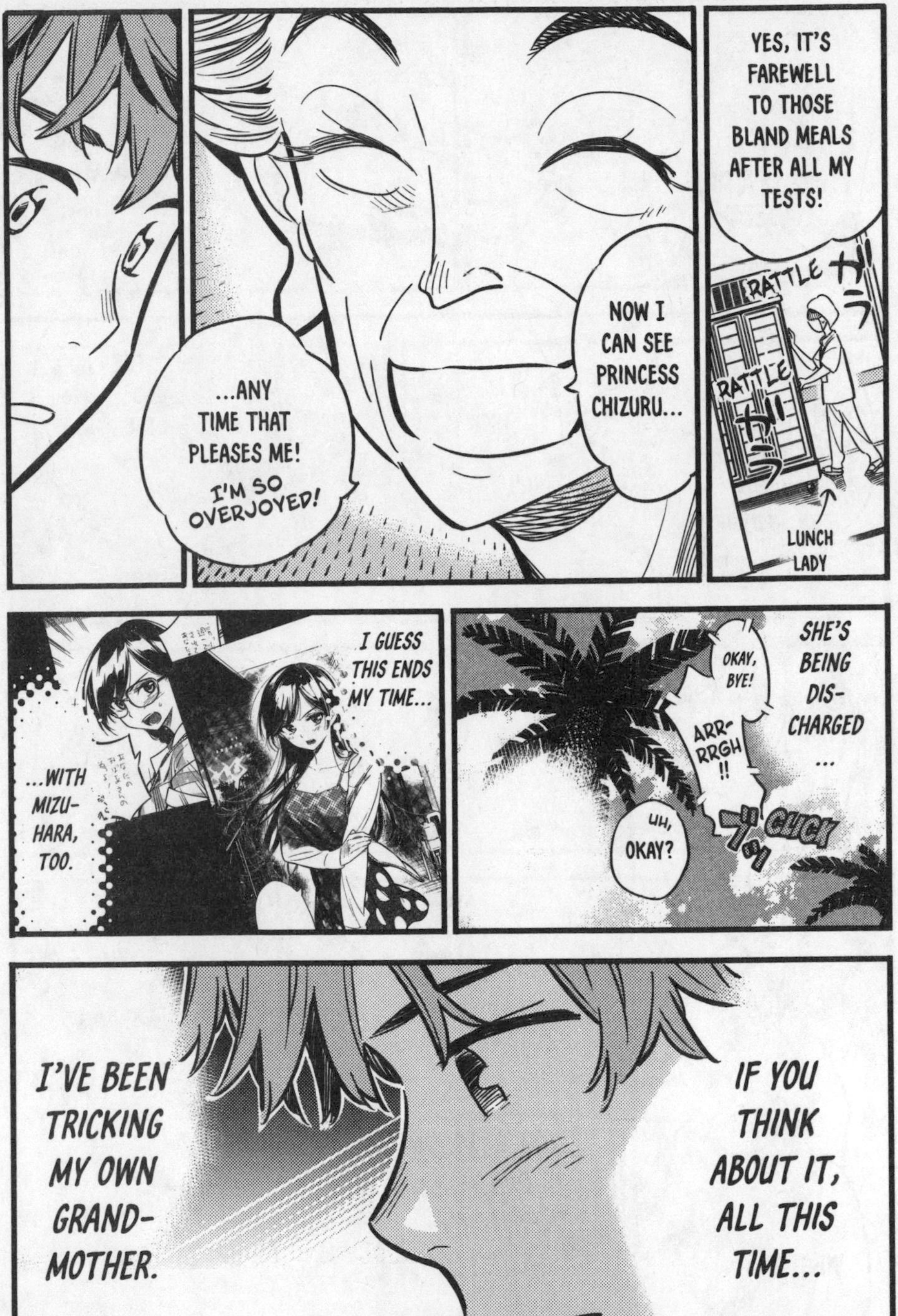
YES, IT'S FAREWELL TO THOSE BLAND MEALS AFTER ALL MY TESTS!
RATTLE ガラ
RATTLE ガラ
LUNCH LADY
NOW I CAN SEE PRINCESS CHIZURU...
...ANY TIME THAT PLEASES ME!
I'M SO OVERJOYED!
SHE'S BEING DIS-CHARGED...
OKAY, BYE!
ARRRRGH!!
UH, OKAY?
CLICK
I GUESS THIS ENDS MY TIME...
...WITH MIZUHARA, TOO.
IF YOU THINK ABOUT IT, ALL THIS TIME...
I'VE BEEN TRICKING MY OWN GRAND-MOTHER.

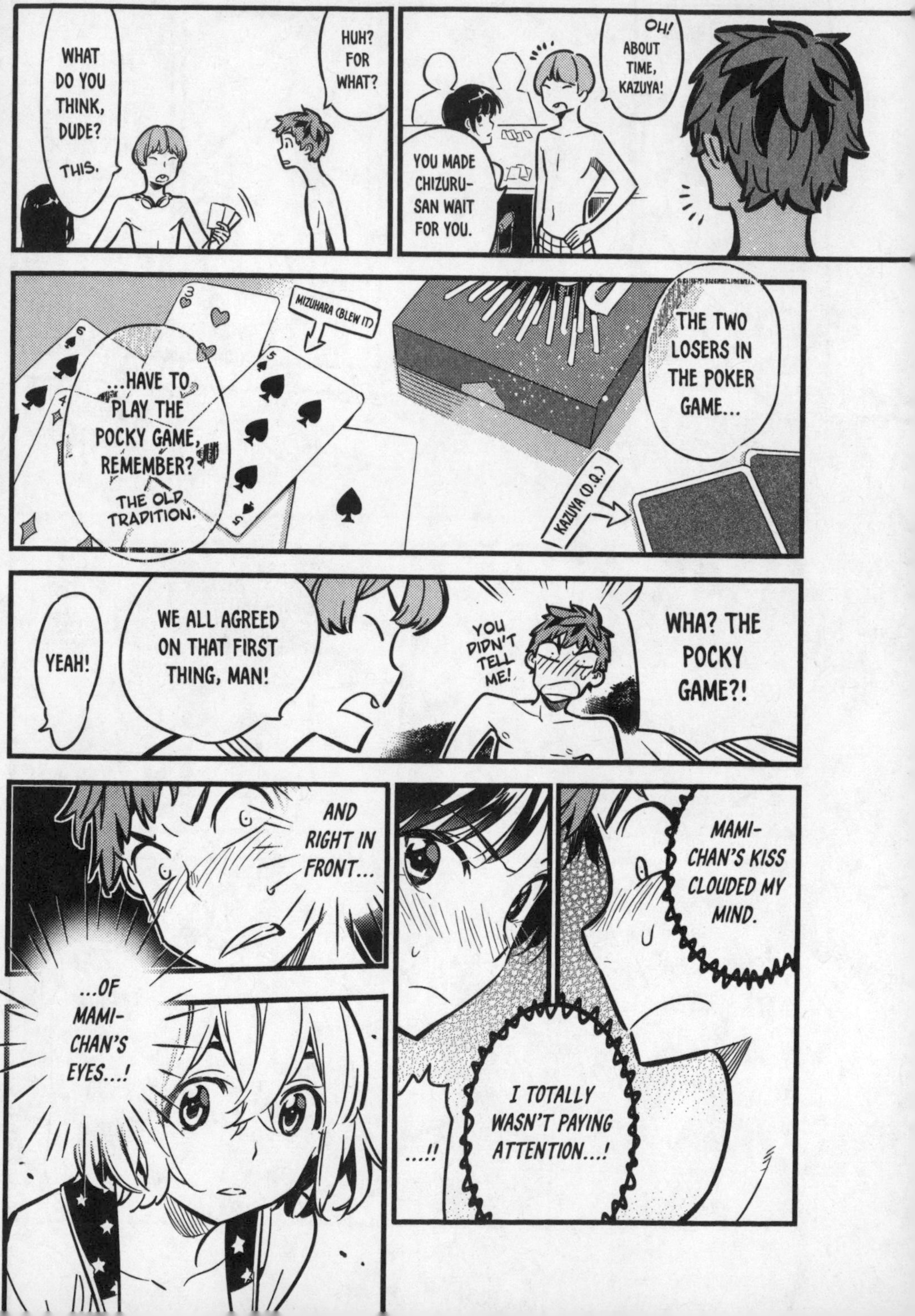

OH! ABOUT TIME, KAZUYA!
YOU MADE CHIZURU-SAN WAIT FOR YOU.
HUH? FOR WHAT?
WHAT DO YOU THINK, DUDE?
THIS.
THE TWO LOSERS IN THE POKER GAME...
KAZUYA (D.Q.)
MIZUHARA (BLEW IT)
...HAVE TO PLAY THE POCKY GAME, REMEMBER?
THE OLD TRADITION.
WHA? THE POCKY GAME?!
YOU DIDN'T TELL ME!
WE ALL AGREED ON THAT FIRST THING, MAN!
YEAH!
MAMI-CHAN'S KISS CLOUDED MY MIND.
I TOTALLY WASN'T PAYING ATTENTION...!
...!!
AND RIGHT IN FRONT...
...OF MAMI-CHAN'S EYES...!

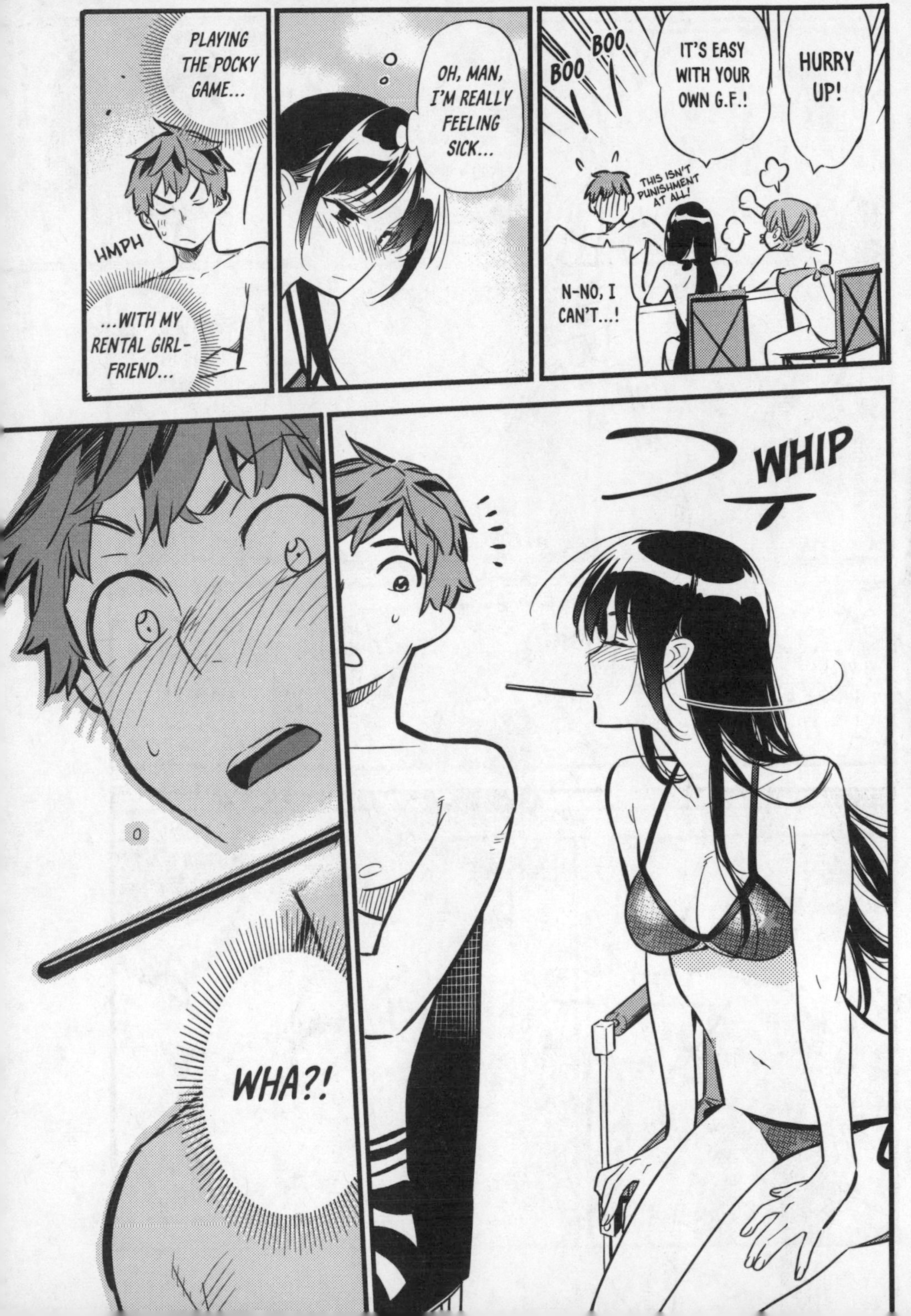
HURRY UP!
IT'S EASY WITH YOUR OWN G.F.!
BOO BOO
THIS ISN'T PUNISHMENT AT ALL!
N-NO, I CAN'T...!
OH, MAN, I'M REALLY FEELING SICK...
PLAYING THE POCKY GAME...
HMPH
...WITH MY RENTAL GIRL-FRIEND...
WHIP
WHA?!

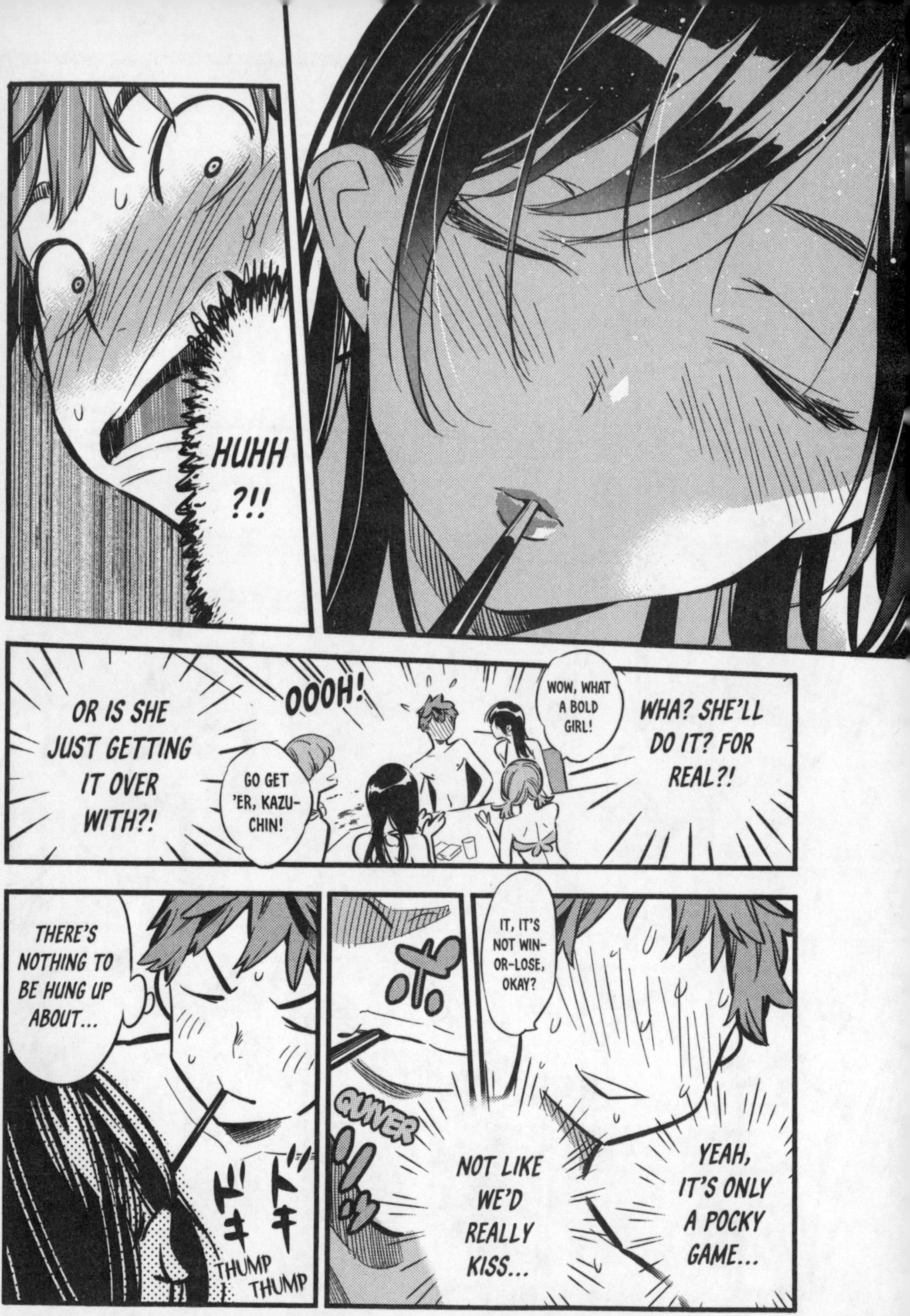
HUHH ?!!
WHA? SHE'LL DO IT? FOR REAL?!
WOW, WHAT A BOLD GIRL!
OOOH!
GO GET 'ER, KAZU-CHIN!
OR IS SHE JUST GETTING IT OVER WITH?!
YEAH, IT'S ONLY A POCKY GAME...
IT, IT'S NOT WIN-OR-LOSE, OKAY?
NOT LIKE WE'D REALLY KISS...
QUIVER
THERE'S NOTHING TO BE HUNG UP ABOUT...
ドキドキ
THUMP THUMP

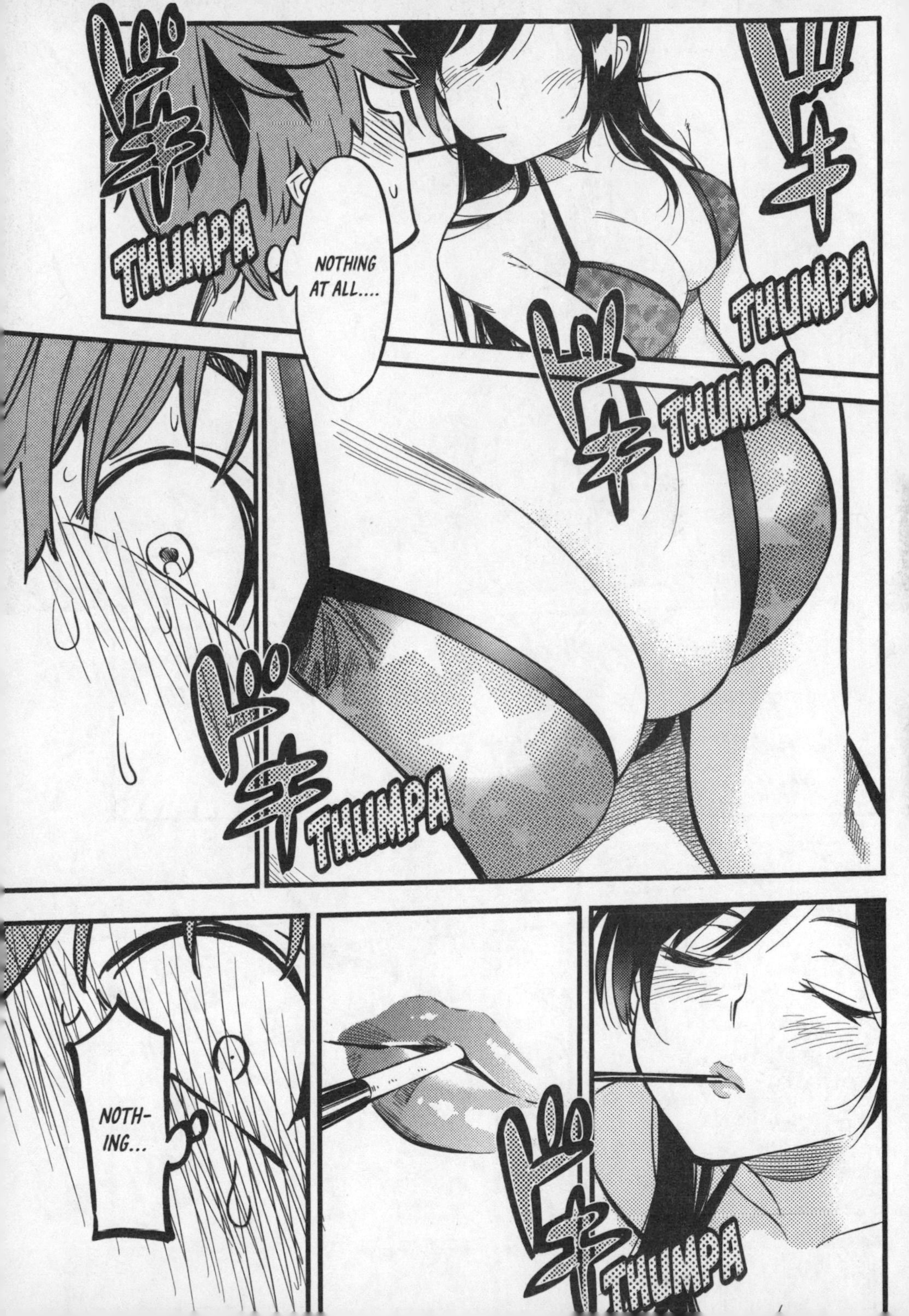
ドキ
THUMPA
NOTHING AT ALL....
ドキ
THUMPA
ドキ
THUMPA
THUMPA
ドキ
THUMPA
ドキ
THUMPA
NOTH-
ING...

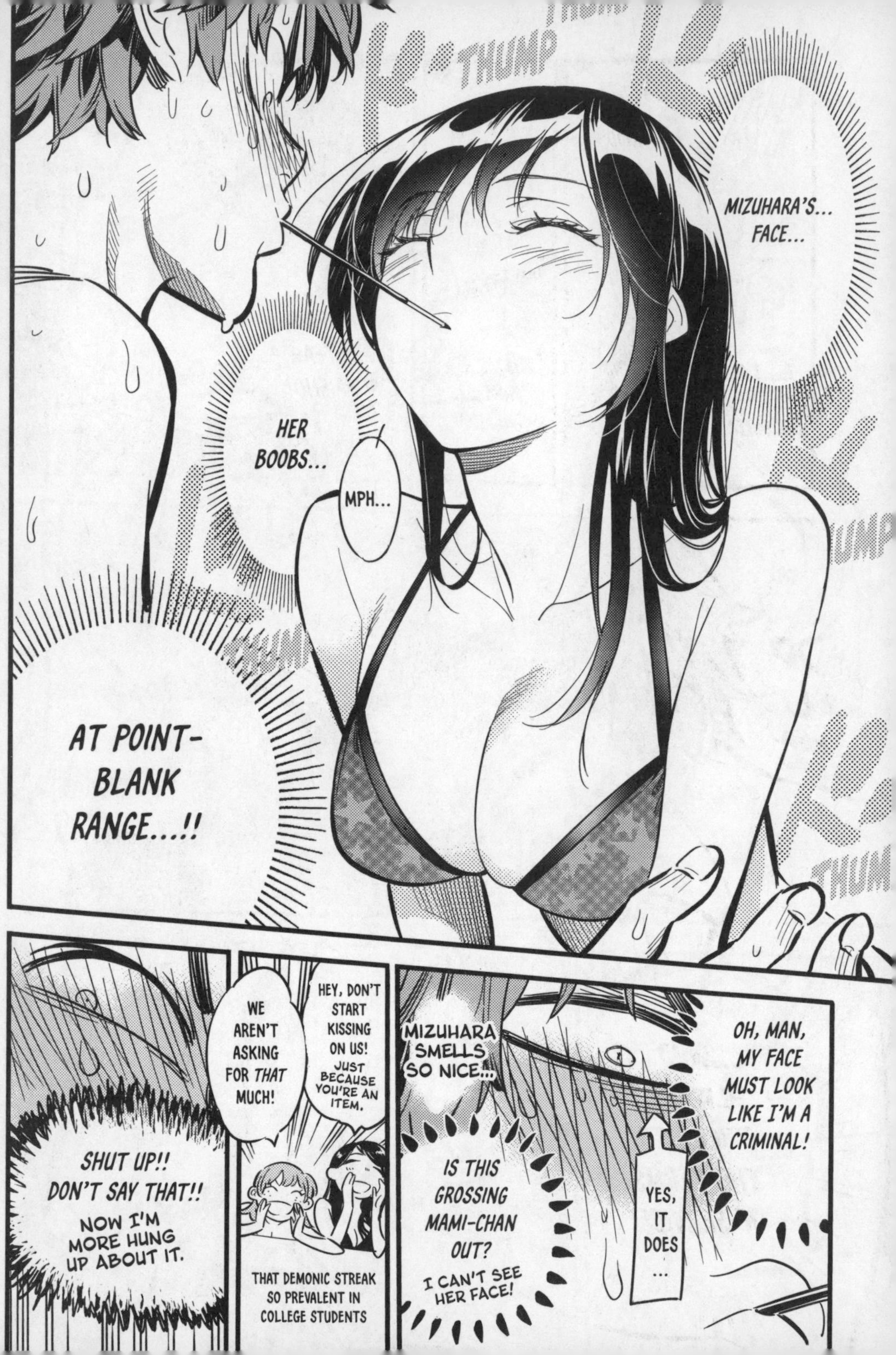
K-THUMP
MIZUHARA'S... FACE...
THUMP
THUMP
HER BOOBS...
MPH...
THUMP
AT POINT-BLANK RANGE...!!
OH, MAN, MY FACE MUST LOOK LIKE I'M A CRIMINAL!
MIZUHARA SMELLS SO NICE...
YES, IT DOES ...
IS THIS GROSSING MAMI-CHAN OUT?
I CAN'T SEE HER FACE!
HEY, DON'T START KISSING ON US!
JUST BECAUSE YOU'RE AN ITEM.
WE AREN'T ASKING FOR *THAT* MUCH!
THAT DEMONIC STREAK SO PREVALENT IN COLLEGE STUDENTS
SHUT UP!! DON'T SAY THAT!!
NOW I'M MORE HUNG UP ABOUT IT.

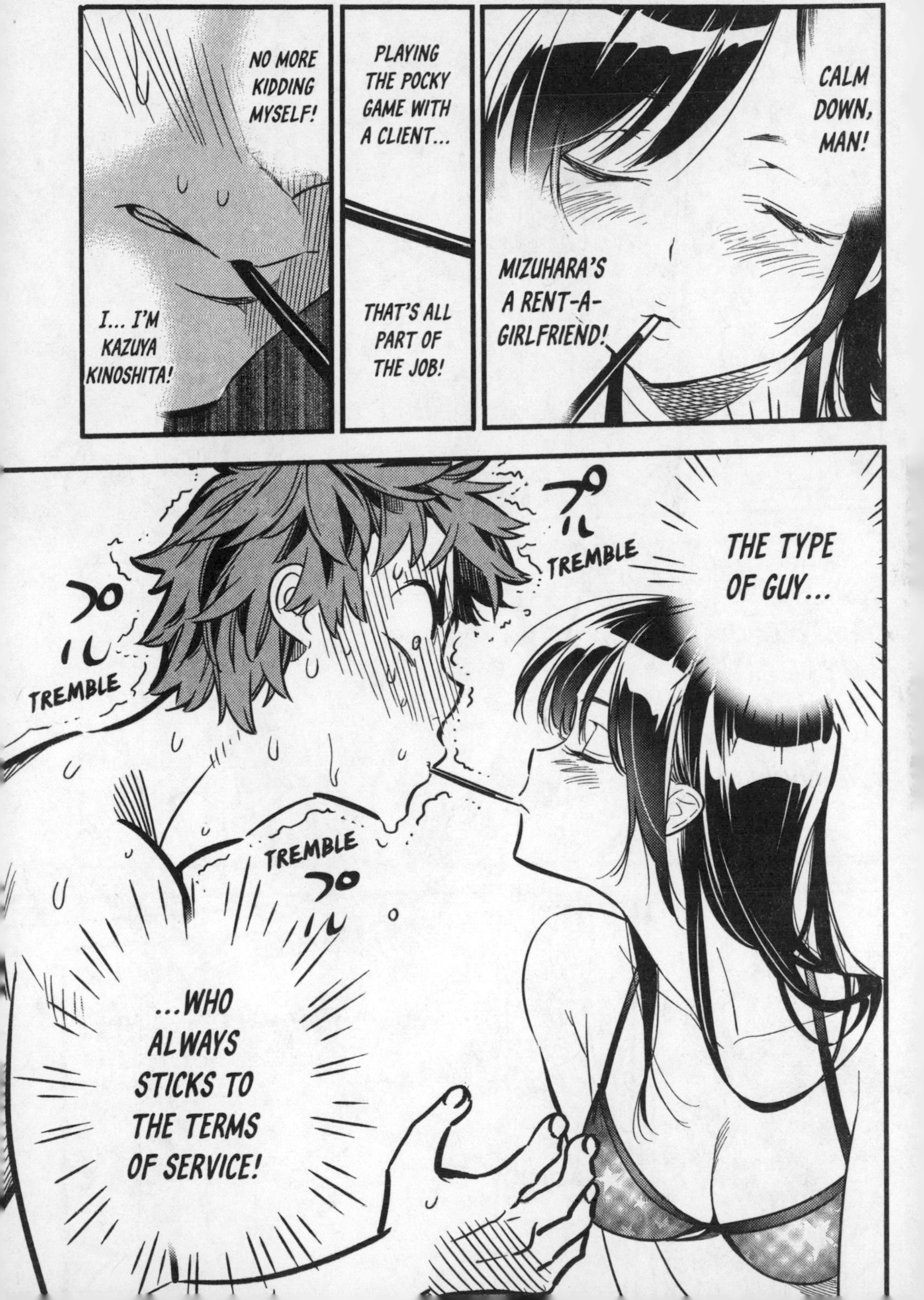
CALM DOWN, MAN!
MIZUHARA'S A RENT-A-GIRLFRIEND!
PLAYING THE POCKY GAME WITH A CLIENT...
THAT'S ALL PART OF THE JOB!
NO MORE KIDDING MYSELF!
I... I'M KAZUYA KINOSHITA!
THE TYPE OF GUY...
プル TREMBLE
プル TREMBLE
プル TREMBLE
...WHO ALWAYS STICKS TO THE TERMS OF SERVICE!

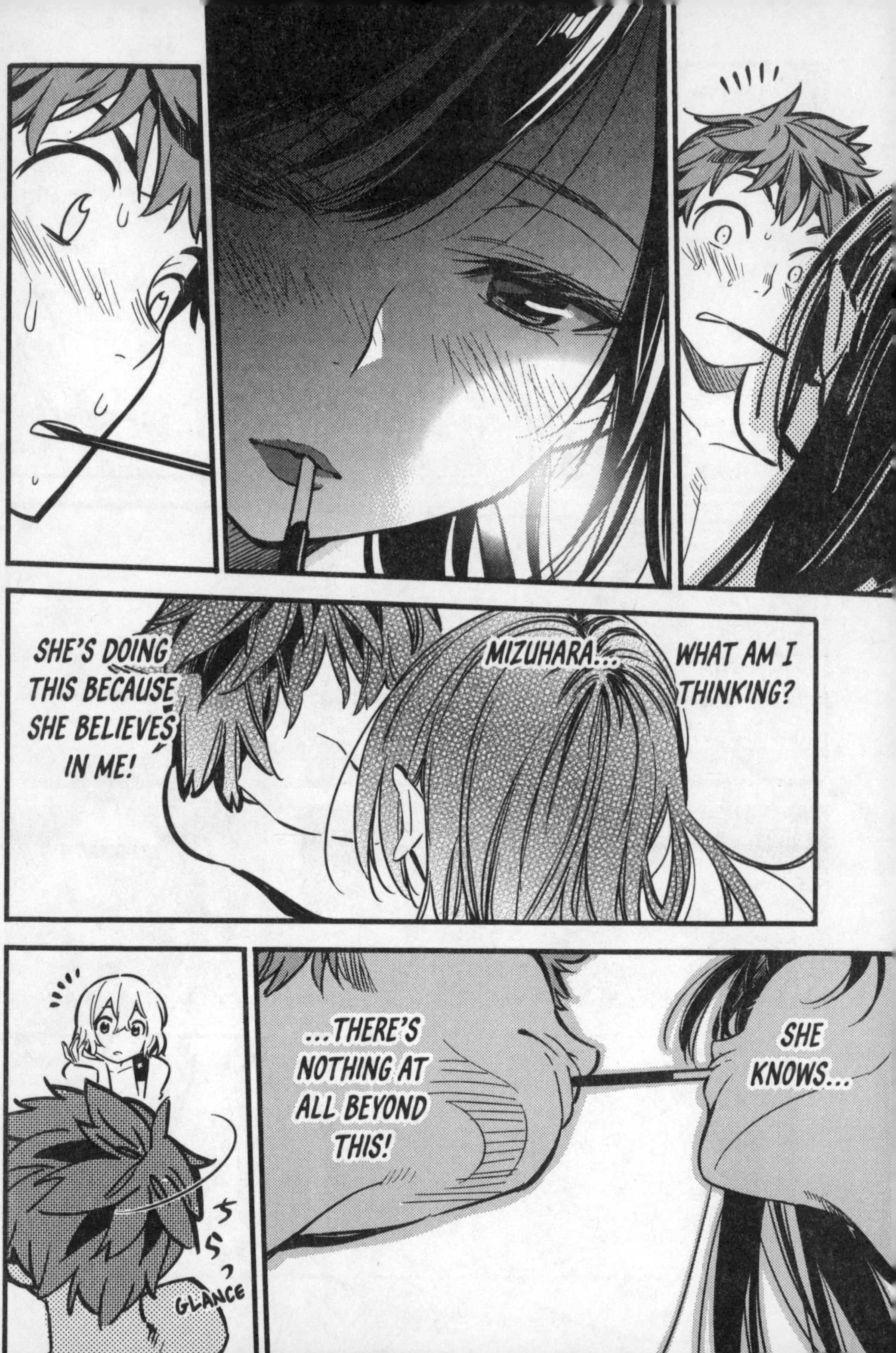
WHAT AM I THINKING?
MIZUHARA...
SHE'S DOING THIS BECAUSE SHE BELIEVES IN ME!
SHE KNOWS...
...THERE'S NOTHING AT ALL BEYOND THIS!
ちらっ
GLANCE

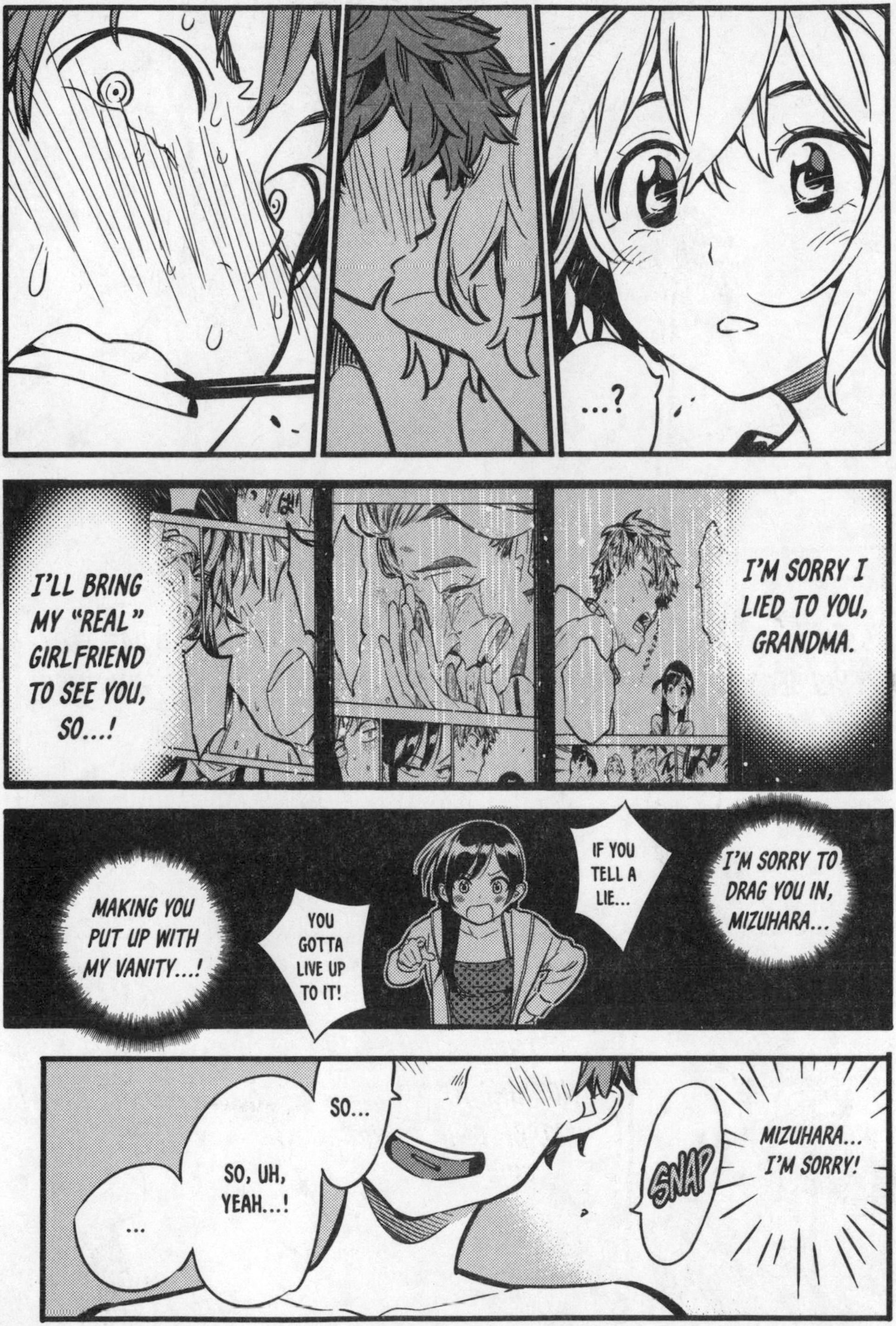
...?
I'M SORRY I LIED TO YOU, GRANDMA.
I'LL BRING MY "REAL" GIRLFRIEND TO SEE YOU, SO...!
I'M SORRY TO DRAG YOU IN, MIZUHARA...
IF YOU TELL A LIE...
YOU GOTTA LIVE UP TO IT!
MAKING YOU PUT UP WITH MY VANITY...!
MIZUHARA... I'M SORRY!
SNAP
SO...
SO, UH, YEAH...!
...

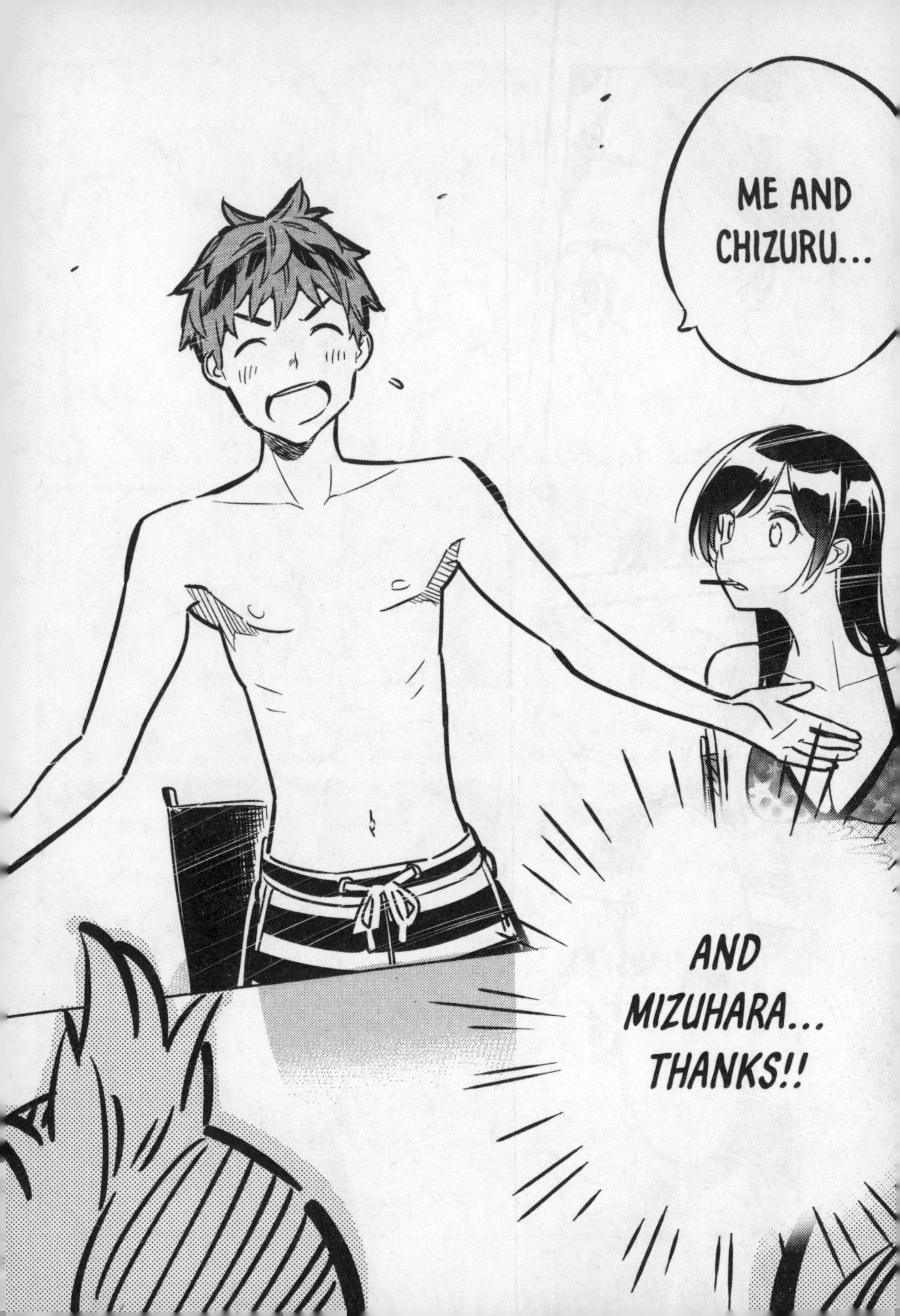
ME AND CHIZURU...
AND MIZUHARA... THANKS!!

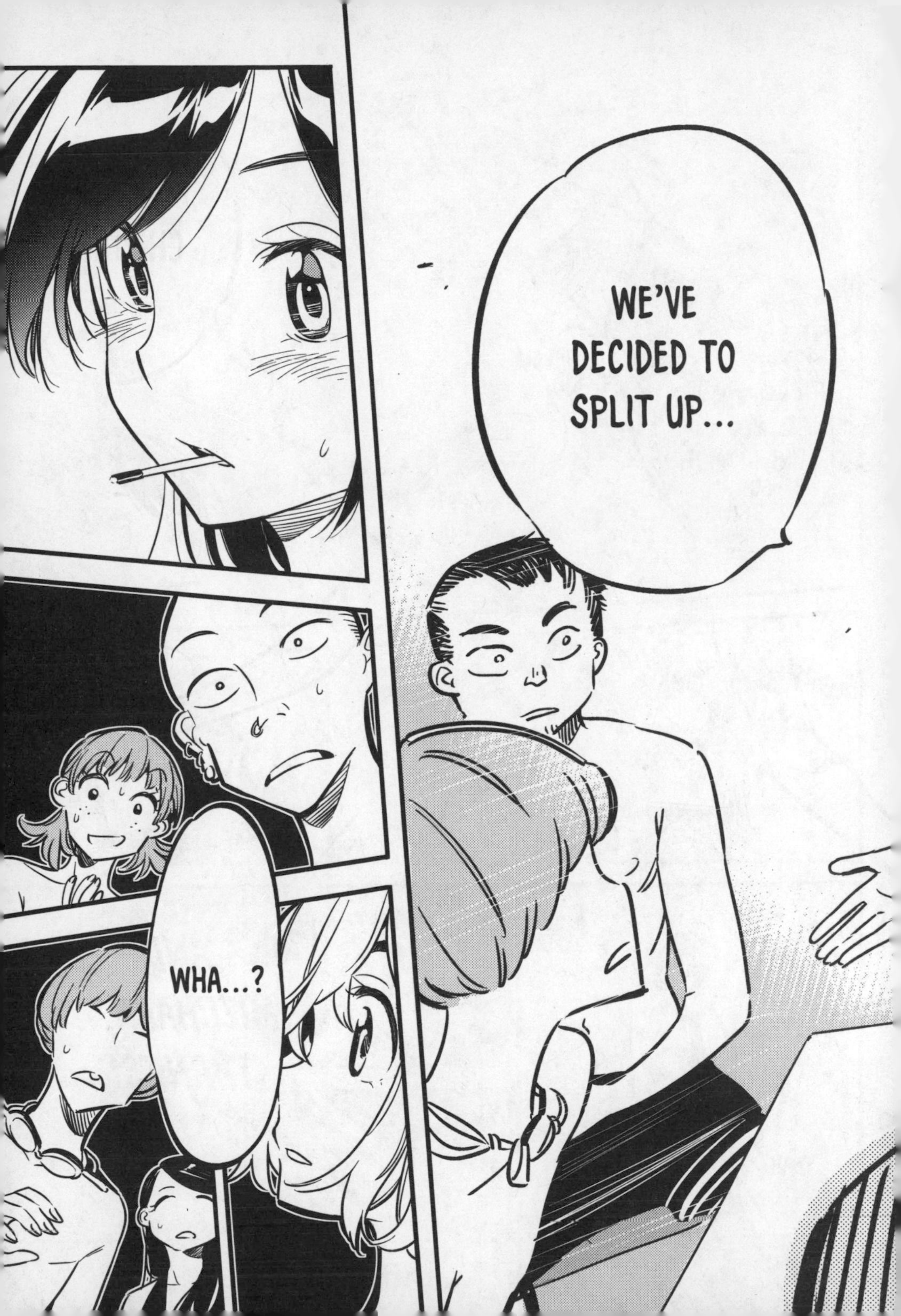
WE'VE DECIDED TO SPLIT UP...
WHA...?

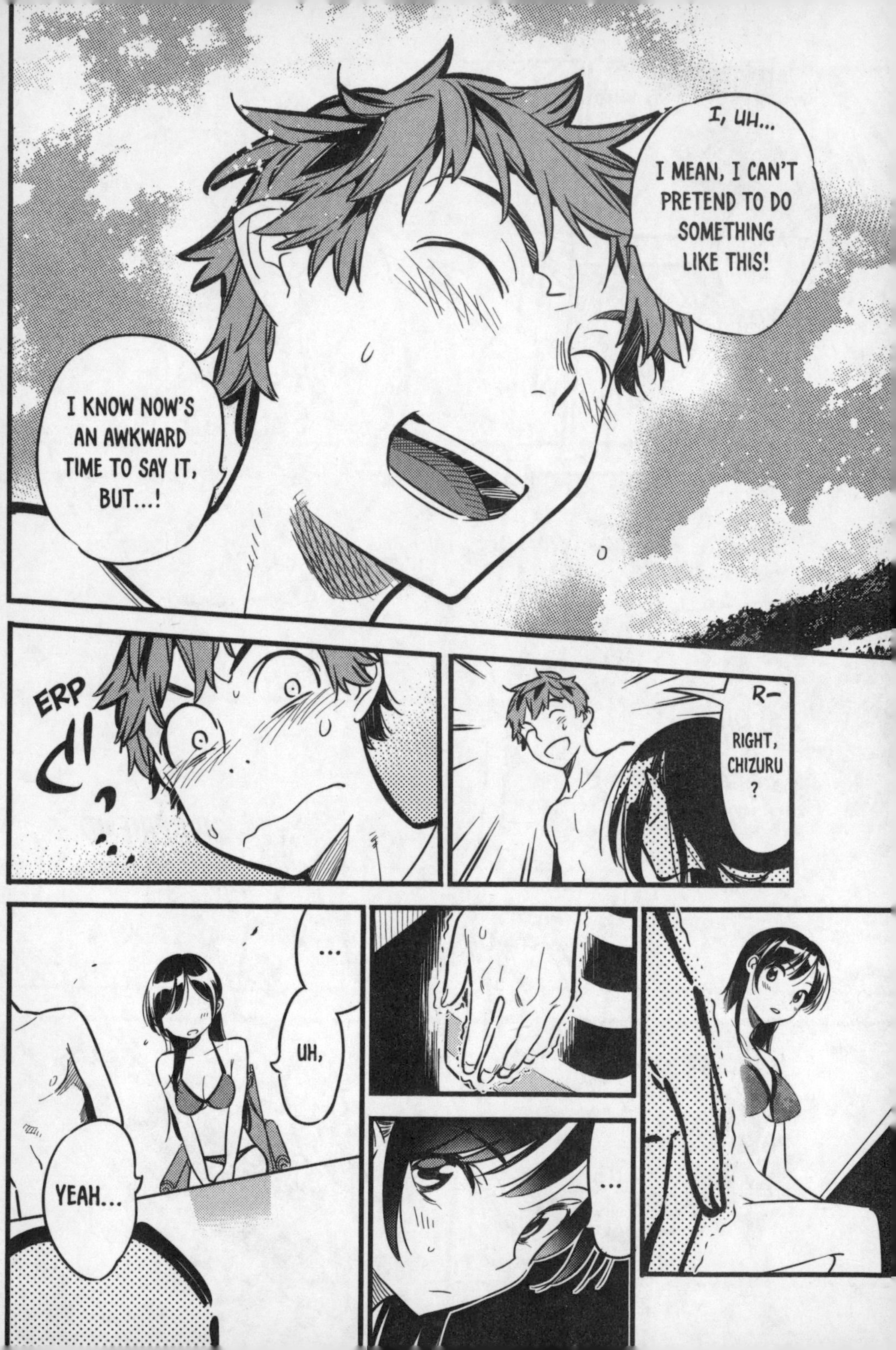
I, UH...
I MEAN, I CAN'T PRETEND TO DO SOMETHING LIKE THIS!
I KNOW NOW'S AN AWKWARD TIME TO SAY IT, BUT...!
R-
RIGHT, CHIZURU?
ERP
...
...
UH,
YEAH...

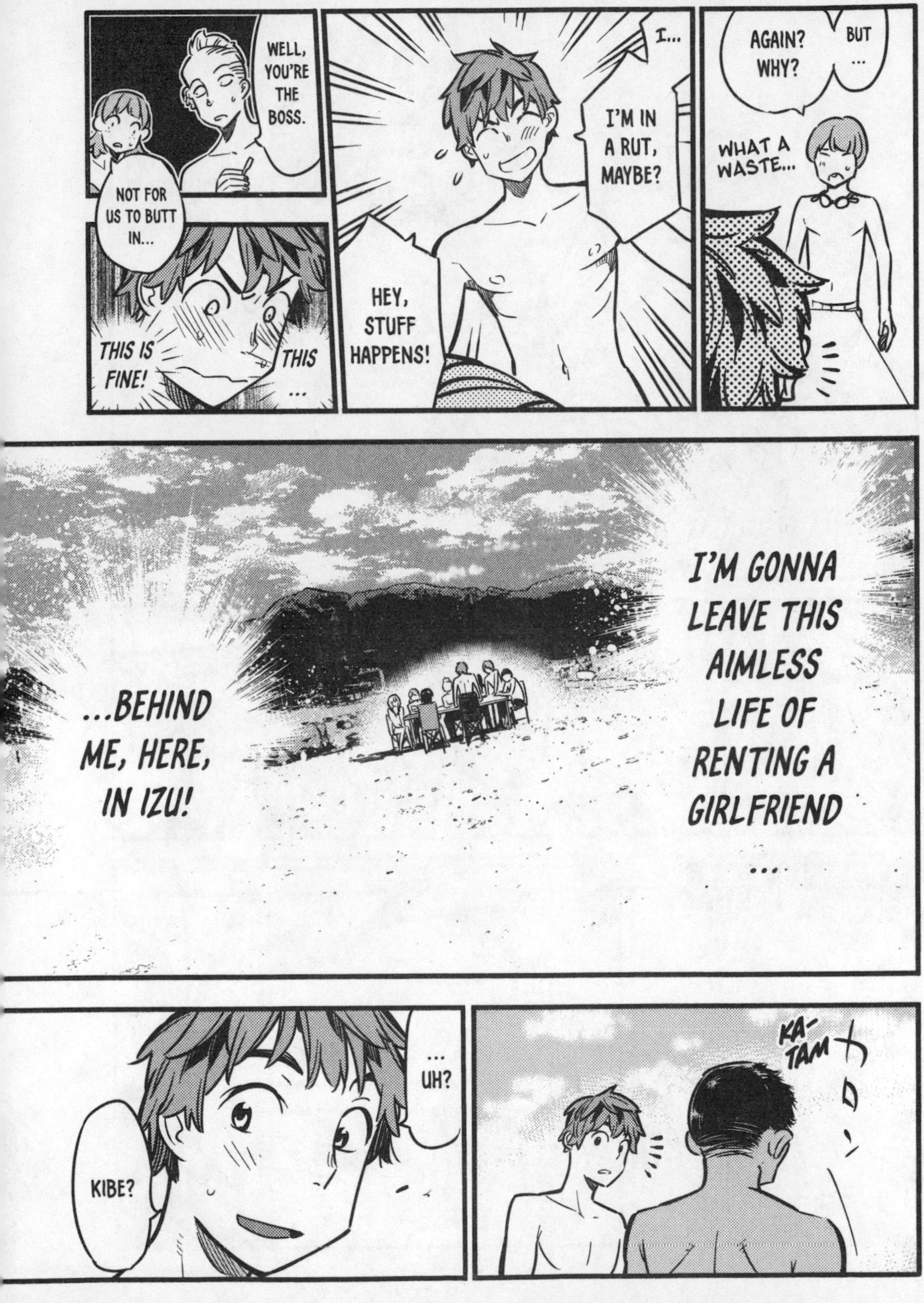
BUT ...
AGAIN? WHY?
WHAT A WASTE...
I...
I'M IN A RUT, MAYBE?
HEY, STUFF HAPPENS!
WELL, YOU'RE THE BOSS.
NOT FOR US TO BUTT IN...
THIS ...
THIS IS FINE!
I'M GONNA LEAVE THIS AIMLESS LIFE OF RENTING A GIRLFRIEND ...
...BEHIND ME, HERE, IN IZU!
KA-TAM
... UH?
KIBE?

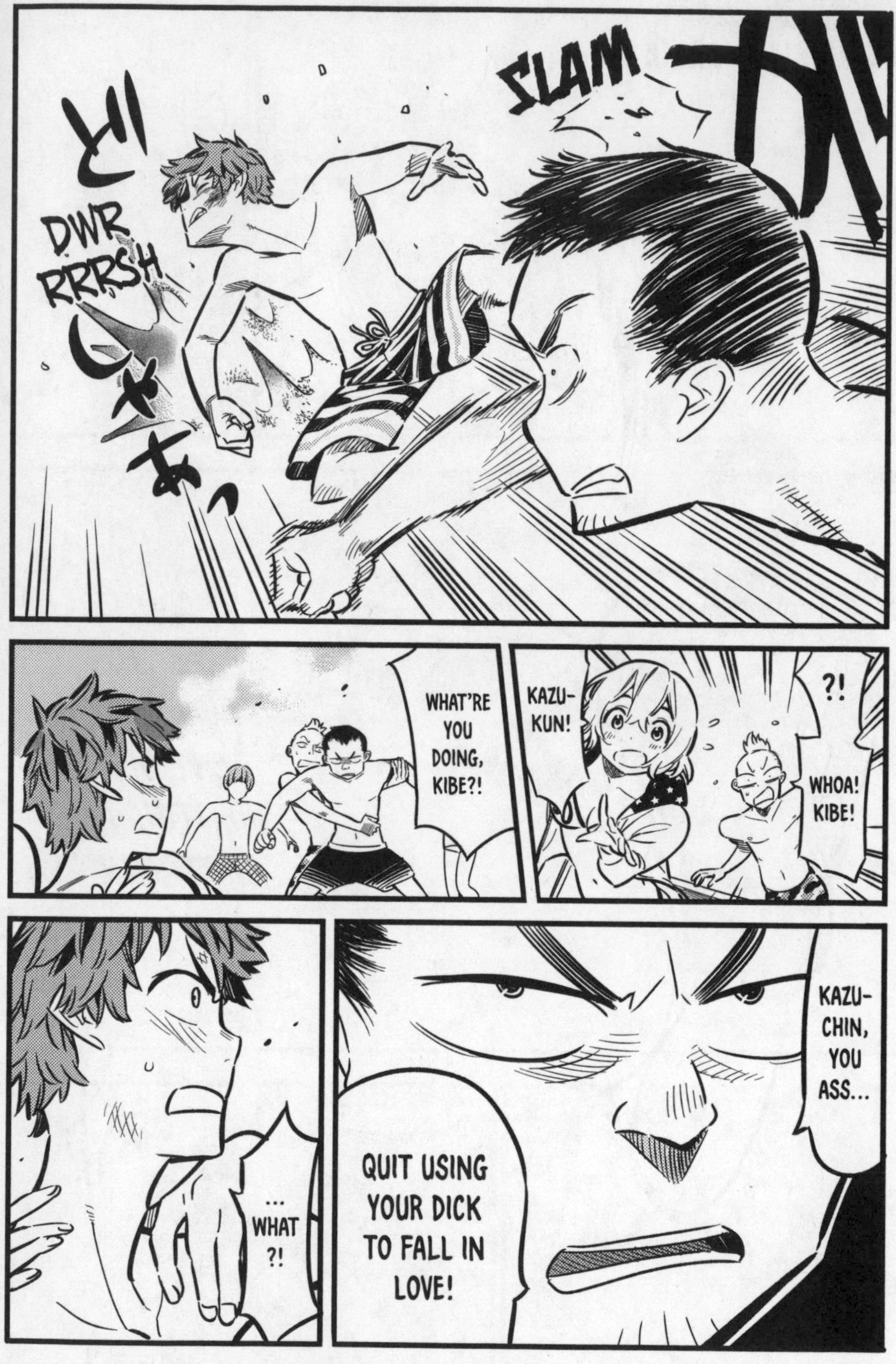
SLAM
DWR RRRSH
?!
WHOA! KIBE!
KAZU-KUN!
WHAT'RE YOU DOING, KIBE?!
KAZU-CHIN, YOU ASS...
QUIT USING YOUR DICK TO FALL IN LOVE!
... WHAT ?!

RATING 12
MY GIRLFRIEND AND A STREET-PUNK FIGHT

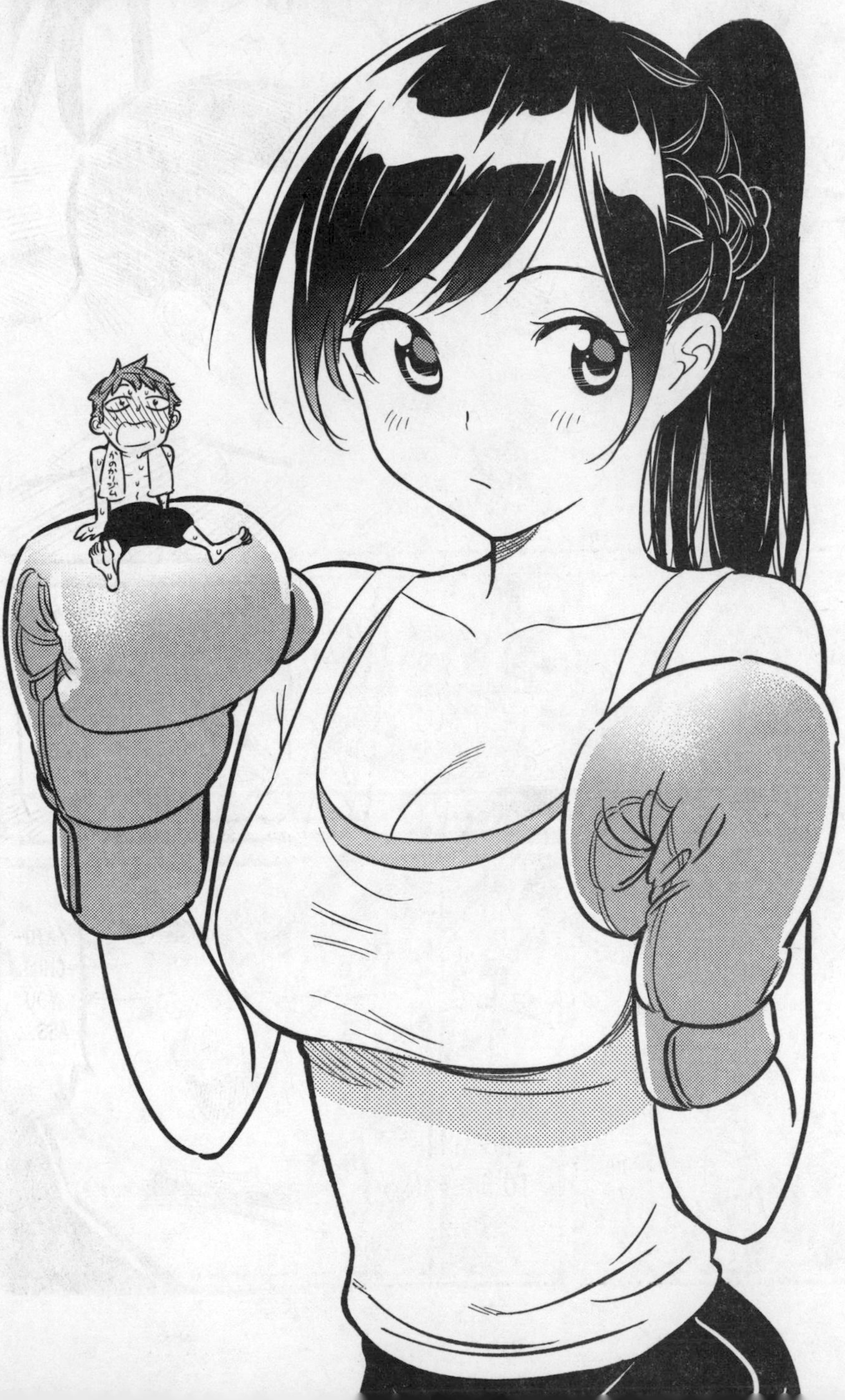

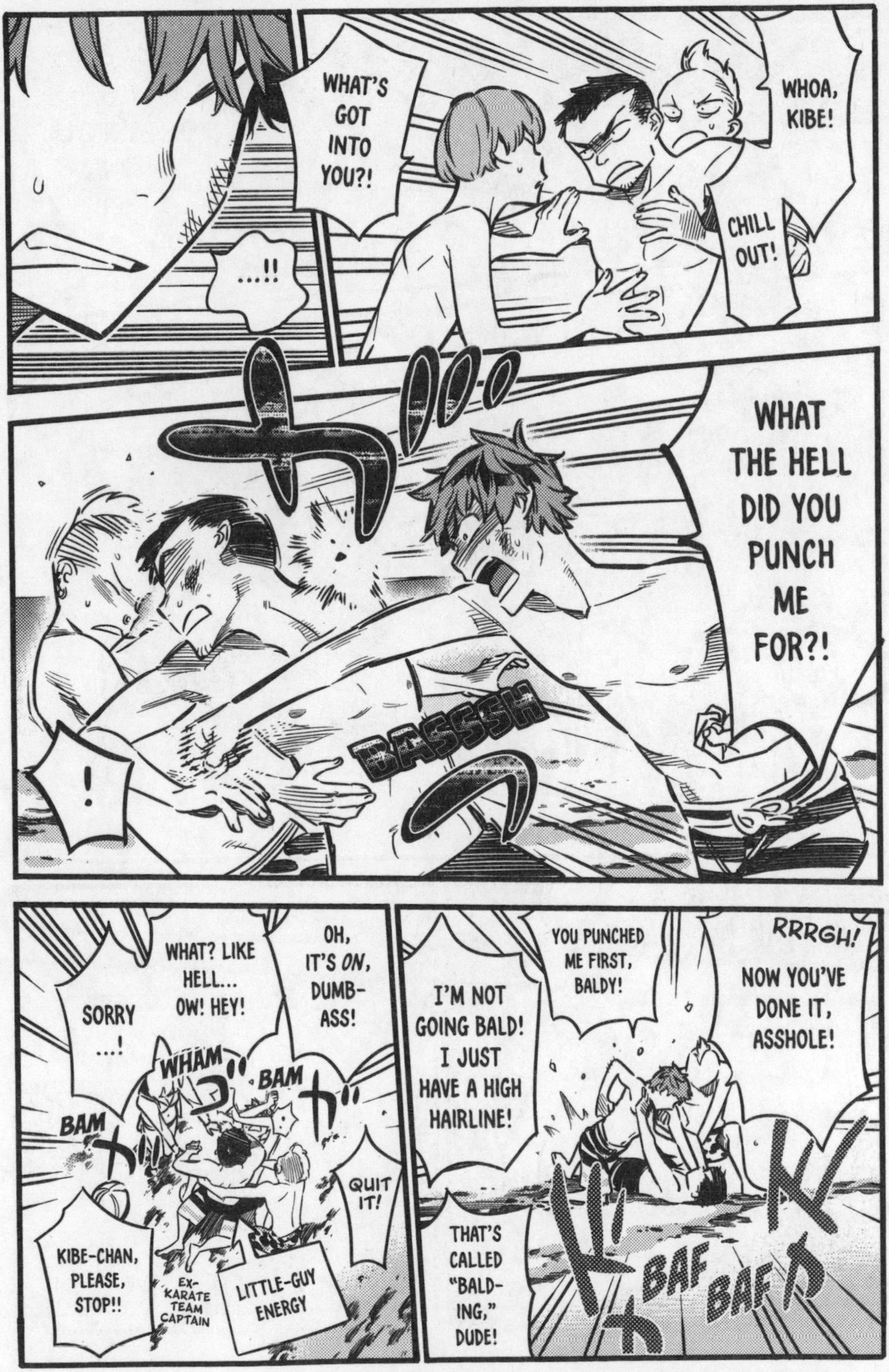
WHOA, KIBE!
CHILL OUT!
WHAT'S GOT INTO YOU?!
...!!
WHAT THE HELL DID YOU PUNCH ME FOR?!
BASSSH
!
RRRGH!
NOW YOU'VE DONE IT, ASSHOLE!
YOU PUNCHED ME FIRST, BALDY!
I'M NOT GOING BALD! I JUST HAVE A HIGH HAIRLINE!
THAT'S CALLED "BALDING," DUDE!
BAF
BAF
OH, IT'S *ON*, DUMB-ASS!
WHAT? LIKE HELL... OW! HEY!
SORRY ...!
BAM
WHAM
BAM
QUIT IT!
LITTLE-GUY ENERGY
EX-KARATE TEAM CAPTAIN
KIBE-CHAN, PLEASE, STOP!!

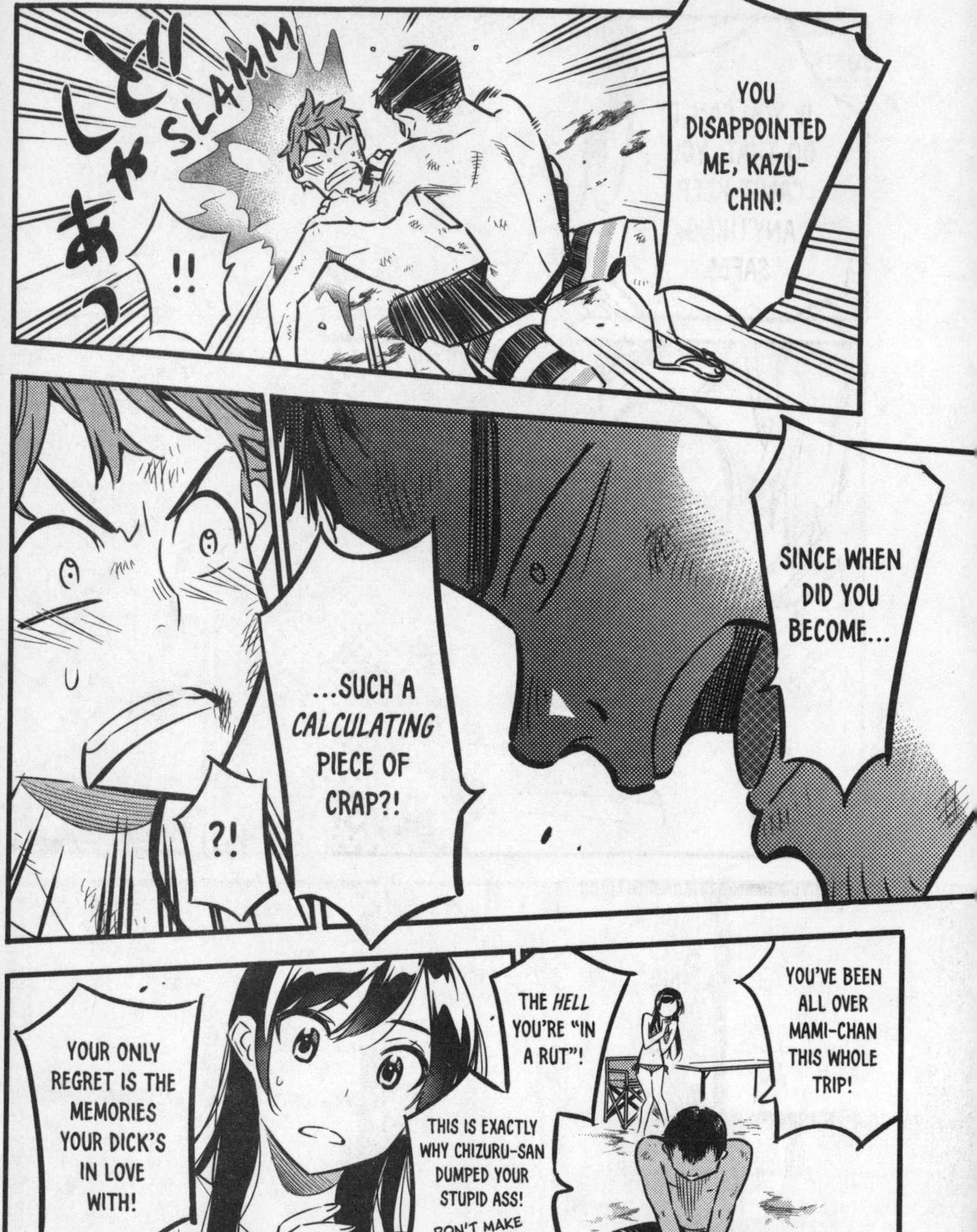

YOU DISAPPOINTED ME, KAZU-CHIN!
SLAMM
!!
SINCE WHEN DID YOU BECOME...
...SUCH A *CALCULATING* PIECE OF CRAP?!
?!
YOU'VE BEEN ALL OVER MAMI-CHAN THIS WHOLE TRIP!
THE *HELL* YOU'RE "IN A RUT"!
THIS IS EXACTLY WHY CHIZURU-SAN DUMPED YOUR STUPID ASS!
DON'T MAKE IT SOUND NICE.
YOUR ONLY REGRET IS THE MEMORIES YOUR DICK'S IN LOVE WITH!

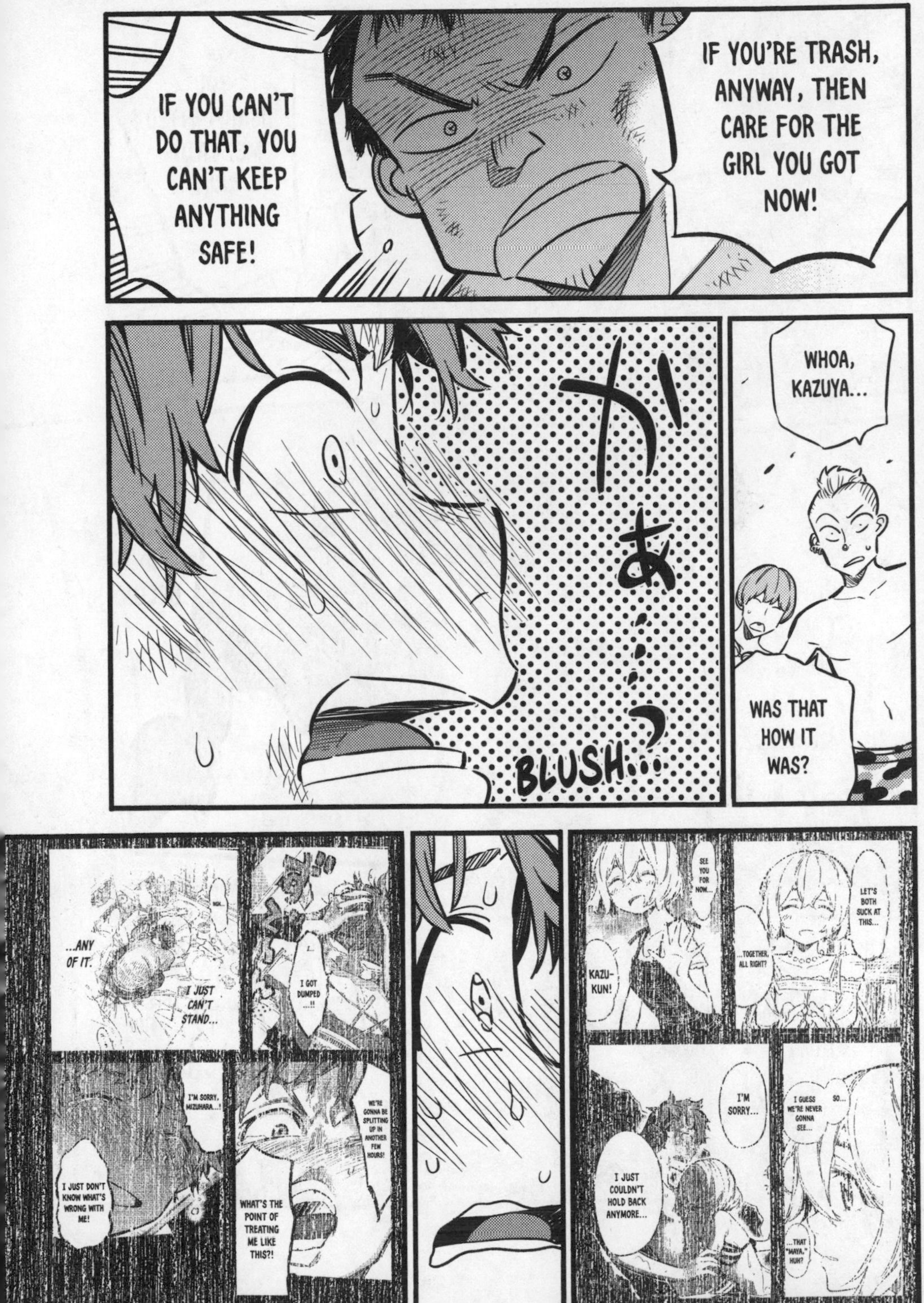
IF YOU'RE TRASH, ANYWAY, THEN CARE FOR THE GIRL YOU GOT NOW!
IF YOU CAN'T DO THAT, YOU CAN'T KEEP ANYTHING SAFE!
WHOA, KAZUYA...
WAS THAT HOW IT WAS?
かぁ…っ
BLUSH...
LET'S BOTH SUCK AT THIS...
...TOGETHER, ALL RIGHT?
SEE YOU FOR NOW...
KAZU-KUN!
SO...
I GUESS WE'RE NEVER GONNA SEE...
...THAT "MAYA," HUH?
I'M SORRY...
I JUST COULDN'T HOLD BACK ANYMORE...
I...
I GOT DUMPED...!!
...ANY OF IT.
I JUST CAN'T STAND...
WE'RE GONNA BE SPLITTING UP IN ANOTHER FEW HOURS!
WHAT'S THE POINT OF TREATING ME LIKE THIS?!
I'M SORRY, MIZUHARA...!
I JUST DON'T KNOW WHAT'S WRONG WITH ME!

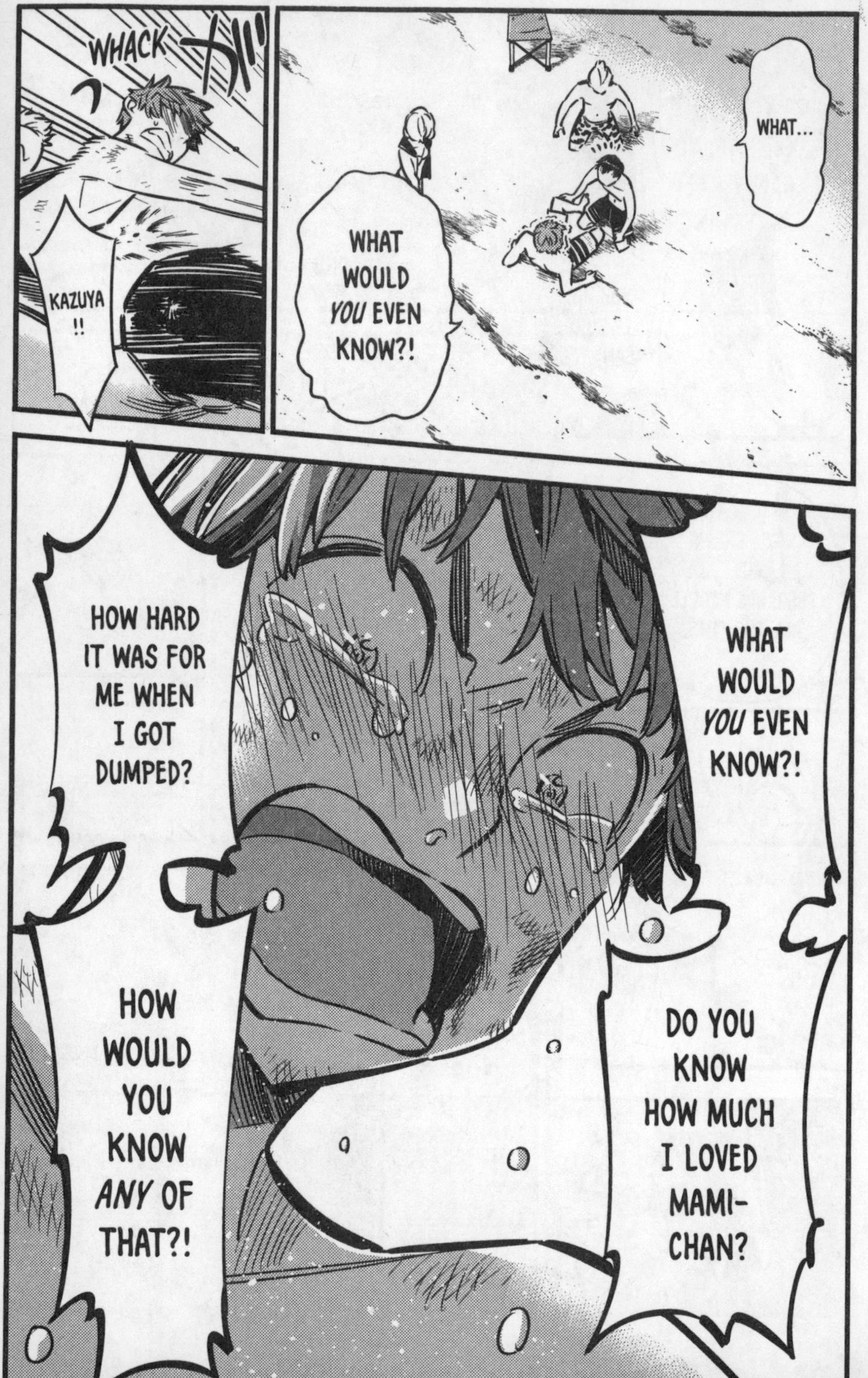
WHAT...
WHAT WOULD YOU EVEN KNOW?!
WHACK
KAZUYA !!
WHAT WOULD YOU EVEN KNOW?!
HOW HARD IT WAS FOR ME WHEN I GOT DUMPED?
DO YOU KNOW HOW MUCH I LOVED MAMI-CHAN?
HOW WOULD YOU KNOW ANY OF THAT?!

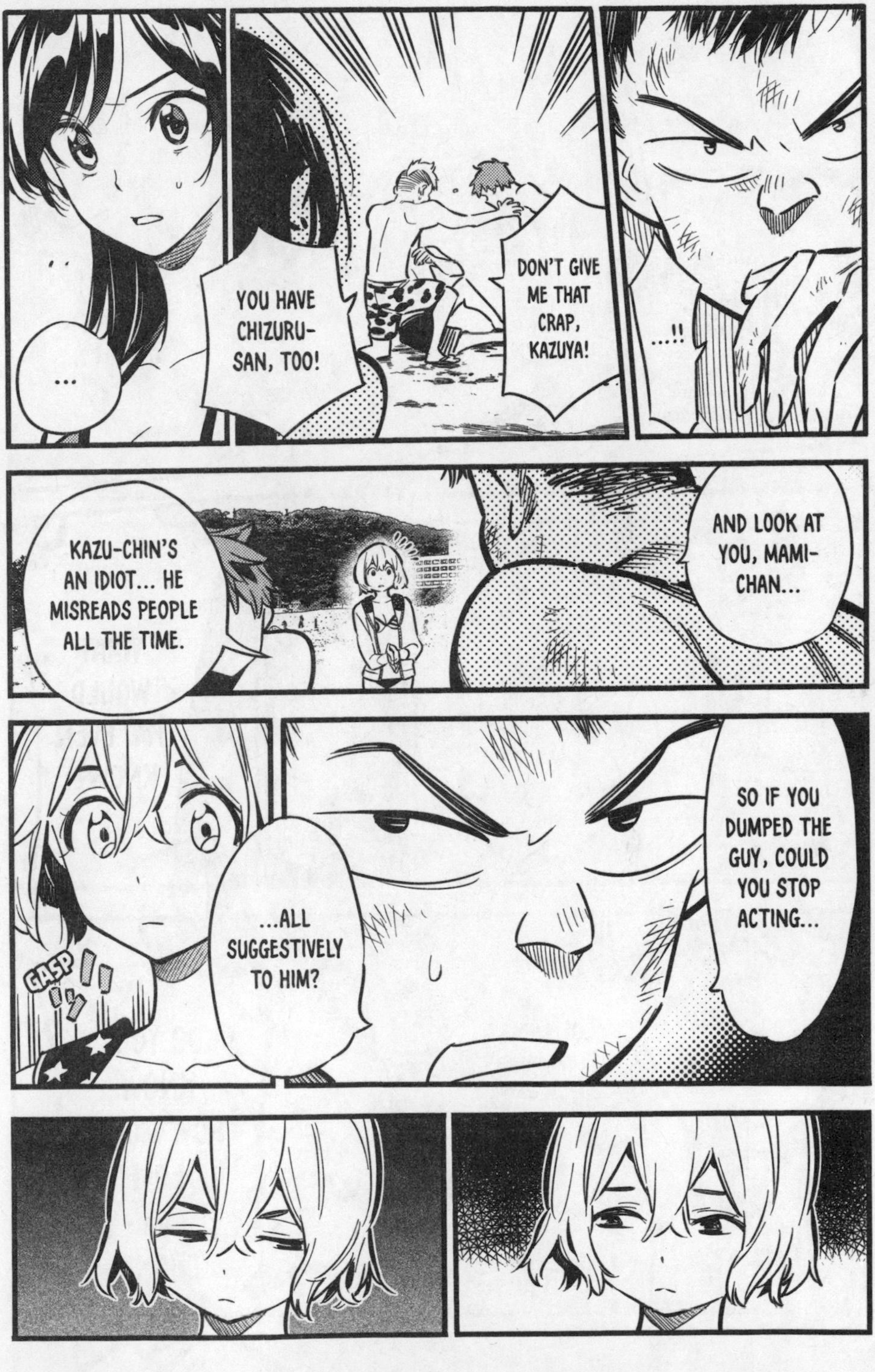
...!!
DON'T GIVE ME THAT CRAP, KAZUYA!
YOU HAVE CHIZURU-SAN, TOO!
...
...
AND LOOK AT YOU, MAMI-CHAN...
KAZU-CHIN'S AN IDIOT... HE MISREADS PEOPLE ALL THE TIME.
SO IF YOU DUMPED THE GUY, COULD YOU STOP ACTING...
...ALL SUGGESTIVELY TO HIM?
GASP

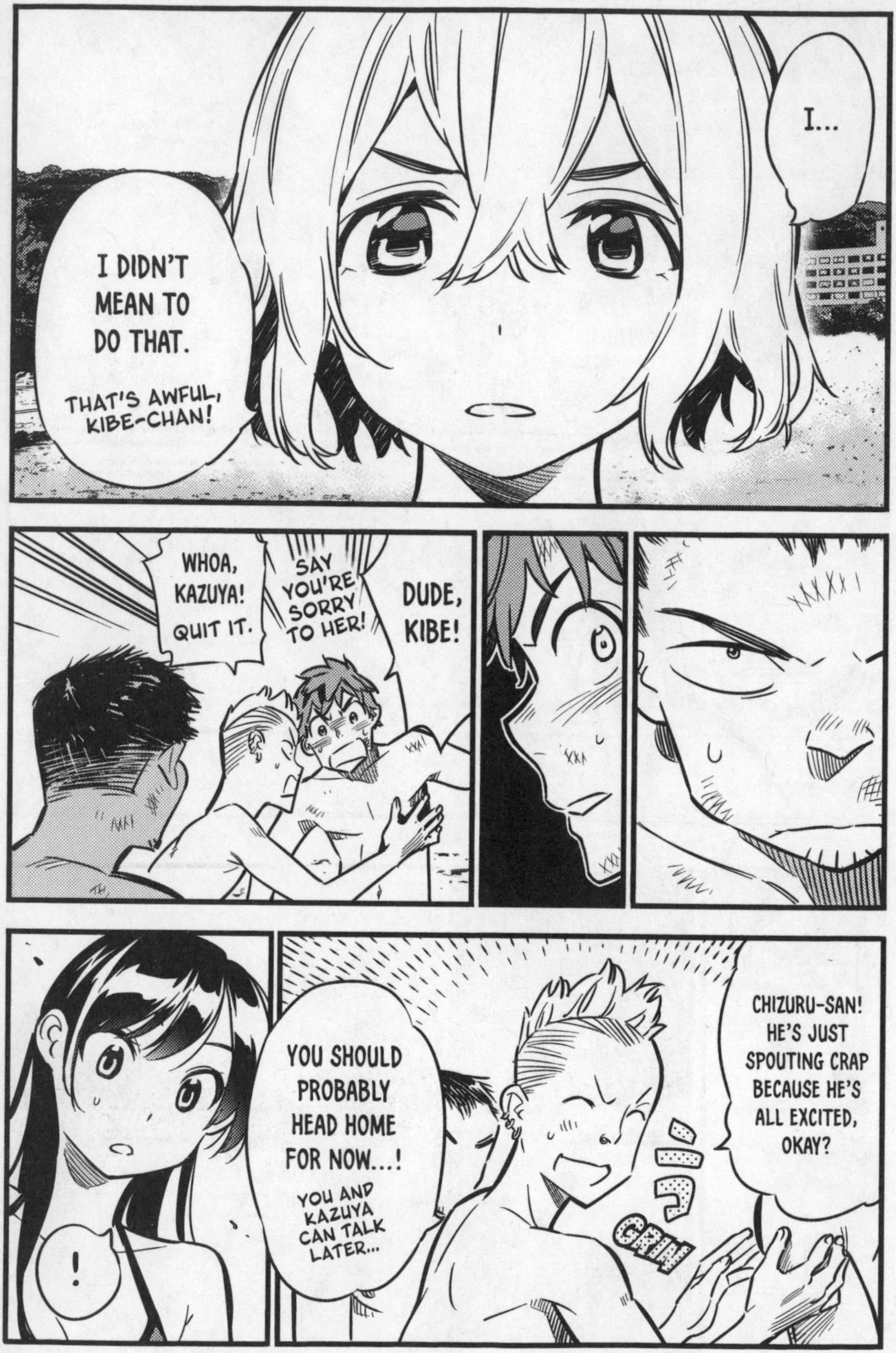
I...
I DIDN'T MEAN TO DO THAT.
THAT'S AWFUL, KIBE-CHAN!
DUDE, KIBE!
SAY YOU'RE SORRY TO HER!
WHOA, KAZUYA! QUIT IT.
CHIZURU-SAN! HE'S JUST SPOUTING CRAP BECAUSE HE'S ALL EXCITED, OKAY?
GRIN
YOU SHOULD PROBABLY HEAD HOME FOR NOW...!
YOU AND KAZUYA CAN TALK LATER...
!

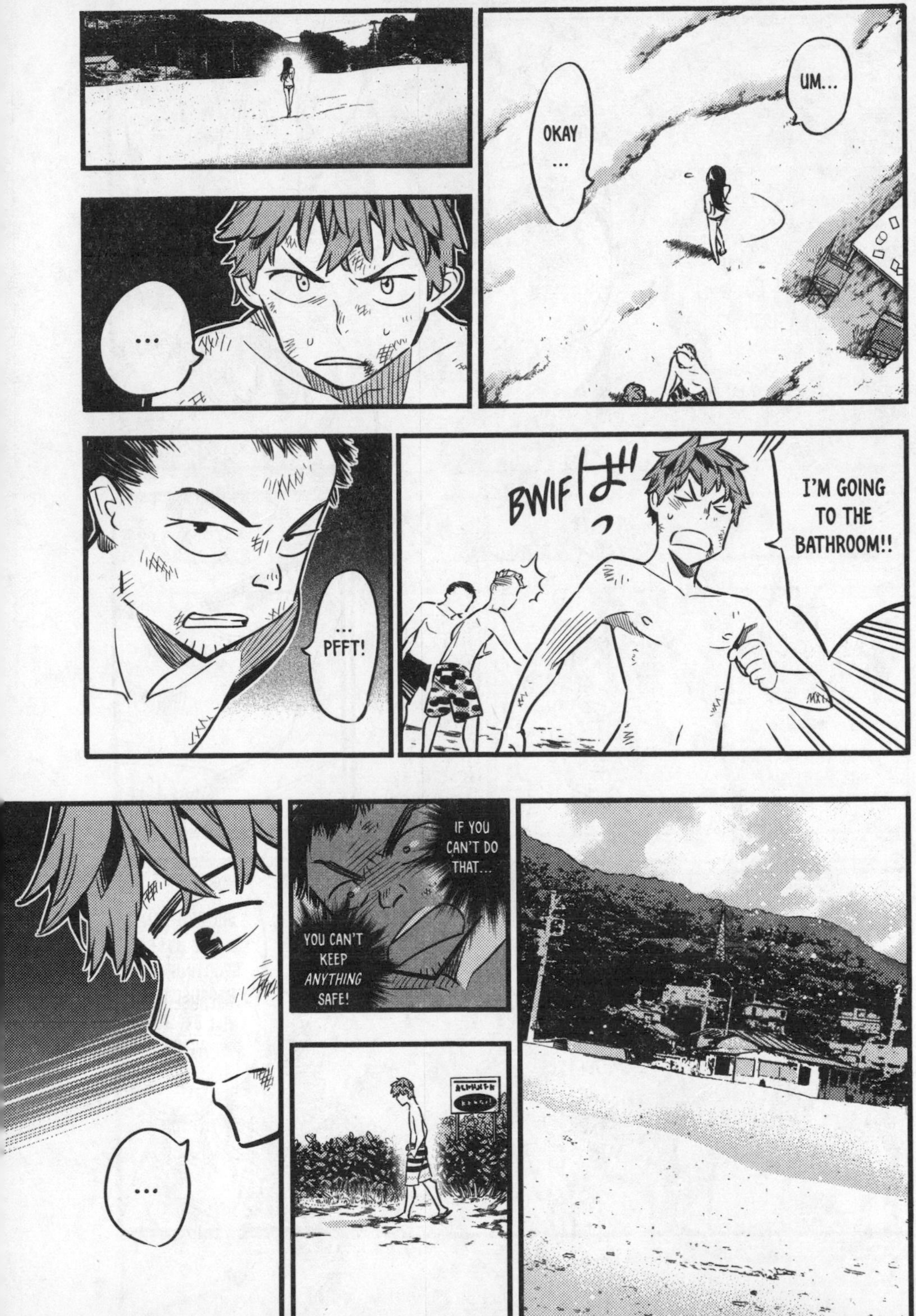
UM...
OKAY ...
...
I'M GOING TO THE BATHROOM!!
BWIF ばっ
... PFFT!
IF YOU CAN'T DO THAT...
YOU CAN'T KEEP *ANYTHING* SAFE!
...

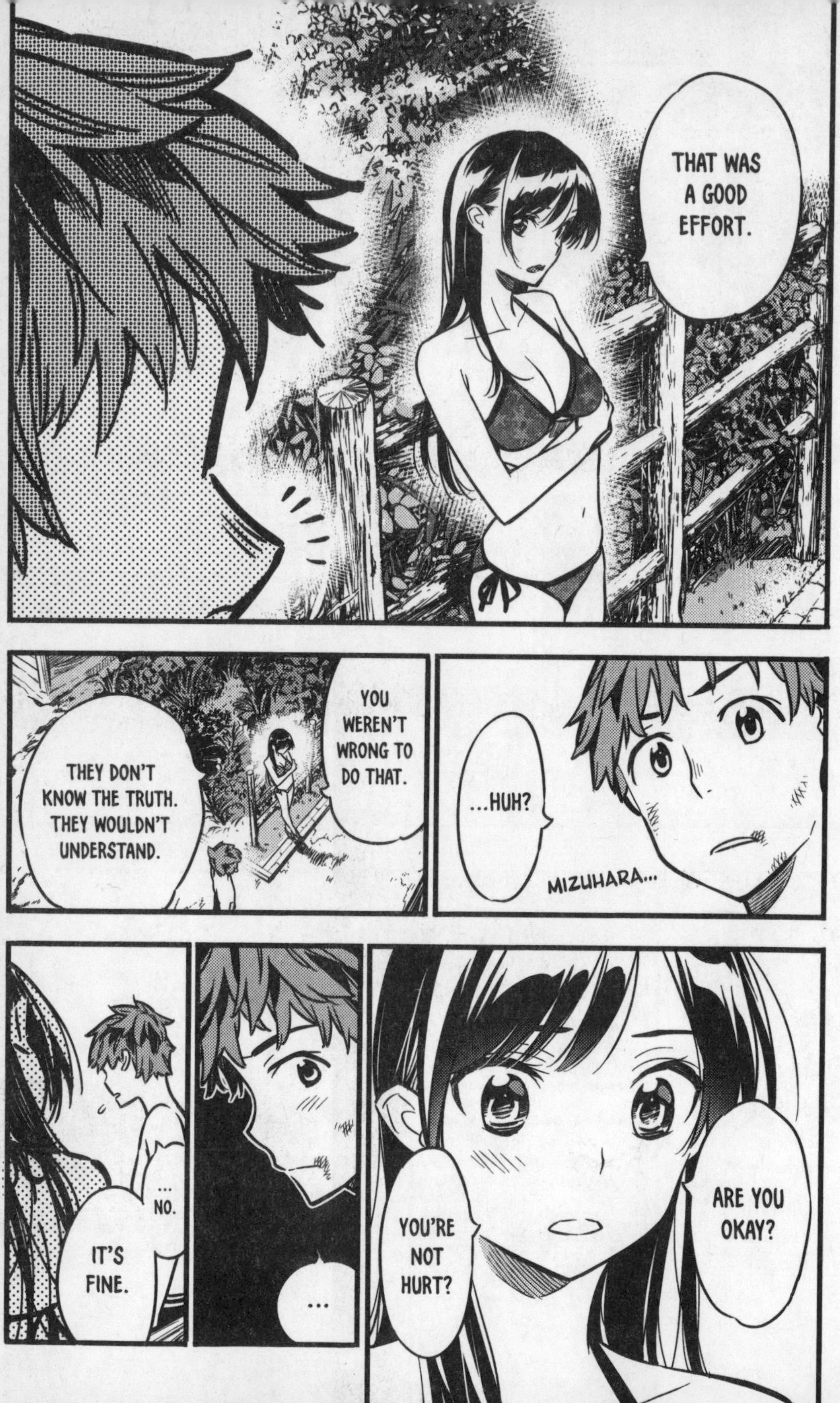
THAT WAS A GOOD EFFORT.
...HUH?
MIZUHARA...
YOU WEREN'T WRONG TO DO THAT.
THEY DON'T KNOW THE TRUTH. THEY WOULDN'T UNDERSTAND.
ARE YOU OKAY?
YOU'RE NOT HURT?
...
... NO.
IT'S FINE.

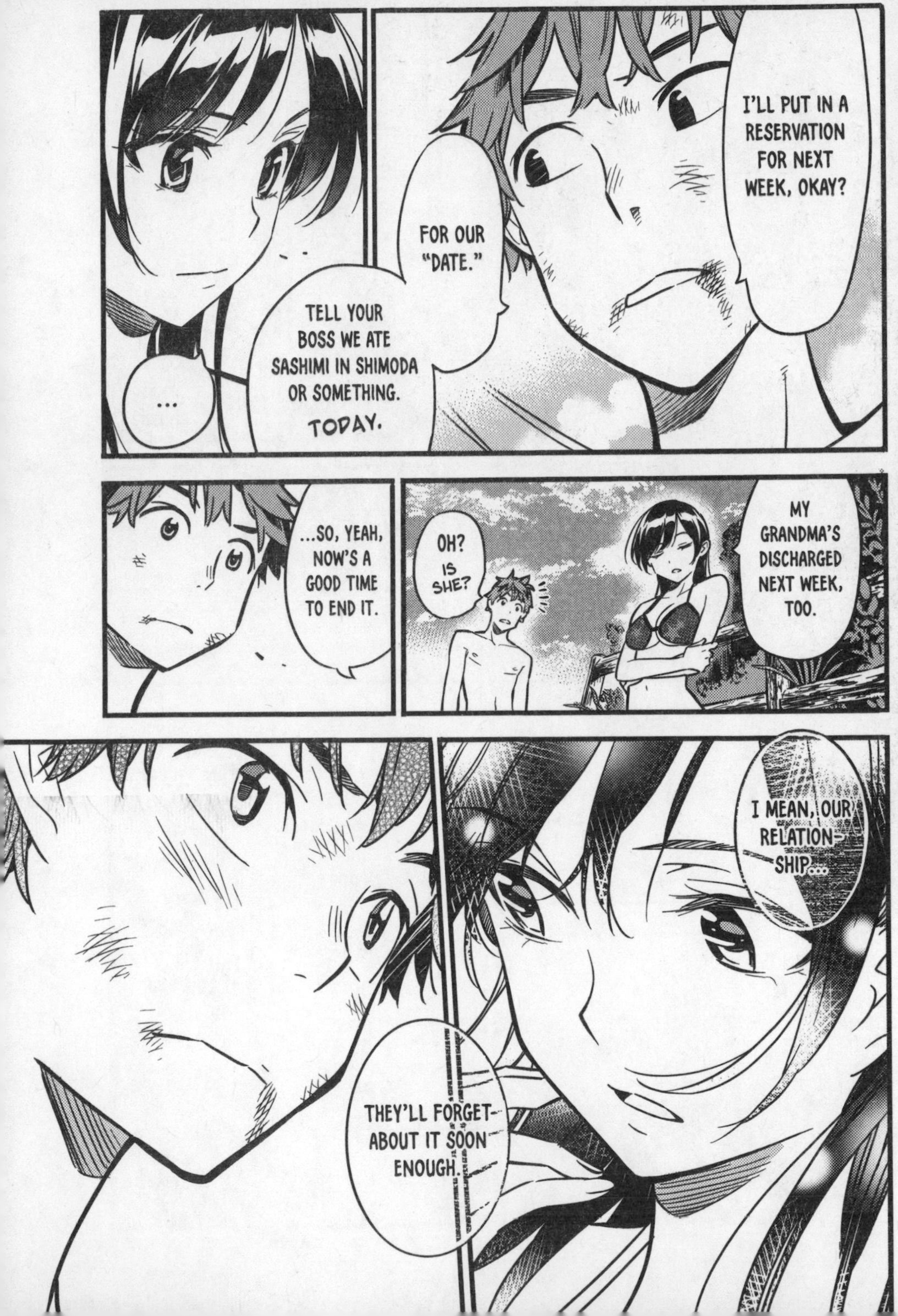
I'LL PUT IN A RESERVATION FOR NEXT WEEK, OKAY?
FOR OUR "DATE."
TELL YOUR BOSS WE ATE SASHIMI IN SHIMODA OR SOMETHING. TODAY.
...
MY GRANDMA'S DISCHARGED NEXT WEEK, TOO.
OH? IS SHE?
...SO, YEAH, NOW'S A GOOD TIME TO END IT.
I MEAN, OUR RELATION-SHIP...
THEY'LL FORGET-ABOUT IT SOON ENOUGH.

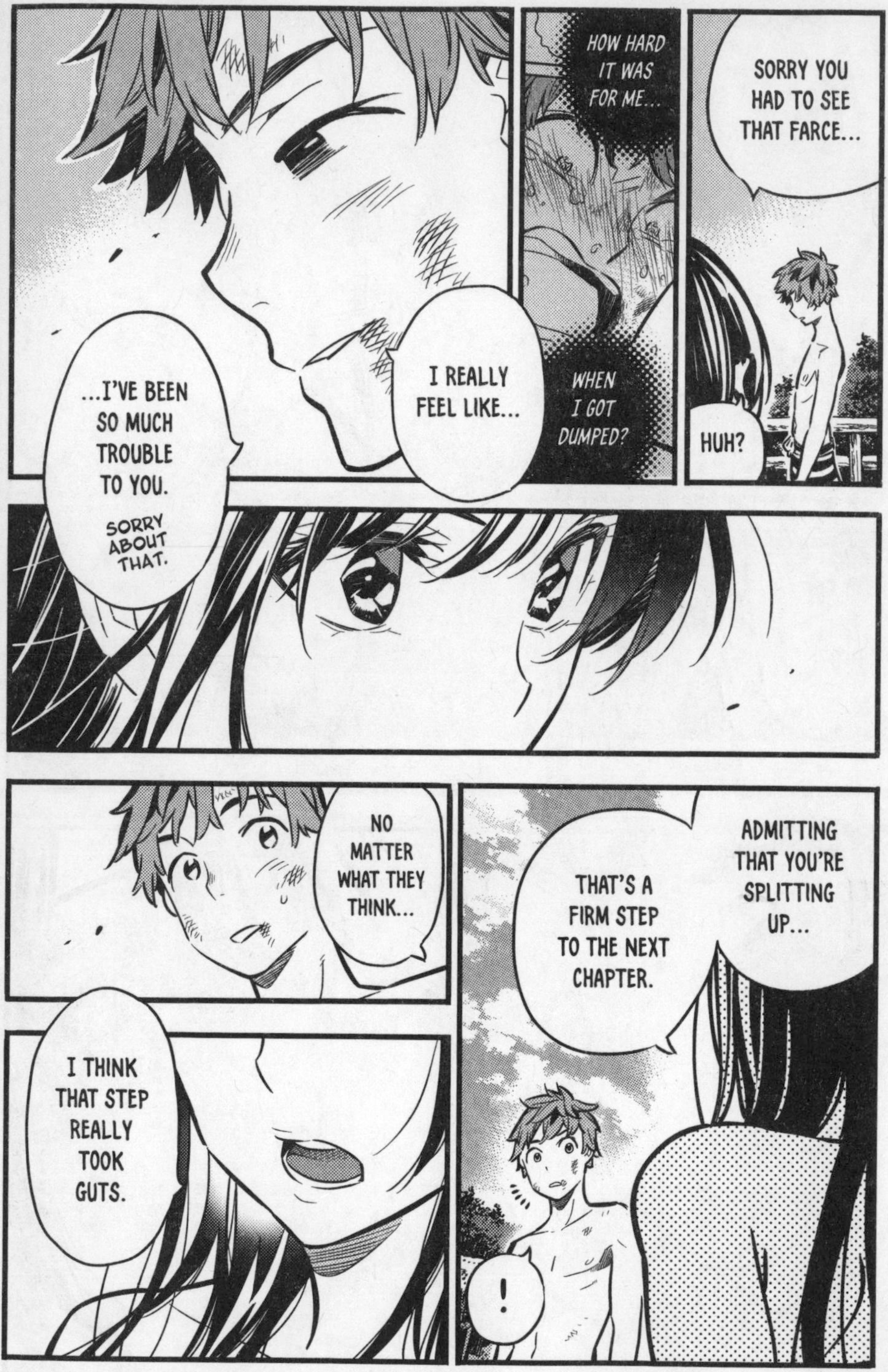
SORRY YOU HAD TO SEE THAT FARCE...
HUH?
HOW HARD IT WAS FOR ME...
WHEN I GOT DUMPED?
I REALLY FEEL LIKE...
...I'VE BEEN SO MUCH TROUBLE TO YOU.
SORRY ABOUT THAT.
ADMITTING THAT YOU'RE SPLITTING UP...
THAT'S A FIRM STEP TO THE NEXT CHAPTER.
!
NO MATTER WHAT THEY THINK...
I THINK THAT STEP REALLY TOOK GUTS.

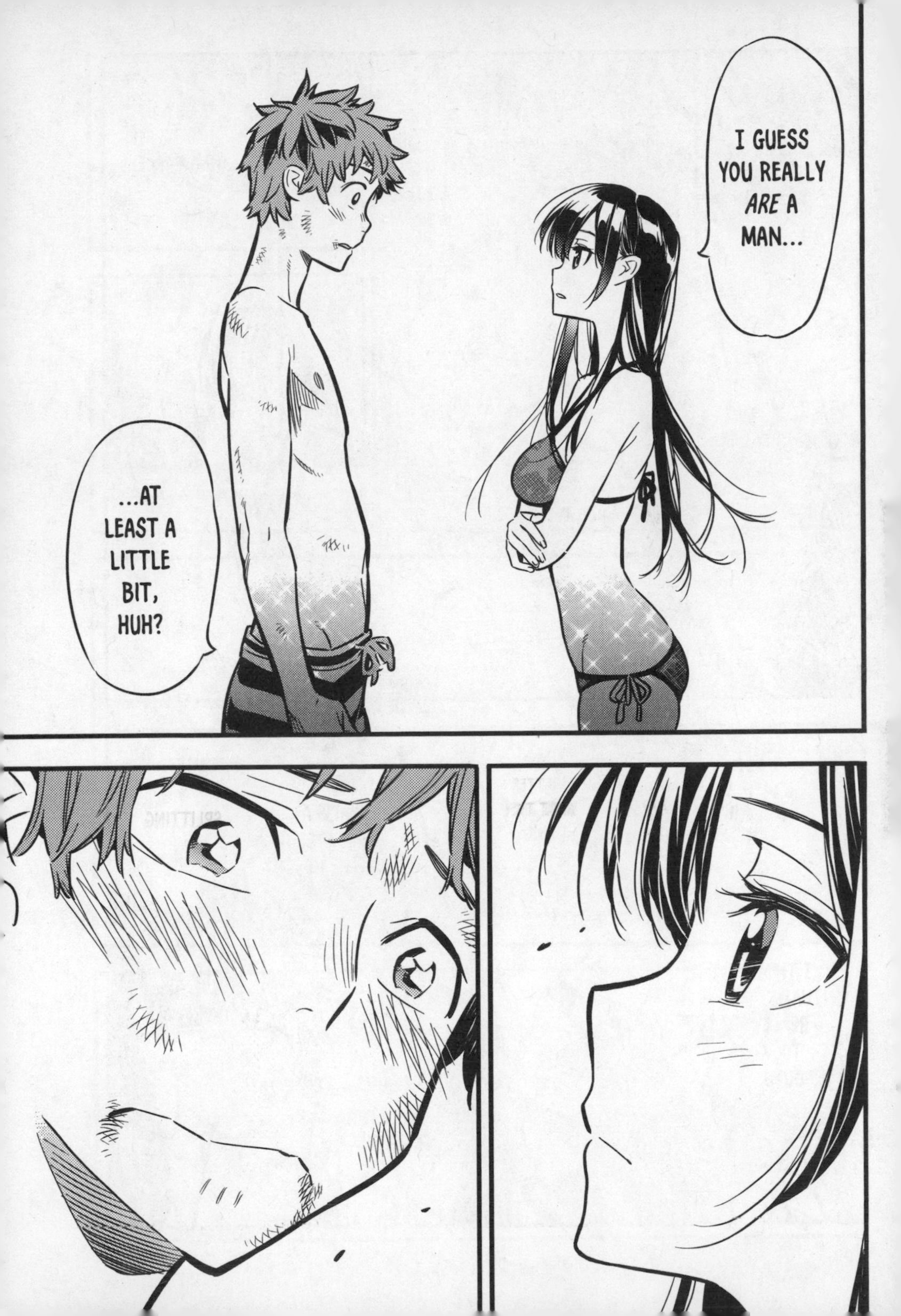
I GUESS YOU REALLY *ARE* A MAN...
...AT LEAST A LITTLE BIT, HUH?

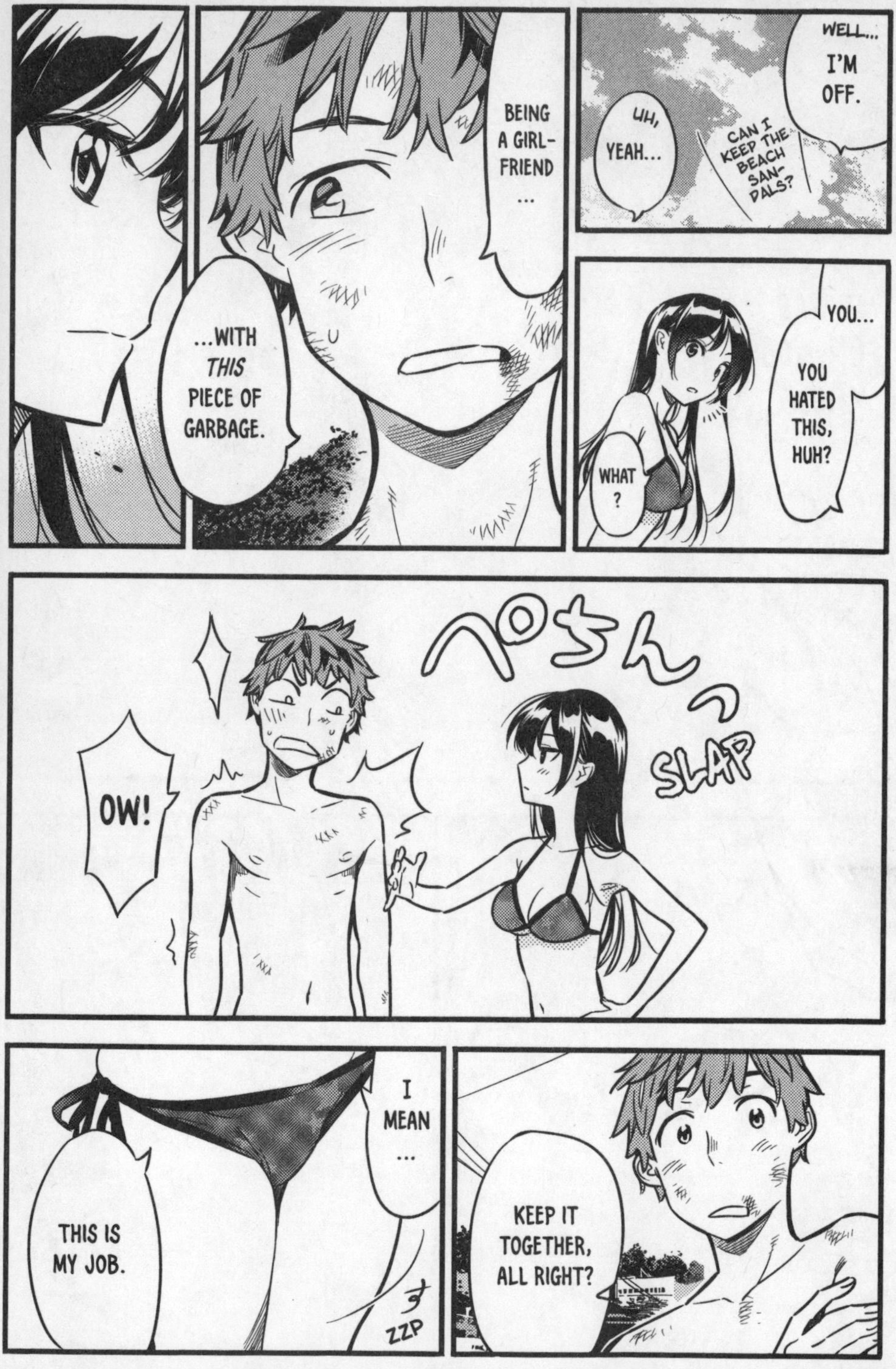
WELL... I'M OFF.
CAN I KEEP THE BEACH SANDALS?
UH, YEAH...
YOU... YOU HATED THIS, HUH?
WHAT?
BEING A GIRL-FRIEND...
...WITH *THIS* PIECE OF GARBAGE.
ぺちんっ
SLAP
OW!
KEEP IT TOGETHER, ALL RIGHT?
I MEAN...
THIS IS MY JOB.
す
ZZP

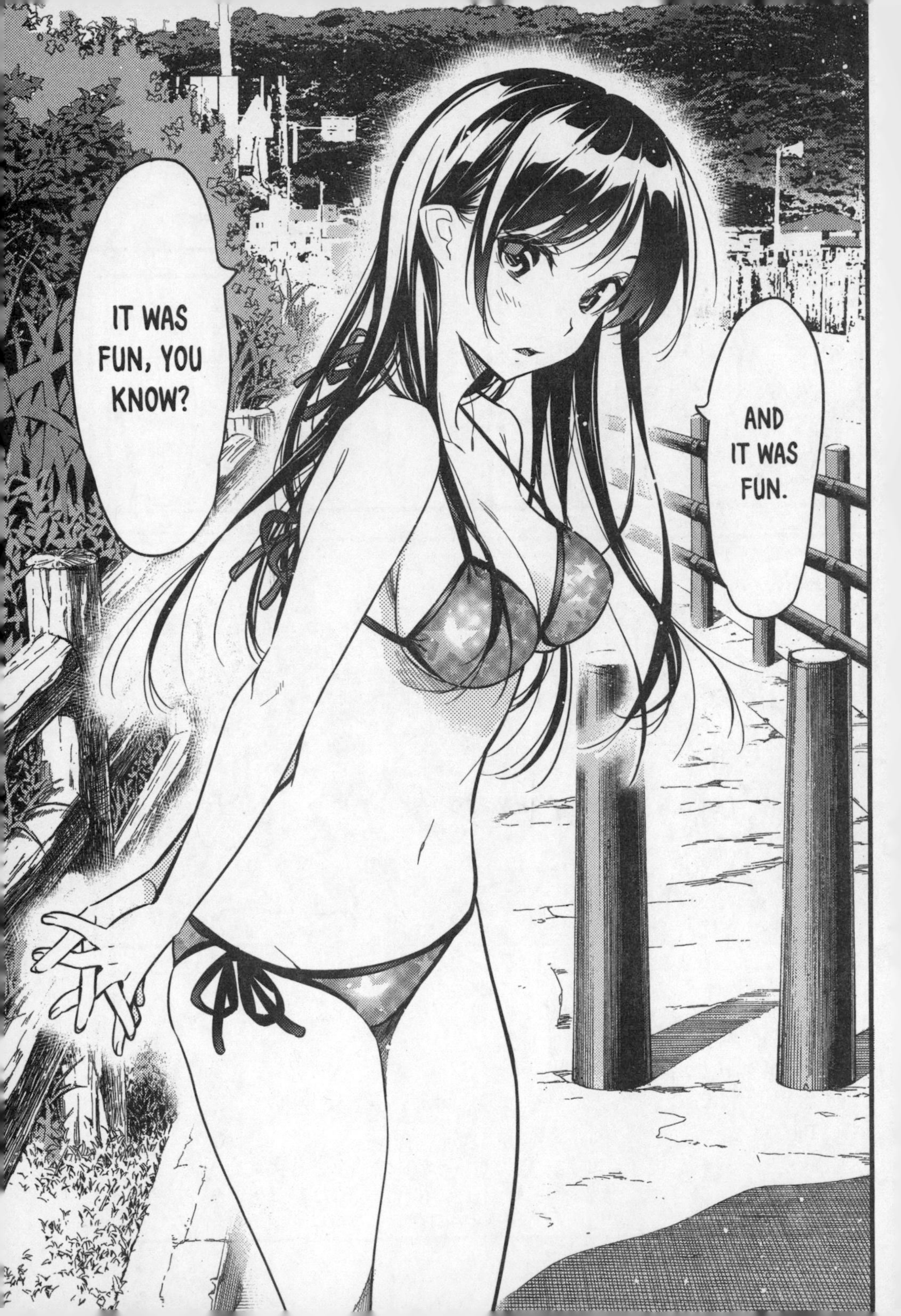
AND IT WAS FUN.
IT WAS FUN, YOU KNOW?

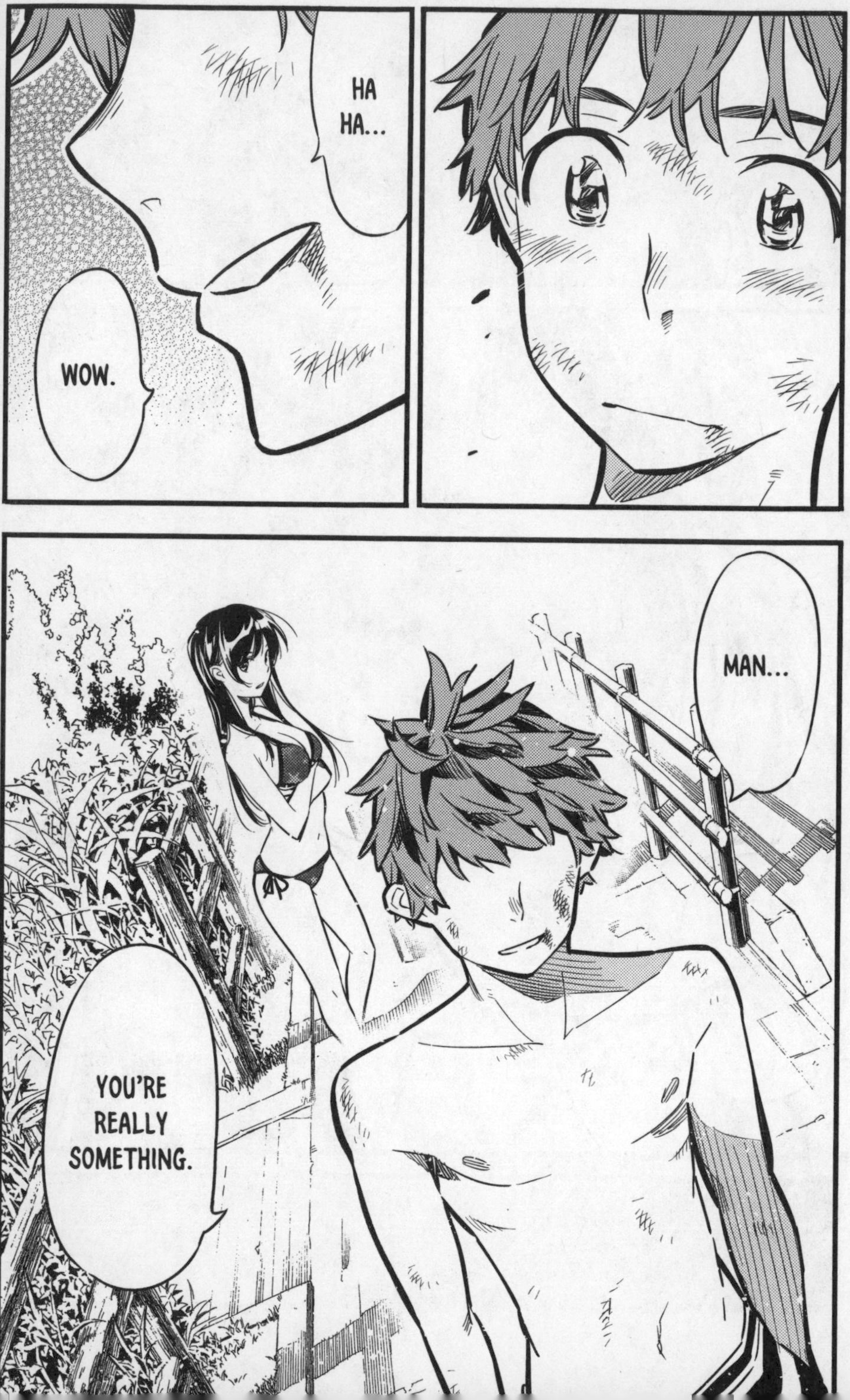
HA HA...
WOW.
MAN...
YOU'RE REALLY SOMETHING.

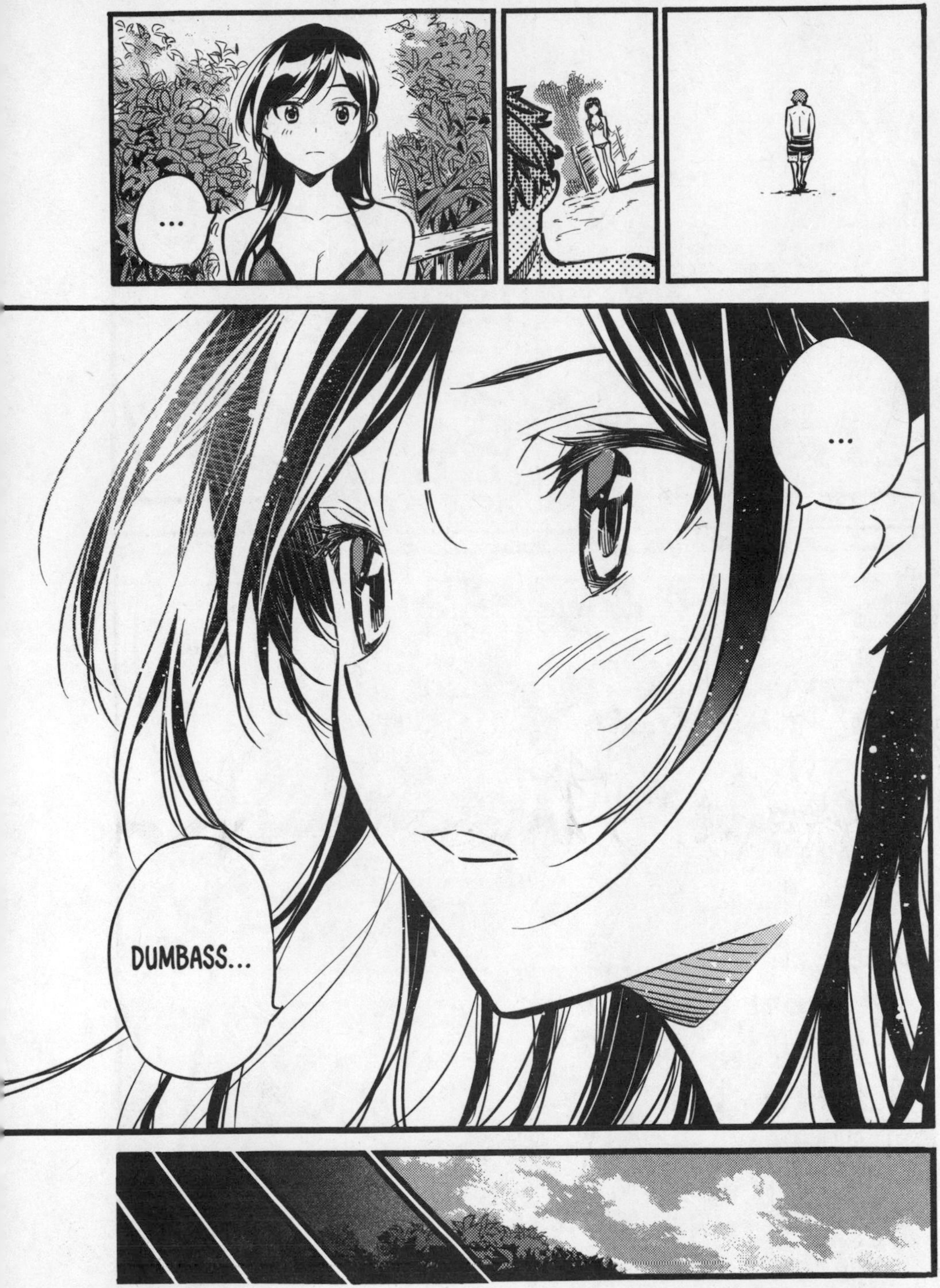
...
...
DUMBASS...

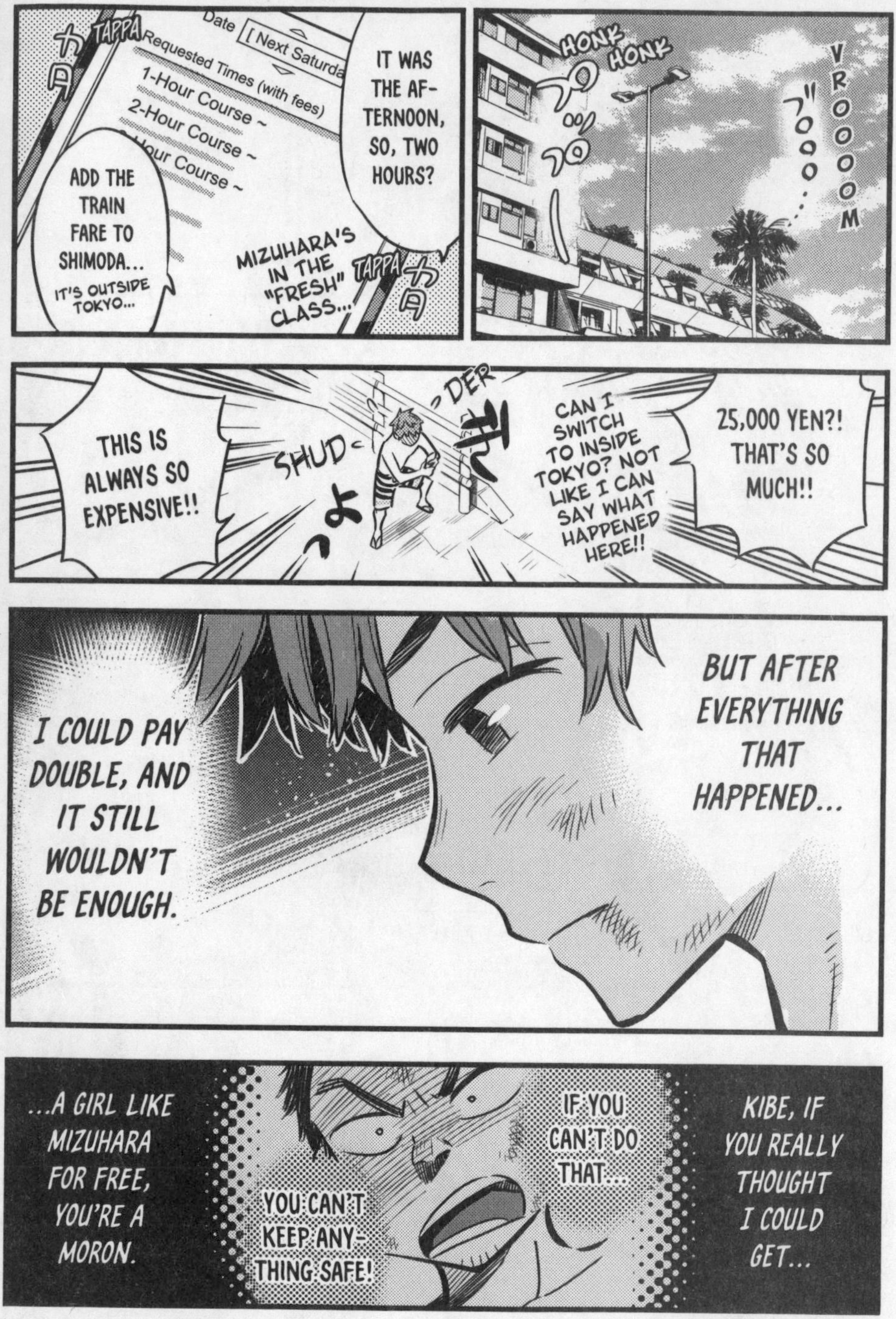
HONK HONK
VROOOOOM
IT WAS THE AFTERNOON, SO, TWO HOURS?
TAPPA
Date [Next Saturda
Requested Times (with fees)
1-Hour Course ~
2-Hour Course ~
Hour Course ~
MIZUHARA'S IN THE "FRESH" CLASS...
TAPPA
ADD THE TRAIN FARE TO SHIMODA...
IT'S OUTSIDE TOKYO...
25,000 YEN?! THAT'S SO MUCH!!
CAN I SWITCH TO INSIDE TOKYO? NOT LIKE I CAN SAY WHAT HAPPENED HERE!!
DER
SHUD
THIS IS ALWAYS SO EXPENSIVE!!
BUT AFTER EVERYTHING THAT HAPPENED...
I COULD PAY DOUBLE, AND IT STILL WOULDN'T BE ENOUGH.
KIBE, IF YOU REALLY THOUGHT I COULD GET...
IF YOU CAN'T DO THAT...
YOU CAN'T KEEP ANYTHING SAFE!
...A GIRL LIKE MIZUHARA FOR FREE, YOU'RE A MORON.

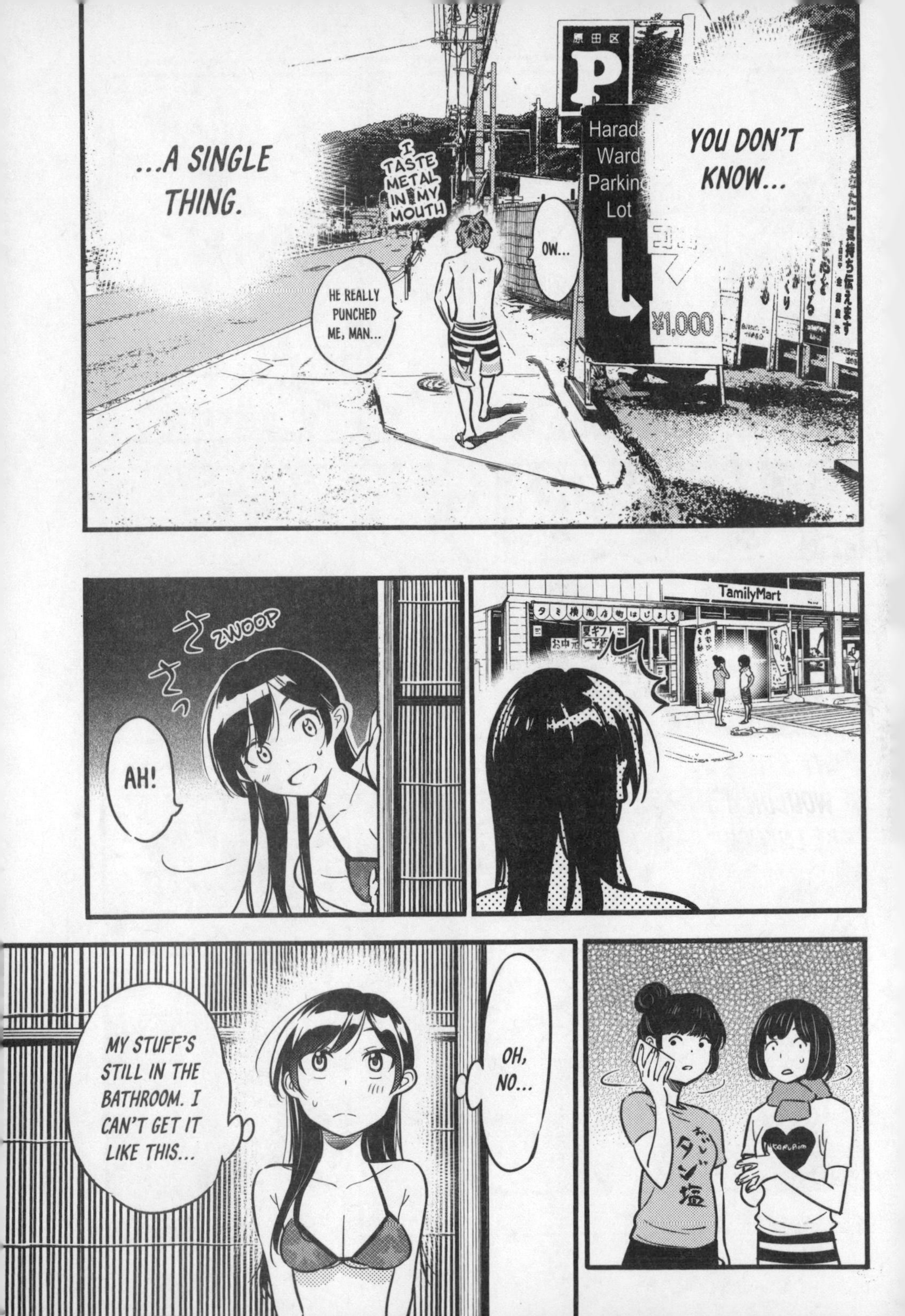
Harada Ward Parking Lot
¥1,000
YOU DON'T KNOW...
...A SINGLE THING.
OW...
I TASTE METAL IN MY MOUTH
HE REALLY PUNCHED ME, MAN...
TamilyMart
ZWOOP
AH!
OH, NO...
MY STUFF'S STILL IN THE BATHROOM. I CAN'T GET IT LIKE THIS...

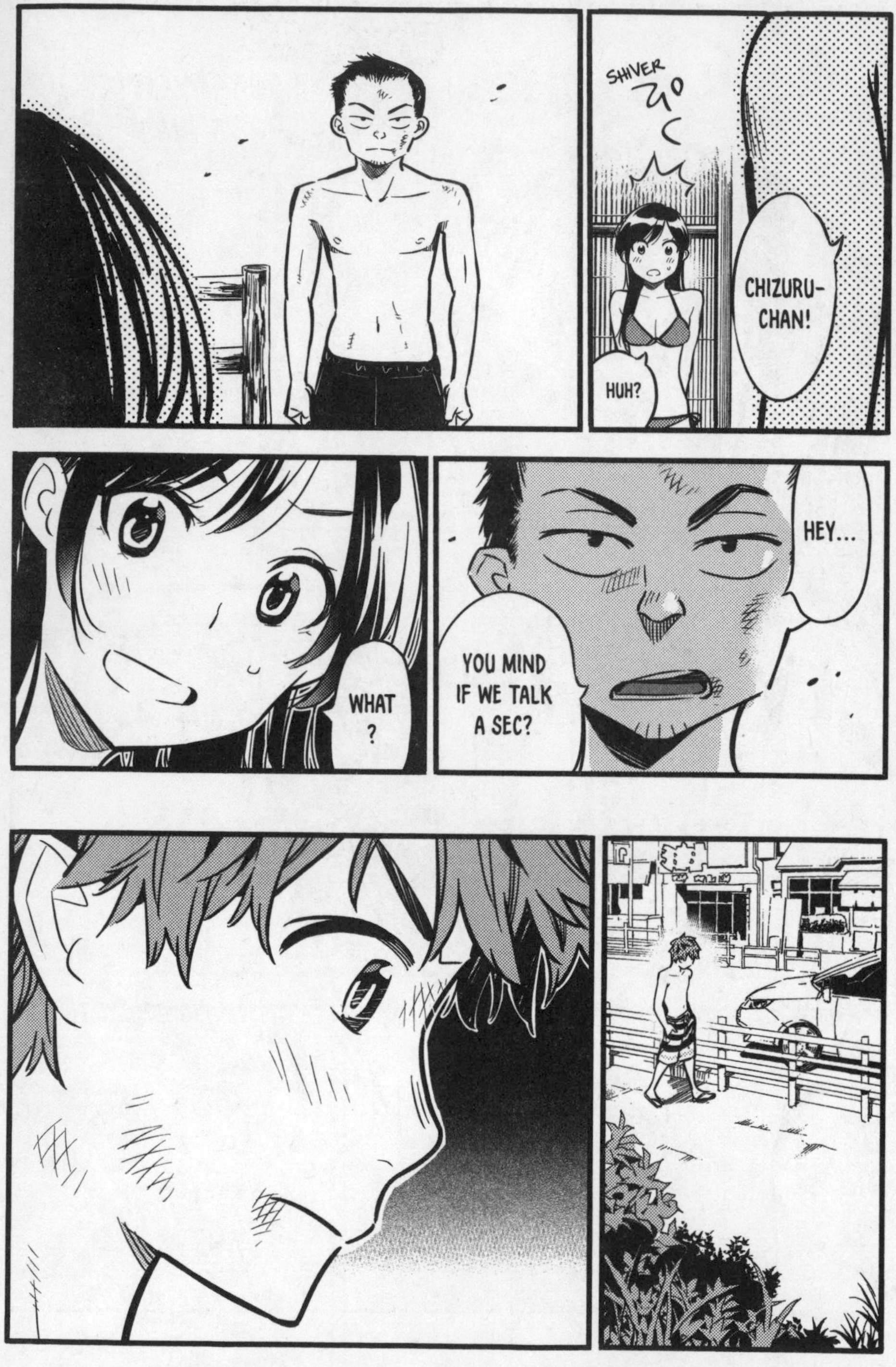
CHIZURU-CHAN!
SHIVER
HUH?
HEY...
YOU MIND IF WE TALK A SEC?
WHAT ?

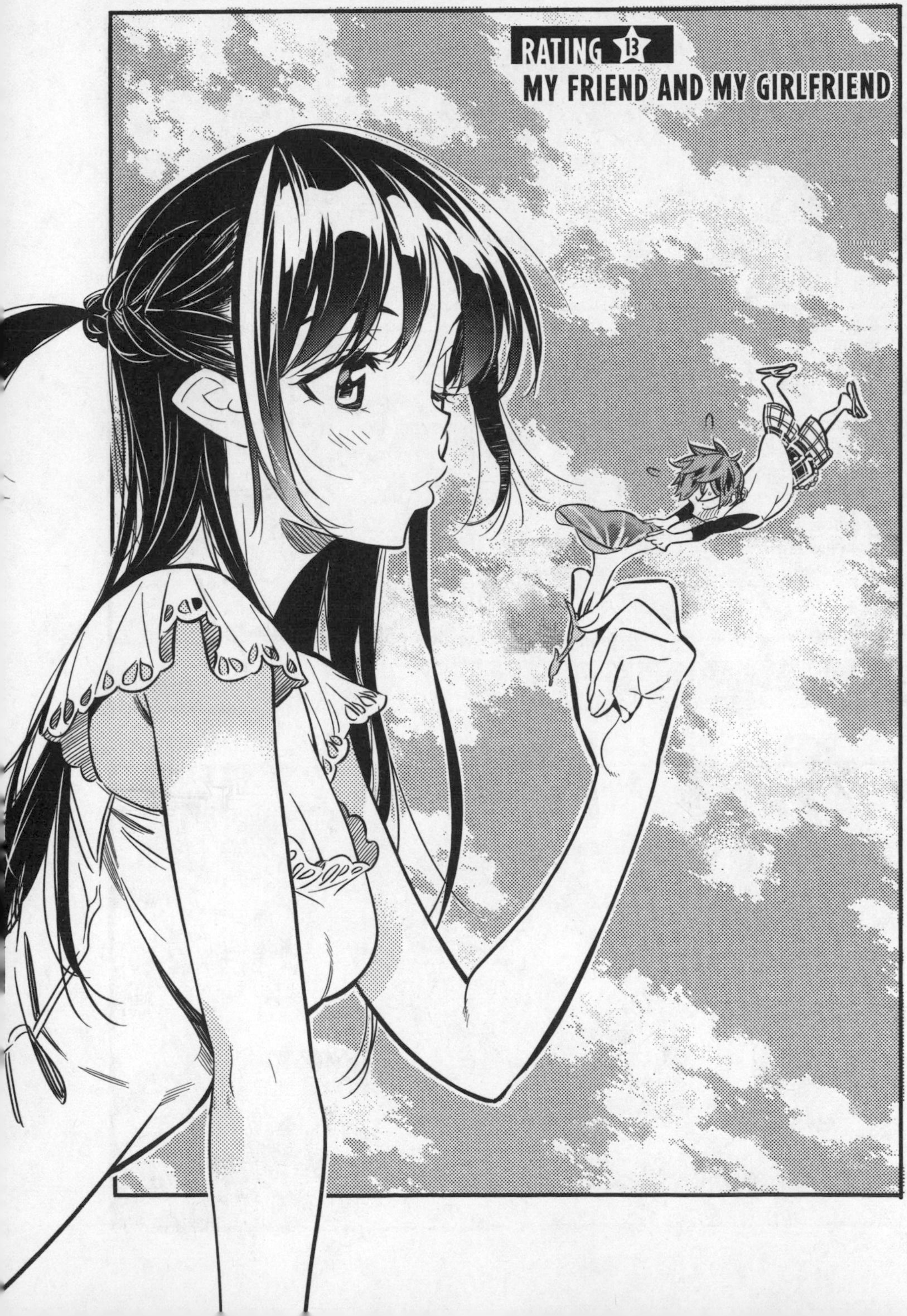
RATING 13
MY FRIEND AND MY GIRLFRIEND

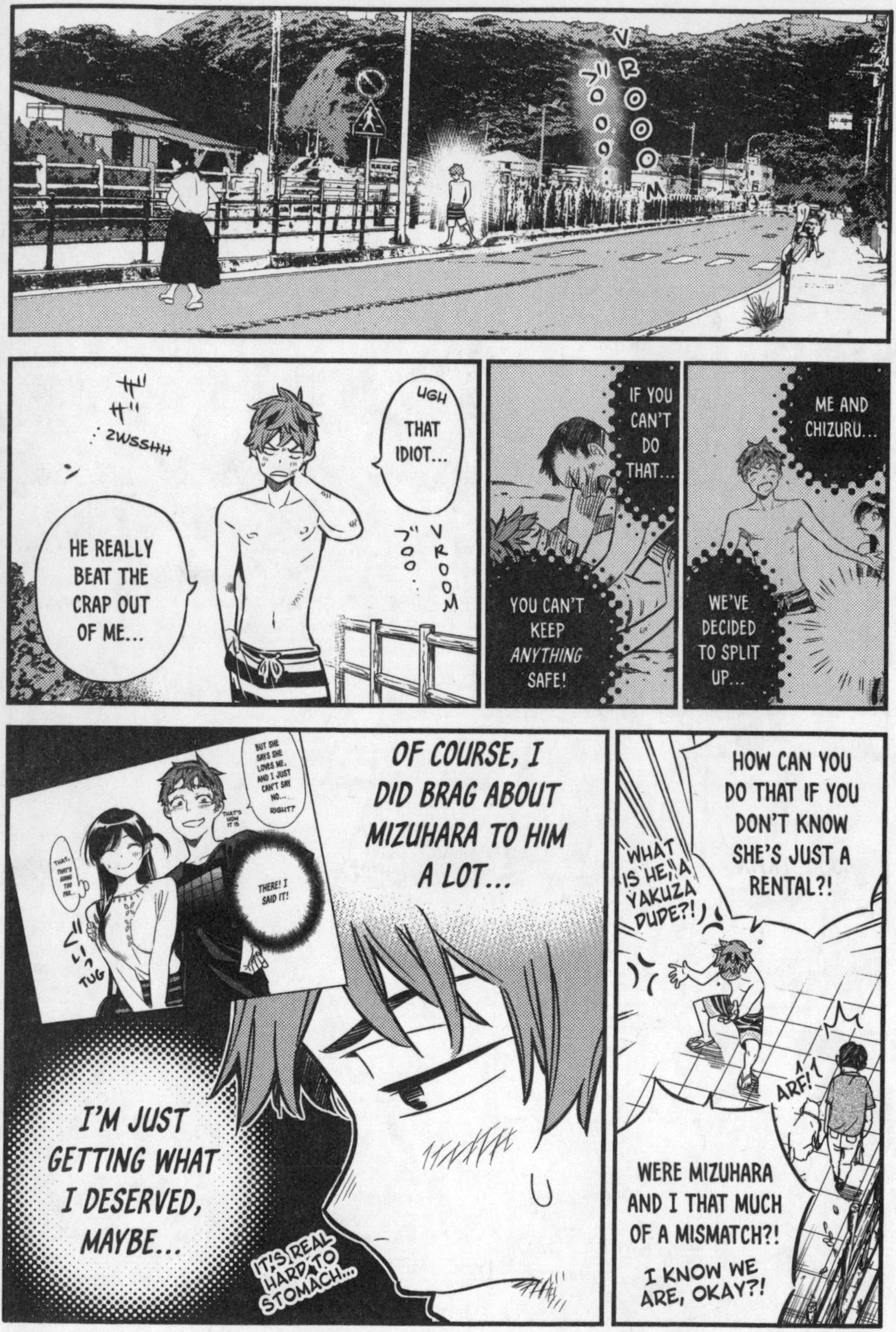
VROOOOM
ME AND CHIZURU...
WE'VE DECIDED TO SPLIT UP...
IF YOU CAN'T DO THAT...
YOU CAN'T KEEP ANYTHING SAFE!
UGH
THAT IDIOT...
ZWSSHH
VROOOM
HE REALLY BEAT THE CRAP OUT OF ME...
HOW CAN YOU DO THAT IF YOU DON'T KNOW SHE'S JUST A RENTAL?!
WHAT IS HE, A YAKUZA DUDE?!
ARF!
WERE MIZUHARA AND I THAT MUCH OF A MISMATCH?!
I KNOW WE ARE, OKAY?!
OF COURSE, I DID BRAG ABOUT MIZUHARA TO HIM A LOT...
BUT SHE SAYS SHE LOVES ME, AND I JUST CAN'T SAY NO... RIGHT?
THAT'S HOW IT IS
THAT, THAT'S GOING TOO FAR...
THERE! I SAID IT!
TUG
I'M JUST GETTING WHAT I DESERVED, MAYBE...
IT'S REAL HARD TO STOMACH...

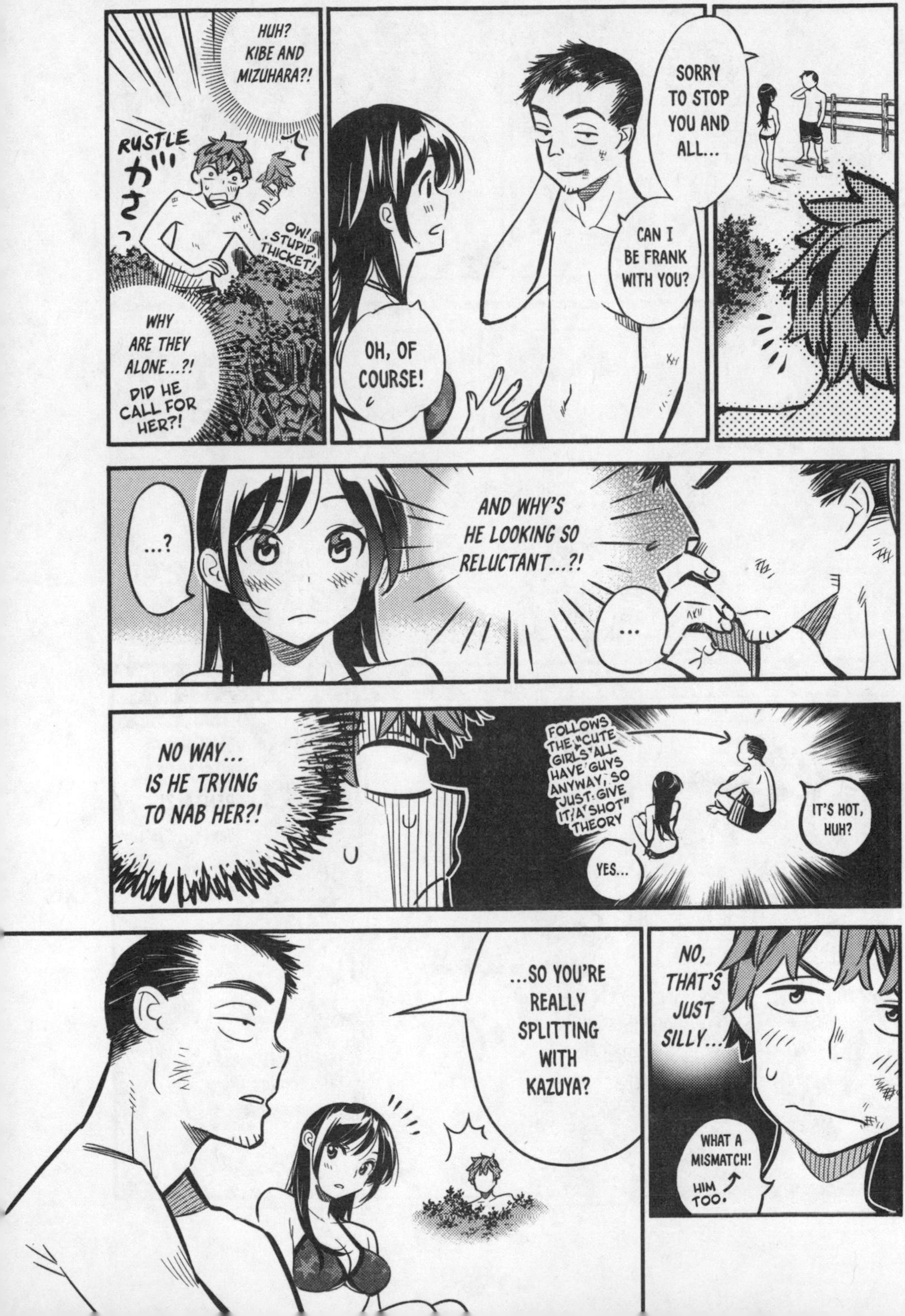
SORRY TO STOP YOU AND ALL...
CAN I BE FRANK WITH YOU?
OH, OF COURSE!
HUH? KIBE AND MIZUHARA?!
RUSTLE
がさっ
OW! STUPID THICKET!
WHY ARE THEY ALONE...?! DID HE CALL FOR HER?!
...
AND WHY'S HE LOOKING SO RELUCTANT...?!
...?
IT'S HOT, HUH?
YES...
FOLLOWS THE "CUTE GIRLS ALL HAVE GUYS ANYWAY, SO JUST GIVE IT A SHOT" THEORY
NO WAY... IS HE TRYING TO NAB HER?!
NO, THAT'S JUST SILLY...
WHAT A MISMATCH!
HIM TOO.
...SO YOU'RE REALLY SPLITTING WITH KAZUYA?

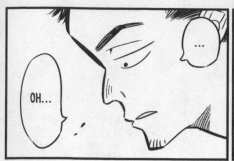

UM...
YEAH ...
...
OH...
WELL, WE'VE BEEN FRIENDS SINCE CHILDHOOD...
DID YOU KNOW?
Y-YEAH ...
I'VE SEEN ALL THE BAD LUCK HE'S HAD WITH GIRLS...
WHEN HE GOT DUMPED THREE TIMES IN A MONTH, *THAT* WAS TOUGH TO WATCH, BUT...
WITH THE SAME GIRL, TOO.
IS NOW THE TIME?! DID YOU NEED TO?!
...
SO WHEN HE INTRODUCED YOU TO ME AS HIS GIRLFRIEND...
I REALLY COULDN'T BELIEVE MY EYES.
SORRY ABOUT THAT.
OH! NO, IT'S FINE...
GEEZ, SORRY.

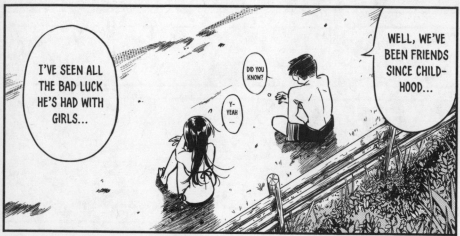

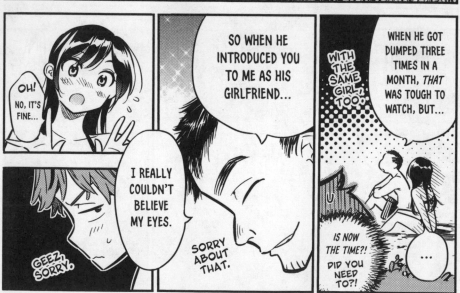

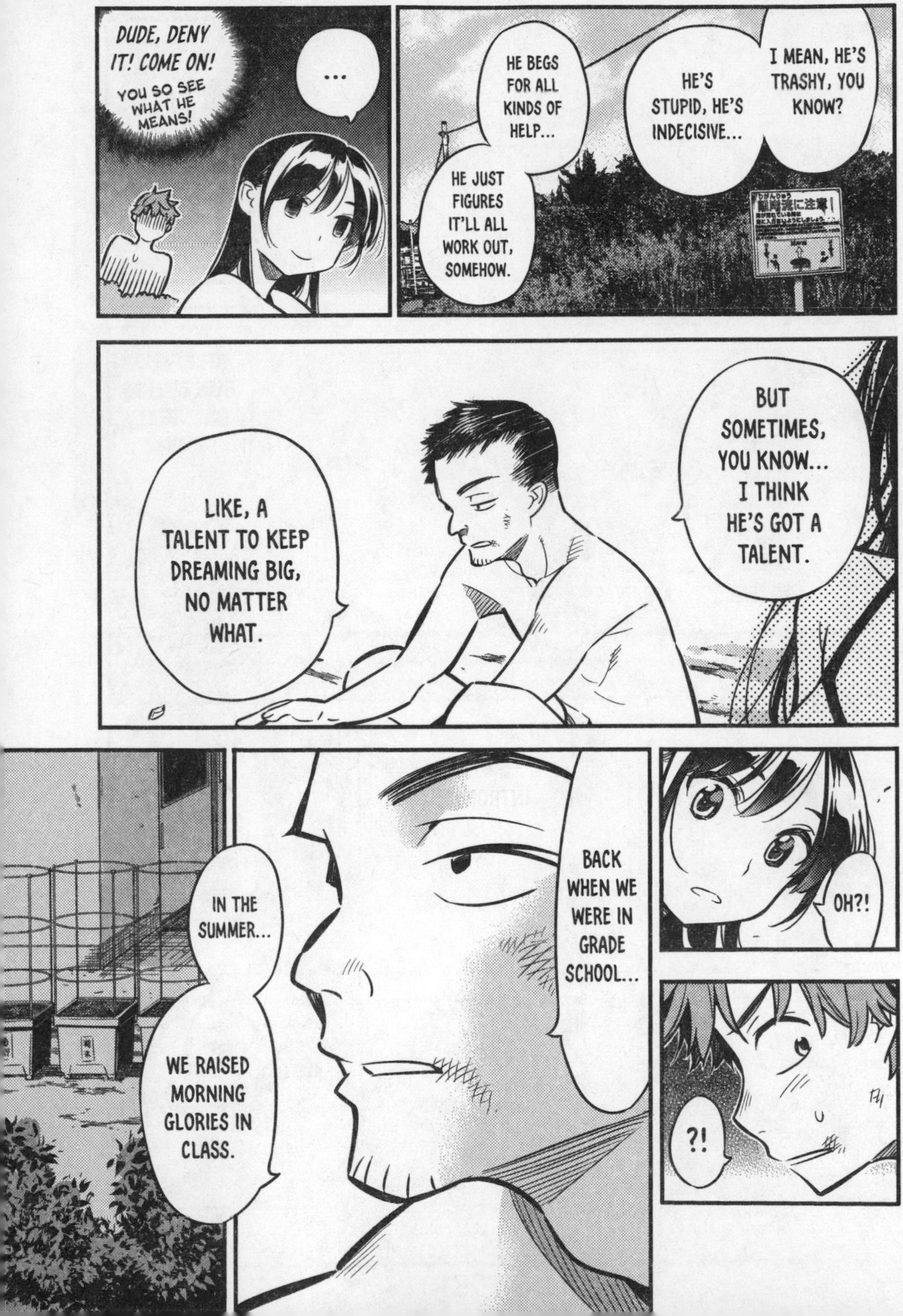
I MEAN, HE'S TRASHY, YOU KNOW?
HE'S STUPID, HE'S INDECISIVE...
HE BEGS FOR ALL KINDS OF HELP...
HE JUST FIGURES IT'LL ALL WORK OUT, SOMEHOW.
...
DUDE, DENY IT! COME ON!
YOU SO SEE WHAT HE MEANS!
BUT SOMETIMES, YOU KNOW... I THINK HE'S GOT A TALENT.
LIKE, A TALENT TO KEEP DREAMING BIG, NO MATTER WHAT.
OH?!
?!
BACK WHEN WE WERE IN GRADE SCHOOL...
IN THE SUMMER...
WE RAISED MORNING GLORIES IN CLASS.

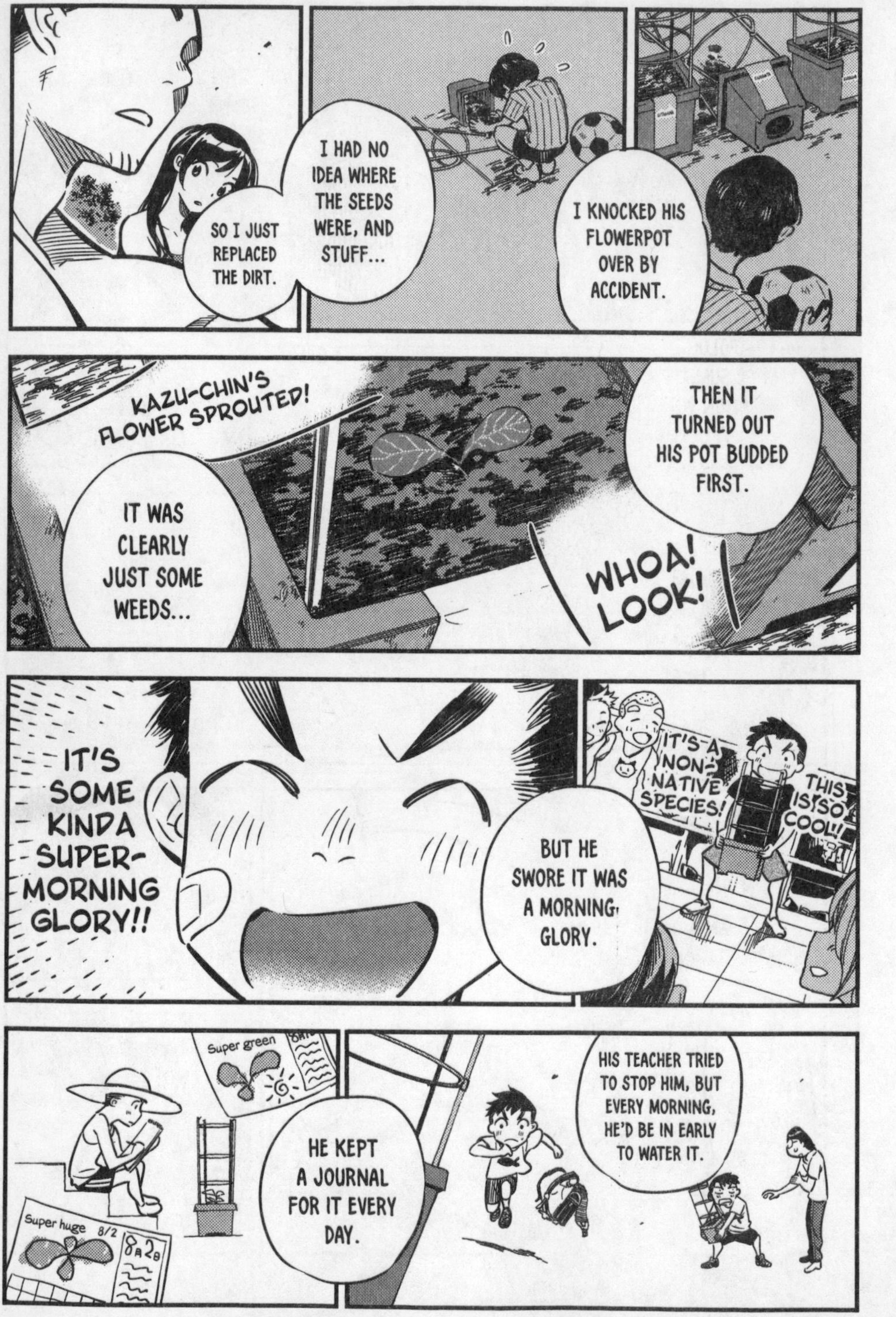
I KNOCKED HIS FLOWERPOT OVER BY ACCIDENT.
I HAD NO IDEA WHERE THE SEEDS WERE, AND STUFF...
SO I JUST REPLACED THE DIRT.
THEN IT TURNED OUT HIS POT BUDDED FIRST.
WHOA! LOOK!
KAZU-CHIN'S FLOWER SPROUTED!
IT WAS CLEARLY JUST SOME WEEDS...
THIS IS SO COOL!!
IT'S A NON-NATIVE SPECIES!
BUT HE SWORE IT WAS A MORNING GLORY.
IT'S SOME KINDA SUPER-MORNING GLORY!!
HIS TEACHER TRIED TO STOP HIM, BUT EVERY MORNING, HE'D BE IN EARLY TO WATER IT.
HE KEPT A JOURNAL FOR IT EVERY DAY.
Super green
Super huge 8/2

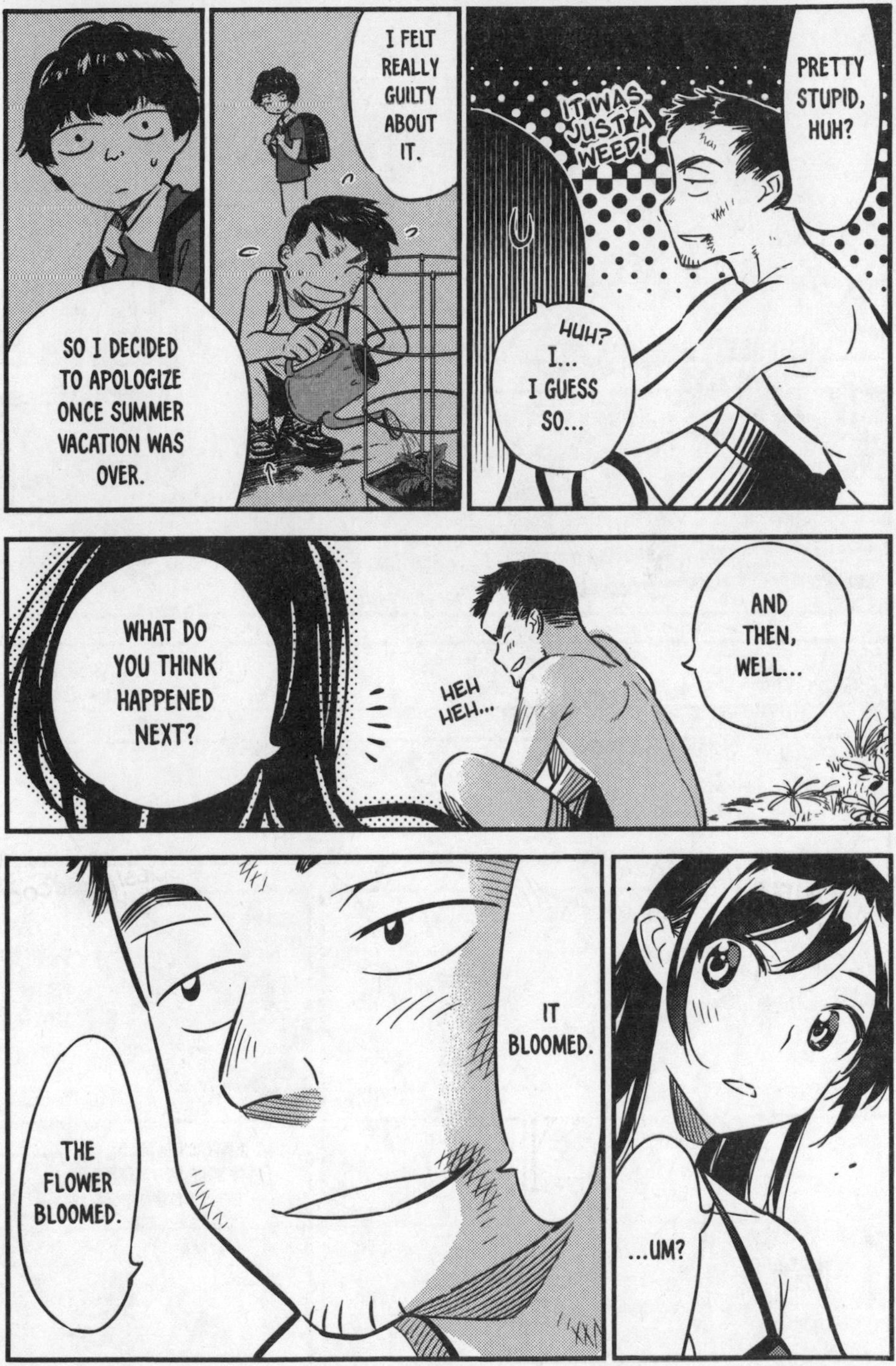
PRETTY STUPID, HUH?
IT WAS JUST A WEED!
HUH? I... I GUESS SO...
I FELT REALLY GUILTY ABOUT IT.
SO I DECIDED TO APOLOGIZE ONCE SUMMER VACATION WAS OVER.
AND THEN, WELL...
HEH HEH...
WHAT DO YOU THINK HAPPENED NEXT?
...UM?
IT BLOOMED.
THE FLOWER BLOOMED.

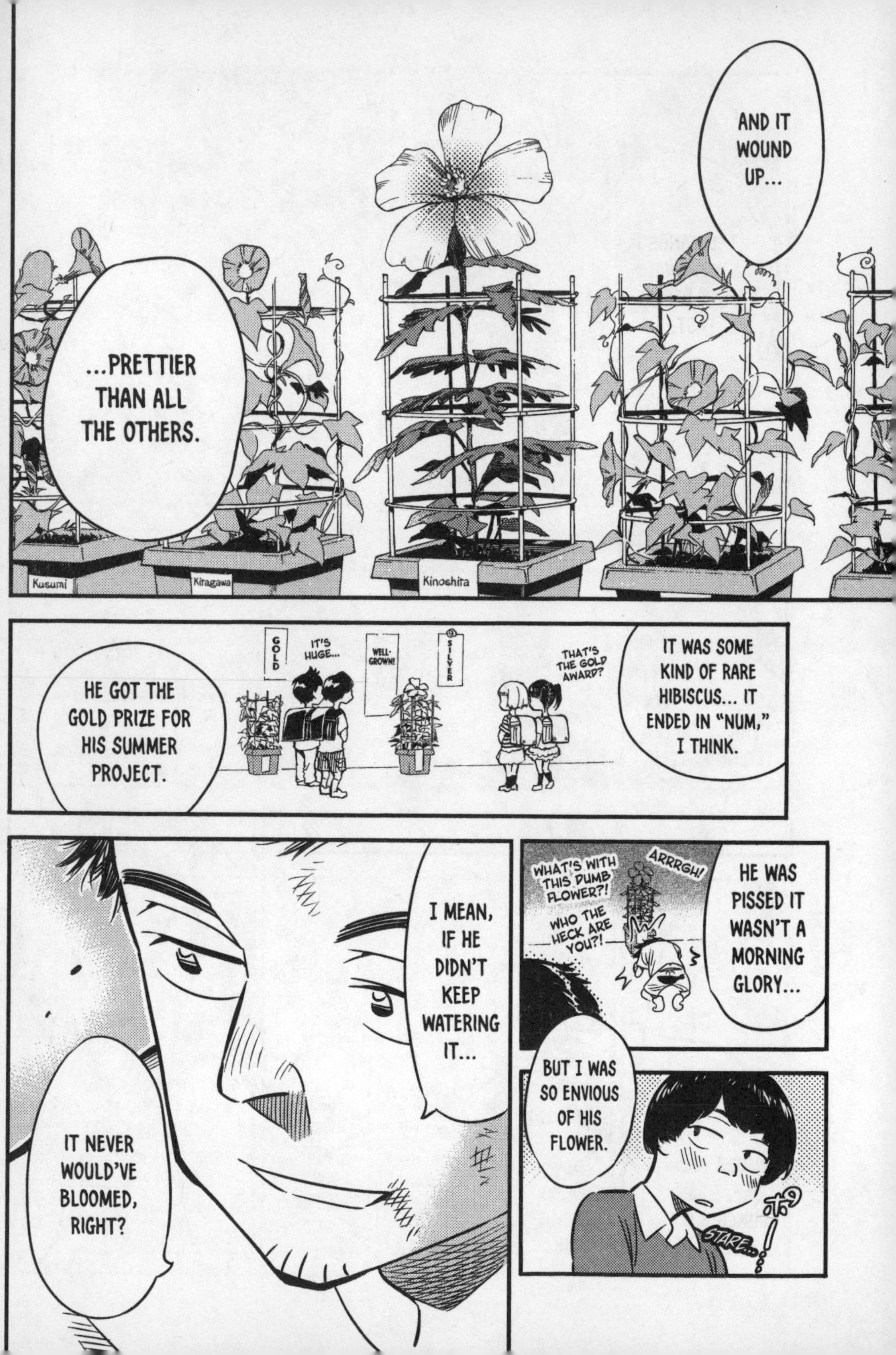
AND IT WOUND UP...
...PRETTIER THAN ALL THE OTHERS.
Kusumi
Kitagawa
Kinoshita
IT WAS SOME KIND OF RARE HIBISCUS... IT ENDED IN "NUM," I THINK.
THAT'S THE GOLD AWARD?
SILVER
WELL-GROWN!
IT'S HUGE...
GOLD
HE GOT THE GOLD PRIZE FOR HIS SUMMER PROJECT.
HE WAS PISSED IT WASN'T A MORNING GLORY...
ARRRGH!
WHAT'S WITH THIS DUMB FLOWER?!
WHO THE HECK ARE YOU?!
BUT I WAS SO ENVIOUS OF HIS FLOWER.
STARE...
I MEAN, IF HE DIDN'T KEEP WATERING IT...
IT NEVER WOULD'VE BLOOMED, RIGHT?

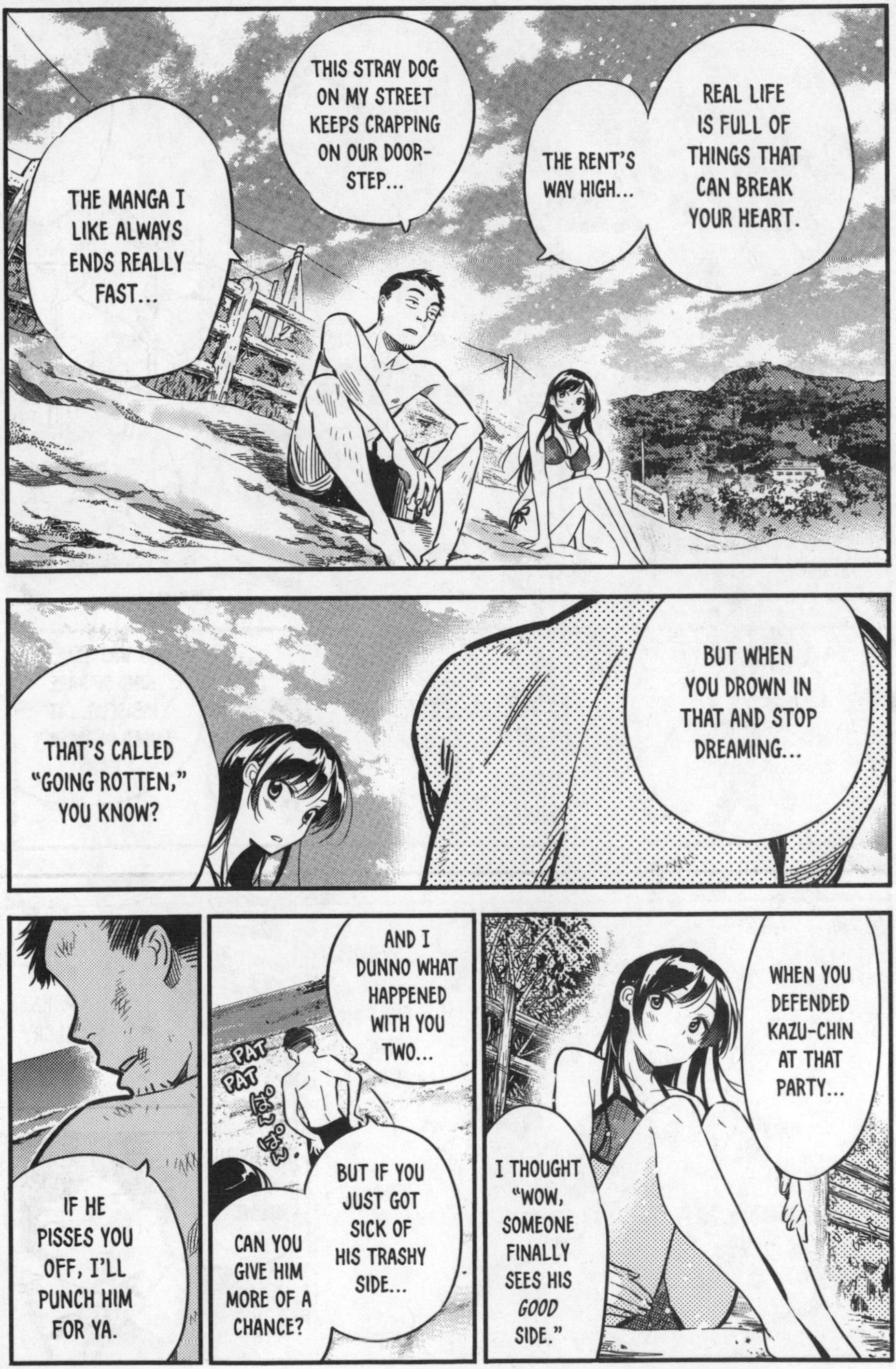
REAL LIFE IS FULL OF THINGS THAT CAN BREAK YOUR HEART.
THE RENT'S WAY HIGH...
THIS STRAY DOG ON MY STREET KEEPS CRAPPING ON OUR DOOR-STEP...
THE MANGA I LIKE ALWAYS ENDS REALLY FAST...
BUT WHEN YOU DROWN IN THAT AND STOP DREAMING...
THAT'S CALLED "GOING ROTTEN," YOU KNOW?
WHEN YOU DEFENDED KAZU-CHIN AT THAT PARTY...
I THOUGHT "WOW, SOMEONE FINALLY SEES HIS *GOOD* SIDE."
AND I DUNNO WHAT HAPPENED WITH YOU TWO...
PAT PAT
ぱんぱん
BUT IF YOU JUST GOT SICK OF HIS TRASHY SIDE...
CAN YOU GIVE HIM MORE OF A CHANCE?
IF HE PISSES YOU OFF, I'LL PUNCH HIM FOR YA.

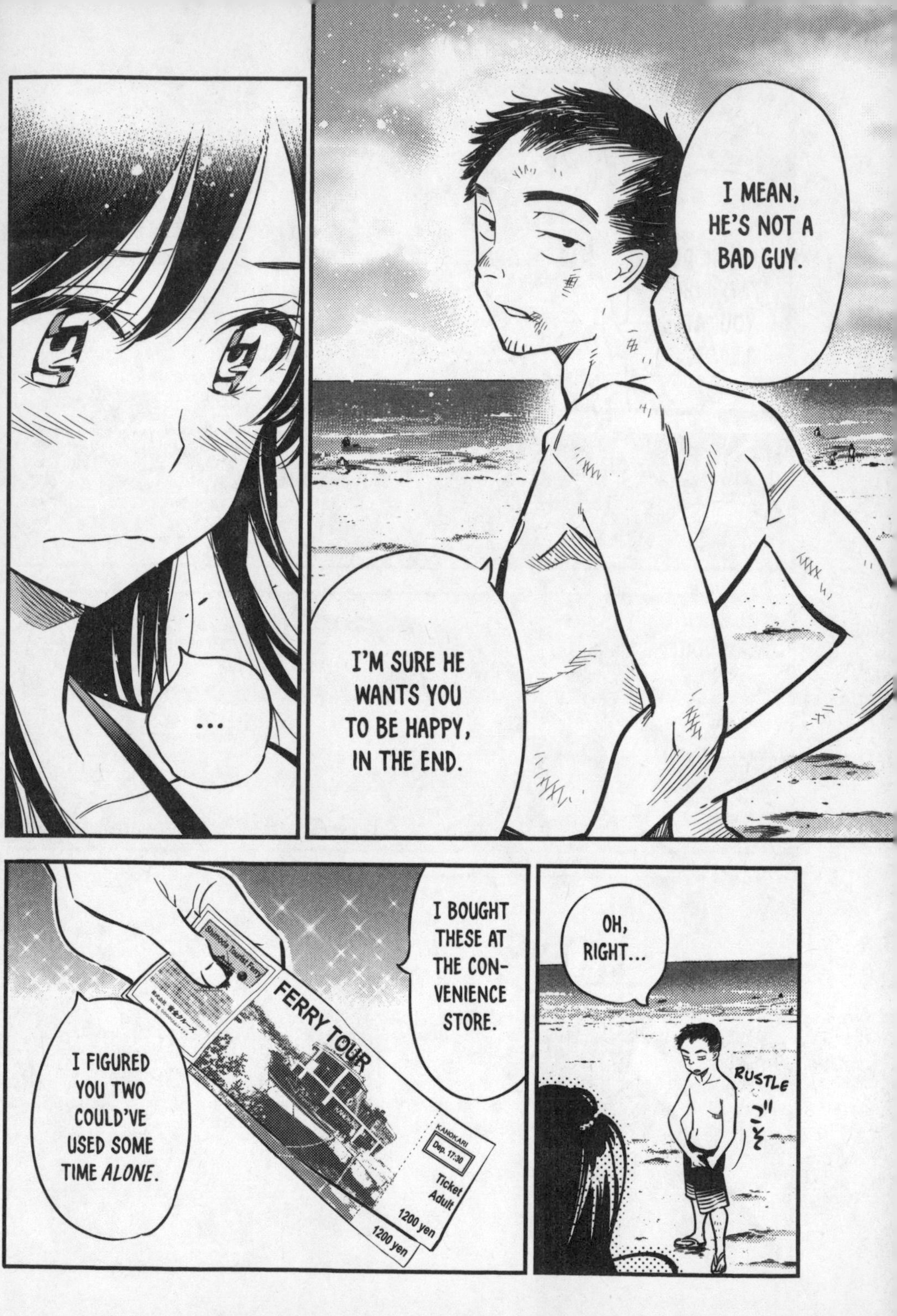
I MEAN, HE'S NOT A BAD GUY.
I'M SURE HE WANTS YOU TO BE HAPPY, IN THE END.
...
OH, RIGHT...
RUSTLE
I BOUGHT THESE AT THE CON-VENIENCE STORE.
FERRY TOUR
KANOKARI
Dep. 17:30
Ticket
Adult
1200 yen
1200 yen
I FIGURED YOU TWO COULD'VE USED SOME TIME ALONE.

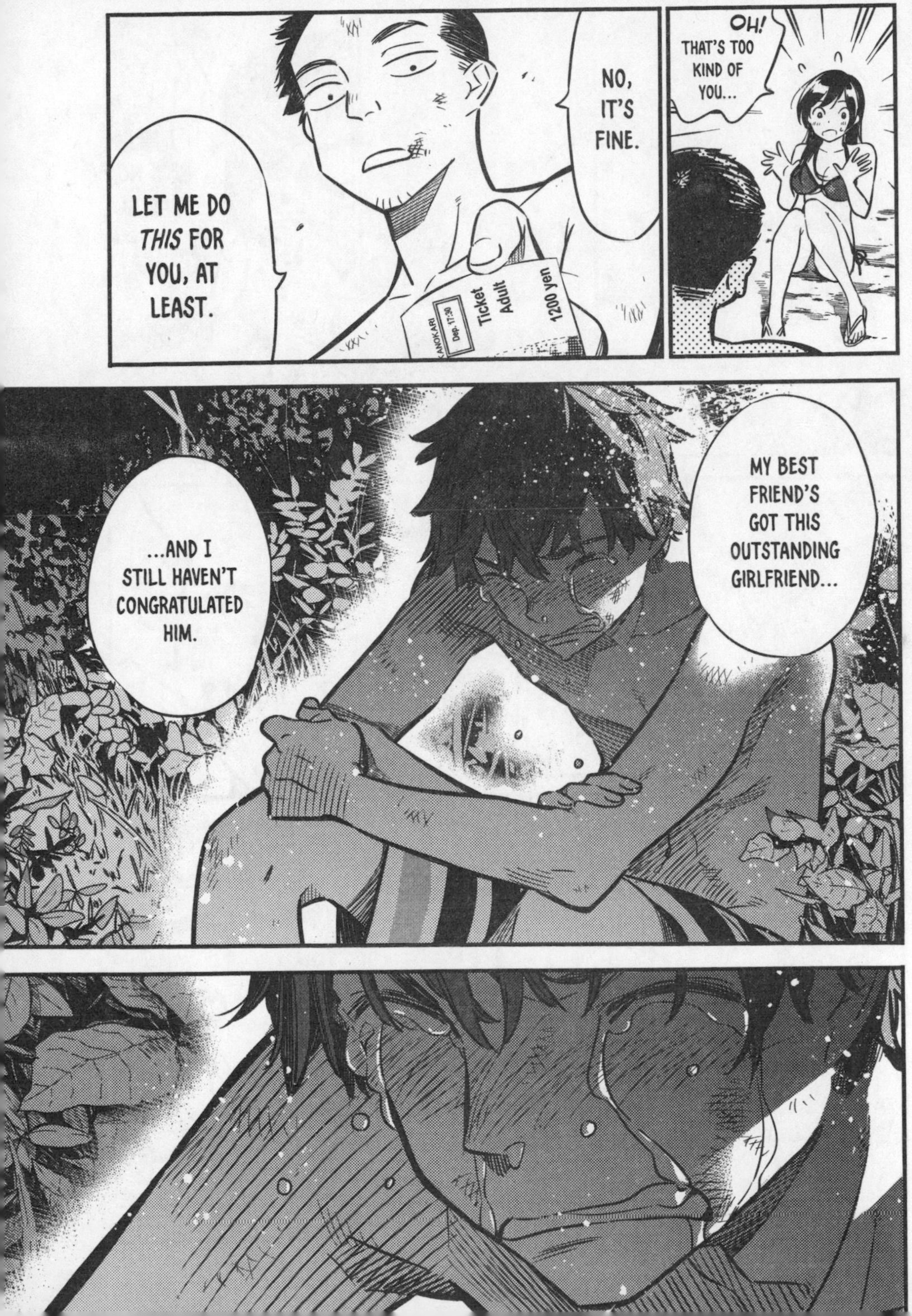
OH! THAT'S TOO KIND OF YOU...
NO, IT'S FINE.
LET ME DO *THIS* FOR YOU, AT LEAST.
KANOKARI
Dep. 17:30
Ticket
Adult
1200 yen
MY BEST FRIEND'S GOT THIS OUTSTANDING GIRLFRIEND...
...AND I STILL HAVEN'T CONGRATULATED HIM.

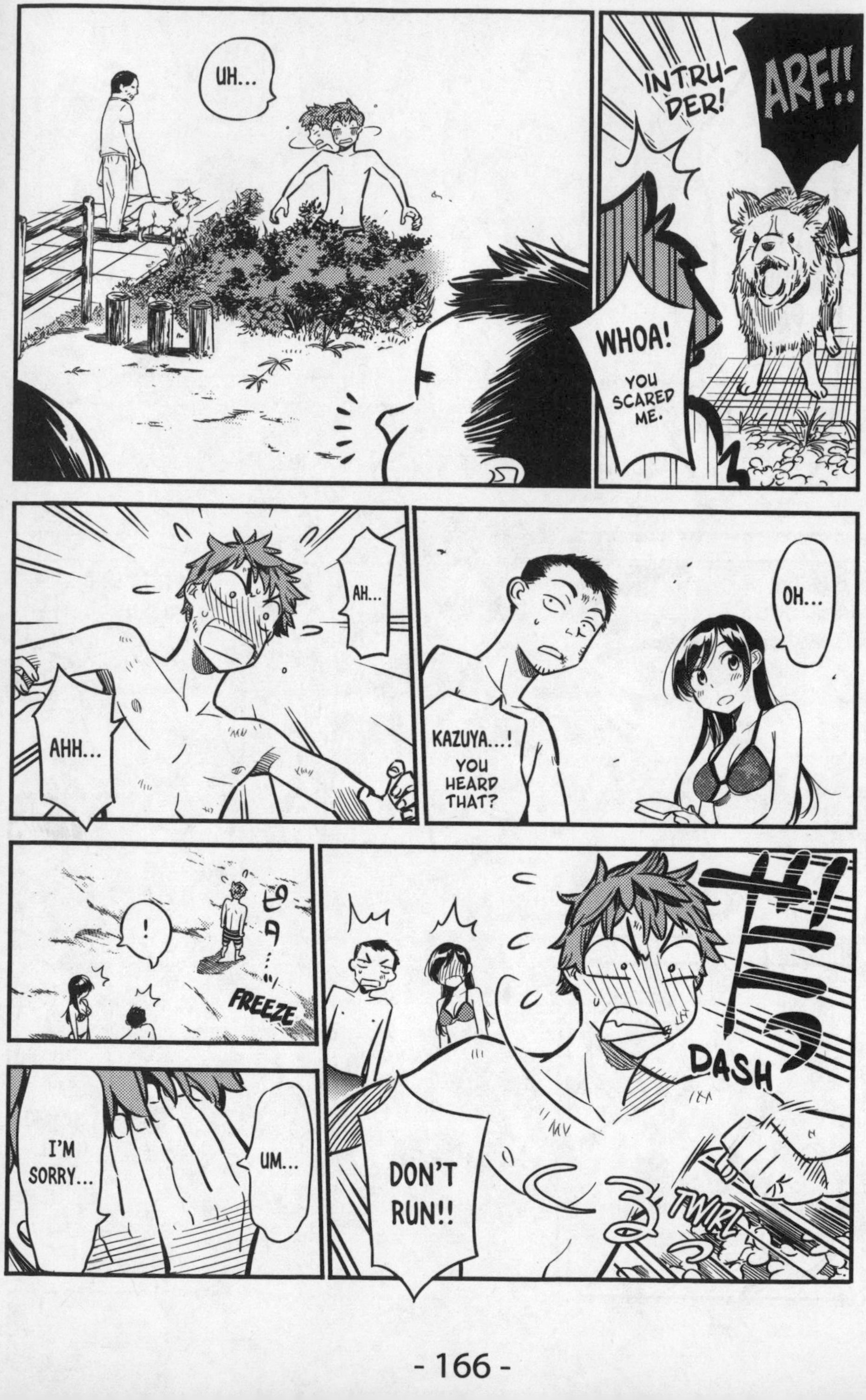
ARF!!
INTRU-DER!
WHOA! YOU SCARED ME.
UH...
OH...
KAZUYA...! YOU HEARD THAT?
AH...
AHH...
DASH
DON'T RUN!!
TWIRL
!
FREEZE
UM...
I'M SORRY...

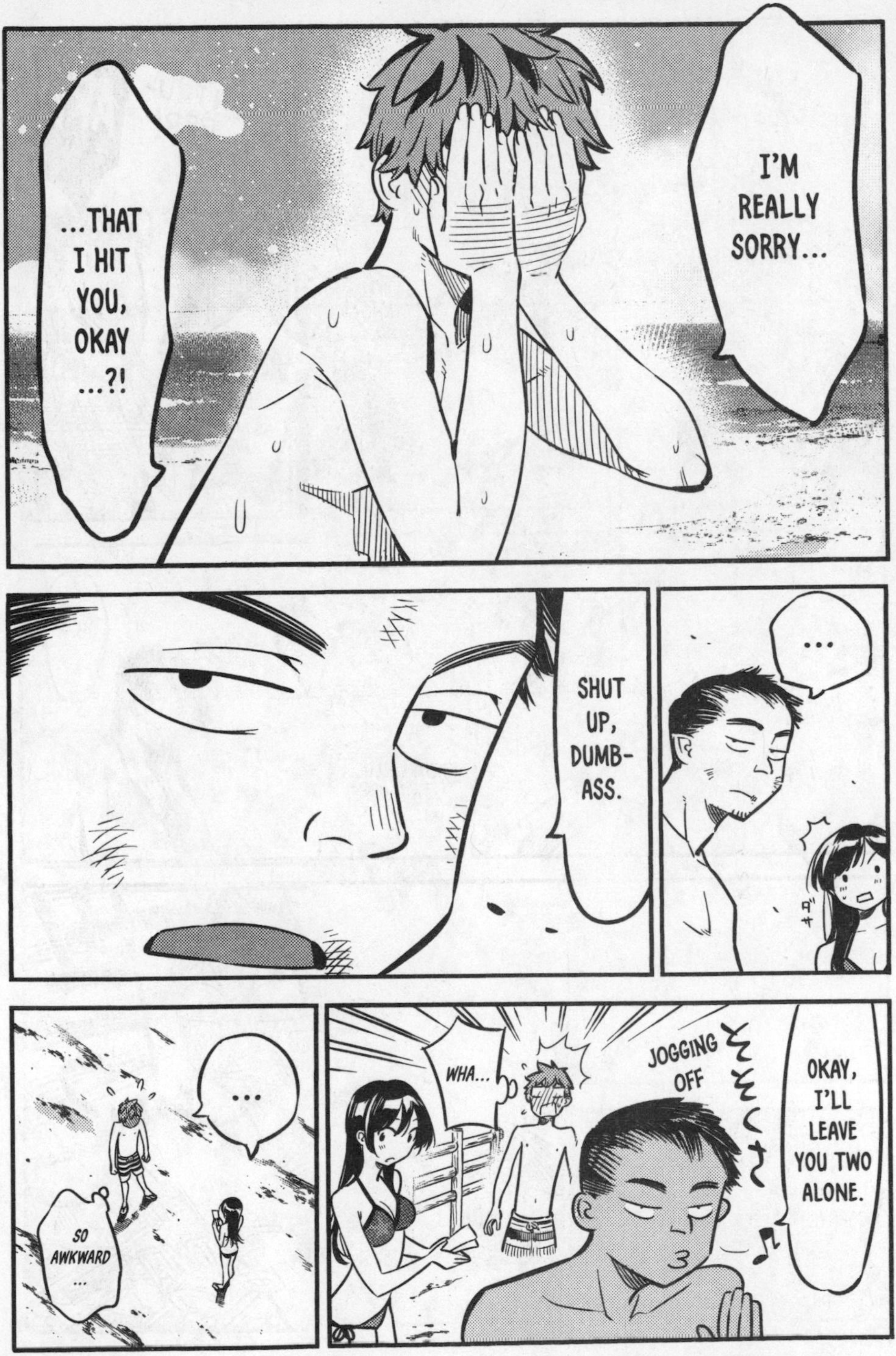
I'M REALLY SORRY...
...THAT I HIT YOU, OKAY ...?!
...
SHUT UP, DUMB-ASS.
OKAY, I'LL LEAVE YOU TWO ALONE.
JOGGING OFF
WHA...
...
SO AWKWARD ...

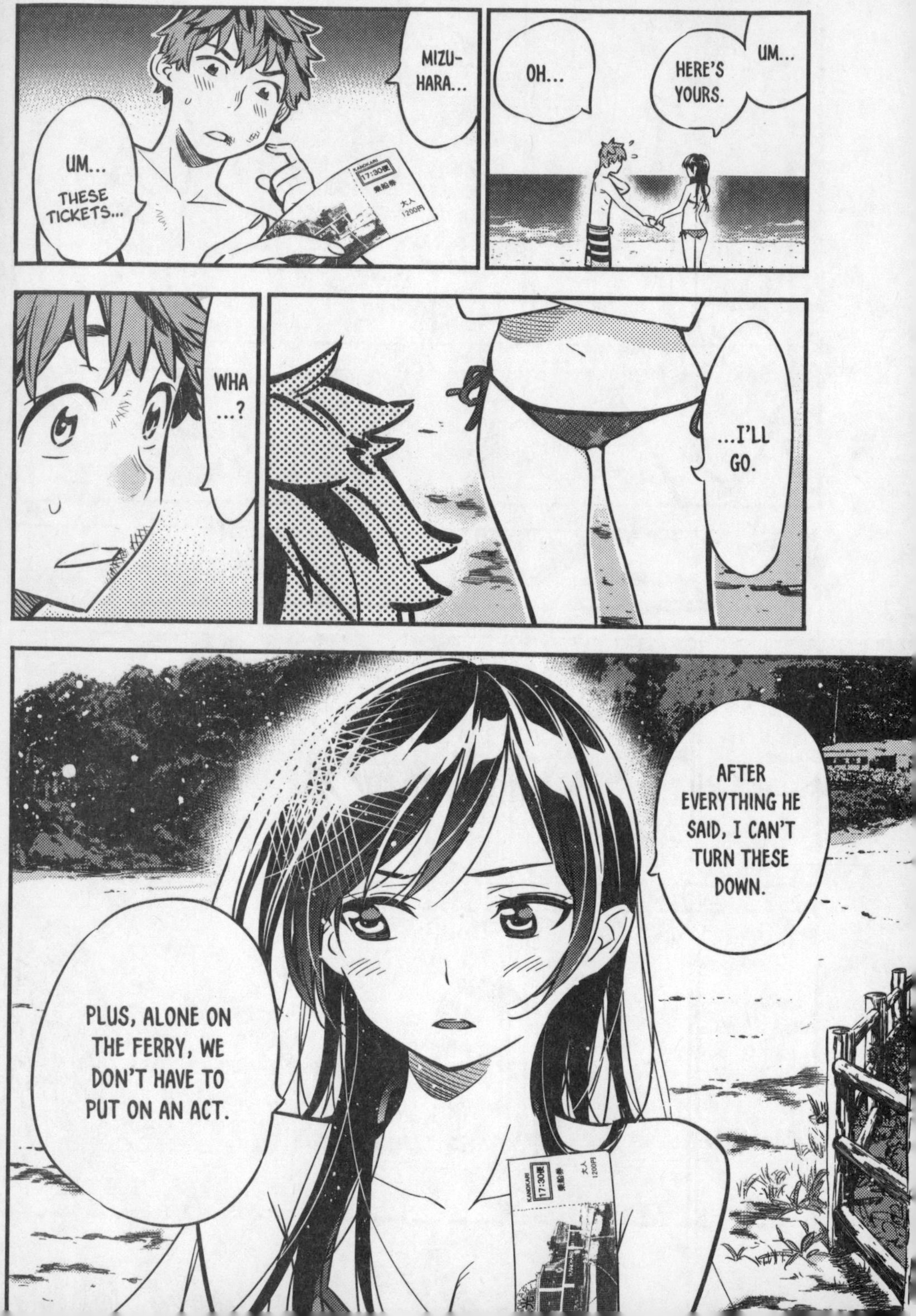
UM...
HERE'S YOURS.
OH...
MIZU-HARA...
UM... THESE TICKETS...
...I'LL GO.
WHA ...?
AFTER EVERYTHING HE SAID, I CAN'T TURN THESE DOWN.
PLUS, ALONE ON THE FERRY, WE DON'T HAVE TO PUT ON AN ACT.

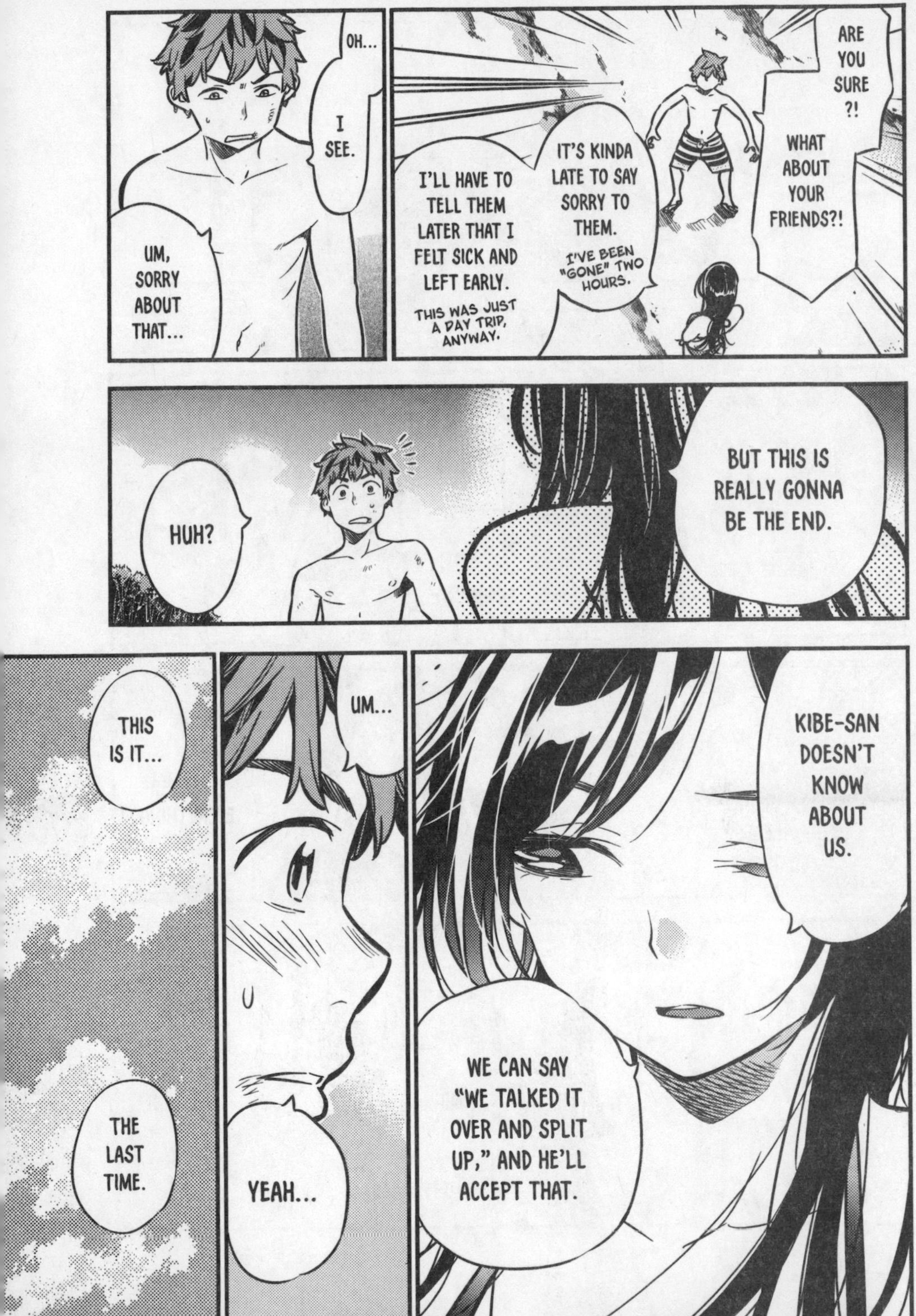
ARE YOU SURE ?!
WHAT ABOUT YOUR FRIENDS?!
IT'S KINDA LATE TO SAY SORRY TO THEM.
I'VE BEEN "GONE" TWO HOURS.
I'LL HAVE TO TELL THEM LATER THAT I FELT SICK AND LEFT EARLY.
THIS WAS JUST A DAY TRIP, ANYWAY.
OH... I SEE.
UM, SORRY ABOUT THAT...
BUT THIS IS REALLY GONNA BE THE END.
HUH?
KIBE-SAN DOESN'T KNOW ABOUT US.
WE CAN SAY "WE TALKED IT OVER AND SPLIT UP," AND HE'LL ACCEPT THAT.
UM...
YEAH...
THIS IS IT...
THE LAST TIME.

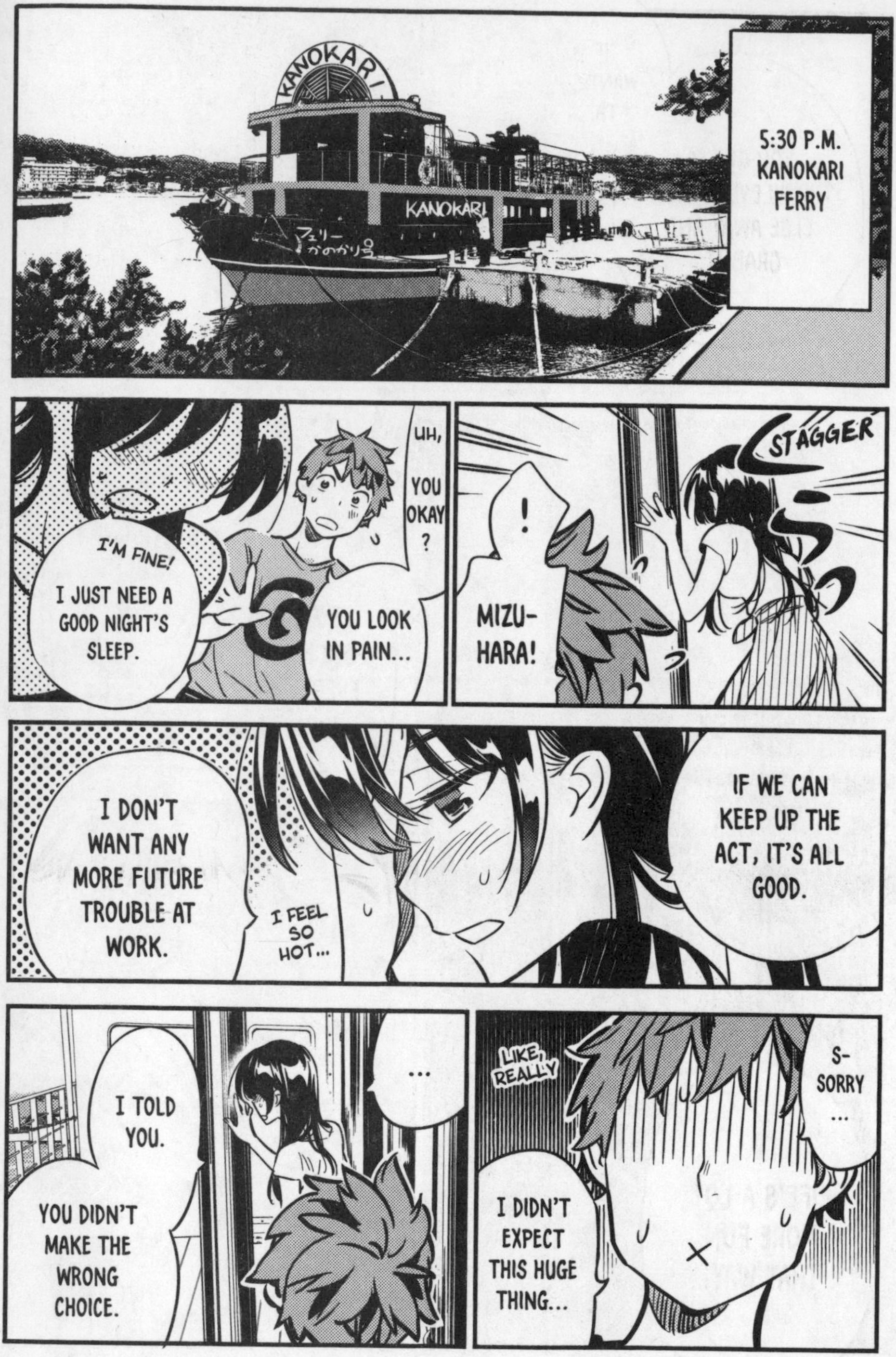
5:30 P.M. KANOKARI FERRY
KANOKARI
KANOKARI
フェリー かのかり号
STAGGER
!
MIZU-HARA!
UH, YOU OKAY?
YOU LOOK IN PAIN...
I'M FINE!
I JUST NEED A GOOD NIGHT'S SLEEP.
IF WE CAN KEEP UP THE ACT, IT'S ALL GOOD.
I FEEL SO HOT...
I DON'T WANT ANY MORE FUTURE TROUBLE AT WORK.
S-SORRY...
LIKE, REALLY
I DIDN'T EXPECT THIS HUGE THING...
...
I TOLD YOU.
YOU DIDN'T MAKE THE WRONG CHOICE.

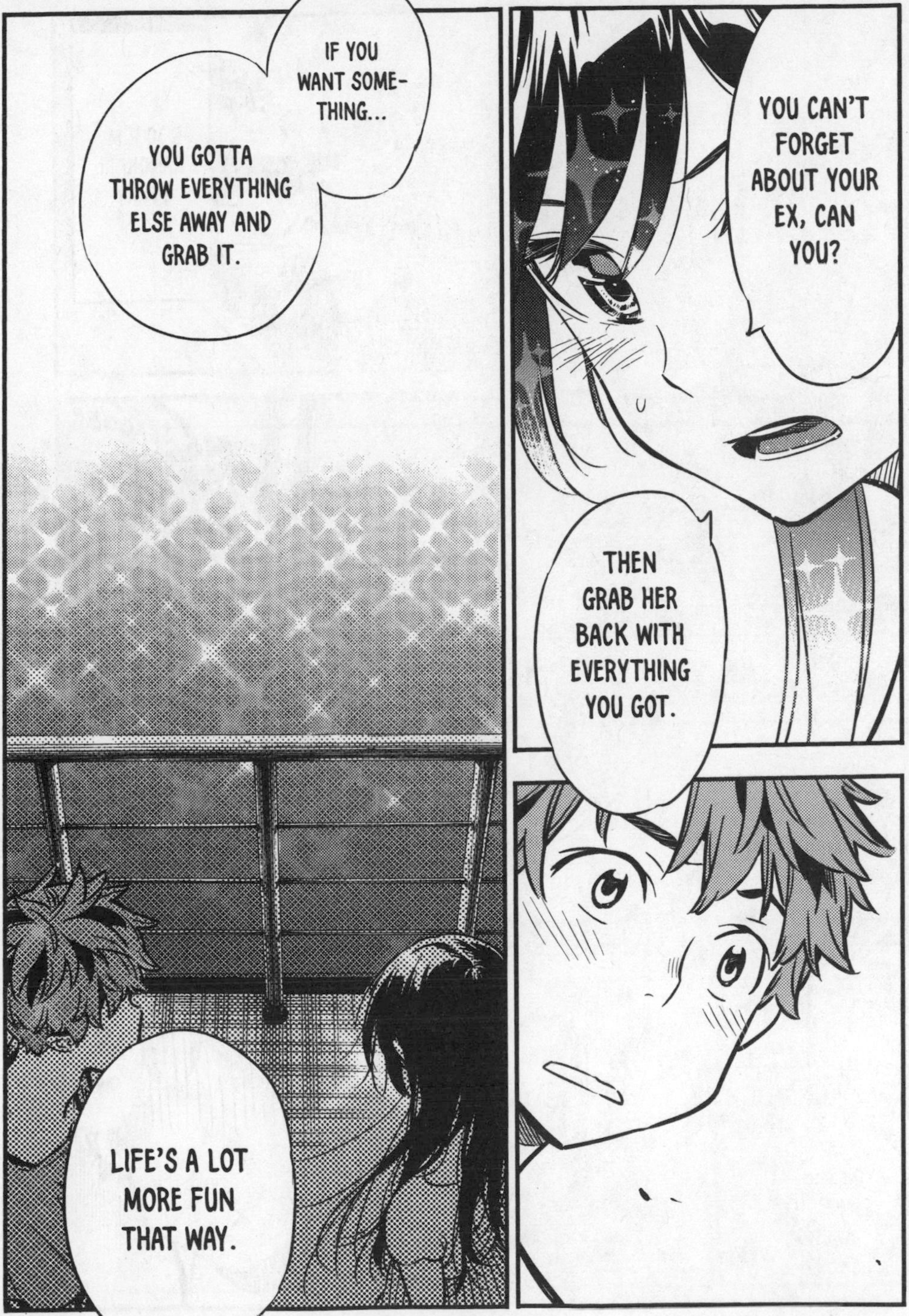
YOU CAN'T FORGET ABOUT YOUR EX, CAN YOU?
THEN GRAB HER BACK WITH EVERYTHING YOU GOT.
IF YOU WANT SOME-THING...
YOU GOTTA THROW EVERYTHING ELSE AWAY AND GRAB IT.
LIFE'S A LOT MORE FUN THAT WAY.

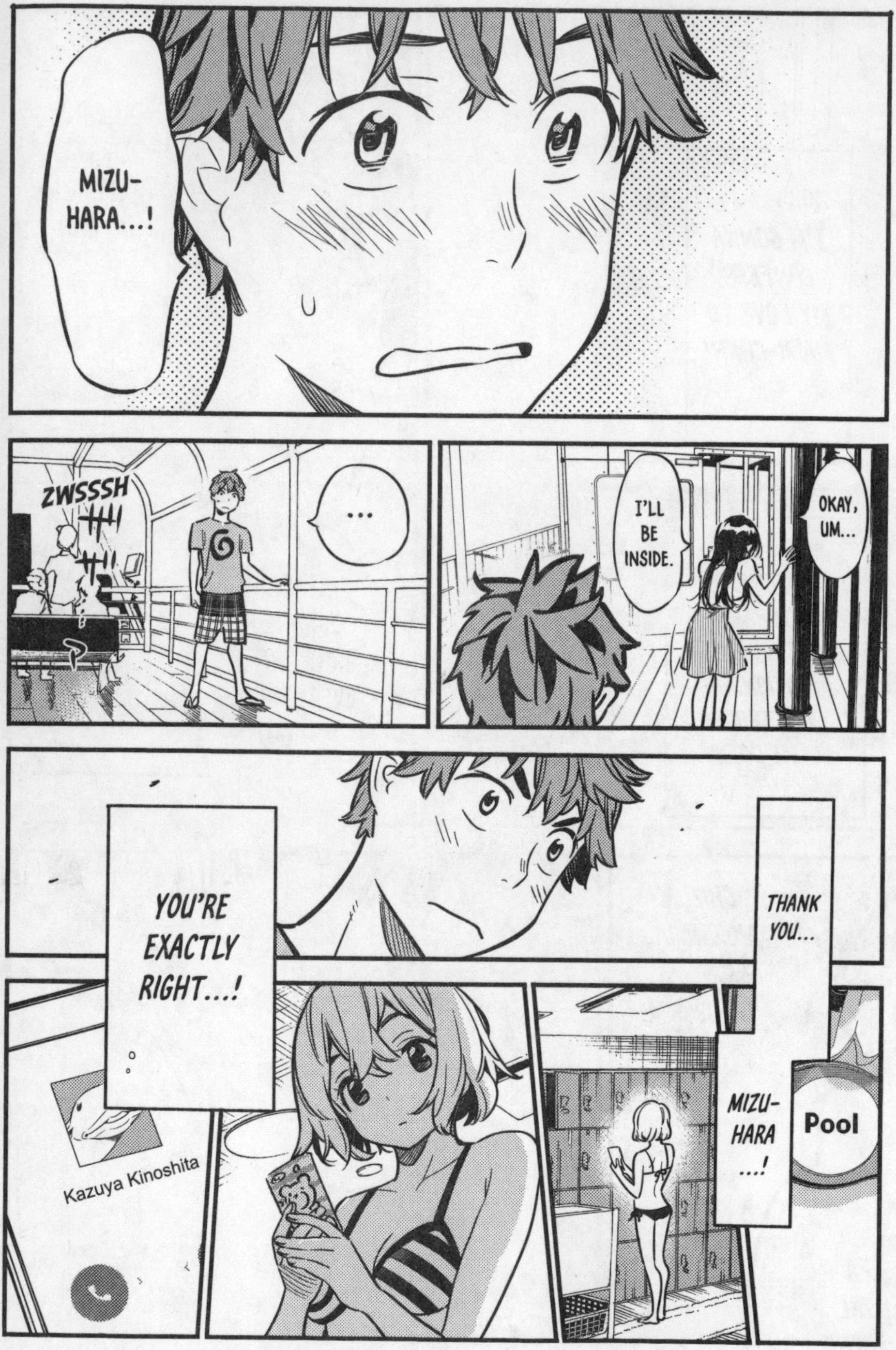
MIZU-HARA...!
OKAY, UM...
I'LL BE INSIDE.
ZWSSSH
...
THANK YOU...
YOU'RE EXACTLY RIGHT...!
Pool
MIZU-HARA...!
Kazuya Kinoshita

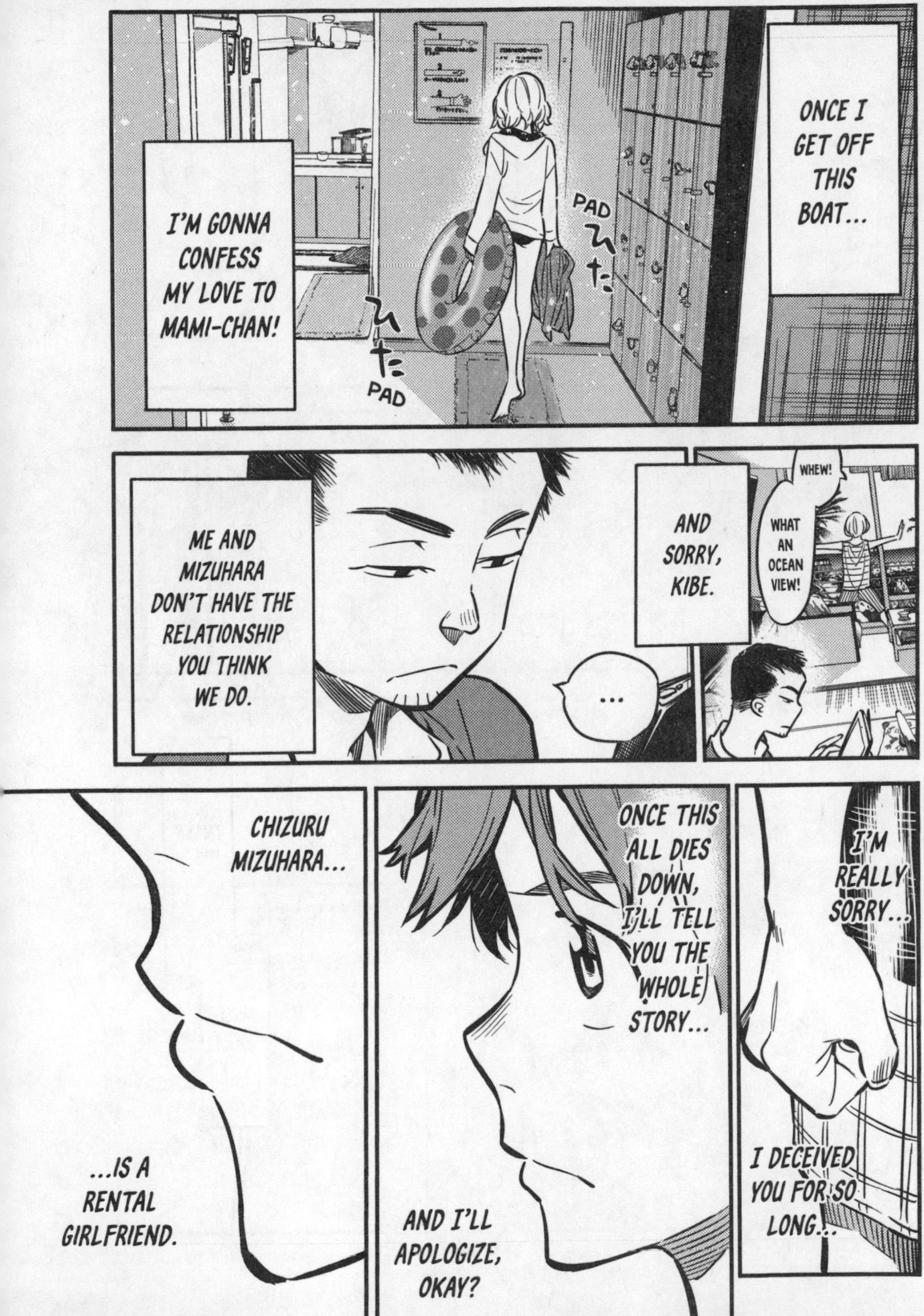
ONCE I GET OFF THIS BOAT...
PAD
I'M GONNA CONFESS MY LOVE TO MAMI-CHAN!
PAD
WHEW!
WHAT AN OCEAN VIEW!
AND SORRY, KIBE.
...
ME AND MIZUHARA DON'T HAVE THE RELATIONSHIP YOU THINK WE DO.
I'M REALLY SORRY...
I DECEIVED YOU FOR SO LONG...
ONCE THIS ALL DIES DOWN, I'LL TELL YOU THE WHOLE STORY...
AND I'LL APOLOGIZE, OKAY?
CHIZURU MIZUHARA...
...IS A RENTAL GIRLFRIEND.

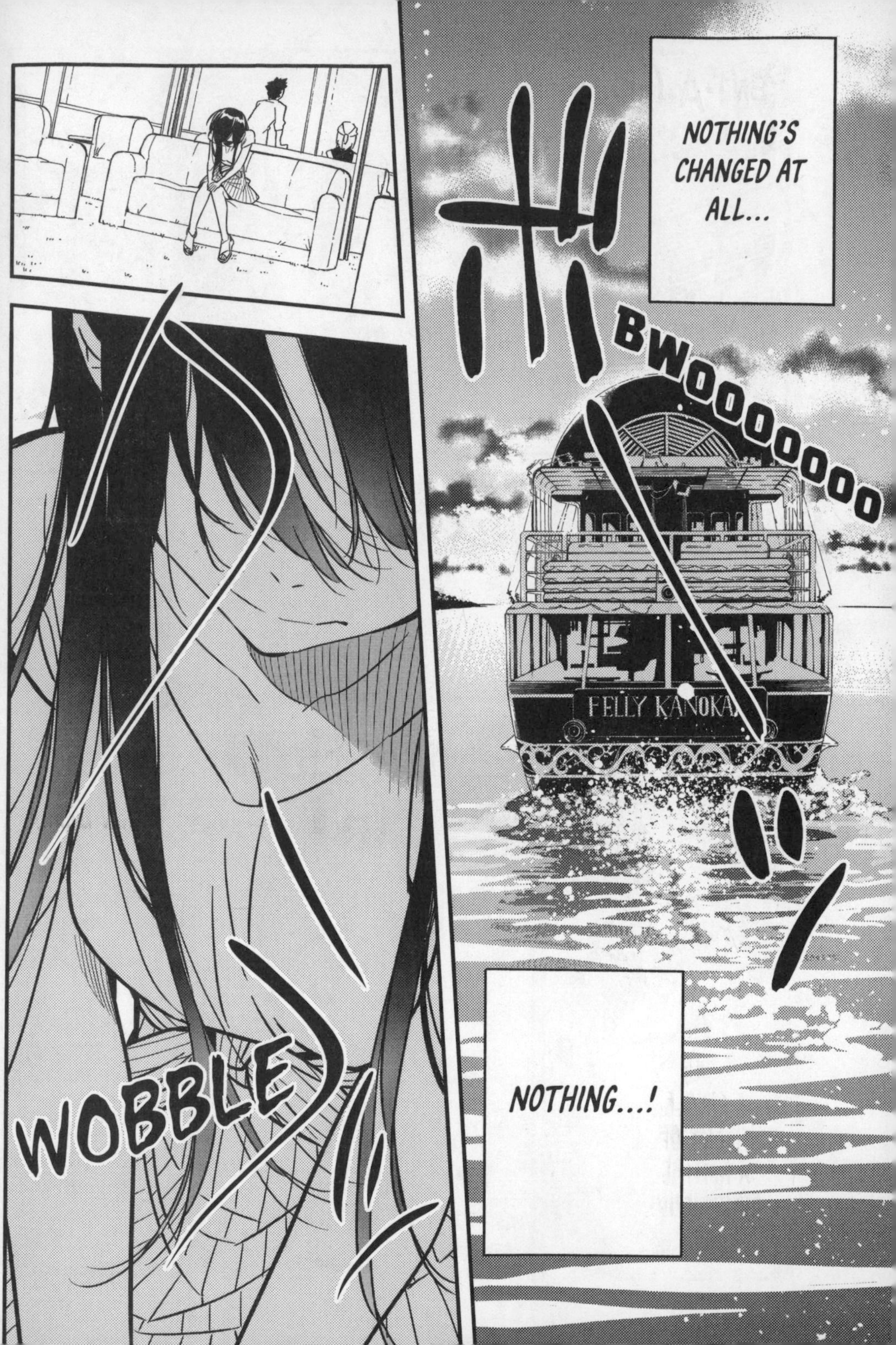
NOTHING'S CHANGED AT ALL...
BWOOOOOOOO
NOTHING...!
WOBBLE

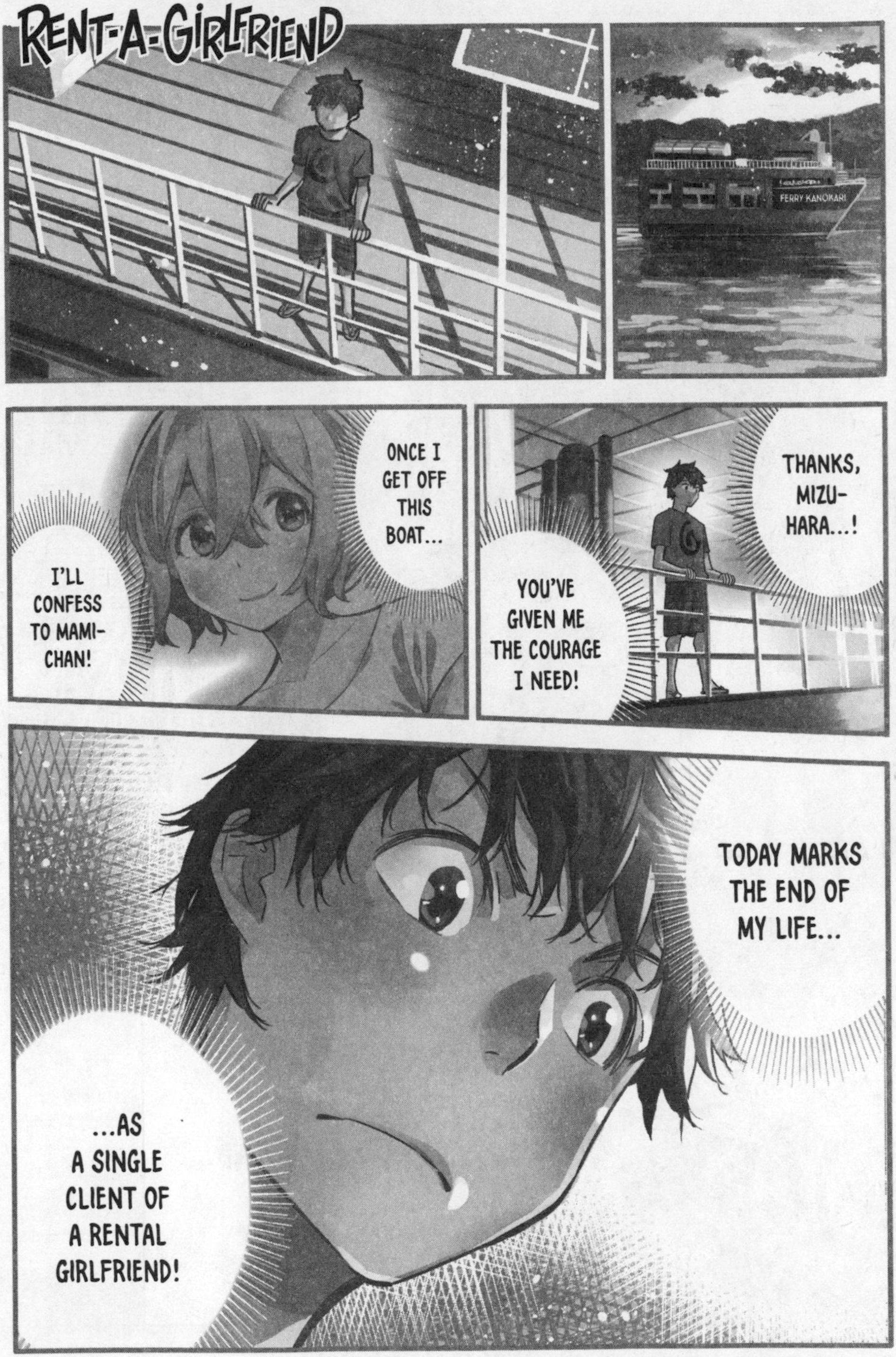
RENT-A-GIRLFRIEND
FERRY KANOKARI
THANKS, MIZUHARA...!
YOU'VE GIVEN ME THE COURAGE I NEED!
ONCE I GET OFF THIS BOAT...
I'LL CONFESS TO MAMI-CHAN!
TODAY MARKS THE END OF MY LIFE...
...AS A SINGLE CLIENT OF A RENTAL GIRLFRIEND!

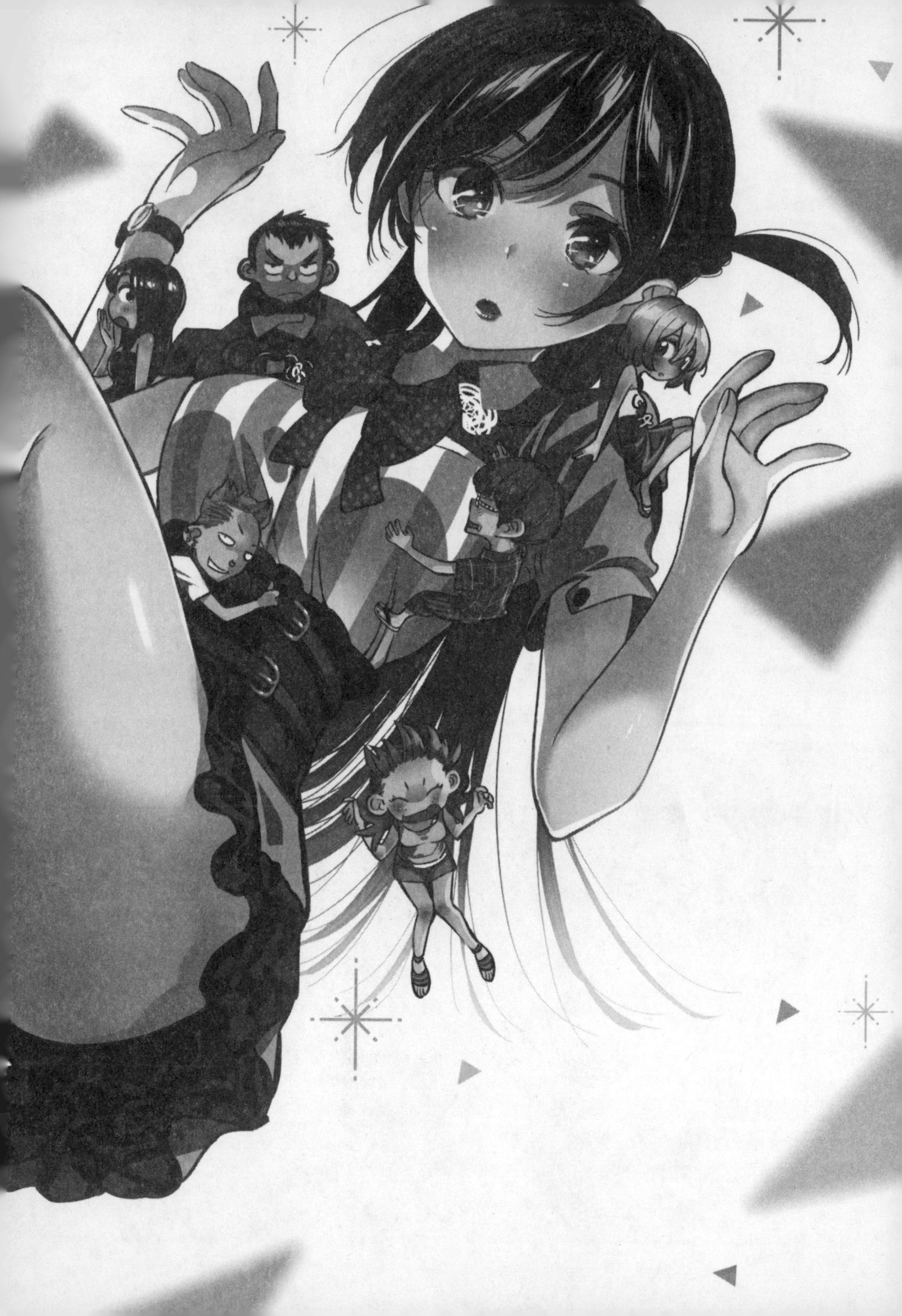

RATING 14
MY GIRLFRIEND AND THE SEA (5)

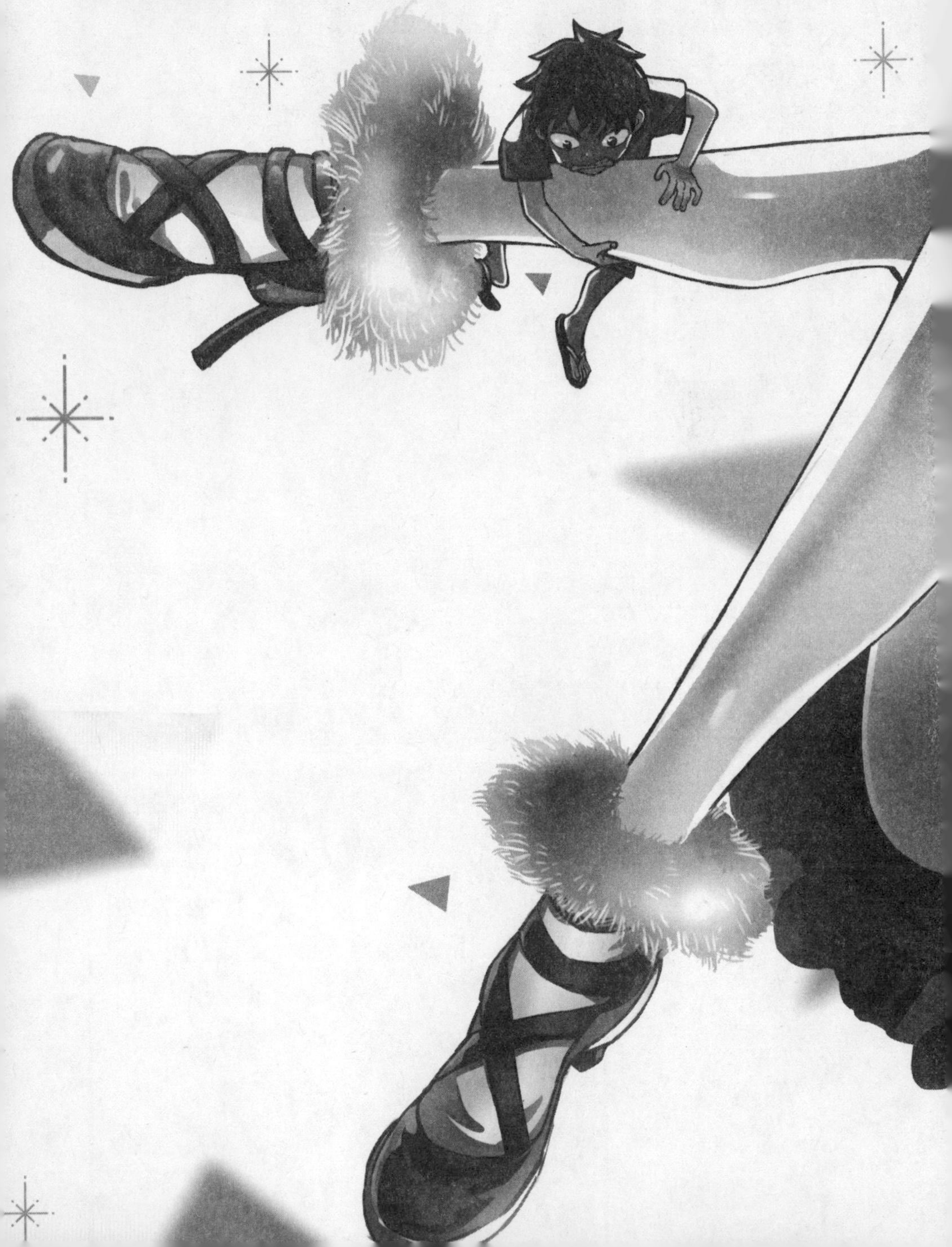

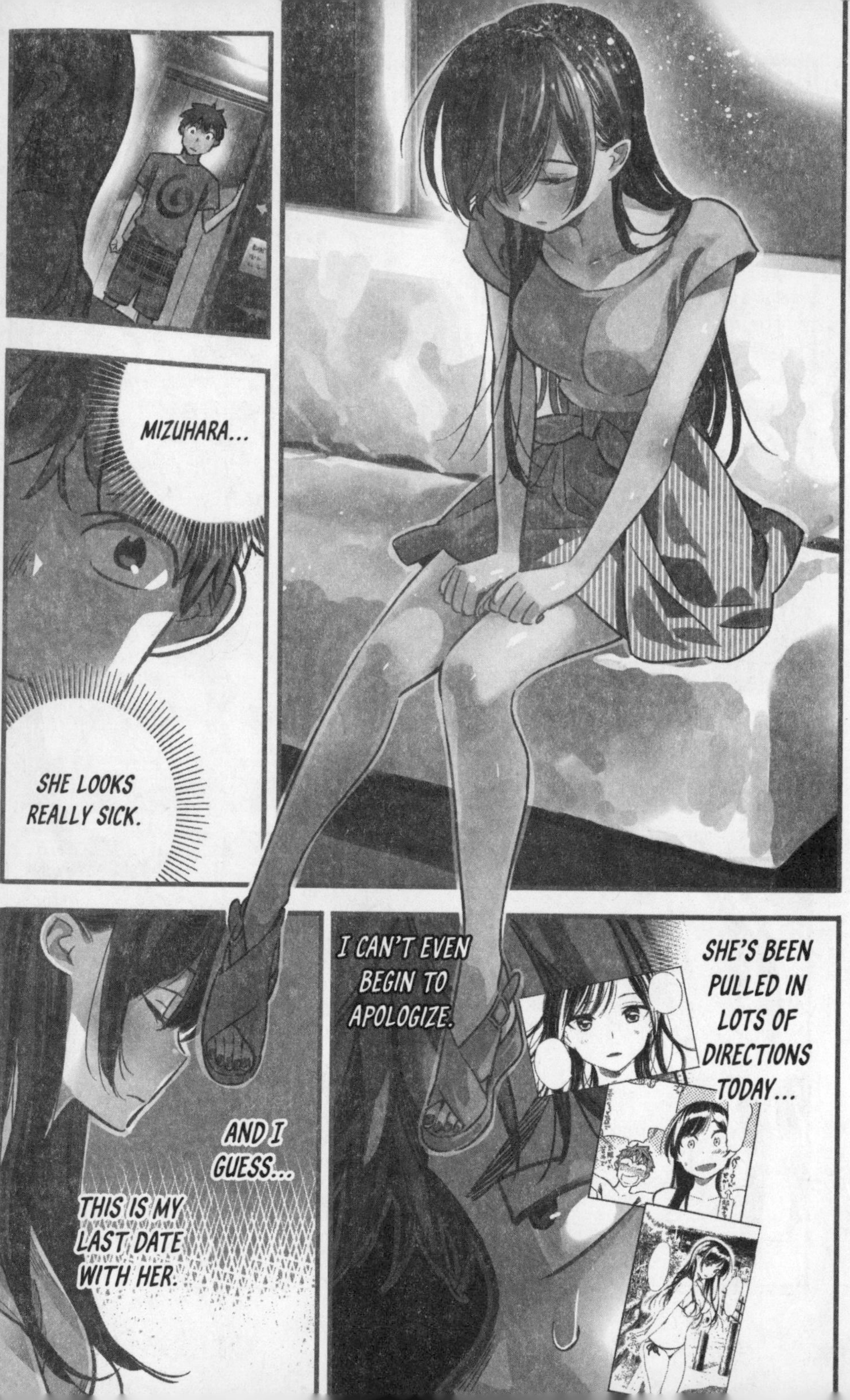
MIZUHARA...
SHE LOOKS REALLY SICK.
SHE'S BEEN PULLED IN LOTS OF DIRECTIONS TODAY...
I CAN'T EVEN BEGIN TO APOLOGIZE.
AND I GUESS...
THIS IS MY LAST DATE WITH HER.

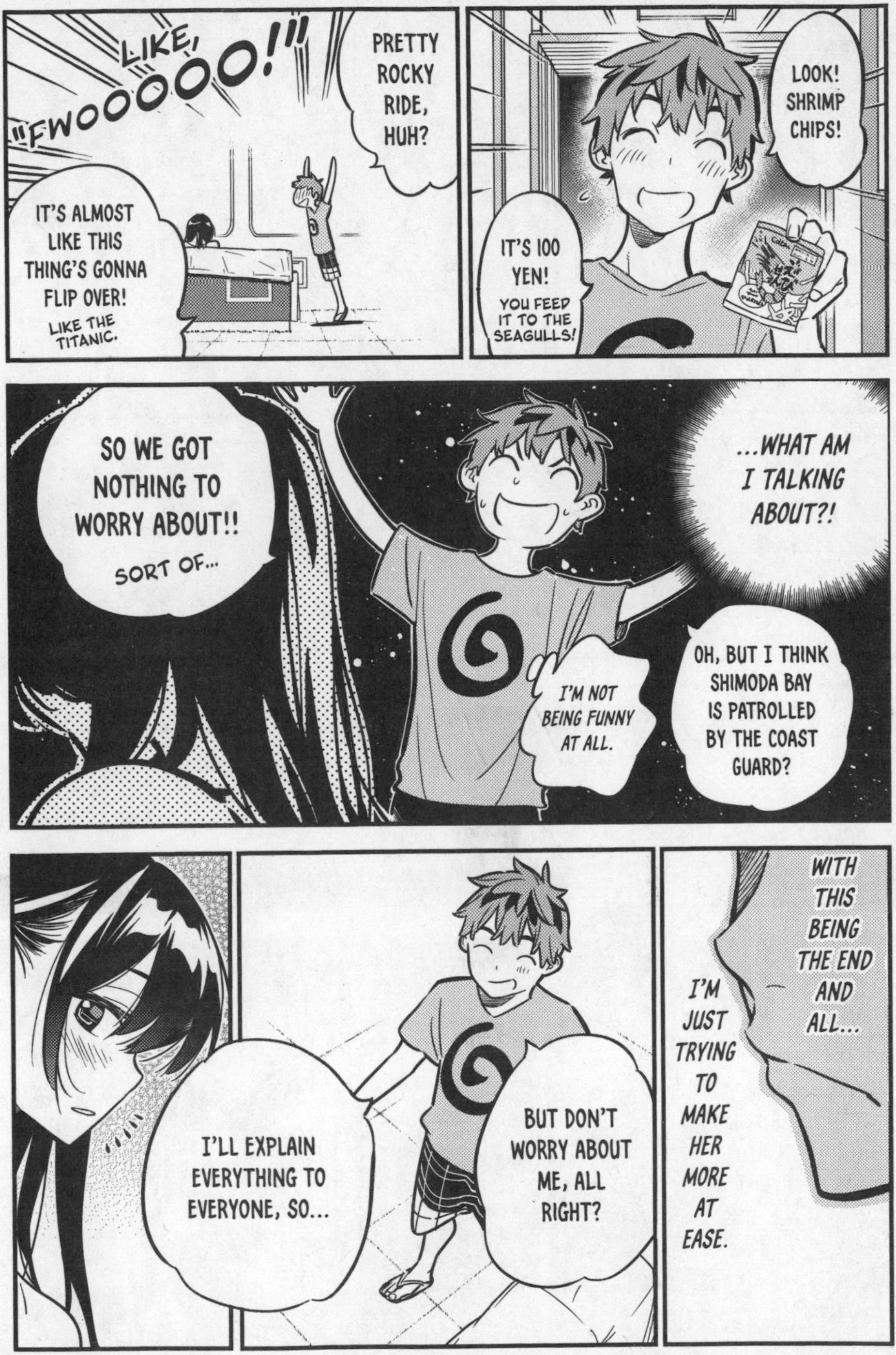
LOOK! SHRIMP CHIPS!
IT'S 100 YEN!
YOU FEED IT TO THE SEAGULLS!
PRETTY ROCKY RIDE, HUH?
LIKE, "FWOOOOOO!"
IT'S ALMOST LIKE THIS THING'S GONNA FLIP OVER!
LIKE THE TITANIC.
...WHAT AM I TALKING ABOUT?!
OH, BUT I THINK SHIMODA BAY IS PATROLLED BY THE COAST GUARD?
I'M NOT BEING FUNNY AT ALL.
SO WE GOT NOTHING TO WORRY ABOUT!!
SORT OF...
WITH THIS BEING THE END AND ALL...
I'M JUST TRYING TO MAKE HER MORE AT EASE.
BUT DON'T WORRY ABOUT ME, ALL RIGHT?
I'LL EXPLAIN EVERYTHING TO EVERYONE, SO...

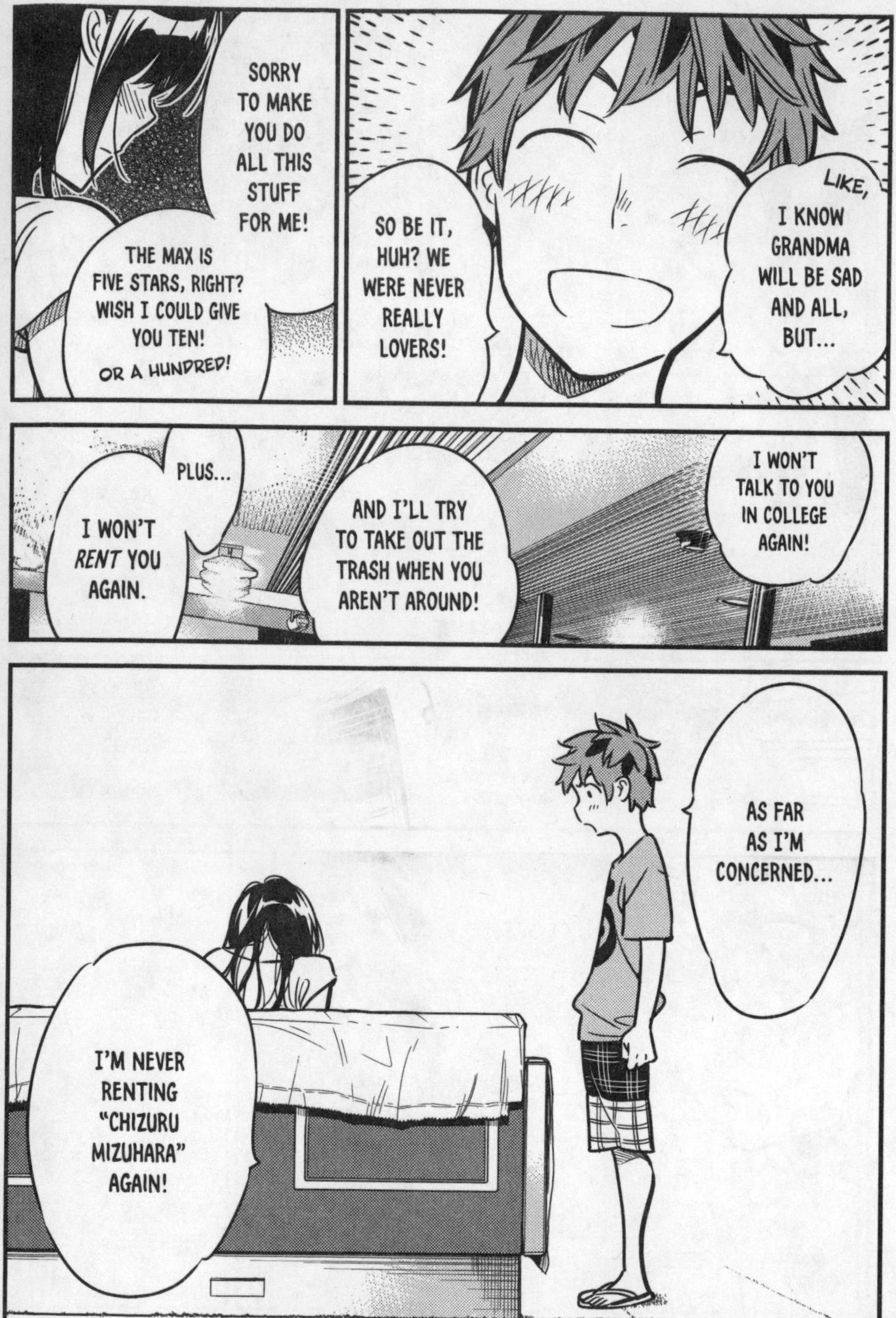
LIKE, I KNOW GRANDMA WILL BE SAD AND ALL, BUT...
SO BE IT, HUH? WE WERE NEVER REALLY LOVERS!
SORRY TO MAKE YOU DO ALL THIS STUFF FOR ME!
THE MAX IS FIVE STARS, RIGHT? WISH I COULD GIVE YOU TEN!
OR A HUNDRED!
I WON'T TALK TO YOU IN COLLEGE AGAIN!
AND I'LL TRY TO TAKE OUT THE TRASH WHEN YOU AREN'T AROUND!
PLUS...
I WON'T *RENT* YOU AGAIN.
AS FAR AS I'M CONCERNED...
I'M NEVER RENTING "CHIZURU MIZUHARA" AGAIN!

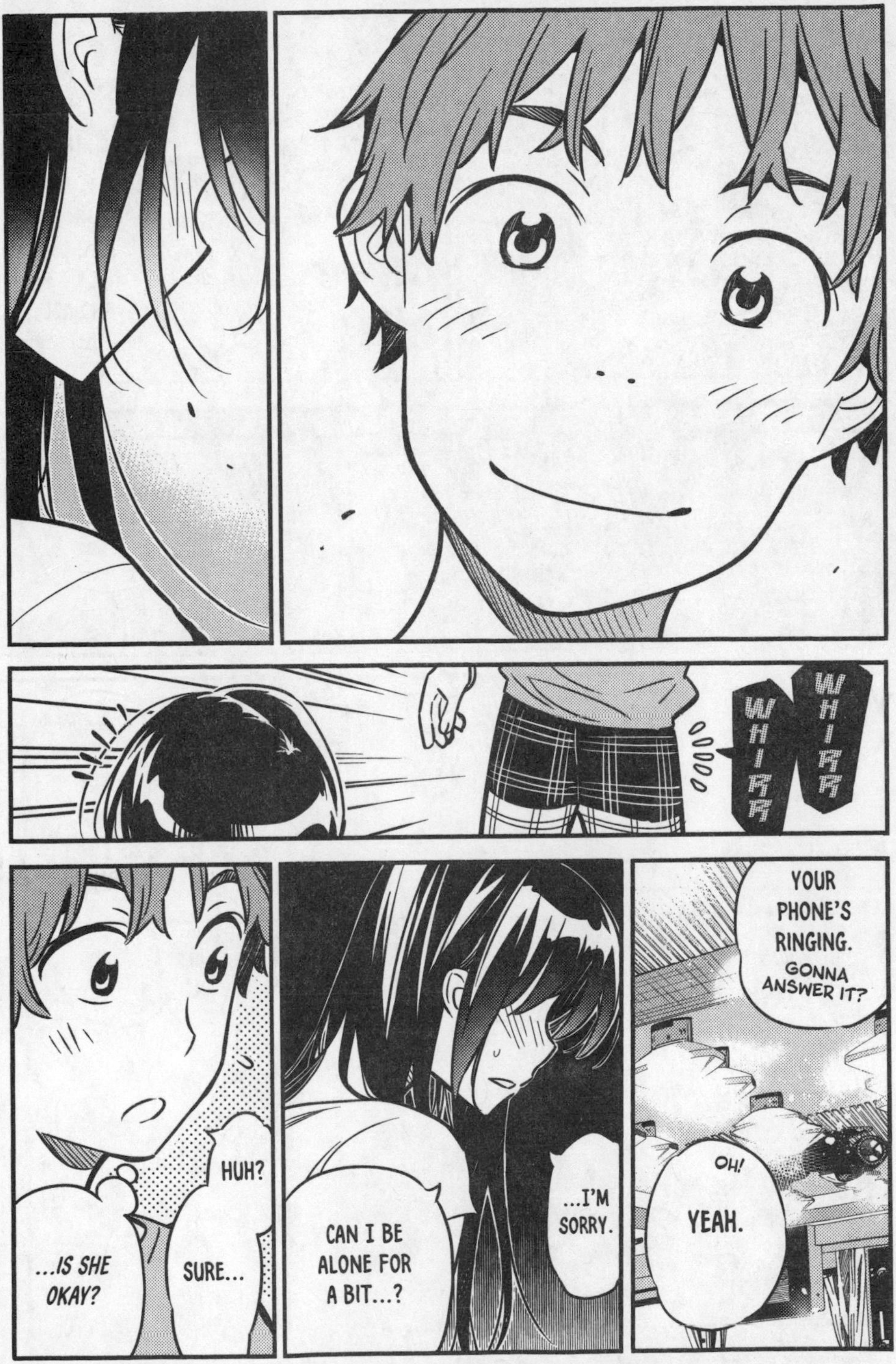
WHIRR
WHIRR
YOUR PHONE'S RINGING.
GONNA ANSWER IT?
OH!
YEAH.
...I'M SORRY.
CAN I BE ALONE FOR A BIT...?
HUH?
SURE...
...IS SHE OKAY?

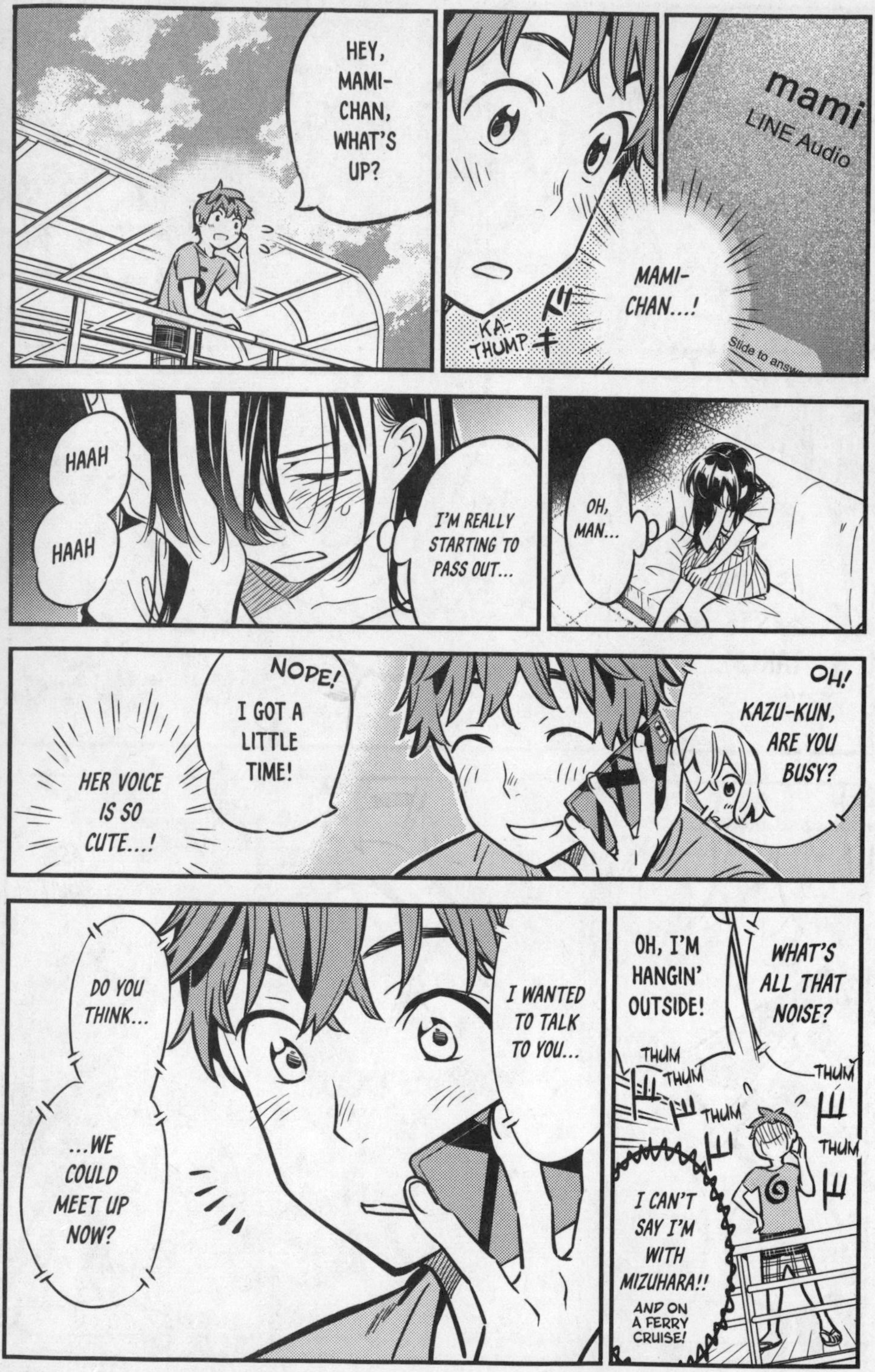
mami
LINE Audio
Slide to answ
MAMI-CHAN...!
KA-THUMP
HEY, MAMI-CHAN, WHAT'S UP?
OH, MAN...
I'M REALLY STARTING TO PASS OUT...
HAAH
HAAH
OH! KAZU-KUN, ARE YOU BUSY?
NOPE! I GOT A LITTLE TIME!
HER VOICE IS SO CUTE...!
WHAT'S ALL THAT NOISE?
OH, I'M HANGIN' OUTSIDE!
THUM THUM THUM
THUM THUM
I CAN'T SAY I'M WITH MIZUHARA!!
AND ON A FERRY CRUISE!
I WANTED TO TALK TO YOU...
DO YOU THINK...
...WE COULD MEET UP NOW?

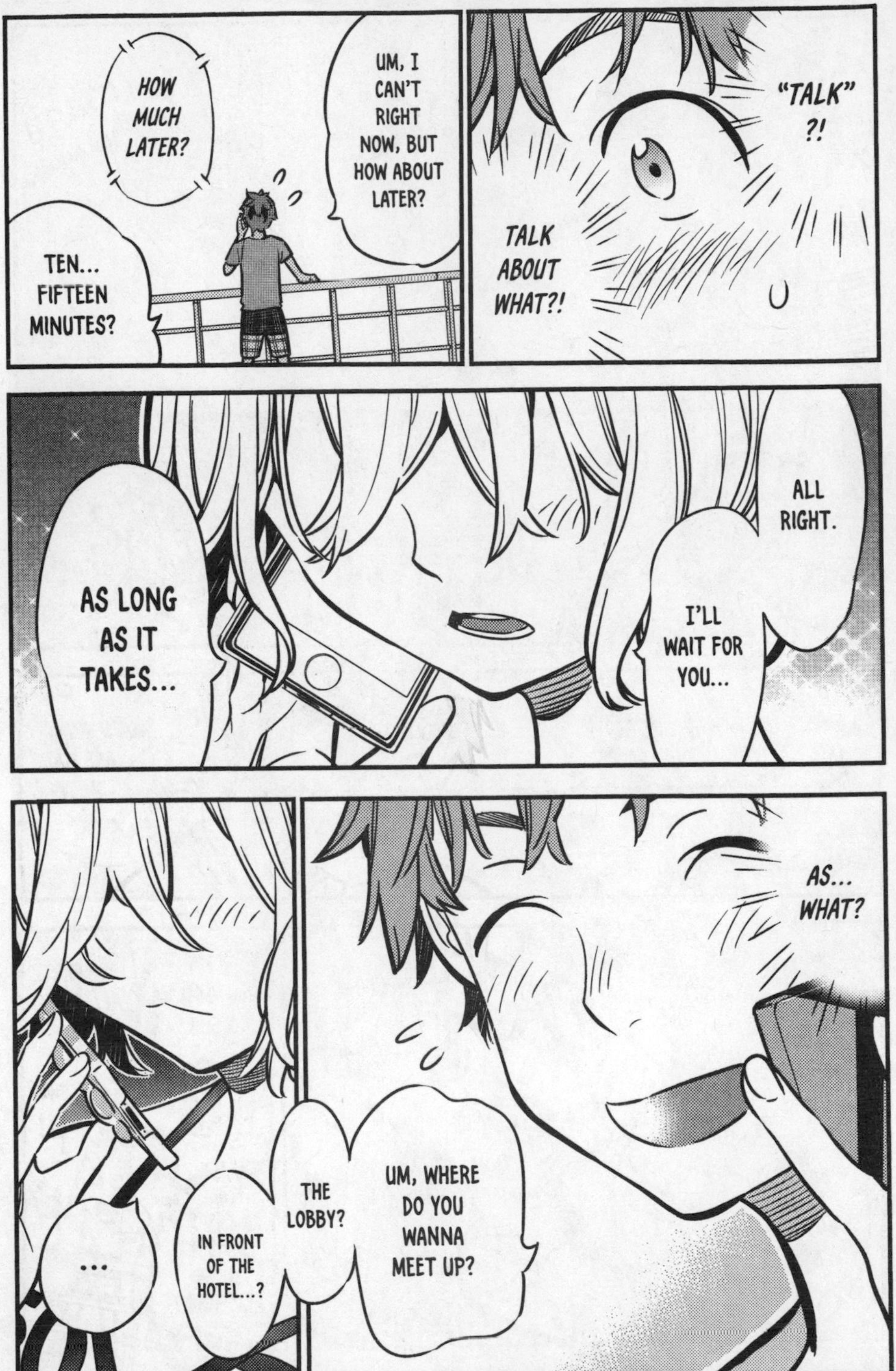
"TALK" ?!
TALK ABOUT WHAT?!
UM, I CAN'T RIGHT NOW, BUT HOW ABOUT LATER?
HOW MUCH LATER?
TEN... FIFTEEN MINUTES?
ALL RIGHT.
I'LL WAIT FOR YOU...
AS LONG AS IT TAKES...
AS... WHAT?
UM, WHERE DO YOU WANNA MEET UP?
THE LOBBY?
IN FRONT OF THE HOTEL...?
...

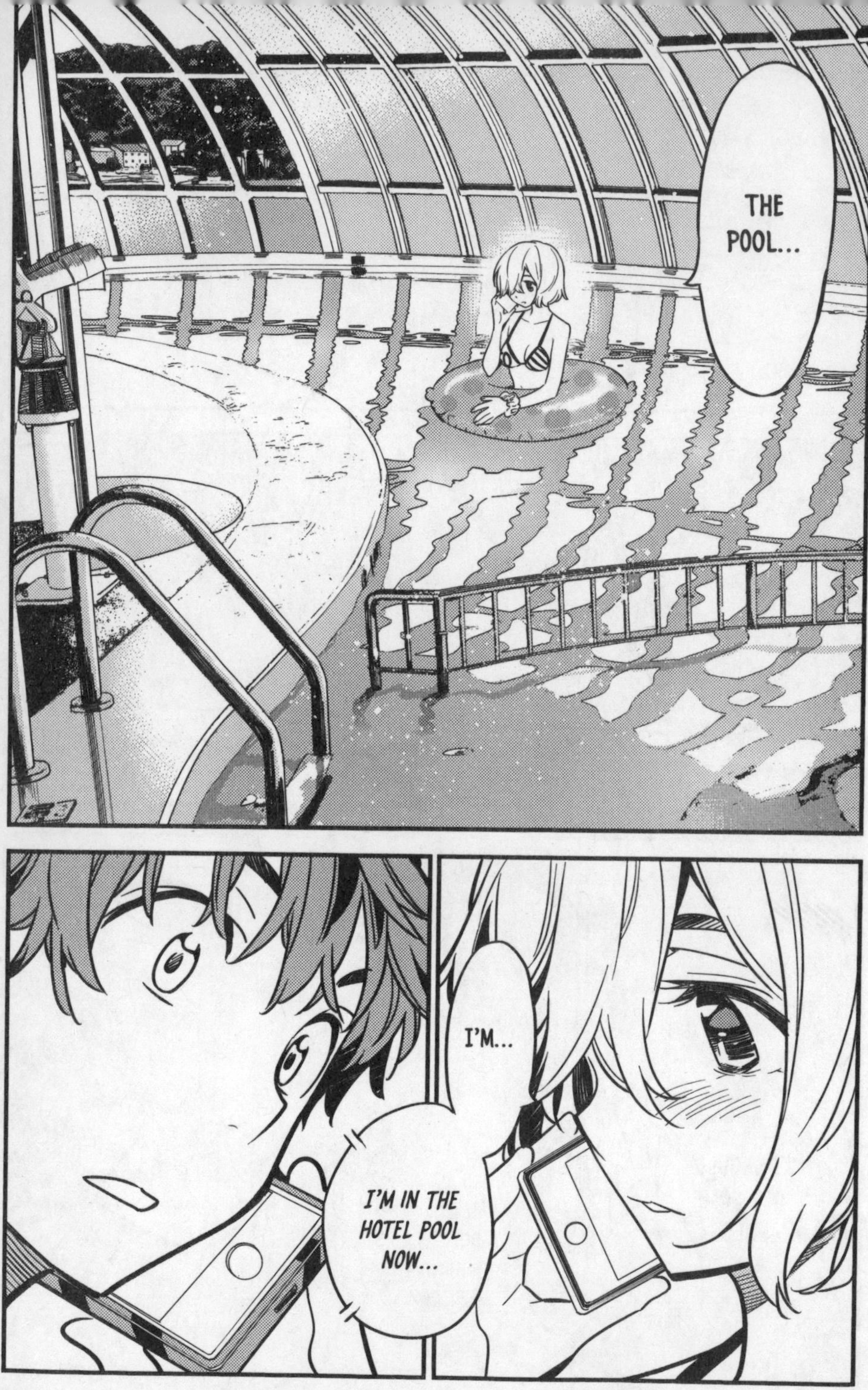
THE POOL...
I'M...
I'M IN THE HOTEL POOL NOW...

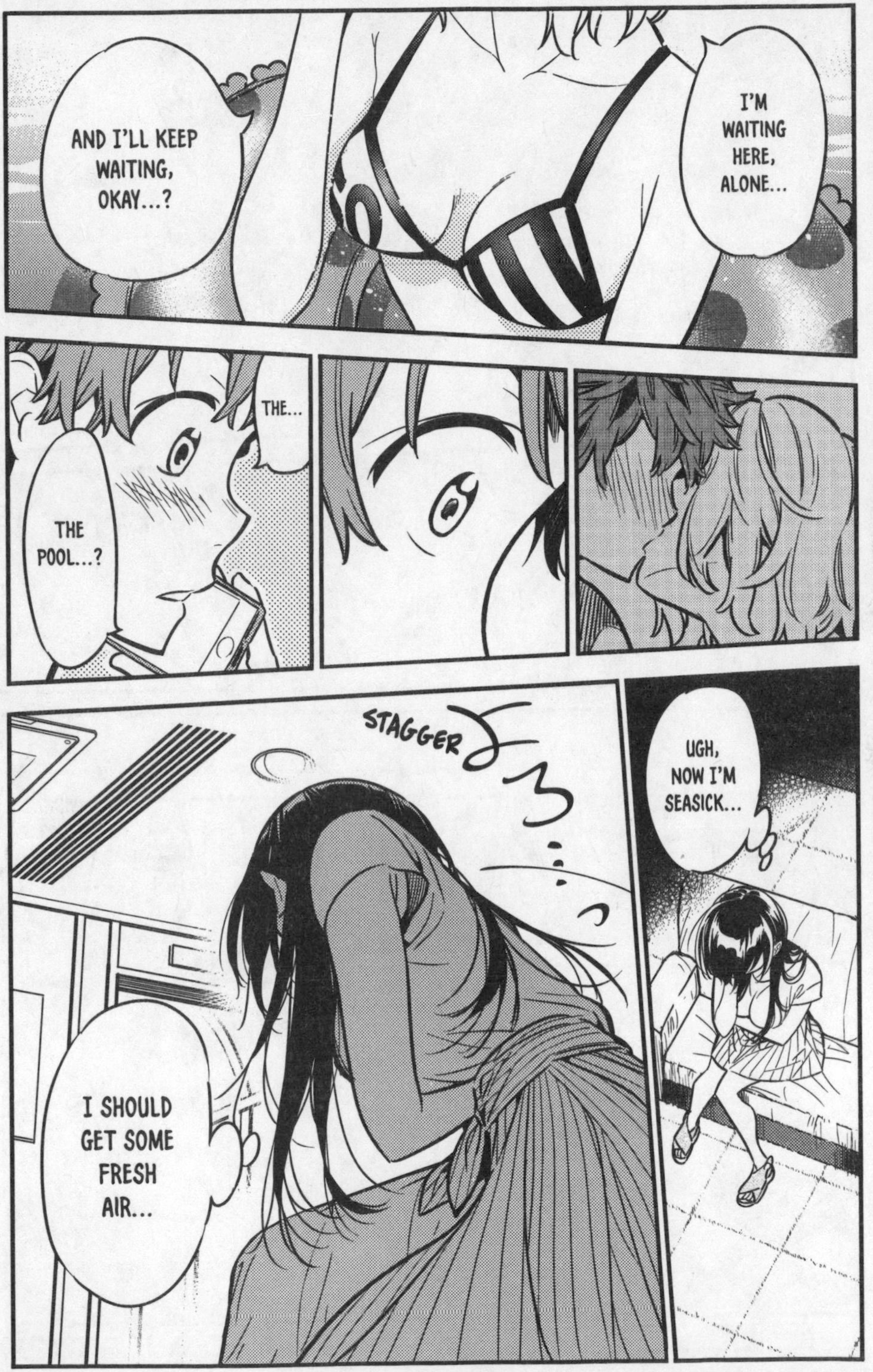
I'M WAITING HERE, ALONE...
AND I'LL KEEP WAITING, OKAY...?
THE...
THE POOL...?
UGH, NOW I'M SEASICK...
STAGGER
I SHOULD GET SOME FRESH AIR...

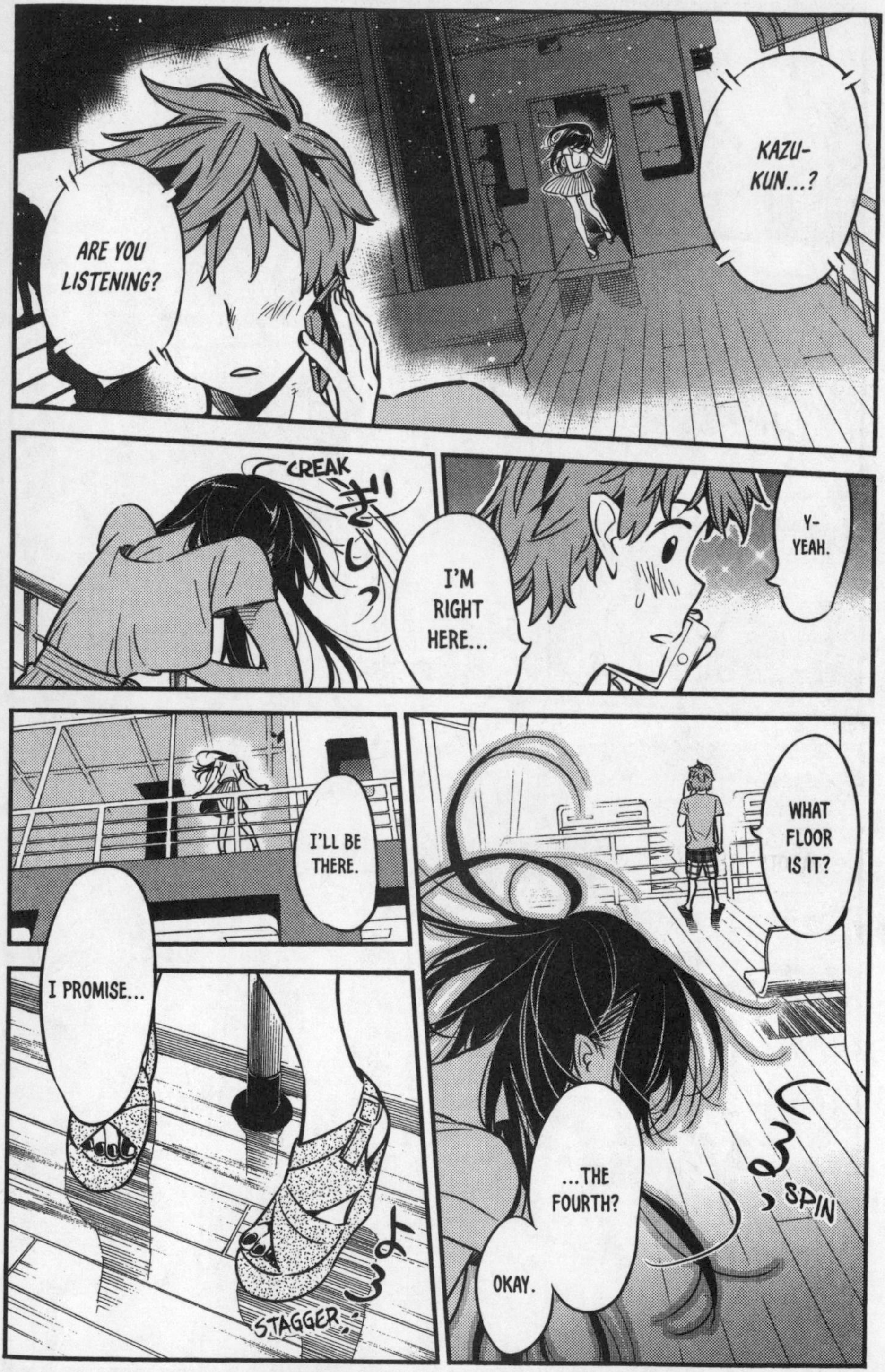
KAZU-KUN...?
ARE YOU LISTENING?
Y-YEAH.
I'M RIGHT HERE...
CREAK
ぎしっ
WHAT FLOOR IS IT?
...THE FOURTH?
くるっ
SPIN
OKAY.
I'LL BE THERE.
I PROMISE...
よろっ
STAGGER

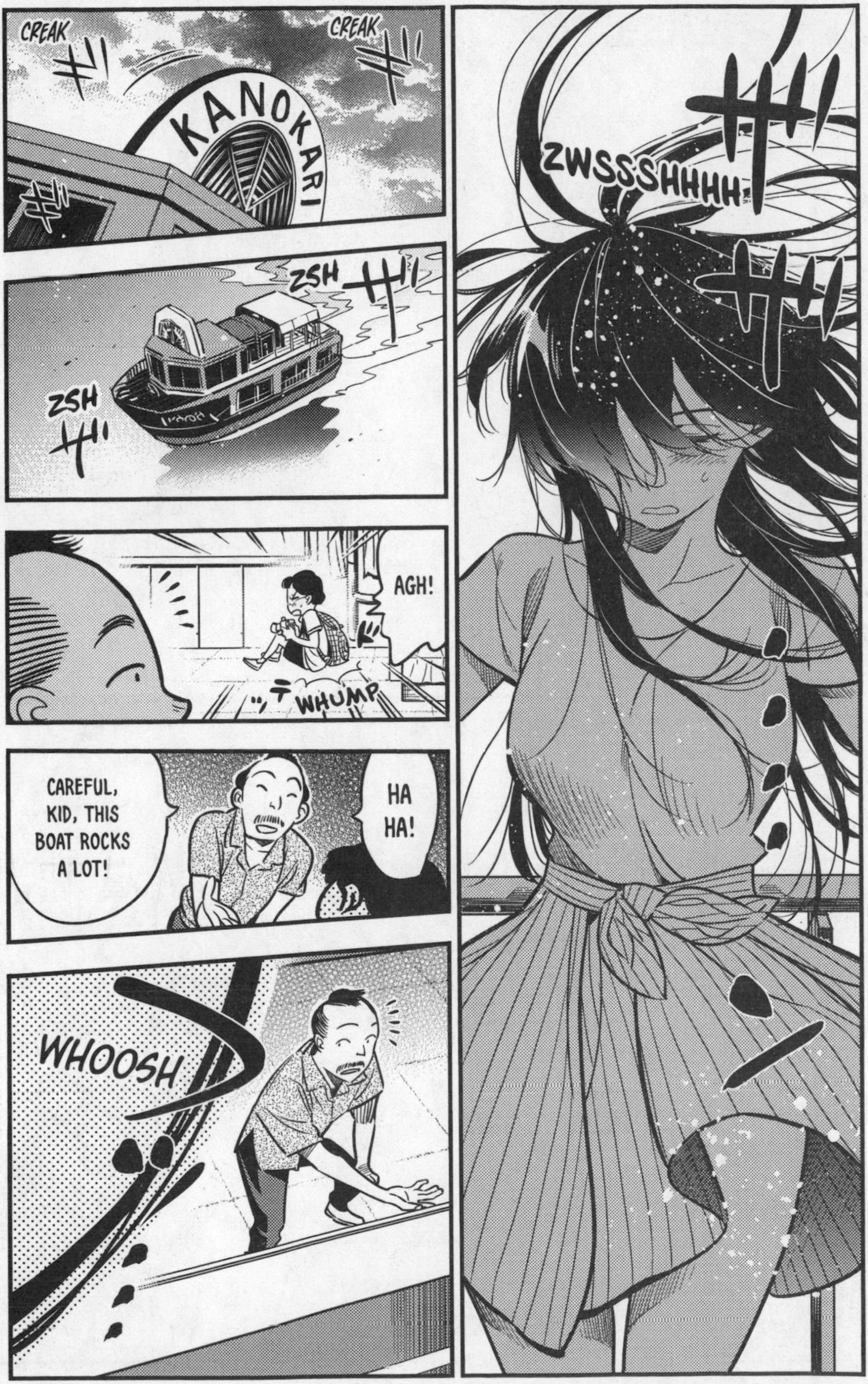
ZWSSSHHHH
CREAK
CREAK
KANOKARI
ZSH
ZSH
AGH!
WHUMP
HA HA!
CAREFUL, KID, THIS BOAT ROCKS A LOT!
WHOOSH

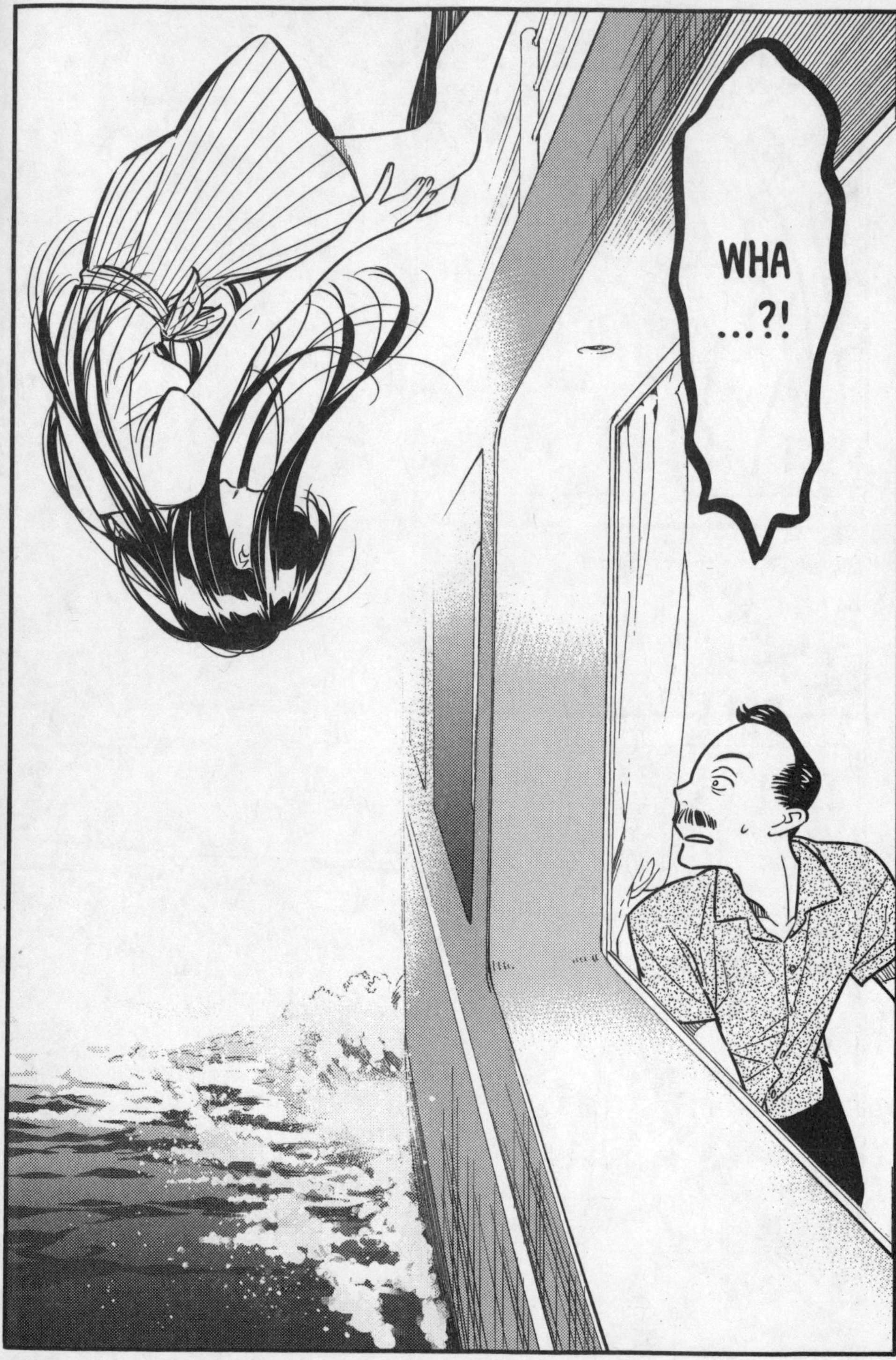
WHA ...?!

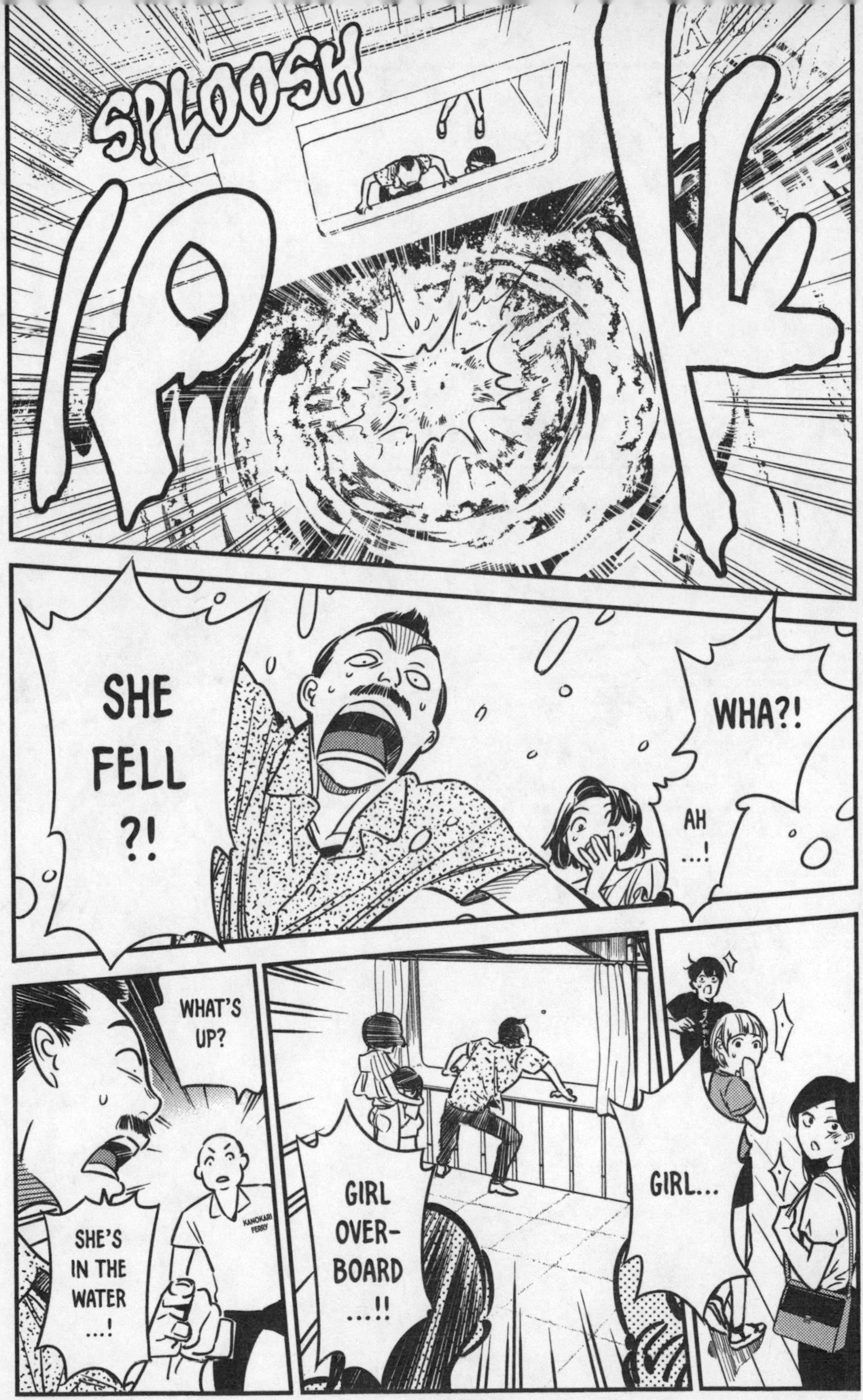
SPLOOSH
WHA?!
AH ...!
SHE FELL ?!
GIRL...
GIRL OVER-BOARD ...!!
WHAT'S UP?
KANOKARI FERRY
SHE'S IN THE WATER ...!

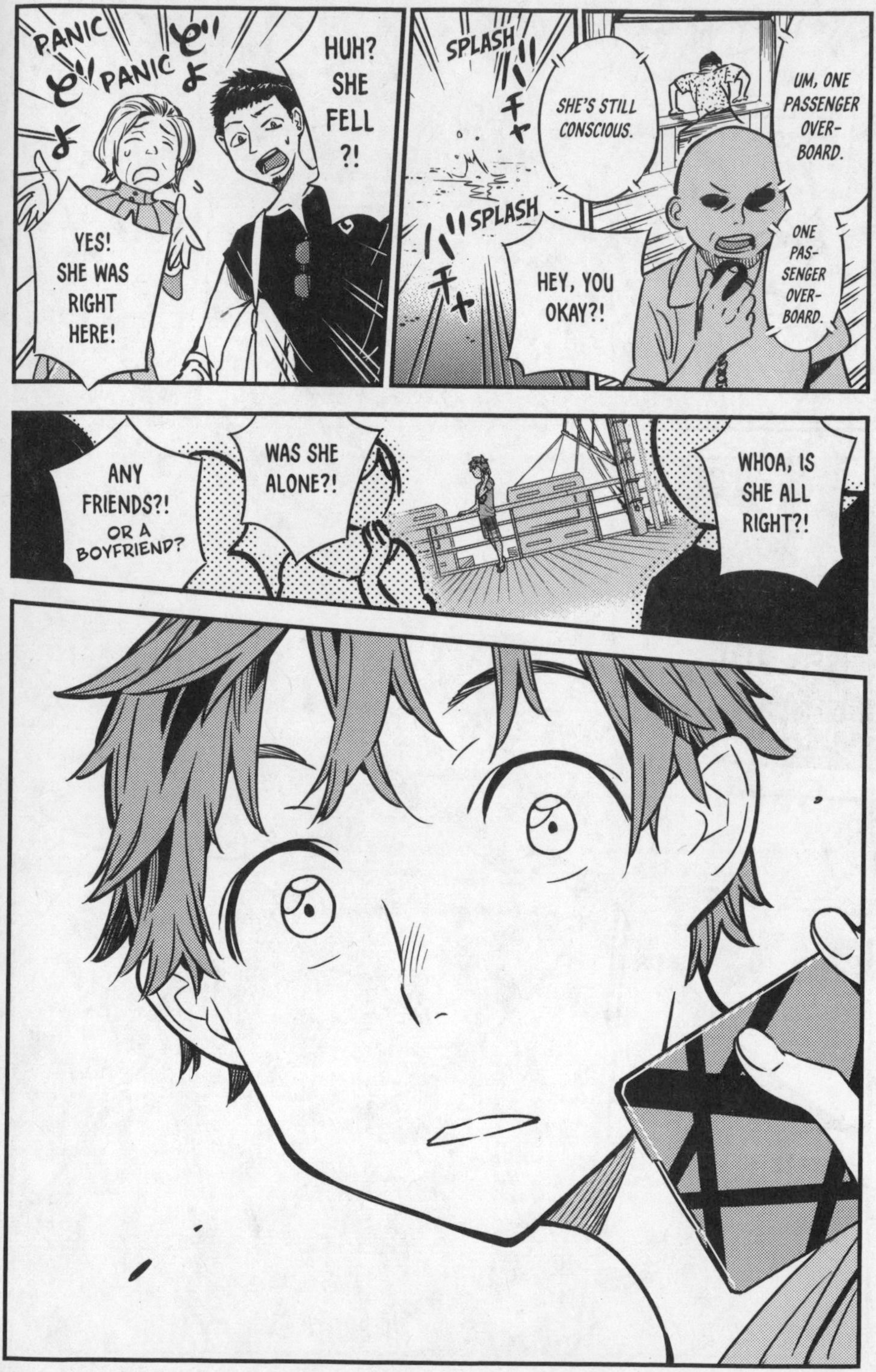
UM, ONE PASSENGER OVER-BOARD.
SHE'S STILL CONSCIOUS.
SPLASH バチャ
ONE PAS-SENGER OVER-BOARD.
HEY, YOU OKAY?!
SPLASH バチャ
HUH? SHE FELL?!
PANIC どよ
PANIC どよ
YES! SHE WAS RIGHT HERE!
WHOA, IS SHE ALL RIGHT?!
WAS SHE ALONE?!
ANY FRIENDS?! OR A BOYFRIEND?

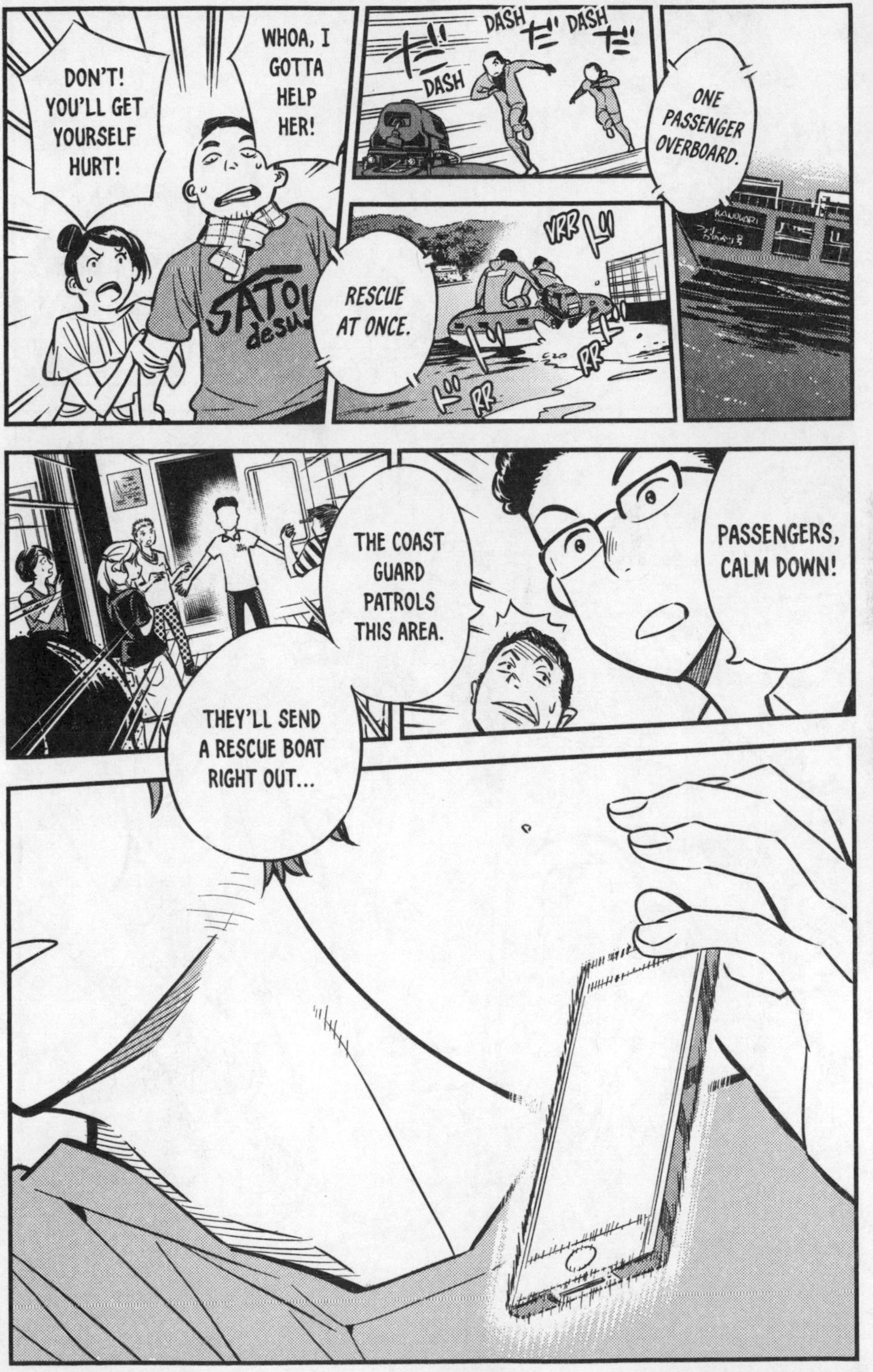
ONE PASSENGER OVERBOARD.
DASH DASH DASH
VRR RR RR
RESCUE AT ONCE.
WHOA, I GOTTA HELP HER!
DON'T! YOU'LL GET YOURSELF HURT!
SATO desu
PASSENGERS, CALM DOWN!
THE COAST GUARD PATROLS THIS AREA.
THEY'LL SEND A RESCUE BOAT RIGHT OUT...

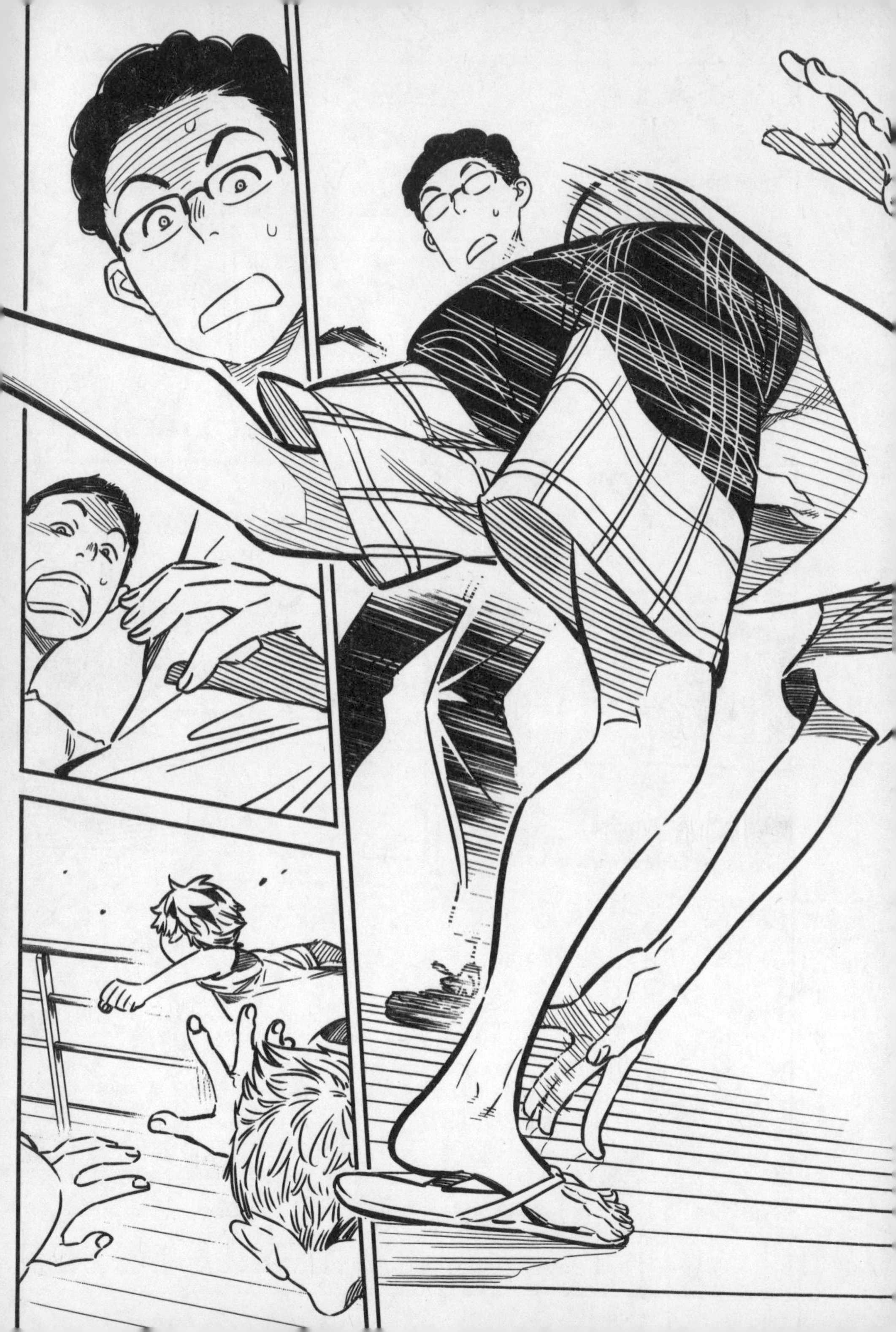

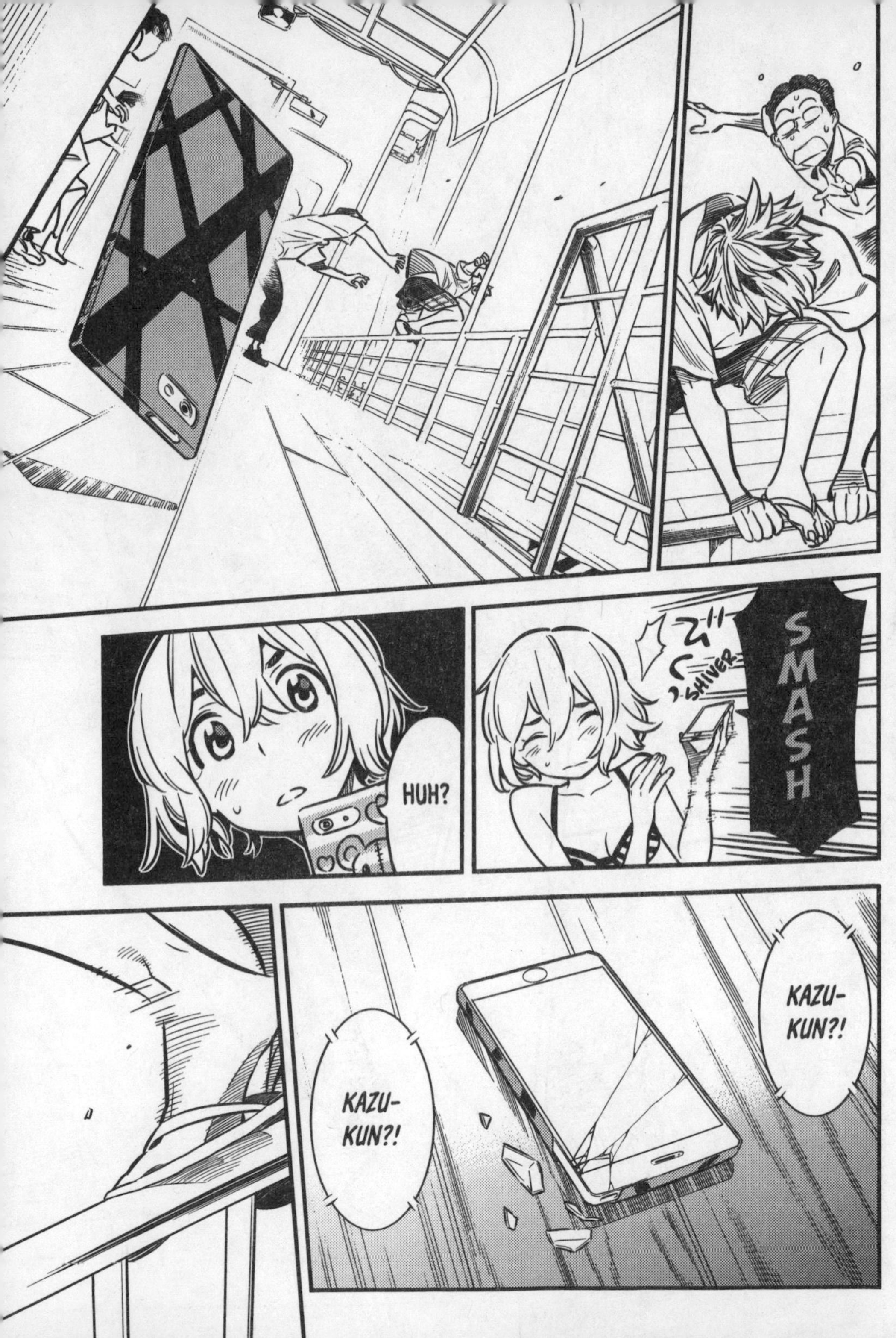
SMASH
SHIVER
HUH?
KAZU-KUN?!
KAZU-KUN?!

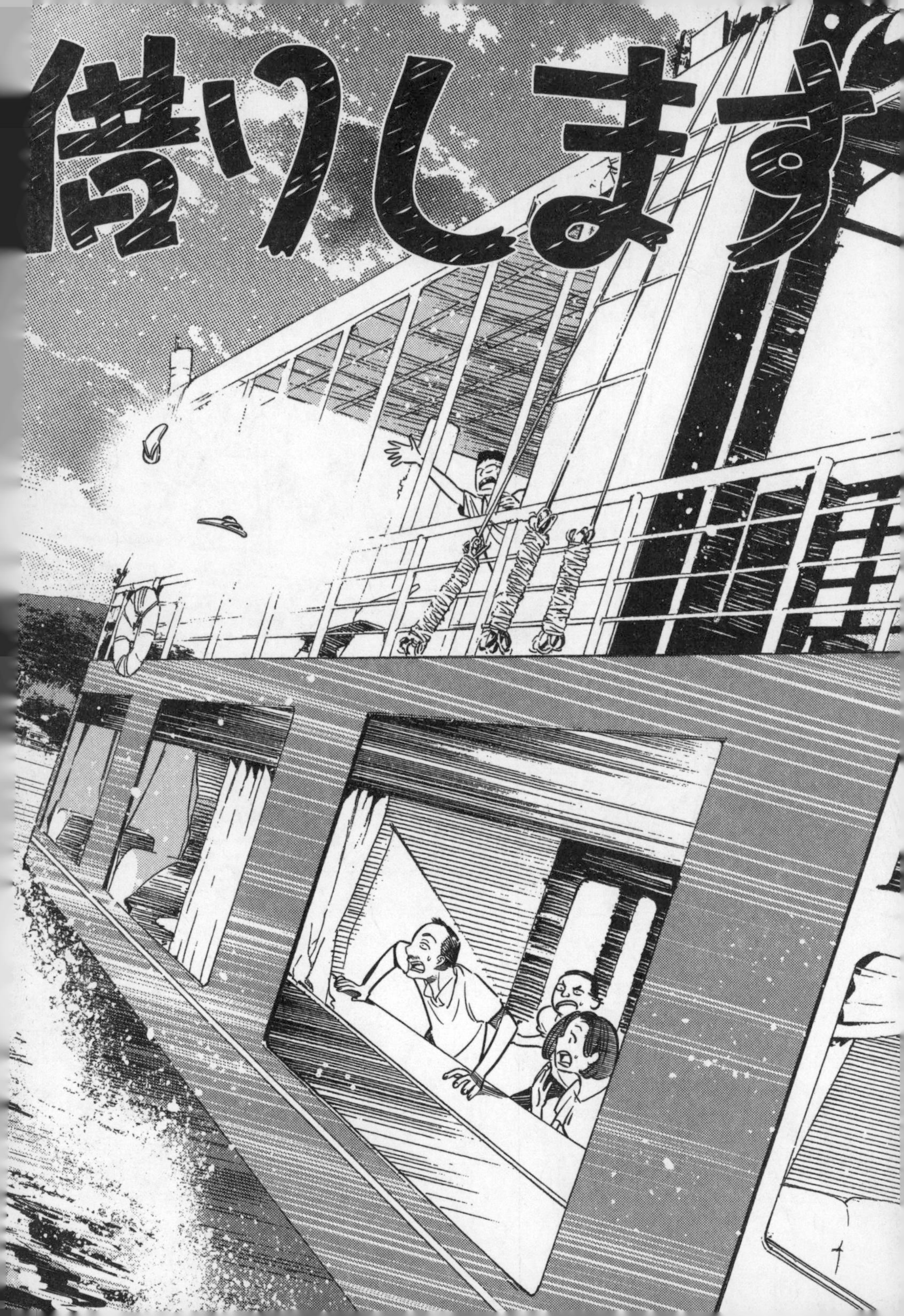
倍りします

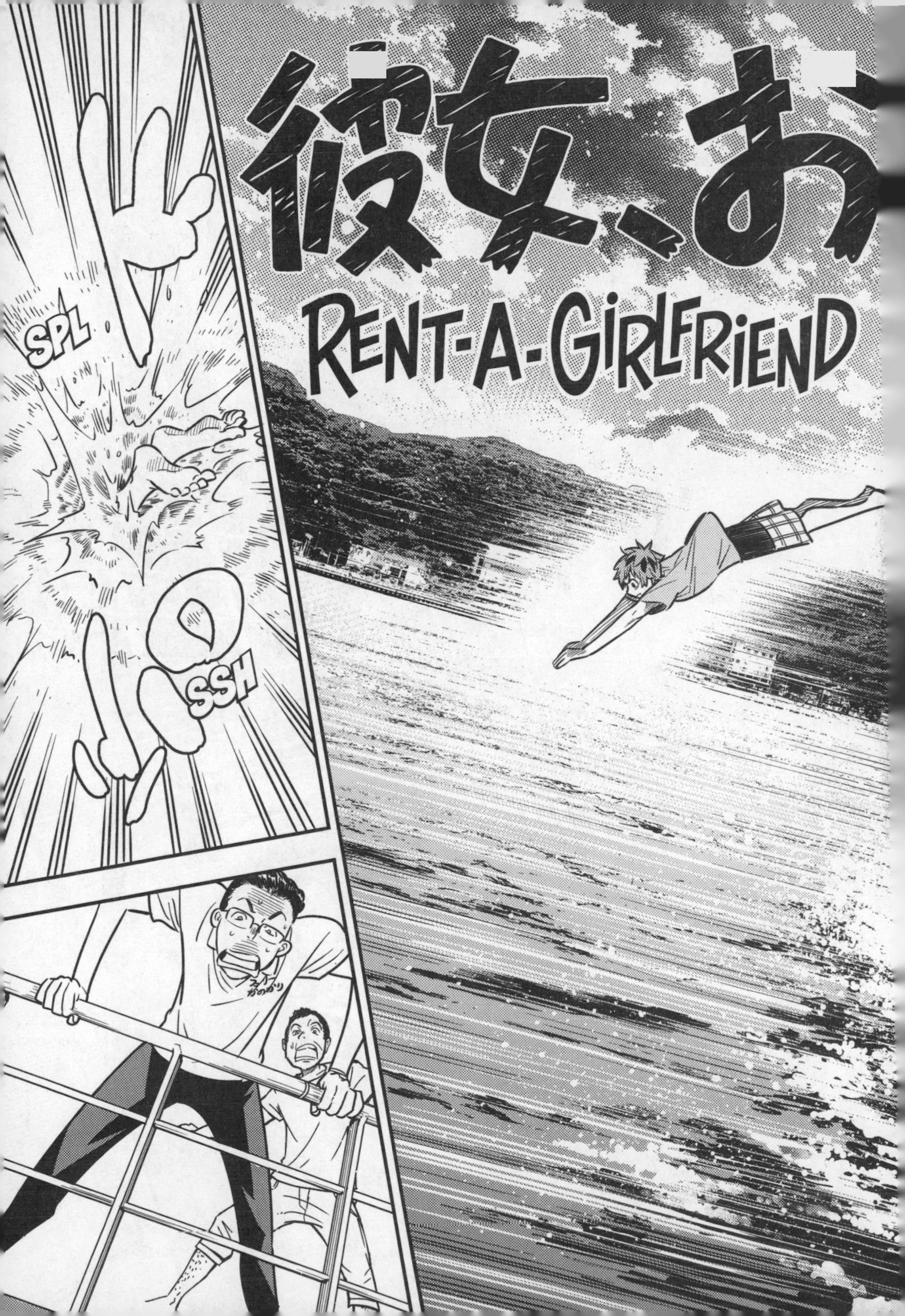
彼女、お
RENT-A-GIRLFRIEND
SPL
SSH

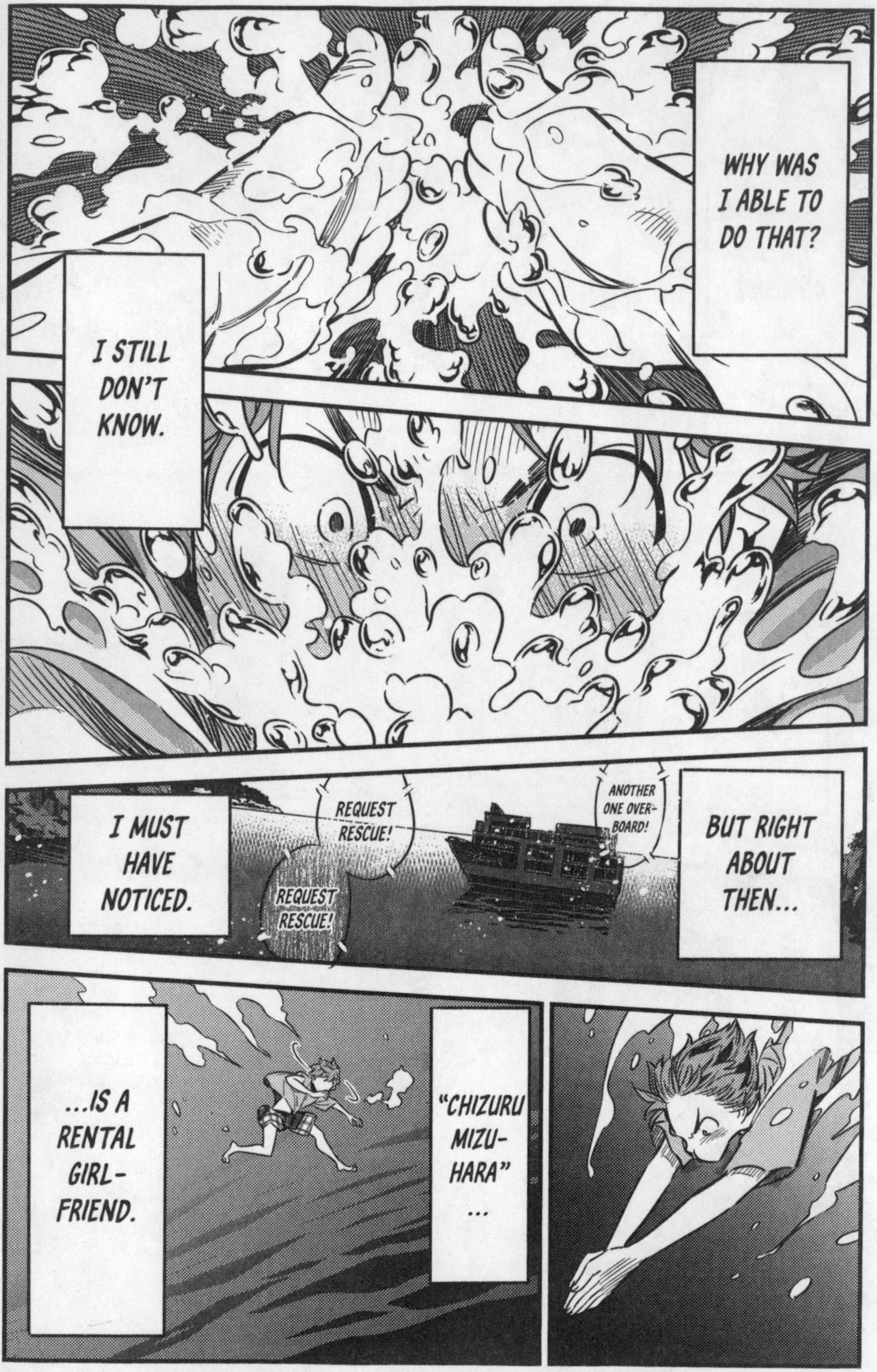
WHY WAS I ABLE TO DO THAT?
I STILL DON'T KNOW.
BUT RIGHT ABOUT THEN...
ANOTHER ONE OVER-BOARD!
REQUEST RESCUE!
REQUEST RESCUE!
I MUST HAVE NOTICED.
"CHIZURU MIZU-HARA" ...
...IS A RENTAL GIRL-FRIEND.

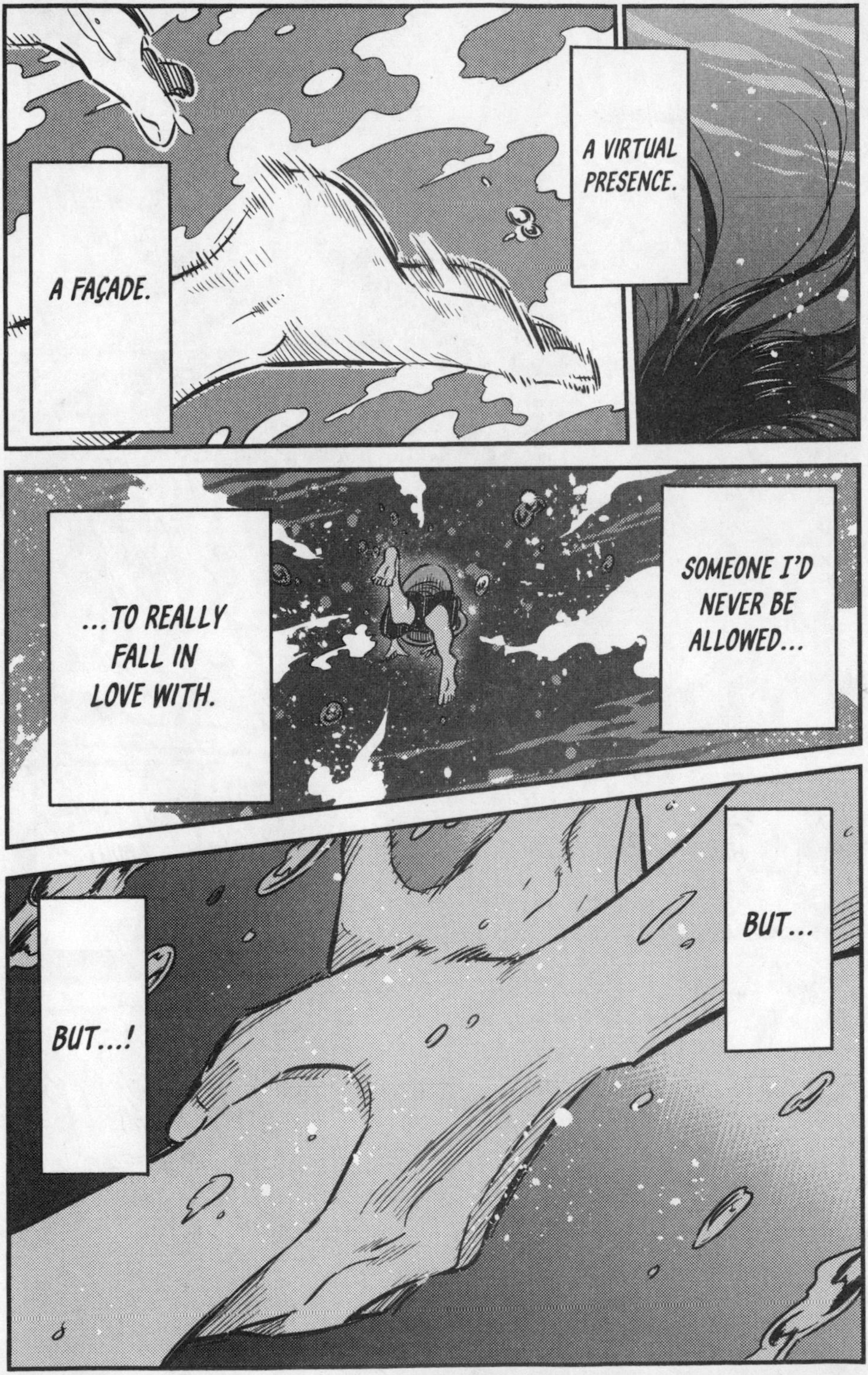
A VIRTUAL PRESENCE.
A FAÇADE.
SOMEONE I'D NEVER BE ALLOWED...
...TO REALLY FALL IN LOVE WITH.
BUT...
BUT...!

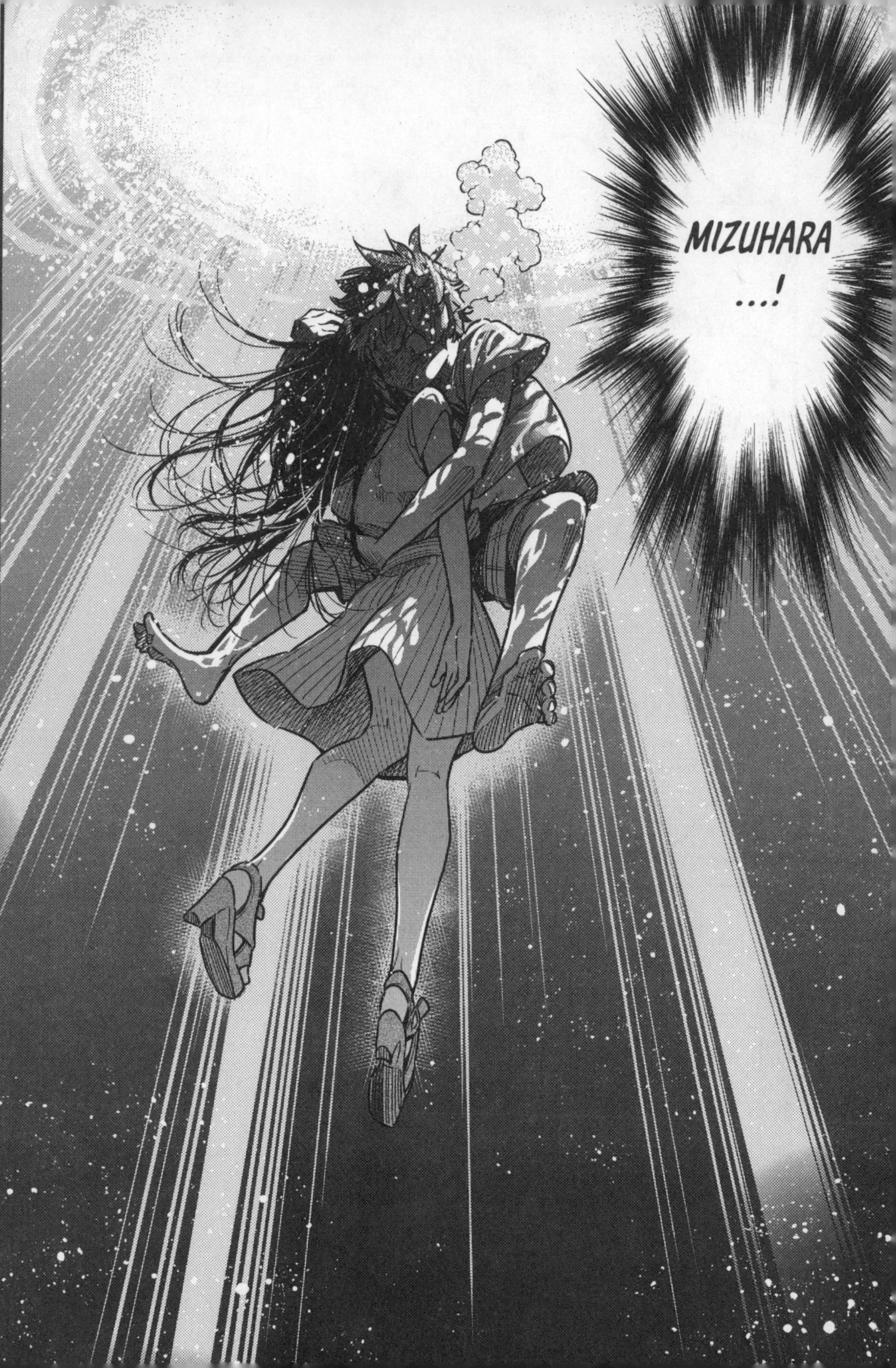
MIZUHARA ...!

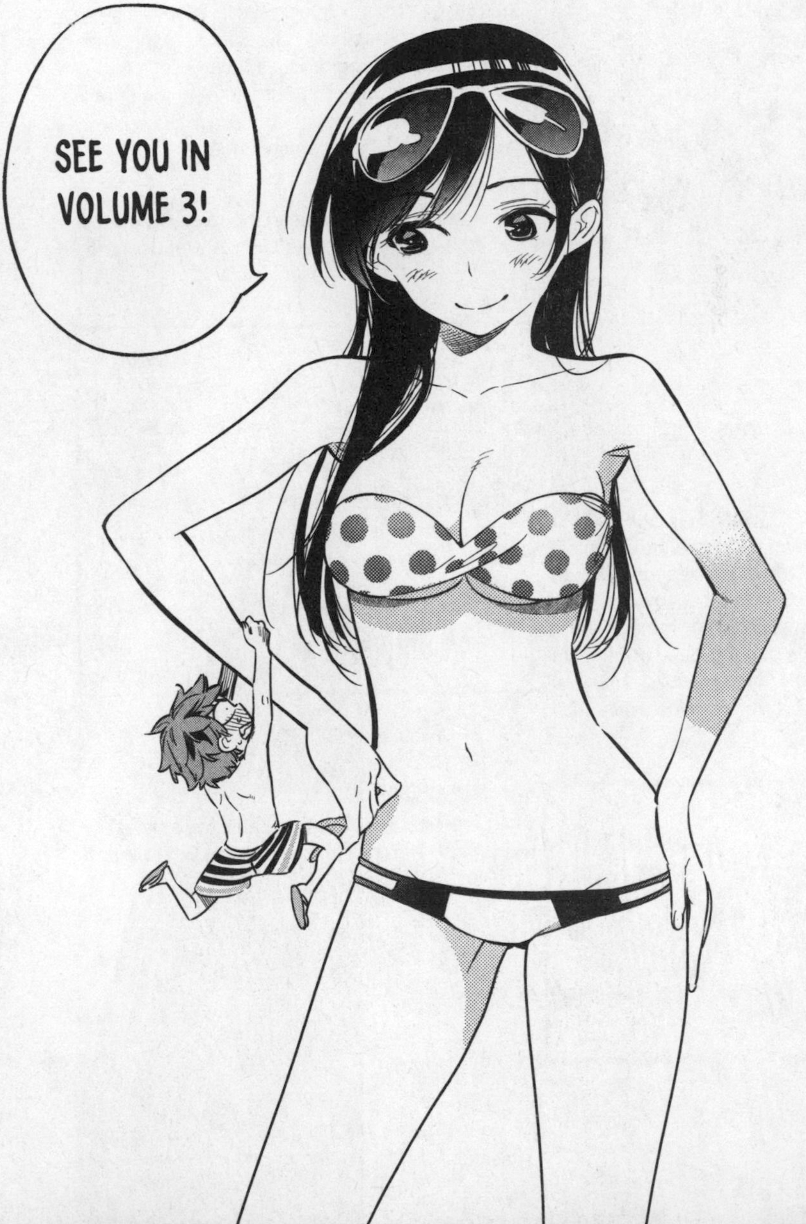
SEE YOU IN VOLUME 3!

TRANSLATION NOTES:

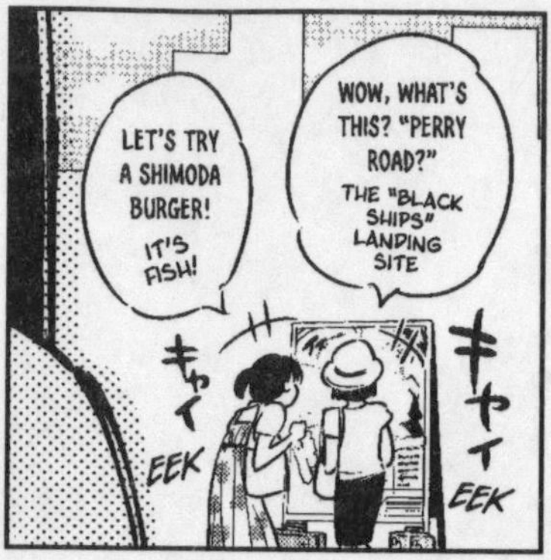
WOW, WHAT'S THIS? "PERRY ROAD?"
THE "BLACK SHIPS" LANDING SITE
LET'S TRY A SHIMODA BURGER!
IT'S FISH!
キャイ
EEK
キャイ
EEK

46, BLACK SHIPS

The "black ships" (*kurofune* or *kurobune*) are the steam-powered war ships headed by American Admiral Matthew Perry that billowed black smoke as they pulled into Tokyo Bay in 1853. This bloodless, threatening "invasion" is responsible for the forced opening of Japan to Westernization, following a period of isolation during the prior 200 or so years of European and American colonial conquests on the Asian continent.

46, SHIMODA BURGER

A kind of burger famous in the Izu town of Shimoda, made with fried fish, soy sauce and brie.

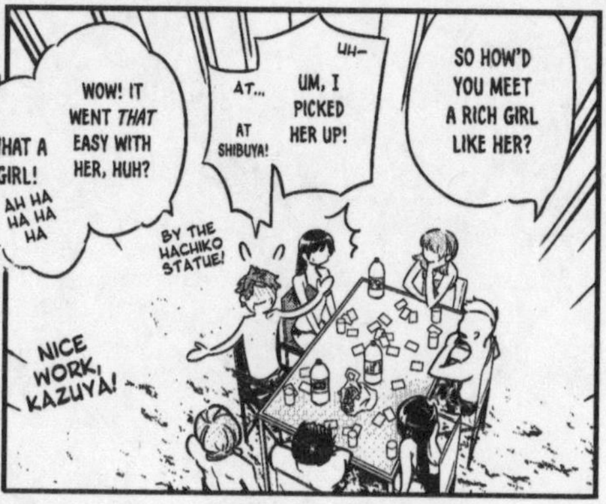
SO HOW'D YOU MEET A RICH GIRL LIKE HER?
UH-
UM, I PICKED HER UP!
AT...
AT SHIBUYA!
WOW! IT WENT *THAT* EASY WITH HER, HUH?
WHAT A GIRL!
AH HA HA HA HA
BY THE HACHIKO STATUE!
NICE WORK, KAZUYA!

97, HACHIKO STATUE IN SHIBUYA

Shibuya is one of the largest and busiest train stations in Tokyo, where a dog named Hachiko was said to wait for his owner every day at the station until he returned. There is a statue in the plaza outside of Shibuya station commemorating Hachiko, who had become a local celebrity.

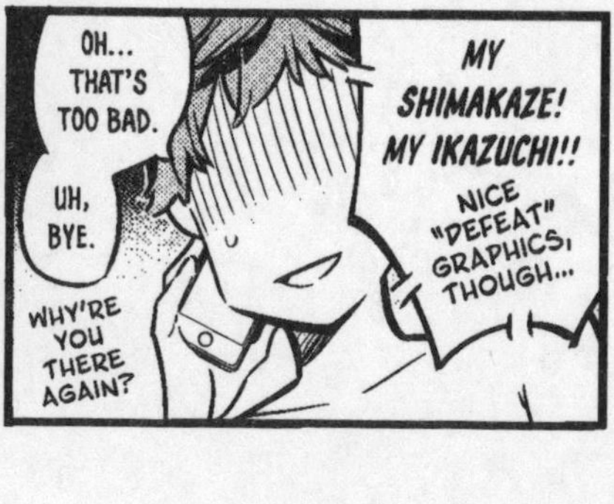
MY SHIMAKAZE! MY IKAZUCHI!!
NICE "DEFEAT" GRAPHICS, THOUGH...
OH... THAT'S TOO BAD.
UH, BYE.
WHY'RE YOU THERE AGAIN?

120, SHIMAKAZE, IKAZUCHI

Both are names of famous battleships used by Japan in the Pacific theater during World War II.

EDENS ZERO
エデンズゼロ

HIRO MASHIMA IS BACK! JOIN THE CREATOR OF *FAIRY TAIL* AS HE TAKES TO THE STARS FOR ANOTHER THRILLING SAGA!

EDENS ZERO © Hiro Mashima/Kodansha, Ltd.

A high-flying space adventure! All the steadfast friendship and wild fighting you've been waiting for...IN SPACE!

At Granbell Kingdom, an abandoned amusement park, Shiki has lived his entire life among machines. But one day, Rebecca and her cat companion Happy appear at the park's front gates. Little do these newcomers know that this is the first human contact Granbell has had in a hundred years! As Shiki stumbles his way into making new friends, his former neighbors stir at an opportunity for a robo-rebellion... And when his old homeland becomes too dangerous, Shiki must join Rebecca and Happy on their spaceship and escape into the boundless cosmos.

KC KODANSHA COMICS

THE SWEET SCENT OF LOVE IS IN THE AIR! FOR FANS OF OFFBEAT ROMANCES LIKE *WOTAKOI*

Sweat and Soap © Kintetsu Yamada / Kodansha Ltd.

In an office romance, there's a fine line between sexy and awkward... and that line is where Asako — a woman who sweats copiously — meets Koutarou — a perfume developer who can't get enough of Asako's, er, scent. Don't miss a romcom manga like no other!

KC KODANSHA COMICS

CAN A FARMER SAVE THE WORLD? FIND OUT IN THIS FANTASY MANGA FOR FANS
OF *SWORD ART ONLINE* AND *THAT TIME I GOT REINCARNATED AS A SLIME!*

I'M STANDING ON A MILLION LIVES

By
Akinari Nao

Original Story by
Naoki Yamakawa

Yusuke Yotsuya doesn't care about getting into high school—he just wants
to get back home to his game and away from other people. But when he
suddenly finds himself in a real-life fantasy game alongside his two gorgeous
classmates, he discovers a new world of possibility and excitement. Despite a
rough start, Yusuke and his friend fight to level up and clear the challenges set
before them by a mysterious figure from the future, but before long, they find
that they're not just battling for their own lives, but for the lives of millions...

KC
KODANSHA
COMICS

A SMART, NEW ROMANTIC COMEDY FOR FANS OF *SHORTCAKE CAKE* AND *TERRACE HOUSE*!

A romance manga starring high school girl Meeko, who learns to live on her own in a boarding house whose living room is home to the odd (but handsome) Matsunaga-san. She begins to adjust to her new life away from her parents, but Meeko soon learns that no matter how far away from home she is, she's still a young girl at heart — especially when she finds herself falling for Matsunaga-san.

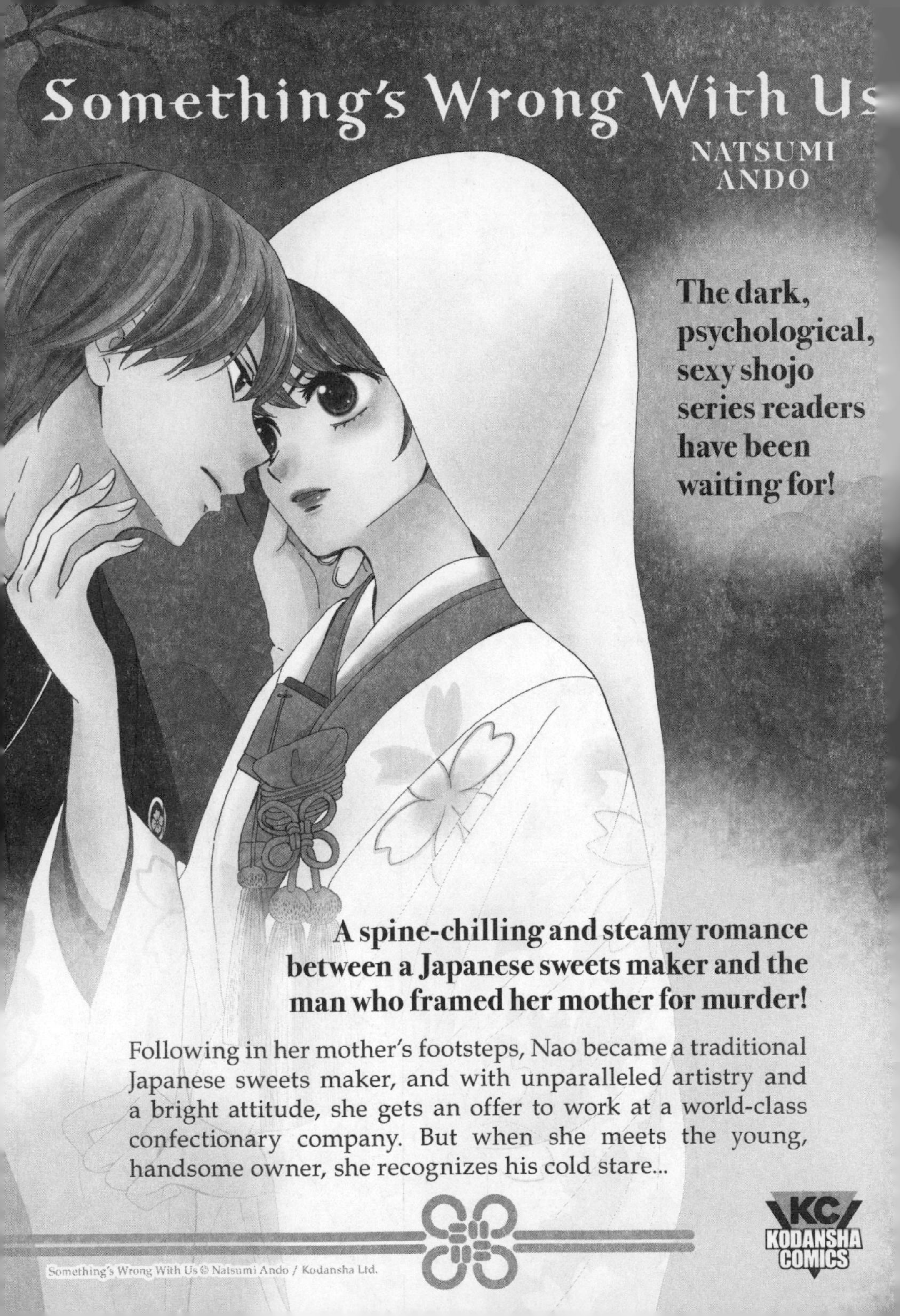
Something's Wrong With Us
NATSUMI ANDO
The dark, psychological, sexy shojo series readers have been waiting for!
A spine-chilling and steamy romance between a Japanese sweets maker and the man who framed her mother for murder!
Following in her mother's footsteps, Nao became a traditional Japanese sweets maker, and with unparalleled artistry and a bright attitude, she gets an offer to work at a world-class confectionary company. But when she meets the young, handsome owner, she recognizes his cold stare...
KC KODANSHA COMICS
Something's Wrong With Us © Natsumi Ando / Kodansha Ltd.

A Kodansha Comics Trade Paperback Original
Rent-A-Girlfriend 2 copyright © 2017 Reiji Miyajima
English translation copyright © 2020 Reiji Miyajima

All rights reserved.

Published in the United States by Kodansha Comics, an imprint of Kodansha USA Publishing, LLC, New York.

Publication rights for this English edition arranged through Kodansha Ltd., Tokyo.

First published in Japan in 2017 by Kodansha Ltd., Tokyo as *Kanojo, okarishimasu*, volume 2.

ISBN 978-1-63236-998-7

Original cover design by Kohei Nawata Design Office

Printed in the United States of America.

www.kodanshacomics.com

9 8 7 6 5
Translation: Kevin Gifford
Lettering: Paige Pumphrey
Kodansha Comics edition cover design by Phil Balsman

Publisher: Kiichiro Sugawara

Director of publishing services: Ben Applegate
Associate director of operations: Stephen Pakula
Publishing services managing editor: Noelle Webster
Assistant production manager: Emi Lotto, Angela Zurlo
Logo and character art ©Kodansha USA Publishing, LLC